T0211265

Lecture Notes in Computer Science 10598

Commenced Publication in 1973
Founding and Former Series Editors:
Gerhard Goos, Juris Hartmanis, and Jan van Leeuwen

More information about this series at http://www.springer.com/series/7408

Alessandro Fantechi · Thierry Lecomte
Alexander Romanovsky (Eds.)

Reliability, Safety, and Security of Railway Systems

Modelling, Analysis, Verification, and Certification

Second International Conference, RSSRail 2017
Pistoia, Italy, November 14–16, 2017
Proceedings

 Springer

Editors
Alessandro Fantechi
Università di Firenze
Florence
Italy

Thierry Lecomte
ClearSy
Aix-en-Provence
France

Alexander Romanovsky
Newcastle University
Newcastle upon Tyne
UK

ISSN 0302-9743   ISSN 1611-3349 (electronic)
Lecture Notes in Computer Science
ISBN 978-3-319-68498-7   ISBN 978-3-319-68499-4 (eBook)
https://doi.org/10.1007/978-3-319-68499-4

Library of Congress Control Number: 2017956780

LNCS Sublibrary: SL2 – Programming and Software Engineering

Printed on acid-free paper

This Springer imprint is published by Springer Nature
The registered company is Springer International Publishing AG
The registered company address is: Gewerbestrasse 11, 6330 Cham, Switzerland

Preface

The RSSRail conference series began in 2016, in Paris, and this year the conference was held in Pistoia, Italy, hosted by DITECFER, the Tuscany-based railway technological district, which formally associates more than 40 enterprises and research bodies, and acts as a reference for many more companies that work in the railway domain.

The RSSRail conference aims to bring together researchers and engineers interested in building critical railway applications and systems, as a working conference in which research advances are discussed and evaluated by both researchers and engineers, focusing on their potential to be deployed in industrial settings.

This is the first international conference focusing on the reliability, safety, and security of railway systems. The conference is devoted to critical problems faced by the modern railway: how to deliver reliable service to passengers and to freight operators, while maintaining very high levels of safety. While it is true that these are problems that the railway sector has faced for almost 200 years, new factors and new trends demand new solutions. One of the biggest challenges stems from ever-increasing automation, driven by requirements for increased capacity and greater efficiency that are further compounded by increased integration of the railway network with other transport systems. The outcome is incorporation of ever more digital systems, with increasing complexity. This, together with the increased openness and interconnection of the railway systems, brings an ever-greater need for effective cyber security, guarding against malicious threats that could compromise both safety and operational performance.

Advanced techniques and tools are needed for modelling, analysis, verification, and validation that can cope with the new more complex systems; these techniques must support rather than impede the development process and must address and ensure:

- Required functionality
- Safety and integrity
- System security
- Adherence to standards

Our aim is to hold a conference that contributes to a range of key objectives. We feel that there is a pressing need to bring together researchers and developers working on railway system reliability, security, and safety to discuss how these requirements can be met in an integrated way. It is also vital to ensure that all advances in research (both in academia and industry) are driven by real industrial needs. This can help ensure that such advances are followed by industrial deployment. Another particularly important objective is to integrate research advances into the current development processes, and make them usable and scalable. Finally, a key goal is to develop advanced methods and tools that will ensure that the systems meet the requirements imposed by the standards and in building the arguments.

We hope that this conference will successfully contribute to all of these objectives.

RSSRail 2017 attracted 34 submissions from 12 countries. In all, 16 papers were accepted after a rigorous review process with every paper receiving at least three reviews. These include 11 technical papers, three industrial experience reports, and two PhD students papers. The papers confirm a wide interest in developing and applying in practice formal modelling and verification techniques as the most cost-effective way to guarantee the safety of today's very complex railway system. Besides these continued research area, two important topics clearly emerge from the accepted papers: the challenges posed to the safety and security of railway systems by the increasing reliance on advanced communication means, and the industrial interest in the expansion of automation and advanced signalling from the sector of main line railways to light rail and urban transit.

Three prominent researchers working on railway engineering, Jens Braband, from Siemens AG, Rail Automation and Honorary Professor of the Technical University of Braunschweig, Germany, Michael Leuschel, from Heinrich Heine Universität, Düsseldorf, Germany, and Aryldo Ar. Russo, from CERTIFER, France, kindly agreed to deliver keynote talks.

We would like to thank the Program Committee members and the additional reviewers for all their efforts. We warmly thank DITECFER, as well as all the industrial sponsors[1], for their help in making it possible to organize this event in Pistoia. We would like to acknowledge the help of Newcastle University staff: Joan Atkinson, Tom Anderson, Wayne Smith, and Dee Carr. We are grateful to Alfred Hofmann from Springer for supporting the publication of these proceedings in the LNCS series. But, most of all, our thanks go to all the contributors and the attendees of the conference for consolidating the success that this conference has experienced since its first edition.

August 2017   Alessandro Fantechi
                                                             Thierry Lecomte
                                                       Alexander Romanovsky

[1] AdaCore, ALSTOM, Altran, Ansaldo STS, ANSYS, ClearSy, ECM, Italcertifer, Sirti, Systerel, VectorCast.

Organization

Conference Chairs

Alessandro Fantechi   University of Florence, Italy
Thierry Lecomte   ClearSy, France
Alexander Romanovsky   Newcastle University, UK

Local Organization Chair

Veronica Bocci   DITECFER, Italy

Conference Organization and Financial Chair

Joan Atkinson   Newcastle University, UK

Web Chair

Wayne Smith   Newcastle University, UK

Organizing Committee

Tom Anderson   Newcastle University, UK
Dee Carr   Newcastle University, UK
Gloria Gori   University of Florence, Italy
Paolo Pacini   DITECFER, Italy

Program Committee

Carlo Becheri   ALSTOM, Italy
Marc Behrens   DB Projekt Stuttgart-Ulm GmbH, Germany
Andrea Bondavalli   University of Florence, Italy
David Bonvoisin   RATP, France
Fares Chucri   SNCF, France
Simon Collart-Dutilleul   IFSTTAR, France
Francesco Flammini   UMUC Europe, Germany
Stefania Gnesi   ISTI-CNR, Italy
Frank Golatowski   University of Rostock, Germany
Anne Haxthausen   Technical University of Denmark, Denmark
Baseliyos Jacob   Deutsche Bahn, Germany
Michael Jastram   Formal Mind, Germany
Alexei Iliasov   Newcastle University, UK
Tim Kelly   University of York, UK

Hironobu Kuruma	Hitachi, Japan
Michael Leuschel	Düsseldorf University, Germany
Gianluca Mandò	Thales, Italy
Jean Marc Mota	Thales R&T, France
Jan Peleska	Verified Systems International, Germany
Ralf Pinger	Siemens AG, Germany
Christophe Ponsard	CETIC, Belgium
Peter Popov	City University, UK
Etienne Prun	ClearSy, France
Matteo Rossi	Politecnico di Milano, Italy
Aryldo Russo	CERTIFER, France
Balazs Saghi	BUTE, Hungary
Kenji Taguchi	AIST, Japan
Jaco van de Pol	University of Twente, The Netherlands
Laurent Voisin	Systerel, France
Kirsten Winter	University of Queensland, Australia

Additional Reviewers

Katrina Attwood	University of York, UK
Davide Basile	ISTI, CNR, Italy
Benjamin Beichler	University of Rostock, Germany
Gautier Dallons	CETIC, Belgium
Renaud De Landtsheer	CETIC, Belgium
Vincenzo Di Massa	Thales, Italy
Mark Douthwaite	University of York, UK
Dominik Hansen	Düsseldorf University, Germany
Sebastian Krings	Düsseldorf University, Germany
Chris Leong	University of York, UK
Thorsten Schulz	University of Rostock, Germany
Romain Soulat	Thales R&T, France
Giorgio Oronzo Spagnolo	ISTI-CNR, Italy
Hannes Raddatz	University of Rostock, Germany
Matteo Tempestini	ALSTOM, Italy

Abstracts of Keynote Talks

Cyber Security in Railways: Quo Vadis?

Jens Braband

Siemens AG, Braunschweig, Germany
jens.braband@siemens.com

Abstract. Some recent incidents and analyses have indicated that possibly the vulnerability of IT systems in railway automation is increasing. Due to several trends, such as digitalization or the use of commercial IT and communication systems, the threat potential has increased. This paper discusses the way forward for the railway sector, how many advantages of digitalization can be realized without compromising safety. In particular topics such as standardization or certification are covered, but also technical issues like SW update.

Keywords: Railway • Cyber security • Safety • Risk assessment • Cyber security requirements

The Unreasonable Effectiveness of B for Data Validation and Modelling of Railway Systems

Michael Leuschel

Institut für Informatik, Heinrich-Heine-Universität Düsseldorf,
Universitätsstr. 1, D-40225 Düsseldorf
michael.leuschel@hhu.de

Abstract. The B method [2] is quite popular for developing provably correct software for safety-critical railway systems, particularly for driverless trains [6]. In recent years, the B method has also been used successfully for data validation.[1] There, the B language has proven to be a compact way to express complex validation rules, and tools such as predicateB, Ovado, or PROB can be used to provide high assurance validation engines, where a secondary toolchain validates the result of the primary toolchain [1, 3–5, 7, 8]. This talk will give an overview of our experience in using B for data validation tasks, as well as for other modelling tasks in the railway domain. We will also touch on subjects such as training and readability. We will examine which features of B make it well suited for the railway domain, but also point out some weaknesses and suggestions for future developments.

Keywords: B method · Data validation · Constraint programming

References

1. Abo, R., Voisin, L.: Formal implementation of data validation for railway safety-related systems with OVADO. In: SEFM Workshops, vol. 8368, pp. 221–236 (2013)
2. Abrial, J.-R.: The B-Book. Cambridge University Press (1996)
3. Ayed, R.B., Dutilleul, S.C., Bon, P., Idani, A., Ledru, Y.: B formal validation of ERTMS/ETCS railway operating rules. In: Ameur, Y.A., Schewe, K. (eds.) ABZ 2014. LNCS, vol. 8477, pp. 124–129. Springer, Heidelberg (2014)
4. Badeau, F., Amelot, A.: Using B as a high level programming language in an industrial project: Roissy VAL. In: ZB 2005. LNCS, vol. 3455, pp. 334–354. Springer, Heidelberg (2005)
5. Badeau, F., Doche-Petit, M.: Formal data validation with Event-B. In: Proceedings of DS-Event-B 2012, Kyoto. CoRR abs/1210.7039 (2012)

---

[1] http://www.data-validation.fr.

6. Essamé, D., Dollé, D.: B in large-scale projects: the Canarsie line CBTC experience. In: Julliand, J., Kouchnarenko, O. (eds.) B 2007. LNCS, vol. 4355, pp. 252–254. Springer, Heidelberg (2007)
7. Lecomte, T., Burdy, L., Leuschel, M.: Formally checking large data sets in the railways. In: Proceedings of DS-Event-B 2012, Kyoto. CoRR abs/1210.6815 (2012)
8. Leuschel, M., Falampin, J., Fritz, F., Plagge, D.: Automated property verification for large scale B models with ProB. Formal Aspects Comput. 23(6), 683–709 (2011)

Safety Certification: Considering Processes Around the World

Aryldo Ar. Russo

CERTIFER, France
aryldo.russo@certifer.eu

Abstract. The theoretical development path of a safety-critical system is for a SILx (where $1 <= x <=4$) => safety standards -> development + independent safety team + ISA -> safety certificate -> OK to operate. This development path, unfortunately, is followed mostly when formally required or imposed by the buyer, line operator, or grant authority, and this formalization is not a reality all around the world. This talk presents the process that is normally applied to certify safety-critical systems, the differences and pitfalls around the world, and briefly discusses the drawbacks and trade-offs of using automatic tools to replace manual development processes.

The main purpose on a railway system is to take passengers from point A to point B in a comfortable a safe way. By comfortable we can understand, besides ergonometric, an on time transport, without disruption, etc… by safe, clearly, a transport that do not kill people. To cope with this last requirement, meaning, safety, it's necessary to use a certain type of system, what's is called safety critical one. And, finally, to demonstrate that this safety critical system can contribute to maintain a certain level of safety on the entire system, the certification process takes place.

The theoretical development path of safety critical system is, for a SILx (where $1 <= x <=4$) => Safety Standards -> development + Independent Safety team + ISA -> Safety Certificate -> OK to operate. In railways, a set of standards exists to support the development, verification & validation and the certification process. These standards are the CENELEC 50126/128/129 (or the equivalent IEC 62278, 62279, 62425). Besides the development lifecycle, these standards determine the 3 pillars that have to exists, in an independent manner, that means, the development team, responsible for define the requirements, design the systems, implement it, etc…, the V&V team or Safety team, responsible for verify that the safety requirements were respected and validate that they were correctly implemented, and the Independent Safety Assessor, responsible for recheck each step of the development and V&V process to identify its compliancy with respect to the standards to the extent of the specific required safety level (SIL).

This development path, unfortunately, is followed mostly when formally required or imposed by the buyer, line operator or grant authority, and this formalization is not a reality all around the world. This talk presents the process that is normally applied to certify safety critical systems, the differences and pitfalls around the world. Most of the time, the requirements to cope with these standards are not well understood, what leads to an endless debate about what should be provided as evidence, the deepness of the analysis that should be performed, and when the assessment should begin. Moreover, there is a misunderstood between "Safety Analysis" and "Safety Assessment".

Finally, this talk briefly discusses the drawbacks and trade-offs of using automatic tools to replace manual development process. More and more the manual development process is being replaced by the use of automatic tools, during the specification phase, like the use of formal methods, during the implementation phase, like automatic code generators, during the test phases, like automatic test cases generators, or automatic test execution and analysis, just to cite a few. Even if those tools help a lot the development, decreasing the time to market, and helping to find hidden bugs, they also have to cope with the safety standards. Depending on the level of interaction of those tools, from a tool that it's just an aid, where no errors can be introduced by the tool itself, to a tool that performs part (or all) of the developer's job, like a code generator, more and more evidences shall be provided to allow the use of such tools. Those tools are classified by the standards as T1, T2 and T3.

Contents

Keynote Talk

Communication Challenges in Railway Systems

Formal Modelling and Verification for Safety

Light Rail and Urban Transit

Engineering Techniques and Standards

Keynote Talk

Cyber Security in Railways: Quo Vadis?

Jens Braband[(✉)]

Siemens AG, Brunswick, Germany
jens.braband@siemens.com

Abstract. Some recent incidents and analyses have indicated that possibly the vulnerability of IT systems in railway automation is increasing. Due to several trends, such as digitalization or the use of commercial IT and communication systems the threat potential has increased. This paper discusses the way forward for the railway sector, how many advantages of digitalization can be realized without compromising safety. In particular topics like standardization or certification are covered, but also technical issues like SW update.

Keywords: Railway · Cyber security · Safety · Risk assessment · Cyber security requirements

1 Introduction

Over the last years, reports on Cyber security incidents related to railways have increased as well as public awareness. For example, it was reported that, on December 1, 2011, "hackers, possibly from abroad, executed an attack on a Northwest rail company's computers that disrupted railway signals for two days" [1]. Although the details of the attack and also its consequences remain unclear, this episode clearly shows the threats to which railways are exposed when they rely on modern commercial-off-the-shelf (COTS) communication and computing technology. Only recently it was reported that the WannaCry virus also affected railway passenger information systems [2].

What distinguishes railway systems from many other systems is their inherently distributed and networked nature with tens of thousands of kilometer track length for large operators. Thus, it is not economical to provide complete protection against physical access to this infrastructure and, as a consequence, railways are very vulnerable to physical denial-of-service attacks leading to service interruptions.

Another feature of railways distinguishing them from most other systems is the long lifespan of their systems and components. Current contracts usually demand support for over 25 years and history has shown that many systems, e.g. mechanical or relay interlockings, last much longer. Cyber security analyses have to take into account such a long lifespan.

Concerning Cyber security another difference to many other application sectors is that railway automation is a highly safety-critical field, which has a rather strict approval regime similar to civil aviation. It seems that so far many Cyber security considerations have been made without this background. While in railway automation harmonized

A. Fantechi et al. (Eds.): RSSRail 2017, LNCS 10598, pp. 3–14, 2017.
https://doi.org/10.1007/978-3-319-68499-4_1

safety standards were elaborated almost two decades ago, up to now no harmonized Cyber security requirements for railway automation exist.

This paper starts with a discussion of the normative and legal background. A short overview of the basic concepts of ISA99/IEC62443 [3] is given. Then several approaches towards Cyber security risk assessment are discussed with particular focus on their applicability to safety-critical systems. Then a Cyber security risk assessment framework is defined which aims to separate Cyber security and safety requirements as well as certification processes as far as possible. This can be beneficial when SW is updated. As an example a particular update-friendly architecture is discussed.

2 Normative Background

In railway automation, there exists an established standard for safety-related communication, IEC 62280 [4]. The first version of the standard was elaborated in 2001. It has proven quite successful and is also used in other application areas, e.g. industry automation. This standard defines threats and countermeasures to ensure safe communication in railway systems. So, at an early stage, the standard established methods to build a safe channel (in security, called "tunnel" or "conduit") through an unsafe environment. However, the threats considered in IEC 62280 arise from technical sources or the environment rather than from humans. The methods described in the standard are partially able to protect the railway system also from intentional attacks, but not completely. Until now, additional organizational and technical measures have been implemented in railway systems, such as separated networks, etc., to achieve a sufficient level of protection.

The safety aspects of electronic hardware and systems are covered by IEC 62425 [5]. However, security issues are taken into account by IEC 62425 only as far as they affect safety issues, but, for example, denial-of-service attacks often do not fall into this category. Questions such as intrusion protection are only covered by one requirement in Table E.10 (unauthorized access). Nevertheless, IEC 62425 provides a structure for a safety case which explicitly includes a subsection on protection against unauthorized access (both physical and informational).

Only recently a survey group for the railway domain has delivered a recommendation that the safety standards like IEC 62425 shall be supplemented by a guideline on Cyber security. Particularly the proposal was made to adapt the ISA99/IEC62443 series, which is a set of standards currently elaborated by the Industrial Automation and Control System Security Committee of the International Society for Automation (ISA) in cooperation with IEC. This standard is not railway-specific and focuses on industrial control systems. It is dedicated to different hierarchical levels, starting from concepts and going down to components of control systems.

Railways are certainly critical national and international infrastructures, so recently national governments, e.g. the USA and Germany, as well as the EU have identified the problem. They have defined clear policies to support the implementation of industry-defined sector-specific Cyber security standards.

How can the gap between information security standards for general systems and railways be bridged? One bridge is provided by the European Commission Regulation

No. 402/2013 on Common Safety Methods [6]. This Commission Regulation mentions three different methods to demonstrate that a railway system is sufficiently safe:

(a) by following existing rules and standards (application of codes of practice),
(b) by similarity analysis, i.e. showing that the given (railway) system is equivalent to an existing and used one,
(c) by explicit risk analysis, where risk is assessed explicitly and shown to be acceptable.

We assume that, from the process point of view, security can be treated just like safety, meaning that threats would be treated as particular hazards. Using the approach under (a), ISA99/IEC62443 may be used in railway systems, but particular tailoring would have to be performed due to different safety requirements and application conditions. By this approach, a code of practice that is approved in other areas of technology and provides a sufficient level of security can be adapted to railways. This ensures a sufficient level of safety.

However, application of the general standards [4] requires tailoring them to the specific needs of a railway system. This is necessary to cover the specific threats associated with railway systems and possible accidents and to take into account specific other risk-reducing measures already present in railway systems, such as the use of specifically trained personnel.

This finally leads to a kind of "Cyber security for safety approach", where the Cyber security objectives and processes are referenced by the technical safety report from IEC

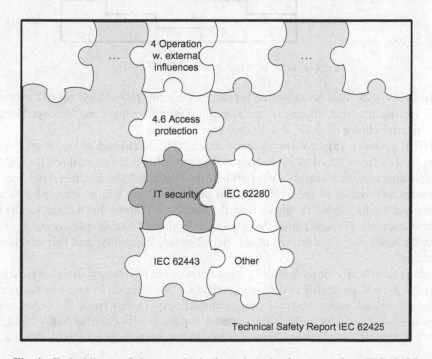

Fig. 1. Embedding on Cyber security in the technical safety report from IEC 62425

62425, see Fig. 1. Other security objectives can also be described in that structure, however the puzzle is not complete today and needs further railway-specific supporting standards and guidelines.

3   Problems with Threat and Risk Analysis for Safety-Related Systems

From the risk analysis point of view, many concepts from safety and Cyber security seem very similar; only the wording seems different. What's called a hazard in safety is called a threat in Cyber security, but the risk analysis processes really look alike. Thus it would be a logic conclusion to apply the same risk assessment techniques to Cyber security. This idea is even more supported by fact that many measures of Cyber security are adapted for safety and residual failure probabilities are computed, e.g. for transmission errors in communication, see e.g. IEC 62280. As a matter of fact this similarity is used in many security standards, ISO 27005 [7] being the most general, but instead of probability the term likelihood is introduced. A commonly used Cyber security risk matrix is shown in Fig. 2.

	Likelihood of incident scenario	Very Low (Very Unlikely)	Low (Unlikely)	Medium (Possible)	High (Likely)	Very High (Frequent)
	Very Low	0	1	2	3	4
	Low	1	2	3	4	5
Business Impact	Medium	2	3	4	5	6
	High	3	4	5	6	7
	Very High	4	5	6	7	8

Fig. 2.   Risk matrix based on ISO 27005

In ISO 27005 "likelihood is used instead of the term 'probability' for risk estimation". It is admitted that "its ease of understanding" is an advantage, but "the dependence on subjective choice of scale" is a disadvantage.

NIST guidance [8] explains in more detail: "The likelihood of occurrence is a weighted risk factor based on an analysis of the probability that a given threat is capable of exploiting a given vulnerability (or set of vulnerabilities). The likelihood risk factor combines an estimate of the likelihood that the threat event will be initiated with an estimate of the likelihood of impact (i.e., the likelihood that the threat event results in adverse impacts). For adversarial threats, an assessment of likelihood of occurrence is typically based on: (i) adversary intent; (ii) adversary capability; and (iii) adversary targeting."

Also scientifically the probabilistic approach does not really apply to Cyber security, e.g. we can't rely on statistical data or experience as we often do in safety as the threat landscape and risk assessment may change immediately if a new vulnerability becomes known. Also the attacks, at least the targeted attacks, don't occur randomly. So as a matter of fact we have both systematic causes as the initiators of a security threat and we have vulnerabilities, flaws in the system or SW engineering, as contributing factors, which also have a systematic nature.

4　Overview of ISA99/IEC62443 Standards

Currently, 10 parts are planned in this standard series covering different aspects for industrial automation and control systems (IACS, the main stakeholders are addressed in brackets):

General (all):

- 1-1 Terminology, concepts and models
- 1-2 Master glossary of terms and abbreviations

Policies and procedures (railway operators)

- 2-1 Establishing an industrial automation and control system security program 2-3 Patch management in the IACS environment
- 2-4 Security program requirements for IACS solution suppliers

System (system integrators)

- 3-1 Security technologies for IACS
- 3-2 Security levels for zones and conduits
- 3-3 System security requirements and security levels

Components (suppliers of Cyber security products)

- 4-1 Product development requirements
- 4-2 Technical security requirements for IACS products

The documents are at different stages of development, some being already international standards, while others are at the first drafting stage. This leads in particular to problems when the documents build on each other, e.g. Part 3-3 [9] with detailed security requirements is published, but it builds on Part 3-2 which defines the security levels and is restarted after a negative vote.

The fundamental concept of the standard is to define foundational requirements (FR) and security levels (SL) which are a "measure of confidence that the IACS is free from vulnerabilities and functions in the intended manner". There are seven groups of FR:

1. Identification and authentication control
2. Use control
3. System integrity
4. Data confidentiality
5. Restricted data flow
6. Timely response to events
7. Resource availability

Each FR group has up to 13 sub-requirement categories which are tailored according to the SL.

5 Security Levels

The default SL assignment for each zone and conduit is based on the attacker capability only:

SL 1: casual or unintended
SL 2: simple means: low resources, generic skills and low motivation
SL 3: sophisticated means: moderate resources, IACS-specific skills and moderate motivation
SL 4: sophisticated means: extended resources, IACS-specific skills and high motivation

The default assignment can be changed based on the results of a threat and risk analysis. For each FR, a different SL may be assigned. There is a distinction between a target SL (as derived by threat and risk analysis), a design SL (capability of the solution architecture) and finally the achieved SL (as finally realized). If either the design SL or the achieved SL does not match the target SL, then additional measures have to be implemented (e.g. physical or organizational) as compensation.

Taking into account the fact that there may also be no Cyber security requirement (SL 0), a SL assignment results in a seven-dimensional vector with $5^7 = 78.125$ possible different assignments. Based on the SL assignment, a standardized set of Cyber security requirements can be found in Part 3-3, which is a great advantage of the approach and which would simplify certification greatly.

Note that there is no simple match between SL and the Safety Integrity Levels (SIL) applied in safety standards. However, the definition of SL 1 is very similar to requirements in the safety field as also safety-related systems have to address topics such as operator error, foreseeable misuse or effects of random failure. So we can conclude that a safety-related system (SIL > 0) should also fulfill the technical requirements of IEC 62443-3-3 as the threats which SL 1 addresses are also safety hazards.

A concise comparison shows that there are some differences in detail. IEC 62443-3-3 contains 41 requirements for SL 1, of which more than half are directly covered by safety standards such as IEC 62425 or IEC 62280, and about a quarter are usually fulfilled in railway safety systems representing good practice. However, another quarter of the requirements are usually not directly addressed in IEC 62425 safety cases. The main reasons are that these requirements do not fall under the "Cyber security for safety" category but address availability requirements in order to prevent denial of service or traceability requirements.

The current proposal is to include all SL 1 requirements from IEC 62443-3-3 in the system requirements specification of any safety-related signaling system. In this way, no additional SL 1 Cyber security certification would be necessary and it would be a contribution to the defense-in-depth principle. Finally, these requirements should find their place in the IEC 62278 standards series.

For the sake of brevity, we are focusing on system aspects in this paper. The first step after system definition would be to divide the system into zones and conduits according to the following basic rules:

- The system definition must include all hardware and software objects.
- Each object is allocated to a zone or a conduit.
- Inside each zone, the same Cyber security requirements are applicable.
- There exists at least one conduit for communication with the environment.

The next step is the threat and risk analysis resulting in SL assignment to each zone and conduit. Here, railway applications might need procedures different from industry automation as factories and plants are usually physically well protected and are not moving.

As soon as the SL is assigned, standardized requirements from IEC 62443-3-3 can be derived. These requirements would be taken over to the railway automation domain without any technical changes. They would define the interface to use pre-certified Cyber security components for the railway automation domain.

Finally, correct implementation of the Cyber security countermeasures according to IEC 62443-3-3 must be evaluated similar to the validation of safety functions.

6 Approaches Towards Cyber Security Risk Assessment

6.1 IEC 62443-3-2 Proposal

Recently, a novel approach towards semi-quantitative Cyber security risk assessment has been proposed in the draft IEC 62443-3-2 [10]. It tried to define the security level as a level of cyber security risk reduction. It used a similar matrix like in Fig. 2, but with a different ranking of risk. But it did not pass the voting as the argumentation was unfounded and was not well integrated with other parts of the standard series. In the review of IEC 62443-3-2 it was recently decided not to propose a particular method for cyber security risk assessment and allocation of SL.

6.2 German DKE 0831-104 Proposal

In a recently published standard for railway automation [11] the approach seems to avoid the uncertainty or infeasibility of credible likelihood estimation, but rather to focus on the capability of the attacker as stipulated by the SL definition. The rationale behind this approach is that the worst case would be a remote attack, which cannot be traced and which has safety impact. This case would deserve the highest Cyber security requirements as such attacks would scale in contrast to attacks that need local or physical access.

In a first step, it must be decided whether the zone or conduit is exposed to malicious attacks at all. If no malicious attacks have to be assumed, then SL 1 is assigned for all FR. Otherwise, the parameters already addressed by IEC 62443 would be assessed separately for each zone and each conduit according to Table 1. This means a score is assigned to each of the parameters resources, know-how and motivation of the attacker.

Table 1. Assessment of attacker capability

Score	2	3	4
Resources (R)	Low	Medium	Extended
Know-how (K)	Common	System-specific	Extended
Motivation (M)	Low	Limited	High

The following railway specific risk parameters should be considered in addition to the parameters already dealt with in IEC 62443, also in comparison with NIST 800-30:

- Attack location (from where can the attack be launched?)
- Traceability of the attack (in the sense of non-repudiation)
- Potential extent of damage (Safety-critical impact)

It is important that a realistic type of attacker is evaluated, rather than an evaluation of which resources, capabilities and motivation an attacker would need for a successful attack. As it has also been demonstrated that in particular the motivation of an attacker and the location of the attack and its traceability are dependent on one another, the evaluation of the attacker's motivation does not need to take place directly, but is covered by the other parameters.

A combination rule is needed to be able to evaluate these two parameters independently. This is specified in Table 2.

Table 2. Preliminary SL assignment

	R2	R3	R4
K2	PSL 2	PSL 3	PSL 4
K3	PSL 3	PSL 3	PSL 4
K4	PSL 3	PSL 4	PSL 4

In particular, the following facts were taken into account:

- According to IEC 62443, an SL x is sufficient to successfully ward off an attacker belonging to the combination Rx, Kx and Mx.
- An attacker who possesses higher resources (Rx) than skills (Kx) could acquire the applicable skills by using his resources.
- The motivation of an attacker and the location of the attack and its traceability are dependent on one another. So no particular direct scale for motivation (Mx) is necessary.

The provisional SL (PSL) listed in Table 2 corresponds to the SL in compliance with IEC 62443 without considering railway specific risk factors.

Generally, several attacker types have to be considered. In this case, the highest PSL of the different attacker types' shall be taken into account. The railway specific parameters have a special importance compared with other application domains and can therefore give rise to adapted SL requirements.

The PSL may then be altered based on railway-specific risk parameters, e.g.

- location of the asset and the attacker (ORT), e.g. does the attacker need access to the site or can the attack be launched remotely, e.g. from home?
- traceability and non-repudiation of the attack (NAC), e.g. is it possible to trace the attacker and to collect sufficient evidence to identify him?
- potential of the attack (POT), e.g. is there no or limited safety implication of the attack?

All these additional variables are binary and are set to 1 if the question can be answered by YES. The final SL is assignment is then by

$$SL = PSL - \text{maximum}\{ORT, NAC, POT\}$$

meaning that the PSL can be reduced if there is at least one railway risk reduction factor present, but not more.

It should be noted that, according to IEC 62443, the assessment would have to be carried out for all seven FR. However, from a railway safety point of view, some of the FR have only little safety impact so that FR such as "Data confidentiality" or "Resource availability" should always be assigned SL 1 as a default. Also, it can be argued that there is no real reason to distinguish between the other FR, because they are not independent, and it is proposed to allocate the same SL to all five remaining FR. This would lead to only four classes for railway signaling applications

- SL 1 = (1,1,1,1,1,1,1)
- SL 2 = (2,2,2,1,2,2,1)
- SL 3 = (3,3,3,1,3,3,1)
- SL 4 = (4,4,4,1,4,4,1)

In the approach presented here, it has to be decided against which kind of attackers the system has to be made secure, which is a decision to be taken by the railway operator and the safety authority. This decision is guided by the parameters in Table 1. The SL then represents the effort which must be made so that the system effectively withstands attacks by these kinds of attackers. Only attackers who exceed this effort considerably might be able to overcome the Cyber security countermeasures. Different kinds of attackers on railway assets have already been researched [12] and the results were compatible with the classification proposed here.

However it may be criticized that this approach concentrates too much on the attacker capability without exploiting all attack scenarios or taking all security aspects into account. In order to satisfy these critics we extend the approach in the next chapter.

7 Combined Approach

We can summarize the analysis so far that the former approach proposed by IEC 62443-3-2 has several systematic flaws which cannot be easily overcome. In particular, the question of calculating Cyber security-related risks is very complex and should be avoided [13]. But we have sketched an approach how to derive the SIL from a safety point of view.

However, the use of risk matrices in Cyber security is so widely used in Threat & Risk Analysis (TRA) that it should be kept, but it should be properly used with the definition of SL in IEC 62443.

We start from the following assumptions (without further justification):

- There exists an agreed risk matrix, like Fig. 2
- We can derive SLs which are defined by the type of attacker and the measures defined by IEC 62443 (like in the previous chapter)

For the sake of the example, we assume the same sample risk matrix as shown from Fig. 2 (but we do not use the criticalities). The precise form of the matrix is not important, however there should be a clear procedure which would be followed based on the classification of the results. Normally color codes green, yellow and red are used ranging from broadly acceptable to intolerable risks.

In a TRA, we would assess all possible threat scenarios and classify them according to their risk. Assume we have defined the SL by the type of attacker, say initially SL is equal to (3,3,3,1,3,3,1). Then, we would start the TRA as a check and should arrive at tolerable risks for safety-related threats (usually green (0–2) or yellow (3–5) fields). For yellow classifications we would only have to reduce risk if it is economically reasonable. If we arrive at red (6–8) classifications, this means we either misjudged the SL in the beginning or we may have scenarios that represent additional Cyber security related risks which are not safety-related. For example this might be a loss of reputation after a data breach. This would mean that we have to define additional security requirements which are not safety-related.

8 Software Patch Management

Software update or software patch management is a topic where fundamental dilemmas between safety and security manifest themselves. Safety-related software undergoes a lengthy and costly approval process with many independent steps such as testing, verification, validation and assessment. Thus, safety-related systems are updated only rarely and infrequently as updating would change the approved software configuration and invalidate the safety case and a new approval process would have to be started. However, in Cyber security, updating or patching occurs frequently, e.g. for COTS operating systems or anti-virus software.

The UK Department for Transport acknowledges these problems in their guidance [14] by stating that safety-related systems "should be updated and patched where this does not violate the safety case". But what if such systems use COTS operating systems? At least it is required that new safety-related systems "can be patched without violating the safety case". However, no concrete solution is presented.

We sketch a solution that even allows the co-existence of a non-safety third-party software and a safety-related software on the same platform. We assume that we have multiple redundant hardware channels and a voter and we distinguish between different kinds of patches for the third-party software: change of configuration data, error correction (without any change of the intended functionality) and new functionality. The solution is as follows:

1. At least one channel (called A channel) contains only the approved safety-related software; at least one (called B channel) additionally contains the third-party software.
2. Initially, the complete system is approved.
3. Before a safety-relevant output is executed, the voter checks that at least one A channel and the majority of B channels have agreed (or produced the same output).
4. The third-party software on the B channels may be updated, if by a change analysis and a system integration test it can be shown that the risk associated with the change is broadly acceptable.

As a consequence, it is ensured that the third-party software cannot influence the safety-related software, as the A channel is not affected by the update. Under normal conditions, a change of configuration data and error correction should always be broadly acceptable in such architecture, so that, in the most frequent cases, the third-party software can be patched. This means that malware protection software may be regularly updated without invalidating the safety case (Fig. 3).

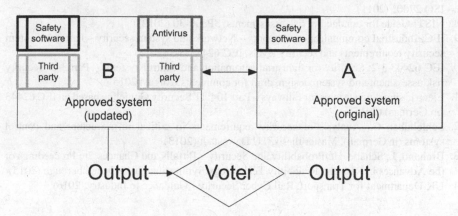

Fig. 3. Update-friendly architecture example

9   Conclusion

This paper has shown a way forward how to deal with cyber security in railways: it should be based on an adaptation of the industry standard ISA99/IEC 62443.

However particular care has to be taken for risk assessment approaches with respect to Cyber security, as currently there is no established approach which combines risk matrices and SL allocation. For this purpose a combined framework for risk assessment with particular focus on railway automation applications has been proposed. The concept aims at the separation of safety and security aspects, as far as possible. This is achieved by integrating safety-related security requirements into the safety process and the safety case.

Finally the particular problem of SW update has been discussed as an example where safety and security have conflicting goals. However it has been shown that this problem cannot be solved by standards but by architecture.

References

1. http://www.nextgov.com/nextgov/ng_20120123_3491.php
2. The Telegraph: Cyber attack hits German train stations as hackers target Deutsche Bahn. http://www.telegraph.co.uk/news/2017/05/13/cyber-attack-hits-german-train-stations-hackers-target-deutsche/
3. ISA 99: Standards of the Industrial Automation and Control System Security Committee of the International Society for Automation (ISA) on information security. http://isa99.isa.org/Documents/Forms/AllItems.aspx
4. IEC 62280 Railway applications, Communication, signaling and processing systems–Safety related communication in transmission systems, September 2010 (CENELEC EN 50159)
5. IEC 62425 Railway applications, Communication, signaling and processing systems – Safety-related electronic systems for signaling, February 2003 (CENELEC EN 50129)
6. Commission Implementing Regulation (EU) No 402/2013 on the common safety method for risk evaluation and assessment and repealing Regulation (EC) No 352/2009, 30 April 2013
7. ISO: Information technology - Security techniques - Information security risk management, ISO 27005 (2011)
8. NIST: Guide for conducting risk assessments, SP800-30 (2012)
9. IEC: Industrial communication networks – Network and system security – Part 3-3: System security requirements and security levels, IEC 62443-3-3 (2015)
10. IEC 62443-3-2: Security for industrial automation and control systems – Part 3-2: Security risk assessment and system design, draft for comments, August 2015
11. Electric signaling systems for railways – Part 104: IT Security Guideline based on IEC 62443 (in German) (2015)
12. Schlehuber, C.: Analysis of security requirements in critical infrastructure and control systems (in German), Master thesis, TU Darmstadt (2013)
13. Braband, J., Schäbe, H.: Probability and Security – Pitfalls and Chances. In: Proceedings of the Advances in Risk and Reliability Technology Symposium 2015, Loughborough (2015)
14. UK Department for Transport: Rail Cyber Security - Guidance to Industry (2016)

Communication Challenges in Railway Systems

LTE System Design for Urban Light Rail Transport

Gianluca Mandò[1]([⊠]) and Giovanni Giambene[2] [iD]

[1] Thales Italia SpA, Via Lucchese, 33, Osmannoro, 50019 Florence, Italy
gianluca.mando@thalesgroup.com
[2] Dipartimento di Ingegneria dell'Informazione e Scienze Matematiche,
Università degli Studi di Siena, Via Roma, 56, 53100 Siena, Italy
giambene@unisi.it

Abstract. This paper deals with the performance of LTE-A (Long Term Evolution-Advanced) cellular networks for supporting operational, safety-critical signaling, and standard IT services for urban transportation. Our interests have been focused on Light Rail Transit (LRT) signaling performance for the Songjiang (China) tramway project. Several stationary and mobility use cases have been considered and mean end-to-end delay and Packet Loss Rate (PLR) key performance indicators have been evaluated. Simulation results highlight that, in stationary conditions, LRT signaling performance requirements are fulfilled, while PLR performance degrades when mobility is introduced. Furthermore, we have evaluated the impact of non-critical IT traffic (e.g., UDP-based video) on TCP-based signaling by demonstrating that signaling throughput is not affected by video in stationary scenarios, whereas, in the presence of mobility, handovers degrade signaling performance, which can be guaranteed only if a QoS-aware scheduler is adopted. In conclusions, our results demonstrate that LTE-A can safely support operative and non-critical applications in urban transportation scenarios, where strong connectivity requirements are crucial.

Keywords: Light rail transit · Safety-critical signaling · LTE

1 Introduction

Reliability, availability and safety play a crucial role for the increasingly use of public transport systems. In this paper, we analyze all major challenges that wireless communication systems are facing today in order to guarantee signaling services for train control, passenger safety, and to allow the coexistence with other new, non-critical applications [1]. Today, traffic control and management of public transportation systems are mainly provided by wireless communication technologies such as GSM-R for railways, TETRA, and WiFi in metro applications. But, if we consider today communication needs for rail transport, we realize that the above technologies have some limitations, mainly due to their inefficiency and limited capacities, thus paving the way to the introduction of new mobile digital technologies.

In this paper, after a brief summary of the existing radio systems used in public transport, we evaluate LTE technology performance for Light Rail Transit (LRT) applications [2]. After defining the main elements of a typical tramway control system, we

© Springer International Publishing AG 2017
A. Fantechi et al. (Eds.): RSSRail 2017, LNCS 10598, pp. 17–33, 2017.
https://doi.org/10.1007/978-3-319-68499-4_2

will describe the simulation of a real urban tram line (Songjiang Line 1 [3]) by using the Ns-3 network simulator [4] and evaluate the performance of an LTE infrastructure for transmitting both control signaling and video traffic.

2   Radio Communications for Urban Transport

Public transport systems can be divided in two main categories, such as: railway transport and Urban Guided Transport (UGT) [5]. The former refers to wheeled vehicles running on rails and is also commonly referred to as train transport. The latter is a public transport system in an urban area with motorized vehicles operated on a guideway (i.e., the vehicles follow a determined trajectory for all or part of their journey). These are, therefore, metro, subways, trams, and LRTs.

Connectivity is one of the key issues for these transport systems. In fact, a moving vehicle cannot obviously be connected to ground-based infrastructure by any other mean than legacy inductive systems or radio communications. In the past, such radio systems have been based on analogue technology, dedicated to voice and not suitable for carrying data. Nowadays, due to the necessity to provide more operational and safety services for train control, passenger security, and new non-critical applications, there is a lot of interest in introducing new digital mobile technologies for urban guided transport systems. In what follows, a survey is presented on the main services provided by radio communication systems for transport systems. Then, a very quick view is given on the state-of-the-art of radio communication technologies for railways and UGT systems.

2.1   Radio Communications Services for Transport Systems

Safety and non-safety services, which are provided today in transport systems through communication technologies, have different Quality of Service (QoS) requirements. They can be classified into three main categories:

- **Safety-critical signaling** for the safe movement of trains and operations. It can be distinguished in two categories: signaling related to the safety of the train itself and public safety signaling, also including voice communications. They generally require a low throughput (up to 100 kbps), but have strong requirements in terms of security, reliability, availability (at least 99.99%), robustness (typically a packet error rate of 10^{-3} for a 200-byte packet) and timing (delay constraints lower than 500–800 ms) [1].
- **Operational non-safety services** for non-critical services for train operation support. They do not have a direct impact on the safety and efficiency, but aim to improve internal railway operations. These services consist of passenger information (to provide contents related to the train location, stations, latest updates on delay and traffic disruption), Closed Circuit TV (CCTV) for security and Internet of Things (IoT) for sensing, communicating and aggregating all information.
- **Non-critical applications for infotainment** that are devoted to providing services to train passengers (e.g., Internet access, advertisement, and movie streaming).

2.2 LTE as a Future Communication Solution for Railway Applications

Today, train operators receive an increasing data traffic demand for signaling, operations, and to provide travel comfort by offering more services to passengers through real-time multimedia data. Technologies such as GSM-R and TETRA, which are ETSI (European Telecommunications Standard Institute) standards, provide an insufficient data rate if we consider today's communication needs for urban transport, while WiFi technologies, although achieving high data rates, have limitations in mobility support and because of interference. LTE is a 4G wireless technology whose standardization started in 2008 by the 3rd Generation Partnership Project (3GPP). Its architecture consists of Base Stations, called eNodeBs (eNBs), which allow connectivity between User Equipment (UE) and Core Network, called Evolved Packet Core (EPC). The introduction of LTE in railway and urban guided transport is an open research issue that is gaining more and more interest from the railway industry.

In a few years, GSM communication systems will be decommissioned as the public communication market is evolving toward LTE. As a consequence, GSM-R also has a foreseeable end of its lifetime [6]. A new system is thus required to fulfill railway operational needs with the capability of being consistent with LTE, offering new services, but still coexisting with GSM-R for a certain period of time. In view of both the performance and the level of maturity of LTE, LTE-Railway (LTE-R) will likely be the next-generation LRT communication systems. Table 1 provides a comparison of LTE with other wireless technologies.

Table 1. Comparison of existing radio communication technologies.

	GSM-R	TETRA	WiFi	LTE
Operational voice support	Yes	Yes	VoIP	VoLTE
Data support	< 10 kbps	< 28.8 kbps	> 10 Mbps	> 10 Mbps
All IP (native)	No	No	Yes	Yes
Vital traffic support	Yes	Yes	No	Yes
P2T/call setup time	1 to 5 s	250 ms	100 ms	100 ms
Handover mechanism	Standard	Standard	Proprietary	Standard
Priorities/pre-emption	Yes	Yes	4 QoS classes/No	9 QoS classes/Yes
Available frequencies	900 MHz UIC	400 MHz PMR	2.4/5 GHz	400 MHz to 3.5 GHz
Cell range	10 km	25 km	< 1 km	1 km
Maturity	End by 2025	Mature	Widely adopted in urban areas	Emerging

3 LRT and Tramway Control System

LRT and tramways are playing an ever more important role in creating environmentally-sustainable cities, enforcing the concept of sustainable mobility within the smart cities contextual environment. It is a kind of urban transportation system for which automation systems for service operation are actually not applied, since these trains share their ways with other vehicles, like buses, cars and even pedestrians. Indeed, the safety in tramways is based on the principle that the train movement is fully controlled by the driver: railway operation is under his responsibility and no level of automation is allowed. Tramway Control System (TCS) is the signaling and control system that provides supervision and control over tramway and LRT networks, including routing and headway management. TCS is a complete signaling and control system that optimizes performances, providing an unprecedented level of supervision and control over tramway and LRT networks, including routing and headway management. It is a modular and scalable system made up of three main building blocks:

- **Traffic Manager** (TM) at the Operation Control Center (OCC) for real-time vehicles localization and circulation management;
- **Interlocking System** (IS), which manages LRT signaling alongside and in the depots. It is usually a fault-tolerant system with a high grade of SIL (Safety Integrity Level) that controls line switches, track circuits, axle counters and signals.
- **On Board Computer** (OBC) to manage on-board signaling, communication and comfort.

The general TCS network architecture (see Fig. 1) consists in a transmission system based on a Gigabit Ethernet Backbone connecting the OCC to the stations and in a radio system to connect the OCC to the trams. Furthermore, TCS allows a safe management of the tram movement at the depot, where electrical switches are monitored and controlled by using the same TCS equipment foreseen for the switch area management in the main line. The main functions of TCS are: automatic vehicle localization, priority management at road and crossing area, train regulation, timetable management, junctions and depot management, and passenger information.

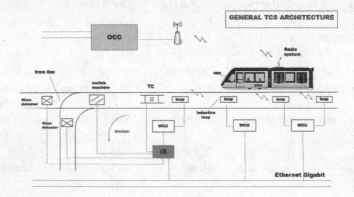

Fig. 1. General TCS architecture.

4   Simulation Approach and Results

For the simulation study carried out in this work, we have assumed an LTE cellular network for the Songjiang Tram Line T1. The details of Songjiang tram lines are provided in Table 2 [3].

Table 2. Characteristics of T1 and T2 tram lines.

Songjiang tram lines T1 & T2	Lines		Total
	Line T1	Line T2	
Length (km)	15.659	15.24	30.941
Stations	23	22 (one station is reserved for future)	45
Trains	15		30
OCC	1		1

First of all we are interested in evaluating the performance in terms of mean end-to-end (e2e) delay and packet loss rate of the signaling traffic from trains to OCC and back, and then we will add a non-critical bandwidth-demanding traffic in order to evaluate the impact of this traffic on signaling traffic. Line T1 is 15.659 km long with 23 stations. At first, 16 trains are provided on the line, but this number will increase to 30 trains during the years. Each train reaches the maximum speed of 70 km/h and its average speed is about 30 km/h. This line is double track; after having reached a terminus point each train goes back to the other terminus. Multiple cells are need in order to cover the whole line T1 with an LTE network. A link budget analysis is then required in order to find the cell range and the number of eNBs to be deployed to cover the target area. We assume that the designed LTE network is dedicated entirely to train traffic.

We model trains as LTE User Equipments (UEs), while the OCC is modelled as a Remote Host and traffic flows are generated in both uplink and downlink directions. We consider the following performance indicators:

- **The mean end-to-end delay (e2e delay)**, calculated as the ratio of the sum of all end-to-end delays for all received packets of a data flow to the number of received packets;
- **The Packet Loss Rate (PLR)**, calculated as the ratio of lost packets to the sum of lost packets and received packets, where lost packets refer to those that were transmitted, but have not been reportedly received or forwarded for a long time.

Transmission Control Protocol (TCP) is used as the transport layer protocol for signaling traffic. TCP provides reliable and ordered delivery of stream of IP packets from one sender to one receiver. LRT signaling traffic is on top of TCP and is intended as the sum of the following traffic flows in downlink:

Traffic position request (32-byte packet size) + Passenger information (128-byte packet size) + Driver logic answer (16-byte packet size) and Time synchronization answer (16-byte packet size).

In uplink, signaling is the sum of the following traffic flows:

Train position request (32-byte packet size) + Route request (16-byte packet size) + Train diagnostic telemetry (32-byte packet size) + Time synchronization request (8-byte packet size).

Both downlink and uplink signaling traffic are modelled (at application level) as a Constant Bit Rate (CBR) traffic having 200-byte packets and data rate of 1600 bps. CBR traffic flows are modelled as ON/OFF traffic processes.

On-board video surveillance is on top of User Datagram Protocol (UDP) that is another common transport layer protocol used in today's Internet. UDP is connectionless and does not provide any sort of reliability, rate limiting or congestion control mechanism to the applications using it, such as video streaming. Table 3(a) summarizes the characteristics of traffic sources and their QoS requirements defined by the train operator. The second phase of this work involves the study of the impact of non-critical traffic (video modelled as CBR traffic having 1000-byte packets and data rate of 1 Mbps) on signaling. Table 3(b) illustrates video traffic characteristics and QoS requirements.

Table 3.   Traffic characteristics and QoS requirements for signaling (a) and video (b) traffic.

Traffic Flow	Signalling Traffic
Packet size	200 bytes
Data Rate	1.6 kbps
Transport layer protocol	TCP (New-Reno version)
Application-level traffic model	CBR
Packet Loss requirement	10^{-3}
Mean E2E delay requirement	50 ms

Traffic Flow	Video Traffic
Packet size	1000 bytes
Data Rate	1 Mbps
Transport layer protocol	UDP
Application-level traffic model	CBR
Packet Loss requirement	10^{-3}
Mean E2E delay requirement	150 ms

(a)   (b)

4.1   Simulator Implementation

We have implemented the LTE scenarios of Songjiang Tram Line T1 using the Ns-3 simulation environment [4]. Ns-3 is an open-source discrete-event network simulator under the GNU GPLv2 license. Ns-3 is primarily used on Linux systems, although support exists for Windows systems as well. To implement the LTE scenario, we have used the Ns-3 LENA (LTE-EPC Network simulAtor) module [7]. LENA is a free opensource LTE network simulator developed by the Centre Tecnològic de Telecomunicacions de Catalunya (CTTC). The LTE model supports Radio Resource Management (RRM), Inter-Cell Interference Coordination (ICIC), dynamic spectrum access and QoS-aware packet scheduling. At radio level, the granularity of the model is at the level of Resource Blocks (RBs), which are the fundamental units of resource allocation. Packet scheduling is done on a Transmission Time Interval (TTI) basis (= 1 ms). An eNB can transmit on a subset of the available RBs, interfering with other eNBs transmitting on the same RBs. The simulator is designed to manage tens of eNBs (each controlling a cell) and hundreds of UEs (corresponding in this case to trains). The simulator can be used to simulate many IP packets flows, but in the LTE simulator, scheduling and radio resource management do not directly work with IP packets, but rather with

Radio Link Control (RLC) packets, obtained by segmentation and concatenation of IP packets at the RLC layer.

4.2 Results: Stationary Trains at Train Depot

This scenario implements the simplest use case where all trains are located at the train depot and turn on signaling traffic all at the same time (data rate 1600 bit/s/train). This situation corresponds to a real case when all trams are started at the same time in the depot (the operational services are activated in the morning) (Fig. 2).

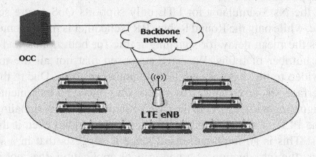

Fig. 2. Stationary trains at train depot.

We consider covering this area with only one eNB with a cell radius of approximately 1 km; thus, all the trains are connected to this cell and exchange data with the OCC. All the trains are modelled as stationary nodes and they are uniformly distributed in the cell. Each simulation run lasted 10 min and was repeated 10 times with different seed numbers in order to achieve reliable results. The main simulation parameters are shown in Table 4 below.

Table 4. Simulation parameters of the stationary scenario.

Parameter	Value
LTE Bandwidth	5 MHz
eNB/UE antenna height	50 m/3.5 m
Cell radius	1 km
eNB/UE antenna gain	18 dBi/0 dBi
eNB/UE Tx Power	26 dBm/23 dBm
Number of trains	15, 20, 25, 30
Simulation repetitions	10

In this scenario, we have found that the mean e2e signaling delay in relation to the number of trains at the train depot is approximately constant in all investigated cases and is below 14 ms and 23 ms (respectively for downlink and uplink) for a number of trains up to 30 at the depot. Uplink delay is a bit higher than downlink because the uplink radio resource scheduling is different from downlink [8]. As for PLR, we have verified that it is negligible for both uplink and downlink, thus fulfilling the requirements of the train operator.

Furthermore, within this depot scenario we have also investigated the impact of non-critical traffic on LRT signaling. In other words, OCC sends a further video flow modelled with 1 Mbps data rate. Both flows share the same LTE resources so that a QoS provisioning mechanism is required in order to prioritize and protect signaling. In LTE, the QoS mechanism is provided using EPS bearers, which carry packet flows between the UEs and a specific packet data gateway (P-GW). Hence, in order to guarantee some specific QoS requirements for a specific application, a dedicated bearer will be established for that application. All the details of each traffic type are summarized in Table 3. Unfortunately, the Ns-3 simulator for LTE only supports QoS-aware schedulers for downlink traffic, while only the Round Robin (RR) scheduler is implemented for uplink. Figure 3 shows the mean delay for signaling traffic for both uplink and downlink in relation to the number of trains. We have supposed that not all the trains activate signaling and video traffic, but only a selected number of them. Due to the congestion of LTE air interface resources caused by video, we noticed an increment of the mean e2e delay for signaling with respect to the case without video. The signaling PLR is still almost zero: the PLR of signaling is not affected by the video even if the number of trains increases. This is an important result since it suggests that in a scenario with stationary trains, the introduction of a non-critical application does not influence the QoS of signaling, which is a vital traffic for train operation and safety.

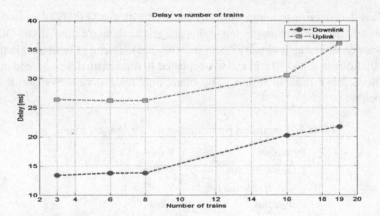

Fig. 3. Signaling traffic delay in relation to the number of trains.

Figure 4 presents the mean delay performance for video. As we can see, due to its high throughput, the mean delay for video is higher than the signaling one.

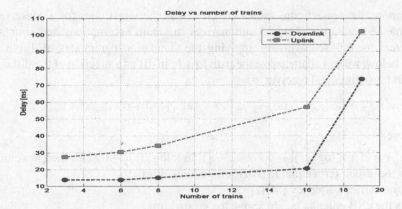

Fig. 4. Video delay in relation to the number of trains.

As for video PLR, it is almost zero in the downlink case until 16 trains are considered at the train depot, since the capacity of an LTE cell is sufficient to support all these traffic flows and a target bit rate is used by the scheduler for each traffic. In the case with 19 trains, the cell capacity is not sufficient so there are packet losses due to congestion. Video PLR requirements defined in Table 3 are not fulfilled in uplink, while they are met in downlink when there is no congestion in the network.

4.3 Results: Cell Planning

The number of eNBs that are needed to cover the tram line with cells of radius R depends on the eNB transmission power according to the link budget analysis. In particular, we use the following equation to determine the cell size R:

$$R[km] = 10^{(P_{tx}+G_{tx}-L_{tx}-P_{min}+G_{rx}-IM-L_{rx}-x)/z} \qquad (1)$$

where:
R is the cell radius
P_{tx} is the transmission power (dBm)
G_{tx}, G_{rx} are transmitter and receiver antenna gains (dB), respectively
L_{tx}, L_{rx} are the losses (dB) at transmitter and receiver, respectively
P_{min} is the minimum receiver power (dBm)
IM is the interference margin (dB)
x, z are terms that depend on the pathloss.

For a given number of trains in transit into the line, we simulate some scenarios where the number of eNBs varies, accordingly to the transmission power, and we evaluate the performance of signaling traffic in terms of mean end-to-end delay and packet loss rate for the communications between trains and OCC. We assume to consider the worst-case conditions for interference: values of the interference margins for both uplink and downlink are chosen as the worst values within a typical range for LTE systems [8].

Furthermore, the noise figure values are chosen as the worst ones for a conservative performance evaluation. Table 5 summarizes the main assumptions and simulation parameters for this scenario. By applying the simulation parameters of Table 5 to Eq. (2) below, we can characterize the path loss L_p in dB as a function of the distance d between transmitter and receiver as:

$$L_p[dB] = 46.3 + 33.9 \times \log_{10}(f) - 13.82 \times \log_{10}(h_b) - F(h_M) + C + [44.9 - 6.55 \times \log_{10}(h_b)] \times \log_{10}(d), \quad (2)$$

where

$F(h_M) = \left[1.1 \times \log_{10}(f)\right] - 0.7 \times h_M - \left[1.56 \times \log_{10}(f)\right] - 0.8$, for medium cities
C is a constant term equal to 0 dB for medium cities
f is the carrier frequency [MHz]
h_b is the eNB antenna height above the ground [m]
h_M is the UE antenna height above the ground [m]
d is the distance between the eNB and the UE [km].

Since uplink is commonly more critical than downlink for the link budget, we determine the cell size R, referring to uplink coverage. In order to define the proper parameters for determining the cell radius R, we can refer to the expected Cell Edge Throughput (CET) or to the minimum receiver power level, P_{min}. Fixing the CET for a single user, we determine the minimum Modulation and Coding Scheme (MCS) index, which has a corresponding Signal-to-Interference and Noise Ratio (SINR) threshold value. Thus, knowing this SINR threshold, the receiver noise figure and the thermal noise, which depends on the number of RBs we assume to allocate to the UE at cell edge, we obtain the minimum receiver power P_{min}, and then R is simply given by (1).

Table 5. Simulation parameters.

Parameter	Value
LTE bandwidth	5 MHz
eNB/UE antenna height	50 m/3.5 m
eNB/UE antenna gain	18 dBi/0 dBi
Type of handover/Handover algorithm	X2-based handover/Strongest cell
CET	1 Mbps
Type of uplink scheduler	Round Robin (RR)
Type of downlink scheduler	Priority Set Scheduler (PSS)
Adaptive modulation and coding	Piro's model
UL/DL receiver sensitivity	−100 dBm/−96 dBm
eNB/UE Tx power	18–48 dBm/23 dBm
eNB noise figure/UE noise figure	5 dB/9 dB
UL/DL interference margin	10 dB/8 dB
Number of trains	16
Tramway line length	15.7 km

Since in our simulation scenario we randomly place 16 trains along the line (8 trains move in a direction and the other 8 trains move in the opposite direction), we can suppose that at most there will be 2 trains at the edge of a cell at the same time. This is only an assumption we have done for our work, but it is of considerable importance in order to define the cell edge throughput and the corresponding number of resource blocks to be allocated to each user. Knowing the CET and the total bandwidth (= 5 MHz in our case, corresponding to 25 RBs), if we consider to have 2 UEs at the cell border, the network could not allocate more than 12 RBs per UE (= train). Assuming an uplink CET of 1 Mbps and allocating 12 RBs, the corresponding MCS index is 6 that corresponds to use a QPSK modulation.

In our Ns-3 simulator, only even MCS indexes from 0 to 28 (out of 30) are considered according to [9]. Each MCS index corresponds to a certain SINR threshold value. So that, knowing the required MCS index to fulfil the CET condition, we can find the corresponding SINR value used by the simulator and the minimum received power P_{min}. In Fig. 5, the MCS level is shown as a function of the SINR level, as implemented in the Ns-3 simulator for the Adaptive Modulation and Coding (AMC) scheme [9].

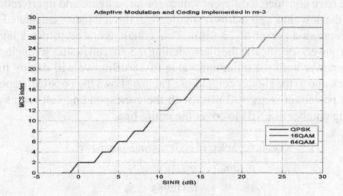

Fig. 5. AMC levels implemented in Ns-3.

In Fig. 6, we provide the graphs for uplink and downlink cell radius. As expected, the higher is the transmission power, the larger is the cell radius. Furthermore, considering the maximum transmission power for UEs equal to 23 dBm, we notice from Fig. 6 that the maximum cell radius is about 0.5 km if we consider the more stringent condition of uplink coverage. This demonstrates that the LTE system is uplink limited. Then, knowing the cell radius, the number of eNBs, N_{eNB}, to be deployed along a tram line according to a linear cellular model is obtained as follows:

$$N_{eNB} = \lceil Length/(2 \times R) \rceil, \tag{3}$$

where h is the total tram line length and $2R$ is the distance between two eNBs (linear cellular model).

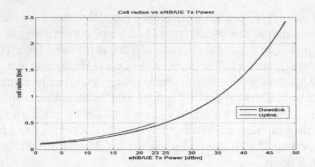

Fig. 6. Cell radius vs. eNB/UE transmission power.

According to the uplink coverage, since the maximum UE transmission power is fixed to 23 dBm, the cell radius is quite small and this has consequence on the minimum number of required eNBs. As shown in Fig. 6, if we limit to have 23 dBm UE transmission power, the cell radius should be about 0.5 km. However, since in uplink and downlink we have considered different values for noise figure and interference margin, we note that the downlink cell radius is smaller than the cell radius calculated for uplink for eNB transmission power of 23 dBm. This entails the need to use a higher eNBs transmission power, specifically the one matching 0.5 km cell radius. Reducing the eNBs transmission power until the minimum value of 18 dBm, we will deploy more eNBs along the track due to the shorter cell radius. Table 6 shows the possible values of eNBs transmission power (in steps of 2 dBs) with the corresponding cell radius R and the corresponding number of eNBs to cover the entire line.

Table 6. Selected eNB transmission power.

$P_{tx}[dBm]$	$R[km]$	N_{eNB}
18	0.312984	26
20	0.358709	22
22	0.411115	20
24	0.471178	17
26	0.540015	15

4.4   Results: Impact of Train Mobility, Handover Performance

We are now going to evaluate the signaling performance when trains move along the tramway line. With the purpose of evaluating the impact that mobility and handovers have on signaling traffic performance [10, 11] in relation to the number of trains and varying the number of eNBs, we firstly consider a simple scenario where few trains are moving along the track and different transmission powers are considered, i.e., different numbers of eNBs are deployed along the track. As shown in Fig. 7, we assume a linear deployment of the eNBs with an inter-eNB distance of $2R$. Trains are moving in the same direction and each train is randomly distributed and travels at a constant speed crossing different eNBs and coming back.

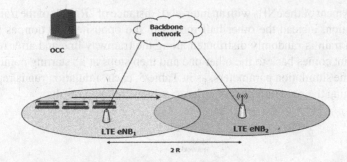

Fig. 7. Handover scenario.

From simulation results not shown here, we have obtained that the mean e2e delays for downlink and uplink for different transmission powers and numbers of trains are not sensitive to the increase in the number of trains and are below 14 ms and 22 ms, respectively, up to 4 trains. Let us now consider the PLR results in Figs. 8(a) and (b). As shown in these graphs, PLR increases when trains have mobility. This increment is mainly due to the handovers that the trains trigger when moving across different cells. Moreover, PLR increases with the number of trains, since more trains trigger handovers at the same time and eNBs do not handle properly the handover procedure and data forwarding. We also notice that the downlink PLR is higher than the uplink one. Regarding this scenario, we can conclude that using higher transmission power for each eNBs could improve the performance at the cost of higher total transmission power in the network. However, increasing the eNB transmission power we reduce the number of cells, thus there could be too congestion and this entails a performance degradation.

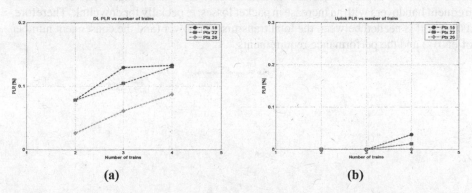

| (a) | (b) |

Fig. 8. Downlink (a) and uplink (b) PLR vs. number of trains and eNB transmission power.

4.5   Results: Impact of the Number of eNBs on Signaling Traffic

In order to evaluate the impact that the eNB deployment has on LRT signaling in an LTE access network, we have fixed the number of trains to 16 in the simulation scenario. Besides, we set different eNB transmission powers, corresponding to different cell radii and numbers of deployed eNBs to cover the entire line. Furthermore, we consider a linear deployment of the eNBs with an inter-eNB distance of $2R$. Half of the trains moves in one direction, instead the other half moves in the opposite direction, as shown in Fig. 9. Each train is randomly distributed along the tramway line and after reaching a terminus point comes back to the other one and then stops at its starting point. Considering the same simulation parameters, as in Table 5, each simulation run is repeated 10 times, changing the seed numbers in order to achieve reliable results.

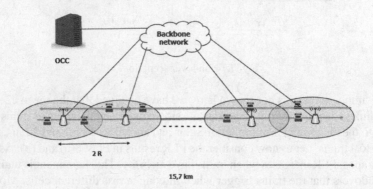

Fig. 9. Simulation scenario topology.

Even if the mean e2e delay is not strongly affected by the number of eNBs deployed, our results show a slight increment in delay for both downlink and uplink when more eNBs are placed. This behavior is mainly due to the more frequent handovers as they will delay transmission and reception of packets. In Fig. 10, instead, we note that the more eNBs are deployed, the higher is the PLR value: this is again due to the more frequent handovers with an increase in packet losses, especially for downlink. Therefore, a trade-off is needed between the total transmission power (and the consequent number of eNBs) and the performance requirements.

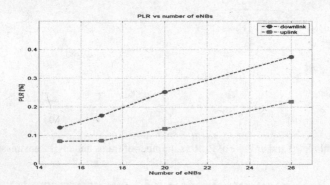

Fig. 10. PLR vs. number of eNBs.

4.6 Results: Impact of the Number of Trains on Signaling Traffic

In this simulation scenario, we consider a deployment with 15 eNBs (considered as a good trade-off solution) and evaluate the performance in relation to the number of trains in the line. We consider the same simulation parameters as in Table 5. Each simulation run is repeated 10 times, changing the seed numbers in order to achieve reliable results.

Even if the number of trains does not strongly affect the mean e2e delay, it has a negative impact on packet loss rate. Indeed, as it can be seen in Fig. 11, the more trains are in the line, the higher the PLR value is; this is mainly due to the more frequent handovers caused by the increment in the number of trains.

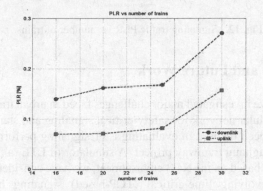

Fig. 11. PLR vs. number of trains.

PLR requirements are met for uplink up to 25 trains and never for downlink. Furthermore, since in the Ns-3 simulator only intra-frequency handovers are supported, additional interference is present in our model, since all eNBs transmit on the same frequency (in real scenarios, there is frequency differentiation among adjacent cells and inter-frequency handovers are adopted).

4.7 Results: Impact of Non-critical Traffic on Signaling

Finally, we are interested in evaluating the impact that non-critical video (500-byte packet) has on signaling when trains are moving. This UDP traffic is modelled as CBR having a data rate of 500 kbps. Compared to the stationary case, there is an increment for both mean e2e delay and PLR: the mean delay continues to match the delay constraint, while the PLR requirement is not met. Figure 12, obtained by varying the number of trains, shows that the PLR of signaling traffic in uplink is significantly degraded, because a QoS-aware scheduler is not used in uplink. Finally, as for the video performance, the mean end-to-end delay and PLR increase with the number of trains, with downlink performance approximately one order of magnitude better than uplink one, because of the use of a QoS scheduler.

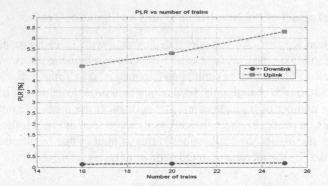

Fig. 12. Signaling traffic PLR vs. number of trains.

5   Conclusions and Future Work

In this paper, we have investigated major challenges faced in urban transportation when using an LTE-A cellular network for safety-critical signaling and standard IT services. Our interests have been focused in evaluating LRT signaling performance using LTE for the citywide Songjiang tramway project. A simulator of LTE railway communications has been built, based on the Ns-3 environment; we have considered several operational scenarios involving time-critical (TCP-based) signaling by differentiating between stationary and mobility use cases. For what concerns PLR in stationary conditions, requirements are fulfilled independently of the number of trains in the depot, while the PLR performance degrades when mobility is introduced. In a second simulation session, we have evaluated the impact of non-critical IT traffic (UDP-based video) on TCP-based signaling. We have obtained that safety-critical signaling throughput is not affected by video in stationary scenarios, whereas, in the presence of mobility, handovers degrade signaling performance that can be guaranteed only if a QoS-aware scheduler is adopted. Results have also shown that QoS requirements are met if there is no congestion in the LTE network.

In conclusions, we have shown that LTE-A radio resources can be safely shared between time-critical and time-non-critical applications, thus allowing the simultaneous use of safety-critical signaling with non-critical traffic such as video surveillance, ticketing, and passenger information. Hence, LTE technology is a good candidate for unified communications in next-generation urban rail infrastructures.

References

1. Bertout, A., Bernard, E.: Next generation of railways and metros wireless communication systems. In: Proceedings of IRSE ASPECT (2012)
2. Sniady, A., Soler, J.: Performance of LTE in high speed railway scenarios. In: Berbineau, M., Jonsson, M., Bonnin, J.-M., Cherkaoui, S., Aguado, M., Rico-Garcia, C., Ghannoum, H., Mehmood, R., Vinel, A. (eds.) Nets4Cars/Nets4Trains 2013. LNCS, vol. 7865, pp. 211–222. Springer, Heidelberg (2013). doi:10.1007/978-3-642-37974-1_17

3. Thales: LRT & Tramway Solution for Optimised Operations and Maintenance. https://www.thalesgroup.com/sites/default/files/asset/document/lrt_tramway_brochure_ld_0.pdf
4. Ns-3 Tutorial: https://www.nsnam.org/docs/release/3.24/tutorial/ns-3-tutorial.pdf
5. Furlan, L., Schmidt, H.: Importance of interchangeability for urban guided transport. Eur. Transp. Res. Rev. **3**(2), 95–101 (2011)
6. Sniady, A., Soler, J.: An overview of GSM-R technology and its shortcomings. In: Proceedings of the 12th International Conference on ITS Telecommunications (2012)
7. Ns-3 Models: https://www.nsnam.org/docs/release/3.24/models/ns-3-model-lib.pdf
8. Holma, H., Toskala, A.: LTE for UMTS: Evolution to LTE-Advanced, 2nd edn. Wiley, Chichester (2011)
9. Ns-3 LTE PHY layer: https://www.nsnam.org/docs/release/3.24/models/html/lte-testing.html#adaptive-modulation-and-coding-tests
10. Sauter, M.: From GSM to LTE-Advanced: An Introduction to Mobile Networks and Mobile Broadband. Wiley, Chichester (2014)
11. Racz, A., Temesvary, A., Reider, N.: Handover Performance in 3GPP Long Term Evolution (LTE) Systems. In: Proceedings of Mobile and Wireless Communications Summit (2007)

A Framework to Evaluate 5G Networks for Smart and Fail-Safe Communications in ERTMS/ETCS

Roberto Canonico[1], Stefano Marrone[2], Roberto Nardone[1], and Valeria Vittorini[1(✉)]

[1] DIETI, Università di Napoli Federico II, Naples, Italy
{roberto.canonico,roberto.nardone,valeria.vittorini}@unina.it
[2] Dip. di Matematica e Fisica, Università della Campania "Luigi Vanvitelli", Caserta, Italy
stefano.marrone@unicampania.it

Abstract. ETCS is an European system for high speed trains control and protection within ERTMS, the European standard for rail traffic management system. ERTMS/ETCS implementations use GSM-R for communications. As GSM-R is becoming obsolete, the adoption of more advanced technologies is investigated for next generation trains. New communication systems for railway infrastructures are expected to overcome the limitations of GSM-R, providing enhanced performance and reliability, as well as safety and security functionality to meet the requirements of the future signalling systems, control and users' applications. While 4G technologies (LTE and LTE-A) are currently tested in a few field trials, railway operators should consider that fifth generation (5G) mobile communications technologies will soon be available. One of the foundational aspects of the 5G architecture is control-plane programmability, achieved through the SDN paradigm. Being aware that in a railway scenario this opportunity can be exploited to dynamically reconfigure the network behavior to better match the communication flows produced by moving trains, we aim at defining a framework, integrating formal modeling and analysis tools and techniques into a network emulator, to evaluate the impact on ERTMS/ETCS safety and security deriving from the adoption of an SDN model in the communication infrastructure. In this paper we describe a first step towards this objective, by presenting a first proof-of-concept implementation of the framework and its use to reproduce a simple railway infrastructure. In our current implementation, Finite State Machines are used to model communication protocols between ERTMS/ETCS entities and to automatically produce code and Promela models. Generated code is directly used to control the network behavior while the Promela model allows to generate and verify a network configuration by model checking.

Keywords: 5G networks · ERTMS/ETCS · Model checking · Model transformation · Network emulation

© Springer International Publishing AG 2017
A. Fantechi et al. (Eds.): RSSRail 2017, LNCS 10598, pp. 34–50, 2017.
https://doi.org/10.1007/978-3-319-68499-4_3

1   Introduction

Train-to-ground communications in today's high speed railways are based on the Global System for Mobile Communications for Railways (GSM-R) standard. As GSM-R is becoming obsolete, different solutions are being investigated for the next generation trains. These solutions must contribute to the control and safe separation of trains and cope with the necessity to answer the dramatic increase in demand for communication services. The winning solution of this challenge will have a great impact on an important market segment including service providers, telecommunication operators and transportation companies.

At the state, the 4G UMTS Long Term Evolution (LTE) technology and its advanced version (LTE-A) are considered in important research and innovation initiatives (e.g., the *Signalling – Innovation Programme 2* of the European Shift2Rail initiative) and in some field trials aimed at testing proprietary solutions [21]. Before switching to a completely new communications infrastructure, however, railway operators should consider that mobile communications are going to experience another evolutionary leap in the next few years. A great research effort, in fact, is currently in place to define a fifth generation (5G) mobile communications standard. 5G networks are expected to support a multitude of diverse services on top of a heterogeneous infrastructure. The 5G architecture is currently designed to be highly flexible for supporting traditional use cases as well as easy integration of future ones. In particular, active 5G research projects suggest that 5G access networks will be based on the emerging *Software Defined Networking* (SDN) paradigm. By pursuing SDN, the network infrastructure will be made easily programmable and hence able to reliably and safely support a number of concurrent multi-tenant applications with diverse requirements. In a railway scenario, 5G networks could support control, monitoring, video-surveillance, infotainment services thanks to control-plane programmability which allows dynamic reconfiguration of the network behavior to better match the communication flows produced by moving trains [1].

This paper presents the preliminary results that we obtained in a research activity aimed at evaluating the opportunities that may derive from the adoption of an SDN model to control the networking infrastructure of next generation railways. In particular, we describe a framework that integrates a network emulator with formal modeling and analysis tools and techniques to evaluate network control strategies specifically tailored for railway communications. The rest of the paper is organized as follows. In Sect. 2 we briefly illustrate the basic concept of control plane programmability that characterizes the SDN paradigm and provide references to related work. In Sect. 3 we describe the framework we have defined, its objectives and its general architecture. Finally, in Sect. 4 we describe a proof-of-concept implementation of the framework and its usage in a simple use case.

2   Background and Related Work

The adoption of 5G communications technologies for future high speed railways has already been proposed in a few recent works, in particular to address the new communications demands of travellers and of security applications (e.g., videosurveillance) [8, 15, 23].

One of the foundational aspects of the 5G architecture is control-plane programmability, achieved through the adoption of the *Software Defined Networking* (SDN) paradigm. The fundamental characteristic of SDN is the separation between control and data plane. In a network device, the *data plane* is responsible of actually forwarding packets from one input port to one (or more) output ports, possibly after a manipulation of some header fields. How this forwarding is performed is responsibility of the *control plane*. In traditional networking, the control plane functionality is embedded in the device itself. With SDN, the control plane functionality is located outside of network devices and is performed by a logically centralized *SDN Controller* entity, i.e. a software system running on a commodity server. A single SDN Controller is usually responsible of controlling many network switches.

In this paper we assume that the SDN paradigm is implemented by means of the well known OpenFlow protocol [14], which is standardized by the Open Networking Foundation (ONF). An *OpenFlow Controller* is an SDN Controller that is able to control the packet forwarding behavior of OpenFlow-enabled switches by inserting *flow entries* into the switches' *flow tables*. A flow entry consists of packet header fields, counters, and actions associated with that entry. The header fields in a flow entry describe to which packets the entry is applicable. A wildcard value may be specified for some of the header fields of packets.

Control plane programmability provided by SDN has been proposed as an instrument to solve emerging networking issues in several contexts. So far, SDN is primarily employed in datacenter networks, to cope with Virtual Machine migrations. However, the same paradigm is also finding useful applications to support *Mobile Cloud Computing* [4] and mobility management (i.e. the ability to quickly configure and manage network resources to accommodate a large number of moving terminals) [22].

Some open issues need to be considered when applying the SDN paradigm to safety- and security-critical domains. An SDN controller needs to update the configuration of a potentially high number of network devices. "Naively updating individual node configurations can lead to incorrect transient behaviors, such as loops, black holes, access control violations, and others" [13]. Hence, research is focusing on efficient techniques for formal verification of control plane strategies and their automatic deployment in network devices in the context of SDN networks. In such networks, efficient paths for each source and destination pair should be automatically computed and defined to improve network management, service performance, survivability and resiliency. Some recent works in this direction propose to integrate a *Path Computation Element* [18] into SDN networks [17]. The need for formal verification of control plane configuration in SDN networks has been recently recognized and addressed in several papers (e.g., [2,6,9,11,12,19,20]). Most of these works apply model checking techniques to prove that SDN programs behave correctly. However, in general, scaling these methods to large networks is challenging and, moreover, they cannot guarantee the absence of errors. To cope with this problem, in [6] the authors adopt symbolic execution properly identifying which inputs would exercise different code paths through an event handler; the framework proposed in [2] requires that admissible network topologies and network-wide invariants are specified through a first-order logic. An ad-hoc language is proposed in [24] for the specification of SDN forwarding policies for which model-checking problems are defined. In [13], the authors investigate the problem of SDN network configuration consistency and propose an approach for synthesizing correct update programs from a formal specification.

In this work we combine formal methods for paths computation and verification of control policies with network emulation. This allows validation of results with real implementations of communicating applications.

3 Framework Definition

3.1 Objectives

This paper proposes a methodological approach and a software architecture for evaluating the impact of 5G networks on signalling (ERTMS/ETCS future systems) as well as on other railway systems, such as surveillance and infotainment systems. The general objective is to provide a framework for the emulation and the verification of different SDN control-planes against the communication flows generated by moving high speed trains. At this aim the framework should provide enhanced capability with respect to common network emulators enabling the seamless integration of evaluation and verification methods and tools. Several users' scenarios can be defined and exploited by the framework. As network programming commonly implements best-effort systems or is specifically focused on non-critical needs, some major objectives are:

- design verification: automatically verify safety, security and correctness properties of SDN controllers according to the ERTMS/ETCS requirements;
- failure handling: automatically derive network re-configuration strategies in case of failure events (e.g., to prevent packets loss affecting vital signalling procedures);
- resources management: automatically derive resource management strategies oriented to maximize the network performance in the fulfillment of specifications and constraints.

In this paper we do not claim to have reached these objectives, as they are the point of arrival of a long-term work, but we provide a proof of concept of how the approach and the tool chain defined in this paper can be exploited to meet them.

3.2 Approach

A model-driven approach is proposed in which all artifacts needed to verification, emulation and analysis purposes can be automatically generated from models. Artifacts can be models, code or analysis results.

The starting point is a formal model of the system behavior and of the network. At the state we focus on signalling protocols. State Machines are used to model the system behavior and the network is modeled by a graph, possibly enriched with information about network nodes and resources.

The ending point is the specification of the emulation scenario and the programs implementing the behavior of both the SDN controller and the railway entities (e.g., the train and the ETCS controller) to be executed by the emulator. In particular, the emulation scenario must reproduce at the network level the exchange of the message packets needed to implement the train-to-ground communication as specified by the system model. The automatic synthesis of these software artifacts is performed by defining and applying proper transformations.

The model of the system behavior and the model of the network are used to:

(a) Derive a new model and a property specification: the capability of a model checker to extract counterexamples of violated properties is exploited to automatically derive traces which specify (re)configuration strategies of the network under given constraints.

(b) Derive a state machine modeling the behavior of the SDN control plane: again we use state machines, in this case as a target formalism; this model also takes into account the (re)configuration strategies referred above. In more details, a configuration strategy provides the rules that the controller must enact for packet routing. Safety and correctness properties can be specified on the controller behavior and checked by translating this state machine into an input model for the model checker.

(c) Perform the automated synthesis of code implementing the emulation scenario and the railway entities: the code to customize the behavior of the SDN controller is directly generated from the state machine produced in (b).

The set of traces produced by the model checker (a) depends on the constraints included in the model and on the specifications used to obtain the counterexamples. Hence, the set may include strategies that fulfill specific requirements, spanning from the definition of alternative routes in case of failures of network nodes or links, to configurations that meet given resource management requirements. Consequently, the resulting state machine (b) and software controller (c) will provide the SDN with the capability to react (at run time) to specified events or conditions, according to what was specified by its state machine model.

3.3   Software Architecture

Figure 1 illustrates a general software architecture of the framework according to the approach described in Sect. 3.2. The architecture has three layers. From the bottom of the figure, the Emulation Layer is in charge of executing a scenario from the real world, the Configuration Layer is in charge of building this scenario and the Specification Layer is in charge of providing the information needed to

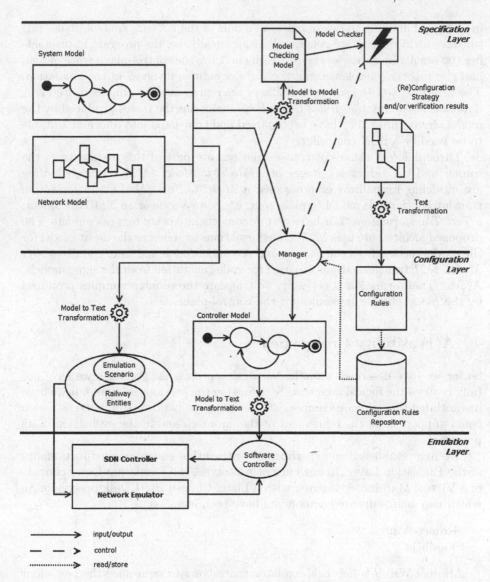

Fig. 1. Framework architecture

build the scenario. The figure also reports the artifacts that are input or output for the software components. The components are: (i) available tools (providing the functionality of the *network emulator*, the *SDN controller* and the *model checker*); (ii) software applications developed to realize the transformations and the management of the process, in particular a software component (*Manager)* is needed to properly invoke the model checker according to the specific objective and work-flow (generation of one or more strategies, verification, etc.). It is also in charge of building the state machine model of the network control-plane; (iii) software artifacts that are generated automatically, i.e. the program implementing the emulation scenario, the program encoding the control-plane state model, and the programs implementing the railway entities involved in the emulation. The *Manager* and the software artifacts are represented by ellipses in Fig. 1. A database (*Configuration Rules Repository*) maintains the traces produced by the model checker after they have been parsed and translated into a format suitable to be used by a SDN controller.

Three different classes of transformations are part of this architecture: the source and the target languages of a *Model-to-Model (M2M) transformation* are modeling formalisms or notations; a *Model-to-Text (M2T) transformation* translates a (formal) model to plain text, e.g. source code or an XML document; a *Text Transformation* translates text documents into other text documents. The proposed architecture uses M2M transformations to generate the input model for the model checker from the *System and Network Models* and from the *Controller Model*. M2T transformations are used for code generation from the same models. A Text Transformation is necessary to translate the counterexamples produced by the model checker into rules for the control-plane.

4   A Feasibility Prototype

So far we have described a methodological approach. At the state we have not fully realized the logical architecture defined in the previous section, but we have instantiated the software components necessary to perform simple trials which could support us in the refinement of the approach and in the evaluation of its potential.

We first established an experimental testbed that embodies the functionality of the Emulation Layer. In our current prototype, the Emulation Layer consists of a Virtual Machine, configured with a Linux Ubuntu 16.04 Desktop system, in which two main software components have been installed:

- Mininet-Wifi;
- Floodlight.

Mininet-Wifi is a network emulator that allows to reproduce the behaviour of a set of end-hosts, switches, as well as WiFi access points and mobile terminals in a single Linux-based machine [7]. It was developed as an extension of Mininet, a network emulator that is largely used by researchers to evaluate SDN solutions. By executing a Python script, Mininet-WiFi is able to reproduce a network scenario composed of both network devices and end-systems. By executing a script, Mininet-WiFi instantiates the emulated nodes and runs real network programs in the emulated hosts. With Mininet-WiFi it is also possible to reproduce node mobility and evaluate, over time, the impact on applications of variable network conditions (e.g. due to handovers). Emulated end-systems may be virtually connected to access point devices through emulated wireless links. Currently, Mininet-WiFi is only able to emulate IEEE 802.11-based wireless networks and not cellular networks. Since our main interest, however, is in evaluating the ability of the fixed part of the network to reconfigure its forwarding rules to follow the train movement, we considered the fact that Mininet-WiFi only reproduces 802.11-based networks not a big issue. Nonetheless, in the future we plan to use other approaches to more faithfully reproduce the behaviour of the *Evolved Packet Core*(EPC) of 4G (LTE) and 5G networks.

Floodlight is a Java-based modular OpenFlow *SDN Controller*. Besides implementing the core functionality of an SDN Controller (e.g. topology discovery), Floodlight includes a number of optional software modules that may be instantiated to customize the behaviour of an SDN network. In particular, by loading the Forwarding module, the network administrator may force into the network a reactive configuration strategy: each time that a packet belonging a new flow arrives to a network switch, the Floodlight controller, knowing the entire network topology, computes the path that the packet should follow to reach its destination and configures the switches along the path accordingly. Such a configuration is not permanent, as flow entries pushed by the Forwarding module are subject to a (configurable) timeout. Alternatively, Floodlight may be used to proactively configure switches by receiving *flow entry* specifications from an external entity, through a REST API. In this latter case, an external program (e.g. a Python script) translates the desired network configuration in a number of flow entries specifications that are formatted as JSON objects and transmitted to the *Floodlight Static Flow Pusher* module by means of HTTP requests.

Then, we have established the formal methods, languages and tools to be used at the Specification Layer in support of the automatic generation of the *Configuration Strategies* and the verification of the controller behavior. A configuration strategy will be translated into *Rules*, i.e. the flow entries used by the *Open-Flow Controller* to control the packet forwarding behavior of network switches. We currently use state machines to model the system behavior, GraphML [5] to describe the network (graph and data of interest) and Spin [10] as model checker.

Spin is a well known on-the-fly model checker for the verification of concurrent systems. The modeling language used by Spin is Promela (Process Meta Language), the properties to be verified are expressed as Linear Temporal Logic formulas. We chose Spin and Promela because some of their features are essential to tackle the problem of modeling the behavior of railway asynchronous communicating systems, in particular they support dynamic creation of concurrent processes, buffered message passing and communication via shared memory. The state machine *System Model* and the GraphML representation are used to derive the Promela model from which the configurations are extracted as counterexamples.

At the state the transformations and the *Manager* have not been implemented yet. Nevertheless, we have performed by hand the main M2M transformation (from the initial models to Promela) and developed the software applications needed to realize the trials, in particular the *Emulation Scenario*, the railway entities and the *Software Controller* (Fig. 1). In our previous works we

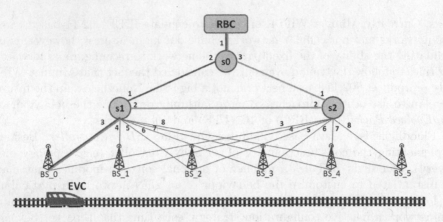

Fig. 2. An example of network scenario and route paths.

have already defined and implemented a number of M2M transformations [3], so that the hand-made construction of artifacts is driven by our previous experience, in particular we have already implemented a complex transformation chain from an extension of state machines to Promela with the aim of generating test cases [3,16].

In this paper we apply the proposed approach to the problem of deriving configurations and emulating a very simple communication scenario between the *Radio Block Centre* (RBC) on the trackside and the *Euro Vital Computer* (EVC) on-board the train. RBC is a computing system at ERTMS/ETCS Level 2 in charge of ensuring a safe inter-train distance on the track area under its supervision. In today's implementation RBC interacts with the on-board system by managing a communication session using the EURORADIO protocol and the GSM-R network.

In the following we assume that the network infrastructure is the one described in Fig. 2. It consists of a two levels hierarchy of switches and a number of base stations located along a linear piece of railway. A top-level switch connects the infrastructure to a fixed station, running the RBC entity. Each of the two switches located at the lower level is connected to six different access points, acting as base stations. In such a network topology, several paths may be exploited to deliver packets from the centralized RBC to the moving EVC entity. Starting from the model of the network and of the communication pattern between RBC and EVC we derive the emulation scenario which reproduces the communication flows in Mininet-WiFi. In our simple scenario RBC just sends messages to the EVC on-board a moving train.

4.1 Specification Layer

The purpose of the Specification Layer is to generate and verify a set of *Rules* to configure the network. The *Configuration Rules* define flow paths on the network from a source node to a target node. The source node represents the network switch that receives the messages from RBC on the trackside. The messages must be delivered to EVC on-board the train. The target nodes represent the base stations located along the railway track that allow EVC to connect to the network. In our current prototype we use the Spin model checker to generate a set of paths from the source node to the target nodes. These paths represent solutions to the packet routing problem according to specified constraints and requirements. In the most general case, this problem is more complex than finding a shortest path on a weighted graph, as not only the network graph topology should be considered but also constraints (e.g., a limited number of flow entries per switch, paths differentiation for different classes of services, or QoS requirements).

From Fig. 2, the three switches are named s0, s1 and s2, the six base stations are numbered from BS_0 to BS_5 and there are fifteen wired links. Local identifiers are used to specify at each node the output ports on which the links are physically attached. We encode the network into a Promela model together with the model representing the communication from RBC to EVC.

Each node is translated into a Promela process type (*proctype*), a link is mapped to two Promela global channels, one for each direction of the communication between the nodes connected by the link. In our first simple trials the

```
int port_number_s0 = 0;
chan s0_s1 = [1] of {bit};
chan s0_s2 = [1] of {bit};
chan s1_s0 = [1] of {bit};
chan s1_s2 = [1] of {bit};

active proctype s0() {
  do
  :: (s1_s0?[1] || s2_s0?[1] || send?[1]) ->
     atomic {
       if
       :: send?1;
       :: s1_s0?1;
       :: s2_s0?1;
       fi;
       if
       :: (port_number_s0==2) ->
          s0_s1!1;
          printf("s0: message received from RBC, sent to s1\n");
       :: (port_number_s0==3) ->
          s0_s2!1;
          printf("s0: : message received from RBC, sent to s2\n");
       :: else ->
          printf("s0: message lost!\n");
       fi;
     }
  od;
}
```

(a)

```
chan send = [1] of {int};
int received=0;

active proctype RBC() {
  send!1;
}

active proctype master() {
  do
  :: (1) -> //s0
  atomic {
    if
    :: (port_number_s0!=2) ->
       port_number_s0=2;
       printf("port_number_s0=2\n");
    :: (port_number_s0!=3) ->
       port_number_s0=3;
       printf("port_number_s0=3\n");
    fi;
  }
  // s1, s2, BS_01 .......
  od;
}

never {
never_step:
  if
  :: (received==1) -> goto end_never;
  :: else -> goto never_step;
  fi;
end_never:
  skip;
}
```

b)

Fig. 3. Promela model (excerpt)

channels may convey bits. Output ports are represented by global integer variables. Figure 3(a) reports the process and the variables used to represent the switch s0.

An additional Promela process models the communication procedure between RBC and EVC. In this case RBC just sends messages to EVC (top of Fig. 3(b)). We want a route from node s0 to the base station to which EVC is connected. This is specified by the Promela process modeling the base station through the variable *received*. Each node waits over the channels on which it can receive messages. When a message is received, the node forwards it using one of its output ports. An additional process (the *master* in Fig. 3(b)) selects for each node the port number to be used to forward the received message. A Promela *never claim* models a linear time temporal logic formula. The *never claim* in Fig. 3(b) requires that the variable *received* never assumes a value equal to 1, i.e. the target base station is never reached. Of course this model just helps finding paths on a graph. More complex problems can be solved by using more complex data types and adding constraints, as mentioned before. In the second trial, the process *master* is used to model the unavailability of nodes.

Trace 1 in Fig. 4(left) reports the counterexample obtained by using the model just described to find a route between the up-level switch s0 and the base station BS_0. Trace 2 in Fig. 4(right) has been obtained by slightly

```
port_number_s0=2
         s0: message received from RBC, sent to s1
    port_number_s1=3
         s1: message received, sent to BS_0
              BS_0: message delivered to EVC!
spin: trail ends after 17 steps
#processes: 11
                    port_number_s0 = 2
                    port_number_s1 = 3
                    port_number_s2 = 0
                    port_number_BS_0 = 0
                    port_number_BS_1 = 0
                    port_number_BS_2 = 0
                    port_number_BS_3 = 0
                    port_number_BS_4 = 0
                    port_number_BS_5 = 0
                    queue 4 (s0_s1):
                    queue 2 (s1_s0):
                    queue 3 (s2_s0):
                    queue 5 (s1_BS_0):
                    queue 1 (send):
                    received = 1
17:        proc 10 (BS_5:1) input.pml:401 (state 18)
17:        proc 9 (BS_4:1) input.pml:378 (state 18)
17:        proc 8 (BS_3:1) input.pml:354 (state 18)
17:        proc 7 (BS_2:1) input.pml:331 (state 18)
17:        proc 6 (BS_1:1) input.pml:308 (state 18)
17:        proc 5 (BS_0:1) input.pml:284 (state 19)
17:        proc 4 (s2:1) input.pml:235 (state 42)
17:        proc 3 (s1:1) input.pml:186 (state 42)
17:        proc 2 (s0:1) input.pml:163 (state 18)
17:        proc 1 (master:1) input.pml:56 (state 95)
17:        proc 0 (RBC:1) input.pml:53 (state 2) <valid end state>
17:        proc - (never_0:1) input.pml:425 (state 5)
11 processes created

                    Trial1 – Trace 1
```

```
switch s1 is down
    port_number_s0=3
         s0: : message received from RBC, sent to s2
    port_number_s2=6
         s2: message received, sent to BS_3
              BS_3: message delivered to EVC!
spin: trail ends after 19 steps
#processes: 11
                    s1_up = 0
                    s2_up = 1
                    port_number_s0 = 3
                    port_number_s1 = 0
                    port_number_s2 = 6
                    port_number_BS_0 = 0
                    port_number_BS_1 = 0
                    port_number_BS_2 = 0
                    port_number_BS_3 = 0
                    port_number_BS_4 = 0
                    port_number_BS_5 = 0
                    queue 4 (s0_s2):
                    queue 2 (s1_s0):
                    queue 3 (s2_s0):
                    queue 6 (s1_BS_3):
                    queue 5 (s2_BS_3):
                    queue 1 (send):
                    received = 1
19:        proc 10 (BS_5:1) input.pml:413 (state 18)
19:        proc 9 (BS_4:1) input.pml:390 (state 18)
19:        proc 8 (BS_3:1) input.pml:365 (state 19)
19:        proc 7 (BS_2:1) input.pml:342 (state 18)
19:        proc 6 (BS_1:1) input.pml:319 (state 18)
19:        proc 5 (BS_0:1) input.pml:295 (state 18)
19:        proc 4 (s2:1) input.pml:246 (state 42)
19:        proc 3 (s1:1) input.pml:197 (state 42)
19:        proc 2 (s0:1) input.pml:174 (state 18)
19:        proc 1 (master:1) input.pml:60 (state 105)
19:        proc 0 (RBC:1) input.pml:57 (state 2) <valid end state>
19:        proc - (never_0:1) input.pml:437 (state 5)
11 processes created
```

Trial2 – Trace 2

Fig. 4. Counterexamples

modifying the *master* process and the *never claim* to extract an alternative path in case of unavailability of s1.

A set of routes is built by varying the problem parameters. They are used to define the behavior of the SDN controller, expressed by a state machine. The proposed approach also exploits model checking to verify properties to be satisfied by the control-plane, but this is not described in this paper.

4.2 Configuration Layer

The primary purpose of the Configuration Layer is to automatically produce a number of artifacts that are needed to configure the underlying Emulation Layer. Our current prototype relies on three kinds of artifacts:

- an *Emulation Scenario*, i.e. a Python script to be executed by the Mininet-WiFi emulator to reproduce the network setup (network topology, physical position of both base stations and motion models for modeling trains);
- a *Software Controller*, i.e. a Python script that takes as input a textual description of the OpenFlow rules corresponding to the desired network behaviour and sends them to the SDN controller through a REST API;
- *Railway Entities*, i.e. a set of executable Java programs that, by exchanging messages through the network, mimic the behaviour of ERTMS/ECTS signalling entities (RBC and EVC).

All of these three artifacts are produced by the Configuration Layer and passed to the Emulation Layer. While our ultimate goal is to produce these artifacts automatically, from the outputs of the Specification Layer, by means of model transformation techniques, as of now they are manually produced.

To control the behavior of the emulated network, switches need to be configured with *flow entries* provided by an OpenFlow controller. The purpose of *flow entries* is to determine the paths that, at a given time, packets should follow to reach the EVC from the RBC, or viceversa. Assuming that a traffic flow of interest may be identified in the network by specific header field values of transmitted

```
import json
import urllib2

flow_entry = {"switch":"00:00:00:00:00:00:00:01",
              "name":"flow-mod-1",
              "cookie":"0",
              "priority":"32768",
              "in_port":"1",
              "active":"true",
              "actions":"output=2"}
url = 'http://127.0.0.1:8080/wm/staticentrypusher/json'
req = urllib2.Request(url)
req.add_header('Content-Type', 'application/json')
req.add_header('Accept', 'application/json')
response = urllib2.urlopen(req, json.dumps(flow1))
```

Fig. 5. Python script to send flow rules to the controller

packets [1], by properly writing these *flow entries*, the network control plane may be able to apply different forwarding policies and routes to specific traffic flows.

Furthermore, since train trajectories are largely predictable, the network control plane may compute in advance such forwarding policies and change them according to proper patterns. In this way, we are able to establish a control strategy that is only partially reactive, and hence more predictable in terms of performance.

In our system, flow entries are passed to network switches by the Floodlight Openflow controller, which, in turn, receives them from an external Python script through the *Static Entry Pusher* REST API. This REST API allows listing, insertion or deletion of flow entries by means of HTTP GET or POST messages

```python
def topology():
    ....
    print '*** Creating endpoints'
    rbc = net.addHost('RBC')
    evc = net.addStation('EVC',position='1000.0,20.0,0.0')
    print '*** Creating base stations'
    bss = list(net.addAccessPoint('BS_' + str(i), ssid="irail",
                    mode="g", channel=bschan[i%2],
                    position=str((i+1)*bsdistance)+
                    ','+str(bsheight)+',0'
            ) for i in range(0,bsnum))
    map(lambda b: b.setRange(bsrange),bss)
    print '*** Creating switches'
    net.configureWifiNodes()
    sm = net.addSwitch('s0')
    ss = list(net.addSwitch('s' + str(i+1)) for i in range(0,swnum))
    switches = list()
    switches.extend(ss)
    switches.append(sm)
    print '*** Buiding Fixed Topology'
    net.addLink(evc,bss[0])
    net.addLink(rbc,sm)
    for j in range(len(ss)-1):
        net.addLink(ss[j],ss[j+1])
    for j in range(len(ss)):
        net.addLink(ss[j],sm)
        for i in range(len(bss)):
            net.addLink(bss[i],ss[j])
    print '*** Starting network'
    net.build()
    dj.start()
    map(lambda b: b.start([dj]),bss)
    map(lambda s: s.start([dj]),switches)
...
```

Fig. 6. Mininet-WiFi script (excerpt)

---

[1] For instance, layer-2 (MAC) and/or layer-3 (IP) addresses, layer-4 (TCP or UDP) port numbers, or a combination of them.

carrying data formatted in JSON syntax. Figure 5 shows a minimal Python script that, by issuing an HTTP POST request to the Floodlight OpenFlow Controller, instantiates into the switch identified by ID 00:00:00:00:00:00:00:01 a flow entry to forward incoming packets from port 1 through output port 2. More complex scripts, not included here for space reasons, have been developed to parse JSON-encoded flow entries and send them to the controller.

4.3   Emulation Layer

The purpose of the Emulation Layer is to reproduce as faithfully as possible the real network conditions in which the communicating entities operate.

The simple network scenario described in Fig. 2 is reproduced in Mininet-WiFi by running a Python script, an excerpt of which is in Fig. 6. A moving node (emulating a train) runs another software module reproducing the behavior of an EVC entity. In the Mininet-WiFi script, such a node is made to move along a linear trajectory parallel to the row of access points. Train movement, hence, will produce, over time, a number of handovers between access points. Figure 7 shows a screenshot of the VM running the Mininet-WiFi emulation script. During the emulation run, the node hosting the EVC component moves from the base station on the left towards the base station on the right, with an emulated constant speed of 100 km/h. While the train moves, the SDN controller dynamically changes the switches configurations according to the precomputed rules generated by the model checker, as explained before. Two xterm windows

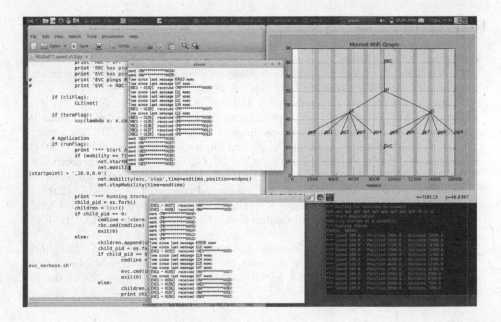

Fig. 7. Mininet-WiFi in execution

show the messages generated by the running RBC and EVC programs. From the log messages it is possible to verify if there is any message lost or disconnection while the train moves. Additionally, timing information regarding the delivered messages are provided and shown.

5   Conclusions

In this paper we propose a methodological approach and a software architecture to evaluate the opportunities that may derive from the adoption of a programmable control plane in the networking infrastructure of future generation railways. Such a paradigm shift opens up the opportunity for efficiently and flexibly managing traffic flows generated from different applications and with different QoS requirements. However, SDN also brings new challenges. In this paper we present a framework that combines formal methods with network emulation to design and validate SDN Controller configurations with realistic applications. In particular, we use the framework to address, in a simple scenario, the problem of automatically creating network configurations that are able to cope with the problem of managing network flows involving signalling messages exchanged by moving trains. Our future work will be aimed at completing the implementation of the framework, at extending the emulation capabilities to reproduce more faithfully the behavior of the network and at applying the framework to evaluate more complex configurations strategies, also considering the case of failures of network devices.

References

1. Ai, B., Guan, K., Rupp, M., Kurner, T., Cheng, X., Yin, X.F., Wang, Q., Ma, G.Y., Li, Y., Xiong, L., Ding, J.W.: Future railway services-oriented mobile communications network. IEEE Commun. Mag. **53**(10), 78–85 (2015)
2. Ball, T., Bjørner, N., Gember, A., Itzhaky, S., Karbyshev, A., Sagiv, M., Schapira, M., Valadarsky, A.: Vericon: towards verifying controller programs in software-defined networks. In: Proceedings of the 35th ACM SIGPLAN Conference on Programming Language Design and Implementation, pp. 282–293 (2014)
3. Benerecetti, M., De Guglielmo, R., Gentile, U., Marrone, S., Mazzocca, N., Nardone, R., Peron, A., Velardi, L., Vittorini, V.: Dynamic state machines for modelling railway control systems. Sci. Comput. Program. **133**, 116–153 (2017)
4. Bifulco, R., Canonico, R.: Analysis of the handover procedure in Follow-Me Cloud. In: 2012 IEEE 1st International Conference on Cloud Networking (CLOUDNET), pp. 185–187 (2012)
5. Brandes, U., Eiglsperger, M., Herman, I., Himsolt, M., Marshall, M.S.: GraphML progress report structural layer proposal. In: Mutzel, P., Jünger, M., Leipert, S. (eds.) GD 2001. LNCS, vol. 2265, pp. 501–512. Springer, Heidelberg (2002). doi:10.1007/3-540-45848-4_59

6. Canini, M., Venzano, D., Perešíni, P., Kostić, D., Rexford, J.: A NICE way to test openflow applications. In: Proceedings of the 9th USENIX Conference on Networked Systems Design and Implementation (2012)
7. Fontes, R.R., Afzal, S., Brito, S.H.B., Santos, M.A.S., Rothenberg, C.E.: Mininet-WiFi: emulating software-defined wireless networks. In: Proceedings of the 2015 11th International Conference on Network and Service Management (CNSM), pp. 384–389. IEEE (2015)
8. Gopalasingham, A., Van Pham, Q., Roullet, L., Chen, C.S., Renault, E., Natarianni, L., De Marchi, S., Hamman, E.: Software-defined mobile backhaul for future train to ground communication services. In: 2016 9th IFIP Wireless and Mobile Networking Conference (WMNC), pp. 161–167 (2016)
9. Guha, A., Reitblatt, M., Foster, N.: Machine-verified network controllers. In: Proceedings of the 34th ACM SIGPLAN Conference on Programming Language Design and Implementation, pp. 483–494. ACM (2013)
10. Holzmann, G.: The SPIN Model Checker: Primer and Reference Manual. Addison-Wesley Professional (2003)
11. Kang, M., Kang, E.Y., Hwang, D.Y., Kim, B.J., Nam, K.H., Shin, M.K., Choi, J.Y.: Formal modeling and verification of sdn-openflow. In: 2013 IEEE Sixth International Conference on Software Testing, Verification and Validation, pp. 481–482, March 2013
12. Majumdar, R., Tetali, S.D., Wang, Z.: Kuai: a model checker for software-defined networks. In: 2014 Formal Methods in Computer-Aided Design (FMCAD), pp. 163–170 (2014)
13. McClurg, J., Hojjat, H., Černý, P., Foster, N.: Efficient synthesis of network updates. In: Proceedings of the 36th ACM SIGPLAN Conference on Programming Language Design and Implementation, PLDI 2015, pp. 196–207. ACM, New York (2015)
14. McKeown, N., Anderson, T., Balakrishnan, H., Parulkar, G., Peterson, L., Rexford, J., Shenker, S., Turner, J.: OpenFlow: enabling innovation in campus networks. SIGCOMM Comput. Commun. Rev. 38(2), 69–74 (2008)
15. Müller, M.K., Taranetz, M., Rupp, M.: Providing current and future cellular services to high speed trains. IEEE Commun. Mag. 53(10), 96–101 (2015)
16. Nardone, R., Gentile, U., Benerecetti, M., Peron, A., Vittorini, V., Marrone, S., Mazzocca, N.: Modeling railway control systems in promela. In: Artho, C., Ölveczky, P.C. (eds.) FTSCS 2015. CCIS, vol. 596, pp. 121–136. Springer, Cham (2016). doi:10.1007/978-3-319-29510-7_7
17. Oliveira, D., Pourvali, M., Bai, H., Ghani, N., Lehman, T., Yang, X., Hayat, M.: A novel automated SDN architecture and orchestration framework for resilient large-scale networks. In: SoutheastCon 2017, pp. 1–6 (2017)
18. Paolucci, F., Cugini, F., Giorgetti, A., Sambo, N., Castoldi, P.: A survey on the path computation element (PCE) architecture. IEEE Commun. Surv. Tutor. 15(4), 1819–1841 (2013)
19. Sethi, D., Narayana, S., Malik, S.: Abstractions for model checking SDN controllers. In: 2013 Formal Methods in Computer-Aided Design, pp. 145–148, October 2013
20. Skowyra, R.W., Lapets, A., Bestavros, A., Kfoury, A.: Verifiably-safe software-defined networks for CPS. In: Proceedings of the 2nd ACM International Conference on High Confidence Networked Systems, pp. 101–110. ACM (2013)
21. Sniady, A., Soler, J.: LTE for railways: impact on performance of ETCS railway signaling. IEEE Veh. Technol. Mag. 9(2), 69–77 (2014)

22. Wang, Y., Bi, J.: A solution for IP mobility support in software defined networks. In: 2014 23rd International Conference on Computer Communication and Networks (ICCCN), pp. 1–8 (2014)
23. Yan, L., Fang, X.: Reliability evaluation of 5G C/U-plane decoupled architecture for high-speed railway. EURASIP J. Wirel. Commun. Netw. **2014**, 127 (2014)
24. Zakharov, V.A., Smelyansky, R.L., Chemeritsky, E.V.: A formal model and verification problems for software defined networks. Autom. Control Comput. Sci. **48**(7), 398–406 (2014)

Systems-Theoretic Likelihood and Severity Analysis for Safety and Security Co-engineering

William G. Temple[1]([✉]), Yue Wu[1], Binbin Chen[1], and Zbigniew Kalbarczyk[2]

[1] Advanced Digital Sciences Center, Illinois at Singapore, Singapore, Singapore
{william.t,wu.yue,binbin.chen}@adsc.com.sg
[2] University of Illinois at Urbana-Champaign, Champaign, IL, USA
kalbar@crhc.illinois.edu

Abstract. A number of methodologies and techniques have been proposed to integrate safety and security in risk assessment, but there is an ideological divide between component-centric and systems-theoretic approaches. In this paper, we propose a new hybrid method for Systems-Theoretic Likelihood and Severity Analysis (STLSA), which combines desirable characteristics from both schools of thought. Specifically, STLSA focuses on functional control actions in the system, including humans-in-the-loop, but incorporates semi-quantitative risk assessment based on existing industry practice. We demonstrate this new approach using the case study of train braking control.

1 Introduction

Until recently, the security of information, communication and control systems has been considered separately from issues of safety during system design. However, there is growing recognition that safety and security properties and related design features may influence one another. This has led to a growing body of work relating to safety and security co-engineering. However, while there are a number of analysis methods available to help designers analyze the safety and security of a system, cyber security threats today are becoming more complex, and attackers can exploit physical phenomena in the system and environment (e.g., Stuxnet), as well as humans-in-the-loop (e.g., phishing) to cause harm. In addition, for systems such as an automated (unattended) metro train, safety features like the emergency braking function could be exploited by cyber attackers to cause large-scale service disruptions. For example, in 2016 in Singapore, the circle line metro train system was affected with intermittent emergency braking of several different trains over the course of more than a week [22]. While the issue was eventually traced to a component failure on an individual train [5], it raises questions about whether such an event could be replicated maliciously.

Those types of complex interactions are challenging to account for using traditional methods for design-stage risk assessment such as fault trees, or failure mode and effects analysis—methods we refer to as component-centric [20]. The Systems-Theoretic Process Analysis for Security approach (STPA-Sec) [23], with

A. Fantechi et al. (Eds.): RSSRail 2017, LNCS 10598, pp. 51–67, 2017.
https://doi.org/10.1007/978-3-319-68499-4_4

its emphasis on control loops, emergent system behavior and qualitative assessment of unsafe or insecure scenarios may offer one path to addressing these challenges. However, following the STPA-Sec process results in the identification of a large number of threat and/or failure modes [16], and that methodology does not provide further guidance on how to address those scenarios. The complexity of today's cyber-physical systems implies a great need for risk-based analysis to help system stakeholders understand the significance of safety/security issues and prioritize remediation. In this paper, we propose a new safety and security co-engineering method, Systems-Theoretic Likelihood and Severity Analysis (STLSA), which provides a top-down view of the functional control structure of a system and enriches threat/failure scenarios with a semi-quantitative risk rating system (severity times likelihood) inspired by a component-centric analysis method [15]. Specifically, we make the following contributions:

- We propose a new hybrid method, STLSA, to leverage advantages of STPA-Sec [23] and FMVEA [15] and address gaps.
- We present a case study applying this method on a realistic train braking system based on information provided from a railway operator.

The outline of this paper is as follows: in Sect. 2 we discuss related work in Safety and Security Co-Analysis; in Sect. 3 we present the Systems-Theoretic Likelihood and Severity Analysis method; in Sect. 4 we apply the STLSA method on a train braking system case study and discuss the results before concluding in Sect. 5.

2   Related Work in Safety and Security Co-Analysis

A number of methods have been proposed to improve the completeness of system risk assessment by covering the interactions between both unintentional/non-malicious failures, and intentional/malicious threats [4,9,12]. Different schools of thought have emerged regarding the appropriate manner of examining a system and evaluating potential hazards and corresponding risks. Many of the approaches in the literature are related to the field of security requirements analysis, which has been an active research area of its own (e.g. [11] and references therein) and often makes use of graphical models and risk assessment. Requirement analysis has been studied in the context of safety critical systems [8] as well. However, in our discussion of related work we focus on research that attempts to explicitly analyze safety and security risks together, often by combining or extending existing approaches from standards or academic literature. Below, we summarize a review and classification of safety/security methods from our earlier position paper [20] before detailing our STLSA approach in later sections.

Table 1 presents a taxonomy of prior work on safety and security co-analysis. In the first column of the table, Security Aware Hazard Analysis and Risk Assessment (SAHARA) [10] and Failure Mode, Vulnerabilities and Effect Analysis (FMVEA) [15] extend existing safety analysis techniques from ISO 26262 and IEC 60812, respectively, by incorporating threat information based on the STRIDE [19] model. In the middle column, the Failure-Attack-CountTermeasure

Table 1. Classification of related work [20]

	Extend	Combine	Alternative
Component-based	SAHARA [10], FMVEA [15]	FACT Graph [14], EFT [6]	
Systems-based		CHASSIS [13]	STPA-Sec [23], STPA-SafeSec [7]

(FACT) Graph [14], and Extended Fault Tree (EFT) [6] are based on a combination of fault tree and attack tree methods. Combined Harm Assessment of Safety and Security for Information Systems (CHASSIS) [13], which involves the combination of use/misuse cases and sequence diagrams, is classified as a systems-based approach because it places more emphasis on interactions between entities (which may include human actors) as opposed to the hardware/software structure of the system. In the last column, System-theoretic Process Analysis for Security (STPA-Sec) [23] and the subsequent STPA-SafeSec [7] approaches emphasize a top-down assessment of a system's functional control structure to identify unsafe/insecure control actions.

In our position paper [20], we advocated combining aspects of STPA-Sec (a systems-theoretic approach) and FMVEA (a component-centric approach). In complex systems, a systems-theoretic approach such as STPA-Sec seems to offer advantages in hazard/threat identification. However, the qualitative nature of the output of STPA-Sec and the large number of causal scenarios generated leads to challenges assessing risk. On the other hand, as a component-centric analysis method, FMVEA provides an assessment process with semi-quantitative ratings which is closer to existing industry practice.

3   Systems-Theoretic Likelihood and Severity Analysis

In this section we describe a new process for identifying and jointly analyzing the risks from safety (hazard/accident) and security (threat) perspectives. The Systems-Theoretic Likelihood and Severity Analysis method combines features from STPA-Sec and FMVEA, and integrates them into a unified analytical process. In this section, we first provide a more thorough introduction of the steps in each of the original methods before presenting the hybrid STLSA method.

3.1   Original STPA-Sec Process

STPA-Sec [23] is a security extension of the System-Theoretic Process Analysis (STPA) method from the safety engineering community, which is itself derived from the System-Theoretic Accident Modeling Process (STAMP). The motivation behind STPA-Sec is to consider the impact of cyber security on system safety from a "strategic" rather than a "tactical" perspective: taking a top-down analysis approach focusing on the functionality provided by a system, and its functional control structure, rather than focusing on threats and attacker properties such as intent and capability.

The process for carrying out STPA-Sec analysis is as follows:

1. Identifying **unacceptable losses** that should be avoided (called, Systems Engineering Foundation in [23]).
2. Modeling the system's **functional control structure** (see Fig. 1)
3. Identifying **unsafe and/or insecure control actions** from the functional control structure using guide phrases (e.g., control provided too early/late)
4. Identifying **causal scenarios** which may be used to define security requirements and constraints.

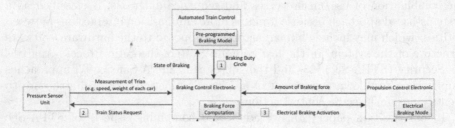

Fig. 1. Partial example of a functional control structure for a train braking system

It should be noted that the output of STPA-Sec analysis is qualitative in nature: a list of control actions in the system that may be unsafe or insecure, and how those control actions may lead to unacceptable losses in one or more causal scenarios. The STPA-Sec approach does not evaluate the relative likelihood or severity of impact for those causal scenarios, which is not fully aligned with current safety/security standards [9,16]. In fact, the authors of [7] motivate their STPA-SafeSec approach in part by noting that the original method does not provide guidance on how to proceed after unsafe/insecure control actions and causal scenarios are identified.

3.2 Original FMVEA Process

FMVEA is an extension of the widely-used Failure Mode and Effect Analysis [15] method for safety risk assessment, as described in IEC 60812 [1]. FMVEA includes security-related information such as vulnerabilities, threat modes (based on STRIDE [19]), and threat effects. As described in [15], the FMVEA analysis process is as follows:

1. Divide a system into components
2. For each component, identify failure modes and/or threat modes
3. Identify the effect of each failure and/or threat mode (includes attack probability)

4. Determine severity of the final effect
5. Identify potential causes/vulnerabilities/threat agents
6. Estimate frequency or probability of occurrence for the failure/threat mode during the predetermined time period
7. Steps 3–6 repeat until there are no more failure modes/vulnerabilities or components left to analyze

We consider FMVEA to be a *component-centric* analysis method, as opposed to STPA-Sec which is *systems-centric*. The authors of [7] adopt a similar taxonomy, considering methods such as traditional FMEA and Fault Tree Analysis as failure-based hazard analysis (i.e., based on component failure), while STPA-Sec is regarded as systems-based hazard analysis. One challenge that component-based methods face is scalability: for large systems, particularly those with complex interactions or emergent behavior, is it sufficient to consider lower level failures and threats? Another challenge is the issue of multiple failures, which are far more plausible in a deliberate attack (security context) as compared with an accidental or random failure (safety context). Finally, in FMEA/FMVEA the *effect* component considers system effects, but the manner in which they are identified is not always made explicit.

An FMVEA case study paper [18] elaborates that components can be either hardware/software, or functions depending on the maturity level of the system design. Similarly, a more recent FMVEA case study [17] includes a three-layer dataflow model of the system as first step in the analysis process, to support the identification of failure modes and effects. If one takes the view that this preliminary system modeling exercise is independent from the documented FMVEA process as described in [15], it raises the question of whether STPA-Sec's functional control structure models could serve the same purpose, and whether the unsafe/insecure control actions would also help to inform FMVEA analysis.

3.3 STLSA Combination

STLSA aims to leverage the high level (functional) control models from STPA-Sec, as well as the guide words and phrases, while introducing a familiar rating process inspired by FMVEA for evaluating the risk of causal scenarios. Risk in this sense is the product of a scenario's severity and the likelihood of occurrence. Severity and likelihood are rated on an ordinal scale (e.g., 1–4), providing a semi-quantitative risk score. In this paper, we use rating scales from existing railway standards and apply the method in a railway case study (see Sect. 4), however other industries (e.g., aviation) may have alternate rating systems that are already familiar to practitioners, and that could be applied within STLSA. Figure 2 depicts the steps in the STLSA analysis process, which we outline in detail below.

Systems-theoretic analysis

We start with an STPA-Sec analysis, with the steps summarized in [23]. However, there are a number of ways in which the functional control structure (step 2),

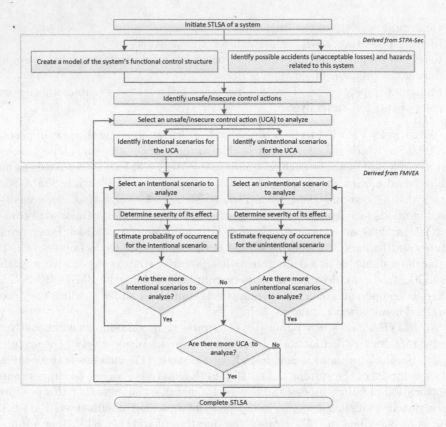

Fig. 2. STLSA: a hybrid method of FMVEA and STPA-Sec

and identification of unsafe/insecure control actions (step 3) are enhanced to better address complex interactions (see Sect. 4 for an example).

– Explicitly indicating which aspects of the functional control structure are in the system and which are in the environment. Connections between the two are indicated with dashed edges.
– Showing multiple instances of actors & components in the system. This is intended to prompt analysts to think about complex failure modes between instances (e.g., multiple trains in a metro, or supposedly identical components behaving differently).
– Applying the extended guide word analysis from [16] (shown in Fig. 3) when identifying causal scenarios for unsafe/insecure control actions. This introduces additional coverage for intentional scenarios (e.g., considering a spoofed controller).

An example of a causal scenario could be *jammed control input* for a train braking control unit, where the italicized text refers to a guide word applied to a generic control loop that is used to aid the assessment process (see Fig. 3).

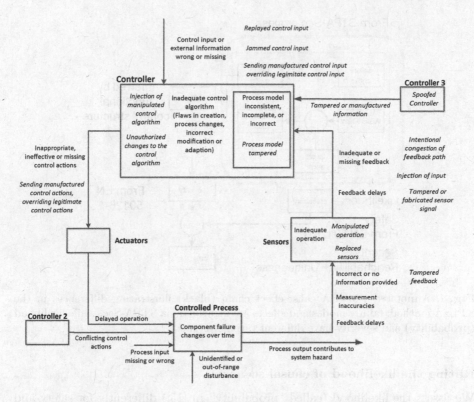

Fig. 3. Control loop with extended guide word (adapted from [16])

Once the causal scenarios for each unsafe/insecure control action are identified, we borrow concepts from FMVEA [15] to assess the risk of each causal scenario in a more nuanced manner.

Severity analysis of causal scenarios

A causal scenario for an unsafe/insecure control action may be thought of as a failure mode in FMVEA. A failure mode has an effect, and that effect has a severity associated with it (see Fig. 4). In STLSA, the effect of a causal scenario may be identified from the functional control structure. The severity of a causal scenario is assigned a rating; in this case we use railway safety standard EN 50126-1 [3] which includes four levels:

1. **Insignificant:** Possible minor injury, and/or system damage.
2. **Marginal:** Minor injuries and/or minor damage to the environment, and/or severe system damage.
3. **Critical:** Severe injures and/or few fatalities and/or large damage to environment, and/ or loss of a major system.
4. **Catastrophic:** Many fatalities and/or extreme damage to the environment.

The classification of severity levels is common between failure (safety) and threat (security) modes.

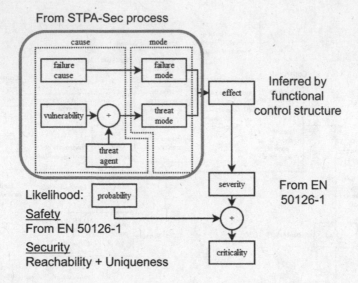

Fig. 4. Annotated FMVEA cause-effect chain (black) illustrating differences in the STLSA method: failure modes and effects are identified via STPA-Sec, while likelihood (probability) and severity have different rating systems.

Rating the likelihood of causal scenarios

We assess the likelihood (called "probability" in [15]) differently for safety and security scenarios, as seen in Fig. 2. In safety scenarios, the likelihood is expressed as a *frequency* score. This is quantified according to a 6-tier event occurrence frequency classification, as suggested in EN 50126-1 [3], ranging from *highly improbable* (1) to *frequent* (6). The descriptions and for each frequency level are listed as follows:

1. **Highly improbable:** Extremely unlikely to occur. It can be assumed that the event may not occur.
2. **Improbable:** Unlikely to occur but possible.It can be assumed that the event may exceptionally occur.
3. **Rare:** Likely to occur sometime in the system life-cycle. Event can reasonably be expected to occur.
4. **Occasional:** Likely to occur sometime in the system life-cycle. Event can reasonably be expected to occur.
5. **Probable:** Will occur several times. Event can be expected to occur often.
6. **Frequent:** Likely to occur frequently. Event will be frequently experienced.

For security related scenarios, however, we adopt an alternative method to assess the likelihood, which is more closely connected to FMVEA. In [15] likelihood is defined as a combination of system susceptibility and threat properties. However, a challenge arises because the STPA-Sec method—the starting point of STLSA—explicitly rejects a threat-based approach (i.e., focusing on a potential adversary's motivation, resources, etc.), arguing instead for a system-centric focus that starts from identifying unacceptable losses.

Therefore, in our STLSA approach, we exclude the Motivation and Capability elements that characterize threats in FMVEA and focus only on the system's susceptibility to a threat, which is characterized by *reachability* ("R") and *uniqueness* ("U"). The likelihood score for security scenarios is given by $R + U$. These are rated according to the following scales:

- **Reachability** (0 = no network, 1 = temporary connected private network, 2 = normal private network, 3 = public network)
- **Uniqueness** (1 = restricted, 2 = commercially available, 3 = standard)

The Reachability and Uniqueness levels describe how easy it is for a potential adversary to connect to and acquire knowledge about the system. This numerical rating system, while simple, allows analysts to incorporate practical information such as the presence of air-gapped networks or the use of proprietary versus commercial-off-the-shelf devices. While *Uniqueness* is classified into 3 levels as suggested in [15], we add one additional classification in *Reachability*, which is called temporary connected private network. This is intended for components that are occasionally connected to network during patching or maintaining periods. Following this change from the original FMVEA, the likelihood rating scale for both intentional and unintentional sources take values up to 6.

Figure 4 illustrates the STLSA process in a different manner from Fig. 2, focusing on the differences from the original FMVEA method. As shown, the upstream aspects of the FMVEA cause-effect chain are replaced with the systems-theoretic modeling in STPA-Sec, while the downstream assessment steps are maintained with modifications to the rating systems. In the next section we go through a case study to illustrate the end-to-end assessment process.

4   Case Study: Train Braking System

A train's braking system is perhaps the most safety-critical of any subsystem, and as a result of this, modern trains have service and emergency braking processes. However, while there are multiple processes of activating and controlling various braking actions, many of the components involved in braking are shared. In addition to the obvious issue of train collision, the braking system should be designed to prevent other undesirable events. Two high-profile incidents from Singapore's mass rapid transit system illustrate the complex safety and security challenges inherent in this system.

Incident 1: Oil leakage on the track. One of the most prominent railway safety incidents in Singapore was a train collision in 1993 [2]. A train that was stationary at the Clementi station was struck by another oncoming train that was unable to stop, injuring 156 passengers. Investigators traced the cause to an oil spill on the track from a maintenance locomotive. The spill had been detected earlier, but delay and miscommunication about clean-up led to a hazard and ultimately an accident. A number of operational changes were made after the accident, including checking all locomotives for oil leakage before and after leaving the depot [21].

Incident 2: Signalling interference from a nearby train. More recently, in late 2016, the automated Circle Line train system in Singapore was afflicted with mysterious service disruptions. Trains would lose the signalling network connection seemingly at random and activate the emergency brake. After a detailed investigation, it was determined that a malfunctioning train was emitting a wireless signal that interfered with nearby trains' connectivity [5, 22].

Based on those incidents, a safety and security co-analysis method needs to be able to model complex system interactions, potentially including multiple instances of the same subsystem (e.g., train) within a larger environment and operational context. At the same time, safety engineers today need to consider both physical hazards and acts of tampering (e.g., oil on the track) as well as cyber threats (e.g., tampering with a train to jam nearby trains). In the case study below we aim to illustrate how the STLSA analysis method can help systems engineers confront these risk assessment challenges.

4.1   System Description

Rolling stock are equipped with both electrical brakes and frictional brakes. Figure 5 shows a typical train with three cars, and overlays the key components of both braking systems. These components and their main functions are:

- ATC: Automatic Train Control. Pre-programmed to initiate service braking.
- BCE: Braking control electronics. Generally in charge of electrical braking and frictional braking at appropriate time.
- BCU: Braking control unit. Activates frictional brake via pneumatic control.
- PCE: Power control electronics. To activate electrical braking.
- EBK/EBR: Emergency brake contractor/Emergency brake relay. De-energized to activate emergency braking.
- Bogie: undercarriage with train wheels

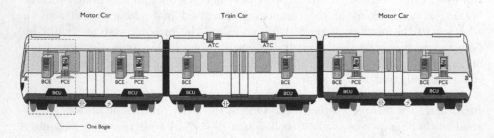

Fig. 5. Topology of the train brake system

Under normal circumstances of service braking, electrical brake is activated in the early phase, then BCUs activate the frictional brake at mid speed to compensate for the decrease in electric braking effort. This control constraint aims to ensure a smooth braking process and it's known as a blending request. When the train speed decreases to below 3 km/hr, full frictional brake would be applied regardless of the receptivity of the traction power system.

Electrical braking is applied for energy saving purpose, since this process boosts power regeneration that kinetic energy of the train converts into electrical energy. In fact, the failure of conducting electrical braking does not have impact to train operation, since the braking force from electrical brake could be fully compensated by frictional braking. However, if frictional brake fails to be conducted properly, train operation will be affected. To specify, a single frictional brake failure of one bogie will not cause the train to stop immediately, and if it is a minor fault, no effects will be exposed to train normal operation, while major fault may affect the train's status, such as overrun.

Unlike normal braking, emergency brake is controlled by a different loop across the trainline, which is called the emergency brake loop. When the emergency brake loop is interrupted (e.g., by a passenger pressing the emergency call button) the train will activate the emergency brake to stop immediately. In an emergency brake scenario only the frictional brake is used, and full brake force is applied. When the emergency brake loop is interrupted, EBK and EBR are de-energized in sequence, which will be sent to BCE to activate frictional brake. The following process of activation of frictional brake from BEC works in the same way as the frictional brake in normal brake.

4.2   Analysis

According to the system description, we construct the control model for the train brake management system as shown in Fig. 6. We first identify the main entities involved in the train brake scenario, including automated controllers, cyber and physical components, as well as human factors (e.g. passengers and station staff). In the hierarchical control structure shown in Fig. 6, the interactions among entities are modeled as control loops, composed of the actions or commands that a controller sends to controlled process, and the responses or feedback that the controller receives from controlled process. In every control loop, any flaws or inadequacies could possibly lead to unsafe control actions and hazardous states in the system.

In Table 2, we list several of the possible accidents related to the train brake management system. Here we focus on safety related losses and exclude other losses like financial or operational losses. Four common accidents (A1 to A4) related to the braking scenario are suggested. For example, if sequential brake processes fail to connect in an appropriate way, train's smooth operation can no more be ensured, and this may cause passengers fall down or even get injured (A1). Another accidental scenario is property damage (A2). For instance, during the regeneration phase of electrical braking, there are risks of damage to traction

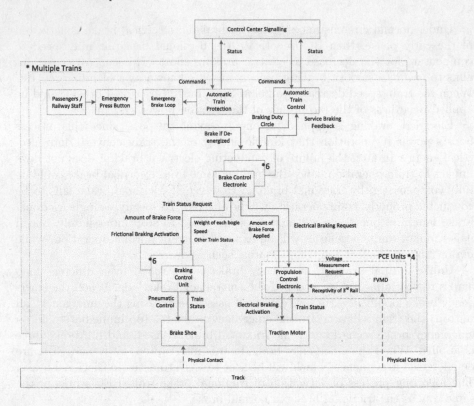

Fig. 6. Hierarchical control loops of a train brake management system

power system when 3rd rail voltage is too high or too low. Similarly, the couplings between cars will be compromised by excessive force if individual bogie does not brake at correct rate. Collision with objects or other trains (A3) is another major type of accident. Additionally, braking failure can cause disruption of availability as well, like the train unexpectedly stops in the middle of a tunnel, or misses the platform (A4).

According to the aforesaid braking accidents, the hazardous scenarios are identified and attached to the related accidents, as shown in Table 2. For example, in train braking phase, individual cars need to sense weight and brake with different force accordingly, since the corresponding equipment like BCE and BCU are dedicated to control the braking process for each bogie. Due to the complex interactions of their control loops, the couplings of cars could suffer from excessive extrusion force or separating force, once there is any inadequate control in this process. This condition could be a significant hazardous scenario (H-1)leading to the damage of relevant equipment (A2), especially for the train with multiple cars.

We further investigate the contexts under which control actions could be unsafe and lead to hazardous status. As per STPA-Sec, unsafe control actions could be categorized into four types: (1) control action not given, (2) control

Table 2. Accidents and system hazards in braking control process

Identified accident
A1. Train decelerates or stops in a sudden way, making passengers fall down and even get injured
A2. Related system or equipment are damaged
A3. Collision with objects or other trains
A4. Train stops at wrong places
Identified hazards and corresponding accidents (in parentheses)
H1. Coupling between adjacent cars is being compromised (A2)
H2. Train is not at the right speed at certain location (A3, A4)
H2-1. Train is overrun
H2-2. Train is underrun
H3. Substantial phases fail to connect smoothly (A1)
H4. Traction power system e.g., 3rd rail, is over voltage (A2)
H5. Procedure continues for a prolonged time (A3, A4)
H6. Train does not stop properly (A3)
H7. Braking phases are conducted with unintended timing, in an unintended amount, or at an unintended location (A3, A4)

action given not correctly, (3) wrong timing or order of control action, (4) control action stopped too soon or applied too long. In this step, to identify unsafe control actions, all the control loops in Fig. 6 are reviewed. Due to the limitation of space, we only show one example under each type (see Table 3).

In Table 3, we highlight the unsafe control action type, the unsafe control actions which could lead to a hazard, and the possible system hazards. For example, an unsafe control action is that too little brake force is performed and transmitted to downstream brake units (UCA-3), which would lead to hazardous system status like wrong speed, compromised couplings, etc. Another example is electrical brake is applied too long and fails to properly stop in time, when the 3rd rail is fully regenerated (UCA-5), and it may cause the damage of related equipment.

Afterwards, with the help of the annotated control graph from [16, 23], we consider intentional and unintentional causal scenarios for each unsafe control action. Table 4 shows a few possible causal scenarios for UCA-3. We distinguish unintentional scenarios and intentional scenarios with the label of "U" and "I" respectively. Unintentional causal scenarios may include safety oriented factors such as possible flaws in the algorithms and models, malfunctions of related components, inadequate or evening missing feedback. While in security perspective, intentional scenarios focus on malicious attacks such as injection of manipulated data, tampered or congested feedback etc.

Table 3. Example conditions under which control actions may lead to hazard

Type	Control action	UCA No.	Unsafe control actions	Possible hazards
Required action not performed	Request electrical braking	UCA-1	Electrical braking request is not preformed by PCE in the train braking scenario	Non-hazardous
	Activate frictional braking	UCA-2	Frictional braking is not activated during the train braking phase	H1, H2-1, H5, H6
Hazardous action performed	Activate frictional braking	UCA-3	Inadequate braking force is performed and transmitted to downstream braking units in frictional braking phase	H1, H2-1, H5, H7
Incorrect timing or order	Activate pneumatic control	UCA-4	Pneumatic control isn't properly be applied at the mid of speed to compensate for the decrease in electrical break effort	H3, H7
Incorrect duration	Activate electrical braking	UCA-5	Electrical braking is preformed too long, and fails to stop before traction power system has been fully regenerated	H4

These scenarios should not be seen as exhaustive checklist which covers all possibilities, but a starting point for further thoughts and investigations. It is also important to note that quite a number of unsafe control actions may share similar causal scenarios, but they happen on different controller and controlled process. That means there are some common causes for unsafe and insecure scenario which calls for extra attention and efforts.

Last, we assess the likelihood of identified causal scenarios with the method suggested in Sect. 3. Specifically, we rate "Reachability" and "Uniqueness" according to the braking management case. The example of evaluation is shown in Table 4 (for UCA-3).

Reachability. Internal cyber components in a train brake management system are not public accessible and best described as a private network. In most of cyber attacks targeting this system, attackers need to manage the control process via a private network connection (reachability = 2).

Uniqueness. Most of train brake systems are restricted and not common for commercial or non-commercial applications (uniqueness = 1). While the process, operation and a few devices such as sensors can be assumed as commercially available (uniqueness = 2).

Table 4. Potential causal scenarios and assessment of UCA-3

ID	Potential causal scenarios	Type (U/I)	S	R	U	p/f score
A	Sensors or related equipment(e.g. BCE, BCU) malfunction	U	1	-	-	5
B	Inadequate control algorithm occur to BCE calculation model, which causes the amount of breaking force is not calculated correctly	U	2	-		2
C	**Unidentified disturbance such as the changes of environment(e.g. the track is oily), makes the braking force in normal circumstance not adequate any longer**	U	3	-	-	2
D	The feedback path to BCE may be congested intentionally, then the train cannot explicitly determine the required brake force for each bogie	I	2	2	1	3
E	Manufactured braking force amount is sent by BCE to the downstream braking equipment, and that forged message overwrites the legitimate braking force	I	3	2	1	3
F	**Maliciously tamper or fabricate readings of relevant devices (e.g. oil gauge,sensors) after creating an unsafe situation of environment**	I	3	2	2	4

Note: Type(U/I)–Type(Unintentional scenario/Intentional scenario); S–Severity; R–Reachability; U–Uniqueness; p/f score–probability/frequency score.

4.3 Discussion

As seen in the analysis above, elements from STPA-Sec and FMVEA can be combined to provide a system-level view of unsafe or insecure control actions with greater support for structured risk assessment in the form of likelihood and severity scores grounded in standards such as EN 50126-1 for railway applications. By reconciling those perspectives on safety/security co-analysis, we arrive at a method that can be used to identify unsafe situations posed by the environment's impact on system control actions (i.e., oil on the track in Table 4) and prioritize high-risk security/safety issues (high S and p/f score) for remediation.

This work represents an initial attempt to reconcile concepts from STPA-Sec with more traditional component-based analysis methods. As such, there are a few limitations we would like to acknowledge. First, it may be possible to incorporate other methods into an STPA-Sec inspired analysis process. We chose FMVEA in this work due to its close alignment with a classical safety/reliability engineering approach used in industry (FMEA). Second, the control structure diagram in Fig. 3, while more expressive than the functional control diagrams used in [23], is also more complex with the addition of multiple instances and environmental interaction. Also, as pointed out in [16], the STPA-Sec process results in a large number of control loops and causal scenarios to analyze. It is our view that these factors point to a need for tool support to assist with creating/maintaining/tracking assessment documentation. This is a topic we will explore in future work.

5   Conclusion

In this paper, we propose a new method for identifying and evaluating safety and security risks. Our Systems-Theoretic Likelihood and Severity Analysis (STLSA) method combines aspects from the systems-theoretic STPA-Sec method, which identifies unsafe/insecure control actions in a system, and component-centric FMVEA method, which is an extension of failure mode and effects analysis from IEC 60812. We illustrate the STLSA process using a railway case study.

Acknowledgements. This work was supported in part by the National Research Foundation (NRF), Prime Minister's Office, Singapore, under its National Cybersecurity R&D Programme (Award No. NRF2014NCR-NCR001-31) and administered by the National Cybersecurity R&D Directorate. It was also supported in part by the research grant for the Human-Centered Cyber-physical Systems Programme at the Advanced Digital Sciences Center from Singapore's Agency for Science, Technology and Research (A*STAR).

References

1. IEC 60812: Analysis techniques for system reliability ? procedure for failure mode and effects analysis (FMEA)
2. First mrt accident (2004). http://eresources.nlb.gov.sg/infopedia/articles/SIP_814_2004-12-31.html
3. BS EN 50126–1. Railway applications-The Specification and Demonstration Reliability, Availability, Maintainability and Safety (RAMS). Part 1: Basic Requirements and Generic Process (2015)
4. Chockalingam, S., Hadziosmanovic, D., Pieters, W., Teixeira, A., van Gelder, P.: Integrated safety and security risk assessment methods: a survey of key characteristics and applications. In: CRITIS (2016)
5. Defence Science and Technology Agency blog. How we caught the circle line rogue train with data (2016). https://blog.data.gov.sg/how-we-caught-the-circle-linerogue-train-with-data-79405c86ab6a#.4fu3jqint
6. Fovino, I.N., Masera, M., De Cian, A.: Integrating cyber attacks within fault trees. Reliab. Eng. Syst. Saf. **94**(9), 1394–1402 (2009)
7. Friedberg, I., McLaughlin, K., Smith, P., Laverty, D., Sezer, S.: STPA-SafeSec: safety and security analysis for cyber-physical systems. J. Inf. Secur. Appl. **34**, 183–196 (2016)
8. Henniger, O., Apvrille, L., Fuchs, A., Roudier, Y., Ruddle, A., Weyl, B.: Security requirements for automotive on-board networks. In: 2009 9th International Conference on Intelligent Transport Systems Telecommunications, (ITST), pp. 641–646. IEEE (2009)
9. Kriaa, S., Pietre-Cambacedes, L., Bouissou, M., Halgand, Y.: A survey of approaches combining safety and security for industrial control systems. Reliab. Eng. Syst. Saf. **139**, 156–178 (2015)

10. Macher, G., Höller, A., Sporer, H., Armengaud, E., Kreiner, C.: A combined safety-hazards and security-threat analysis method for automotive systems. In: Koornneef, F., Gulijk, C. (eds.) SAFECOMP 2015. LNCS, vol. 9338, pp. 237–250. Springer, Cham (2015). doi:10.1007/978-3-319-24249-1_21

11. Massacci, F., Paci, F.: How to select a security requirements method? a comparative study with students and practitioners. In: Jøsang, A., Carlsson, B. (eds.) NordSec 2012. LNCS, vol. 7617, pp. 89–104. Springer, Heidelberg (2012). doi:10.1007/978-3-642-34210-3_7

12. Piètre-Cambacédès, L., Bouissou, M.: Cross-fertilization between safety and security engineering. Reliab. Eng. Syst. Saf. **110**, 110–126 (2013)

13. Raspotnig, C., Karpati, P., Katta, V.: A combined process for elicitation and analysis of safety and security requirements. In: Bider, I., Halpin, T., Krogstie, J., Nurcan, S., Proper, E., Schmidt, R., Soffer, P., Wrycza, S. (eds.) BPMDS/EMMSAD -2012. LNBIP, vol. 113, pp. 347–361. Springer, Heidelberg (2012). doi:10.1007/978-3-642-31072-0_24

14. Raspotnig, C., Karpati, P., Katta, V.: A combined process for elicitation and analysis of safety and security requirements. In: Bider, I., Halpin, T., Krogstie, J., Nurcan, S., Proper, E., Schmidt, R., Soffer, P., Wrycza, S. (eds.) BPMDS/EMMSAD - 2012. LNBIP, vol. 113, pp. 347–361. Springer, Heidelberg (2012). doi:10.1007/978-3-642-31072-0_24

15. Schmittner, C., Gruber, T., Puschner, P., Schoitsch, E.: Security application of failure mode and effect analysis (FMEA). In: Bondavalli, A., Di Giandomenico, F. (eds.) SAFECOMP 2014. LNCS, vol. 8666, pp. 310–325. Springer, Cham (2014). doi:10.1007/978-3-319-10506-2_21

16. Schmittner, C., Ma, Z., Puschner, P.: Limitation and improvement of STPA-sec for safety and security co-analysis. In: Skavhaug, A., Guiochet, J., Schoitsch, E., Bitsch, F. (eds.) SAFECOMP 2016. LNCS, vol. 9923, pp. 195–209. Springer, Cham (2016). doi:10.1007/978-3-319-45480-1_16

17. Schmittner, C., Ma, Z., Schoitsch, E., Gruber, T.: A case study of fmvea and chassis as safety and security co-analysis method for automotive cyber-physical systems. In: ACM Workshop on Cyber-Physical System Security, pp. 69–80. ACM (2015)

18. Schmittner, C., Ma, Z., Smith, P.: FMVEA for safety and security analysis of intelligent and cooperative vehicles. In: Bondavalli, A., Ceccarelli, A., Ortmeier, F. (eds.) SAFECOMP 2014. LNCS, vol. 8696, pp. 282–288. Springer, Cham (2014). doi:10.1007/978-3-319-10557-4_31

19. Shostack, A., Lambert, S., Ostwald, T., Hernan, S.: Uncover security design flaws using the STRIDE approach. MSDN Mag., November 2006. https://msdn.microsoft.com/magazine/msdn-magazine-issues

20. Temple, W.G., Wu, Y., Chen, B., Kalbarczyk, Z.: Reconciling systems-theoretic and component-centric methods for safety and security co-analysis. In: Tonetta, S., Schoitsch, E., Bitsch, F. (eds.) SAFECOMP 2017. LNCS, vol. 10489, pp. 87–93. Springer, Cham (2017). doi:10.1007/978-3-319-66284-8_9

21. The Straits Times. Oil spillage led to mrt train collision, Panel (1993). http://eresources.nlb.gov.sg/newspapers/Digitised/Article/straitstimes19931020-1.2.2

22. The Straits Times. Train's faulty signals behind circle line woes (2016). http://www.straitstimes.com/singapore/transport/trains-faulty-signals-behind-circle-line-woes

23. Young, W., Leveson, N.: Systems thinking for safety and security. In: ACSAC, pp. 1–8. ACM (2013)

Formal Modelling and Verification for Safety

Formal Modelling Techniques for Efficient Development of Railway Control Products

M. Butler[1], D. Dghaym[1], T. Fischer[2], T.S. Hoang[1], K. Reichl[2], C. Snook[1(✉)], and P. Tummeltshammer[2]

[1] ECS, University of Southampton, Southampton, UK
{mjb,dd4g12,t.s.hoang,cfs}@ecs.soton.ac.uk
[2] Thales Austria GmbH, Vienna, Austria
{tomas.fischer,klaus.reichl,peter.tummeltshammer}@thalesgroup.com

Abstract. We wish to model railway control systems in a formally precise way so that product lines can be adapted to specific customer requirements. Typically a customer is a railway operator with national conventions leading to different variation points based on a common core principle. A formal model of the core product must be precise and manipulatable so that different feature variations can be specified and verified without disrupting important properties that have already been established in the core product. Cyber-physical systems such as railway interlocking, are characterised by the combination of device behaviours resulting in an overall safe system behaviour. Hence there is a strong need for correct sequential operation with safety "interlocks" making up a process. We utilise diagrammatic modelling tools to make the core product more accessible to systems engineers. The *RailGround* example used to discuss these techniques is an open source model of a railway control system that has been made available by Thales Austria GmbH for research purpose, which demonstrates some fundamental modelling challenges.

Keywords: Event-B · iUML-B · ERS · Interlocking

1 Introduction

A railway control system is a safety-critical cyber-physical system where common principles are well established and adopted on a broadly generic infrastructure, but with an abundance of feature variations across national boundaries. In order to be able to offer a configurable, yet certified, product it is therefore essential to adopt an efficient product development process that allows a verified core product to be adapted to specific solutions. We propose a model-based approach that will support such a development process.

Motivation. Our motivation is to model railway control systems in a formally precise way so that product lines can be adapted to specific customer requirements. Typically a customer is a railway operator with national conventions

© Springer International Publishing AG 2017
A. Fantechi et al. (Eds.): RSSRail 2017, LNCS 10598, pp. 71–86, 2017.
https://doi.org/10.1007/978-3-319-68499-4_5

leading to different variation points based on a common core principle such as *Interlocking* (IXL). A formal model of the core product therefore must be precise and manipulatable so that different feature variations can be specified and verified without disrupting important properties that have already been established in the core product. Such properties include the safety principles of a technology and we assume that they have already been proven to ensure safety. For example, in our IXL model, we assume that if conflicting paths are exclusively enabled, this is sufficient to ensure that trains do not collide. In future work, we envisage using various *domain-specific languages* (DSLs) so that customers can precisely specify their specific feature requirements. For now, we focus on modelling the core system.

We model the core system using notations that are accessible to systems engineers. These engineers have extensive domain knowledge, are skilled at specifying systems in the railway domain and usually have experience in semi-formal modelling tools such as UML and SysML. They are generally less experienced at formal modelling and proof. For this reason we utilise graphical representations of the formal model. To fully understand the model, and to debug models when proofs do not discharge automatically, it is necessary to understand the formal notation. Formal methods specialists are needed to help with proof and specific modelling difficulties, but the main content of the models must be accessible to less specialised systems engineers and other stakeholders.

Event-B and extensions. The Event-B modelling method [1] is suitable for this formal modelling task because it allows us to verify (core) properties while leaving certain features underspecified, and subsequently refine the model to fully specify those features in a consistent manner with respect to the abstract model. Event-B has strong tool support for verification and validation in the form of theorem provers and model-checkers. Diagrammatic modelling notations and tools are available which aid model accessibility. We use the iUML-B class diagrams and state-machines [15,18,19] in conjunction with *Event Refinement Structure* (ERS) [5,6] to visualise event refinement structures.

RailGround. For research and illustration purposes we use an example railway interlocking specification called RailGround [14]. RailGround is provided as an open specification and model for this purpose. This is a simplified version of interlocking systems, built specifically for research on formal validation and verification of railway systems [14]. This example is used as part of the rail use case of the European project *Enable-S3* [4].

Contribution. *Cyber-Physical Systems* (CPS) such as the railway interlocking, are made up of many disparate devices with interrelationships. They are characterised by the combination of device behaviours resulting in an overall safe system behaviour. Hence there is a strong need for correct sequential operation with safety "interlocks" making up a process. To model CPS we start by modelling the entity relationships of the devices using an iUML-B class diagram, we then model the individual behaviour of instances of these entities using iUML-B state-machines.

However, this is not sufficient to show the overall system process. To show this we add the ERS view which shows the process based on the sequences of events involved in the interaction of all devices.

Our contribution is an approach for modelling CPS using diagrammatic notations for the three views above: Entity-Relationships, Entity-Behaviour and System Process. Our approach utilises an integration of iUML-B and ERS.

Structure. In Sect. 2 we describe the requirements of the RailGround system and introduce the modelling notations and tools that we use to model it. In Sect. 3 we describe our model of the RailGround system in order to illustrate the use of the formal modelling notations. Section 4 discusses related work to our approach and the case study. In Sect. 5 we reflect on the effectiveness and benefits of combining the modelling notations and indicate future work.

Dataset. The Event-B model illustrating this paper is available as a dataset here: https://doi.org/10.5258/SOTON/D0184. The required Rodin and plug-in configuration is given in a 'readme' file within the dataset.

2   Background

We first present some background information on the case study including its requirements in Sect. 2.1. Subsequently, we give a brief overview of the Event-B method in Sect. 2.2, of iUML-B in Sect. 2.3, and of ERS in Sect. 2.4.

2.1   RailGround

The example used in this paper is based on RailGround, a formal model of a railway interlocking system using Event-B, which was developed by Thales Austria GmbH [14]. Railway systems, in general, aim at providing a timely, efficient and most importantly a safe train service. This requires a reliable command and control system that ensures a train can safely enter its specified path. In the system under consideration, the railway topology consists of a set of connected elements, which are protected by signals passing information to the trains. The safety of a train is ensured by allowing its path to be set, only if it does not conflict with the current available paths. The following requirements are extracted and simplified from [14]. For illustration, we will consider the network topology with one track and two points as in Fig. 1. Note that we focus on modelling the system functional safety here. This is a subset of the overall system safety functionality. In particular, technical measures from other domains to achieve the desired *Safety Integrity Level* (SIL) are not considered.

Railway Topology. The railway topology is formed by a set of *Rail Elements*. A rail element is a unit which provides a physical running path for the trains, i.e. rails (e.g. track, points, crossing). A *Rail Connector* is a port of a rail element used to define the element's connectivity via *Rail Segments* as well as to link

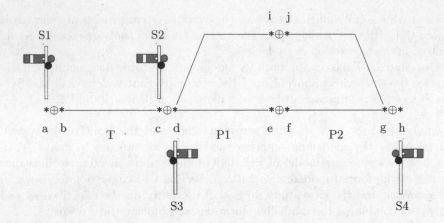

Fig. 1. An example railway topology [14]

this element with the adjacent ones via rail links. Depending on its type, each rail element usually has 2 to 4 rail connectors. Each rail connector belongs to exactly one rail element. Typically, a rail element is made up of one or more *Segments*. A rail segment is a connection from an element's rail connector to another connector of the same rail element.

REQ 1 The network topology is a set of rail elements.

REQ 2 A rail element has 2 to 4 rail connectors. Each rail connector belongs to exactly one rail element.

REQ 3 A rail segment is a connection from a rail connector of some rail element to another rail connector of the same rail element.

In Fig. 1, there are three rail elements, namely T (a track), P1, P2 (points). The connectors are a, b, ..., h and associate with the rail elements as follows:

$$T \mapsto \{b, c\}, P1 \mapsto \{d, e, i\}, P2 \mapsto \{f, j, g\}.$$

The segments are $\{bc, cb, di, id, de, ed, jg, gj, fg, gf\}$. The relationship between the rail elements and the segments are as follows:

$$T \mapsto \{bc, cb\}, P1 \mapsto \{di, id, de, ed\}, P2 \mapsto \{jg, gj, fg, gf\}.$$

Element Positions. For each rail element, an *Element Position* is a distinct situation of that rail element. Furthermore, each element position defines the set of possible element connections (defined by segments) for that particular rail element.

REQ 4 For each rail element, there is a set of possible element positions

REQ 5 Each rail element and position correspond to a set of rail segments

For example, a set of points has three possible positions POS_X (in transition), POS_L (left), POS_R (right). Consider the points P1, position POS_X corresponds to an emptyset of segments, POS_L corresponds to segments $\{di, id\}$, and POS_R corresponds to segments $\{de, ed\}$.

Paths. A path is a sequence of rail segments, with the constraint that two rail segments of the same rail element are not allowed within one path. A path can be activated so that trains are allowed to be on that path.

REQ 6 A path is a sequence of rail segments.
REQ 7 Two rail segments belonging to the same element are not allowed within one path.

Consider the example in Fig. 1, a path could be the following sequence of segments [bc, di, jg], or [gf, ed, cb].

Path Life-Cycle. A set of paths are pre-defined in the network. Before becoming active, a path must be requested. As soon as all conditions for the path (e.g., rail elements must be in the required position to establish its path), a requested path can be activated. As a train moves along a path, rail elements that are no longer in use can be released. An active path can be removed only after all its rail elements are released. A rail element position can only be changed if the rail element is not part of an active path.

REQ 8 A requested path can become an active path when all conditions for that path are met
REQ 9 An active path can be removed only after all its rail elements are released.
REQ 10 A rail element position can only be changed if it is not part of an active path.

In the example network topology, we can have the following paths R1–R4, with the following associations:

R1 ↦ [bc, de, fg], R2 ↦ [bc, di, jg], R3 ↦ [gf, ed, cb], R4 ↦ [gj, id, cb].

Vacancy Detection. In order to detect trains on the network, the system is equipped with *Track Vacancy Detection* (TVD). Each segment belongs to exactly one TVD section. A TVD section is either vacant or occupied. A TVD section is occupied if there is some train on some segment belonging to that TVD section.

REQ 11 Each segment belongs to exactly one TVD section.
REQ 12 A TVD section can be either in vacant or occupied state.

Signals. A *Signal* is an entity capable of passing information to trains. A signal is associated with a rail element for a particular traversal direction. A signal aspect is an (abstract) information conveyed by a signal. *Signal Default* is a predefined aspect of signals. Trains are assumed to obey the signals, in particular, stop at a signal containing default aspect.

REQ 13 A signal may be set to an aspect other than default, only if there is an active element after this signal.

REQ 14 A signal is associated to a connector and hence to a specific location within the topology, i.e., the information passed by the signal are only valid to a specific direction which in this case will be the segment starting at the signal connector.

In Fig. 1, we have 4 signals, S1–S4 associated with different connectors as follows.

$$S1 \mapsto a, S2 \mapsto c, S3 \mapsto d, S4 \mapsto h$$

Safety Properties. Safety in this model is ensured by the paths which are active. The paths can only be set if all its elements are in the right positions. Safety is ensured by preventing paths to be requested if there are other paths requiring the same elements.

REQ 15 Two active paths cannot overlap
REQ 16 An active path must have all its elements in the right positions
REQ 17 A path can be requested if it is disjoint from other active or requested paths.

2.2   Event-B

Event-B [1] is a formal method for system development. Main features of Event-B include the use of *refinement* to introduce system details gradually into the formal model. An Event-B model contains two parts: *contexts* and *machines*. Contexts contain *carrier sets*, *constants*, and *axioms* that constrain the carrier sets and constants. Machines contain *variables* v, *invariants* I(v) that constrain the variables, and *events*. An event comprises a guard denoting its enabling-condition and an action describing how the variables are modified when the event is executed. In general, an event e has the following form, where t are the event parameters, $G(t, v)$ is the guard of the event, and $v := E(t, v)$ is the action of the event[1].

$$e == \text{any t where } G(t,v) \text{ then } v := E(t,v) \text{ end}$$

A machine in Event-B corresponds to a transition system where *variables* represent the states and *events* specify the transitions. Contexts can be *extended* by adding new carrier sets, constants, axioms, and theorems. Machine M can be *refined* by machine N (we call M the abstract machine and N the concrete machine). The state of M and N are related by a *gluing invariant* $J(v, w)$ where v, w are variables of M and N, respectively. The gluing invariant specifies the consistency between the abstract and concrete machines and must be maintained by the execution of both machines. Intuitively, any "behaviour" exhibited by N can be simulated by M, with respect to the gluing invariant J. Refinement in Event-B is reasoned event-wise. Consider an abstract event e and the corresponding concrete event f. Somewhat simplifying, we say that e is refined by f if

---

[1] Actions in Event-B are, in the most general cases, non-deterministic [8].

f's guard is stronger than that of e and f's action can be simulated by e's action, taking into account the gluing invariant J. More information about Event-B can be found in [8]. Event-B is supported by *Rodin platform* (Rodin) [2], an extensible toolkit which includes facilities for modelling, verifying the consistency of models using theorem proving and model checking techniques, and validating models with simulation-based approaches.

2.3   iUML-B

iUML-B [15,18,19] provides a diagrammatic modelling notation for Event-B in the form of state-machines and class-diagrams. The diagrammatic elements are contained within an Event-B model and generate or contribute to parts of it. For example a state-machine will automatically generate the Event-B data elements (sets, constants, axioms, variables, and invariants) to implement the states, and contribute additional guards and actions to existing events. iUML-B Class diagrams provide a way to visually model data relationships. Classes, attributes and associations are linked to Event-B data elements (carrier sets, constants, or variables) and generate constraints on those elements. In iUML-B class diagrams, a class represents some set of instances and the class may be used to show relationships with other classes. Usually the set of instances is given by an Event-B data element, but in some scenarios it is useful to construct a set using an expression as the class name.

2.4   Event Refinement Structures

In Event-B, behaviour can be decomposed during refinement into a combination of new and refining atomic events. However, the relationship between the events at different refinement levels is not explicit, for this we use ERS [5,6] diagrams. ERS, is a tree-like structure, inspired by Jackson Structure Diagrams (JSD) [10], that provides a graphical extension of Event-B to represent event decomposition explicitly. In addition to specifying event decomposition, an ERS diagram can explicitly represent control flow. Similar to JSD diagrams, the ordering of events is read from left-to-right. In addition to sequencing ERS provides different combinators that support iteration, choice and different forms of non-deterministic interleaving.

3   RailGround Model Using iUML-B and ERS

In this section we describe our version of the RailGround model which is modelled in iUML-B and ERS. For each refinement level we discuss the iUML-B class diagram and state-machine (where applicable) and then describe the behaviour of that refinement level, including the refinement relationships of events, using an ERS diagram.

The overall ERS diagram of the RailGround model is illustrated in Fig. 2. The root of the diagram represents the name of the system and it is parametrised by p of type PATH to show the possible interleaving of different paths. The different regions represent the different refinement levels. One of the refinement levels (**Rails**) does not change the event refinement structure, hence the second region represents two refinement levels. Events of the RailGround model are represented by the leaf nodes of the tree, where an event connected to its parent by a dashed line is a newly added event, while a solid line represents a refining event which is identified by the keyword **refines** in the Event-B model.

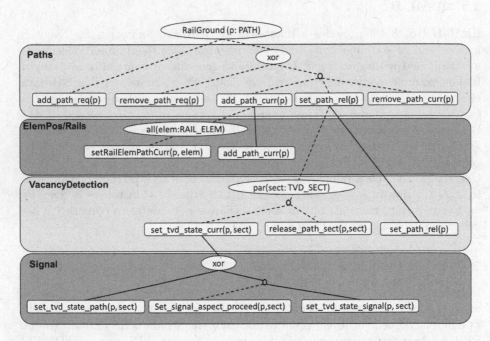

Fig. 2. Event Refinement of the RailGround model shown in ERS (solid lines: refining events, dashed lines: new events)

The refinement sequence adopted for the iUML-B model is as follows:

1. Paths - abstract representation of the path of a train through a rail network (REQ 15, REQ 17).
2. ElemPos - positioning of elements in the rail network to put a path in the right state (REQ 1, REQ 4, REQ 8, REQ 9, REQ 10, REQ 16).
3. Rails - connectivity of elements and their organisation into segments (REQ 5, REQ 6, REQ 7).
4. Vacancy detection - the ability of elements in the rail network to detect when they are occupied by a train (REQ 11, REQ 12).
5. Signal - signals that inform trains to stop or proceed through a path (REQ 2, REQ 3, REQ 13, REQ 14).

The reasons for choosing this sequence are

- The exclusive reservation of a path is the primary concept upon which interlocking safety is based. Therefore it is important to model this first when the model is simple, so that it is easier to validate.
- More detail about the operation of paths is introduced next (Element positioning, Rails).
- The occupation of a path is an important concept that can be introduced as soon as paths are sufficiently modelled.
- Signals are a design detail which can vary depending on customer. It is therefore more convenient to introduce this late.

Paths. Our first abstract model introduces the notion of paths through a rail network. Paths are reserved for exclusive use ensuring that trains cannot collide. Paths are a conceptual device used by the control system, which are related to a set of physical elements in the railway system. The iUML-B class diagram, Fig. 3a, defines a finite given set PATH of paths and an association, Path_Exc of paths that conflict with each other. Axioms constrain this association so that paths do not conflict with themselves and the association is symmetric. The iUML-B state-machine, Fig. 3b defines the behaviour of paths. A path is initially requested (add_path_req) and can then be made active (add_path_curr), followed by released (add_path_rel) and then removed (remove_path_curr). Paths that have been made active but not yet removed are called current. This is represented by superstate path_curr which allows us to specify the state invariant that for all current paths, none of their conflicting paths are also current. This is the safety principle of interlocking systems. It is ensured by a guard on add_path_curr. There is also the possibility remove_path_req of un-requesting a path without it ever becoming current.

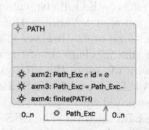
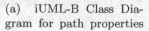
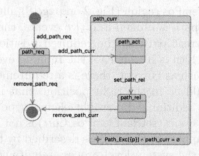

(a) iUML-B Class Diagram for path properties

(b) iUML-B State-machine for path behaviour

Fig. 3. Abstract model of paths through a rail network

The process involved at this abstract level of the model is represented by the **Paths** region in Fig. 2 on page 8. The RailGround model starts by adding a required path, then there is a choice (indicated by *xor*) between either removing the path or making it the current path. If the path p is added as current, then it can be followed by releasing the path, after which the path can be removed from the current paths. At this level, since there is only one (conceptual) device and no refinement, the ERS diagram has a close correspondence with the iUML-B state-machine diagram.

Element Position. In the first refinement we introduce the idea that elements need to be in a particular position for a path. This corresponds to physical devices such as railway "points". We define a constant function Path_Elem_Pos (Fig. 4a) which, for each path, gives a functional mapping from elements to positions. That is, the position that each element of the path needs to be in for that path to be ready. We also define a default position Default_Elem_Pos for each element. Variable functional associations are defined for the current position rail_elem_pos_curr and current path rail_elem_path_curr of each rail element. Two RAIL_ELEM class methods are provided to set the position, rail_elem_pos_curr, of a particular element. Method setRailElemPos_Curr sets the position when the element is not involved in a path, and method setRailElemPath_Curr sets the element to the appropriate position for a given path. The current path of an element is set and reset when the path is made current and released respectively (i.e. these actions are added to the relevant state-machine transitions). Two class invariants are added to class RAIL_ELEM. The first states that, if an element belongs to a current path, then that element must have a defined position for that path according to Path_Elem_Pos. The second ensures that the element is currently in the correct position according to Path_Elem_Pos. Two state invariants in state path_req (Fig. 4b) require that the requested path has no elements in common with another requested path and no elements in common with a current path.

The ElemPos region (Fig. 2 on page 8), illustrates how the atomicity of adding a current path is broken into two events, the first sets the rail elements position of the current path to the required position, followed by adding the path as current, which is in this case the refining event (solid line). However in order to add the path as current, there is a requirement that all elements of the required path should be in the right position, that is why we apply the *all* combinator adding an additional dimension, elem of type RAIL_ELEM, to the ERS model. The other new event (setRailElemPos_Curr) is not associated with a path and therefore does not appear in the process described by the ERS diagram. The ERS diagram visualises the system level process requirement that the positioning of elements must be completed before the path becomes *current*. This is not apparent in the iUML-B model which focusses on the behaviour of individual devices (PATH and RAIL_ELEM). The fact that setRailElemPath_Curr is a preliminary (stuttering) event leading to add_path_curr is made clear in the ERS diagram. Arguably, this is shown in the iUML-B state-machine by adding setRailElemPath_Curr as a transition on the source state, path_req of add_path_curr but the event refinement

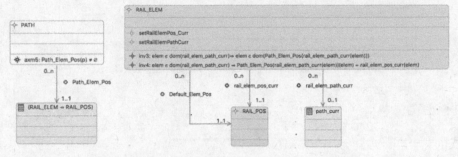

(a) iUML-B Class Diagram for element position

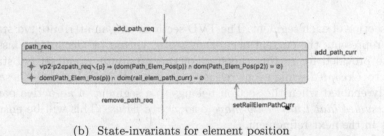

(b) State-invariants for element position

Fig. 4. First refinement introducing element positioning

relationship is not as explicit as in the ERS diagram. On the other hand, the ERS diagram does not illustrate state constraint information such as the requirement that setRailElemPath_Curr is only performed while the associated path is in the state path_req.

Rails. In the second refinement we introduce a stronger relationship describing the physical construction of paths using rail segments. To do this we introduce a given set RAIL_SGMT (Fig. 5) with a functional association Rail_Sgmt_Elem to RAIL_ELEM. An association Path_Segmt gives the subset of RAIL_SGMT that makes up each path. Class axioms specify various constraints to ensure the new segment representation is consistent with other configuration data.

In this refinement, we extended the context to introduce details about the rail's connectivity using segments, which only resulted in changing the model's behaviour by adding some invariants and guards to the existing events relating connectivity to the element position. Consequently, there were no changes to the structure and ordering of events, which remains the same as the ElemPos region.

Vacancy Detection. In the third refinement (Fig. 6) we introduce the detection of trains as they occupy rail segments. A new given set TVD_SECT is introduced to represent TVD sections that can detect when they are occupied. A many-to-one relationship TVD_Seg_Sect from RAIL_SGMT to TVD_SECT specifies the

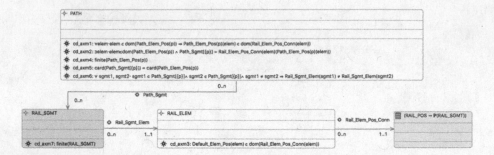

Fig. 5. Second refinement introducing rail segments

TVD section of each segment. The TVD sections own an attribute tvd_state_curr which represents the current occupancy state: *Vacant* or *Occupied*. Class methods are provided for setting the state of this attribute: event set_tvd_state_curr sets it to *Occupied* while event release_path_sect sets it to Vacant. These events are only enabled when the section belongs to a segment of an active path, *i.e.*, *it is assumed that trains only move over active paths.* (This will be ensured by signals in the next refinement.)

At the **Vacancy Detection** level (Fig. 2 on page 8), we break the atomicity of set_path_rel, which releases the current active path. Here we introduce the *par* combinator which allows the interleaving of its instance values zero or more times before its follow-on event executes. In this case, the *par* shows the possibility of occupying a TVD section (set_tvd_state_curr) then leaving it (release_path_sect) before releasing an active path. This ensures that all TVD sections are vacant before releasing the path. The ERS diagram visualises the system level process requirement leading to releasing a path which is not so explicit in the iUML-B.

Fig. 6. Third refinement introducing detection of trains

Signals. In the final refinement (Fig. 7) we introduce signals that control the entry of trains wanting to use a path. The given set (class) SIGNAL has a variable attribute signal_aspect_curr which represents the current aspect and a constant attribute Signal_Aspect_Avail that provides the set of available aspects for that signal. Note that the only specific signal aspect defined at this level is Signal_Aspect_Default which represents the signal's stop aspect. Other aspects may by introduced at later stages when tailoring the specification to a particular product. Class method set_signal_aspect_proceed sets the aspect of the signal to proceed (i.e., not default) while method set_tvd_state_signal sets the signal back to default as the corresponding connected section becomes occupied. Signals are related to paths via connectors. This is modelled by class (Elem_Ctor) and the associations Signal_Ctor and Path_Ctor_Beg. Signals are also related to *Track Vacancy Detection* (TVD) sections via their connectors and the association Sgmt_Ctor. A class invariant cdm_inv2 ensures that a signal is only set to a non-default value when there is an active path at the rear of the signal.

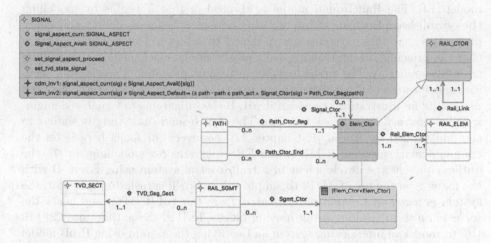

Fig. 7. Fourth refinement introducing signalling

In the **Signals** region of Fig. 2, we split set_tvd_state_curr into two cases using the *xor* combinator. In the first case the TVD section is part of a path but is not protected by a signal (set_tvd_state_path). In the second case the section is protected by a signal. In this latter case we need to set the signal's aspect to proceed first. Then it is possible to occupy that section (set_tvd_state_signal), in which case we also set the signal's aspect back to default to indicate that the section is now occupied. Again the ERS diagram compliments the iUML-B model by visualising the system level process details of signal setting and how it interacts with TVD occupation.

4   Related Work

Our approach combines a state-based modelling notation (iUML-B) with a process-based notation (ERS). Essentially, iUML-B diagrams captures the complex data aspect of the system and their evolution, while ERS diagrams represent the behavioural aspect of the system, in particular sequencing of events. In this sense, this is similar to various existing approaches combining state-based and process-based notations, e.g., CSP and Z [21], CSP and B [3,16], CSP and Event-B [17], etc. In particular, these approaches also support development of systems via (separate) refinement of the state-based model and the process-based model. In our work, both iUML-B and ERS get there semantics by transforming them to Event-B and can contribute to the underlying Event-B model, hence their meanings are given entirely using Event-B. This is in contrast with the above mentioned approaches where essentially combining the different formalisms. As a result, the semantics of these approaches are given using more expressive notation such as *Unifying Theories of Programming* (UTP), for example [13].

We illustrate our approach on a case study based on the RailGround model [14]. The RailGround model is atypical in that it begins by modelling the established principals of interlocking systems without modelling the safety properties that those systems are designed to achieve. The reason for this is that the principles of interlocking are a proven design mechanism for controlling trains in a safe way. The model focusses instead on providing a precise and accurate specification of the interlocking product-line. The same case study has been used in [9] for illustrating the use of iUML-B class-diagrams to visualise domain-specific *Abstract Data Types* (ADTs). The RailGround case study is similar to the one tackled by Abrial [1, Chapter 17], however, our focus here is on the complementary usage of iUML-B and ERS diagrams for modelling. In [7], the authors present the development of a train control system using Event-B with the focus is on the use of ADTs to simplify the modelling task. In particular, the system is based on *Commnications-based Train Control* (CBTC) and hence the focus is on train tracking using moving blocks. In [11], the authors use CSP||B [16] to model an interlocking system and verifying the system using ProB model checker [12]. In [20], the authors present an approach for formal development of interlocking systems using a DSL to specify the configuration data of the interlocking system. The data is then used to generate a concrete behaviour model of the interlocking system from a generic behavioural model and concrete system properties from generic properties. The concrete properties and the concrete system are then verified using SMT-based bounded model checking (BMC) and inductive reasoning. In both [11, 20], refinement is not considered.

5   Conclusion

In this paper we present an alternative development to the RailGround interlocking system, which was originally developed by Thales Austria GmbH using plain Event-B. Our approach is based on a combination of a state-based (iUML-B) and a process-based (ERS) approach. The RailGround model contains several complex entity relationships to represent the railway topology. By separating the entity relationship model, illustrated by the class diagrams, from the behavioural model, we are making the modelling process more efficient. The class diagram allows us to explore different abstractions efficiently compared with specifying these data relationships textually in Event-B. The behavioural model of the system is represented by both the state-oriented state-machines and the process-oriented ERS diagrams. The statemachines give a view of the behaviour which is local to a particular type of entity. ERS makes the system level ordering of the transitions more visible. ERS also explicitly represents the event decomposition and their refinement relationships. In our developments, we used the iUML-B graphical tool which also automatically generates part of the Event-B model, making the modelling process more intuitive and efficient for engineers. Here, we only used the ERS as a visualisation to avoid the duplication of control variables generated by both ERS and state-machines. However, the ERS and state-machine views of behaviour complement each other and facilitate the modelling process.

The presented approach, which is based on different visualisations from different perspectives makes the model more understandable and easier to communicate, but also simplifies the model and is thus cheaper to verify and validate, which is a primary goal of the Enable-S3 project. This is a huge benefit for any further model adaptation and modifications, which are inevitable due to long product life time (25+ years). In future work we will do some trials to assess the complexity of making changes to the model with and without visualisations.

Future work. In this paper, our focus is on building an approach for the generic modelling of the core system. Currently iUMLB and ERS specify control flow from different perspectives. We are looking at a tool integration of ERS with iUML-B to have a common generation mechanism of Event-B.

We have started to complement the approach with DSLs for specifying customer-specific variations in feature requirements. For example, a DSL for specifying signalling has been developed. The DSL is precise enough to perform a certain amount of static-checking, but easily understood by the customer's domain experts. The signalling specification is translated into an Event-B machine which is proven to refine the generic signalling required by the core product model. We are developing composition and instantiation mechanisms so that we can isolate the generic signalling requirements as a separate component in the core product model. This component structuring of the model helps to address scalability and re-use as well as facilitating customer specific feature variants in order to efficiently obtain a complete and verified model of a customer specific product.

Acknowledgement. This work has been conducted within the ENABLE-S3 project that has received funding from the ECSEL Joint Undertaking under Grant Agreement no. 692455. This Joint Undertaking receives support from the European Union's HORIZON 2020 research and innovation programm and Austria, Denmark, Germany, Finland, Czech Republic, Italy, Spain, Portugal, Poland, Ireland, Belgium, France, Netherlands, United Kingdom, Slovakia, Norway.

References

1. Abrial, J.-R.: Modeling in Event-B: System and Software Engineering. Cambridge University Press, New York (2010)
2. Abrial, J.-R., Butler, M., Hallerstede, S., Hoang, T.S., Mehta, F., Voisin, L.: Rodin: An open toolset for modelling and reasoning in Event-B. Softw. Tools Technol. Transf. **12**(6), 447–466 (2010)

3. Butler, M., Leuschel, M.: Combining CSP and B for specification and property verification. In: Fitzgerald, J., Hayes, I.J., Tarlecki, A. (eds.) FM 2005. LNCS, vol. 3582, pp. 221–236. Springer, Heidelberg (2005). doi:10.1007/11526841_16
4. The Enable-S3 Consortium. Enable-S3 European project (2016). www.enable-s3.eu
5. Dghaym, D., Trindade, M.G., Butler, M., Fathabadi, A.S.: A graphical tool for event refinement structures in event-B. In: Butler, M., Schewe, K.-D., Mashkoor, A., Biro, M. (eds.) ABZ 2016. LNCS, vol. 9675, pp. 269–274. Springer, Cham (2016). doi:10.1007/978-3-319-33600-8_20
6. Fathabadi, A.S., Butler, M., Rezazadeh, A.: Language and tool support for event refinement structures in Event-B. Formal Aspects Comput. **27**(3), 499–523 (2015)
7. Fürst, A., Hoang, T.S., Basin, D.A., Sato, N., Miyazaki, K.: Large-scale system development using abstract data types and refinement. Sci. Comput. Program. **131**, 59–75 (2016)
8. Hoang, T.S.: An introduction to the Event-B modelling method. In: Romanovsky, A., Thomas, M. (eds.) Industrial Deployment of System Engineering Methods, pp. 211–236. Springer, Heidelberg (2013)
9. Hoang, T.S., Snook, C., Dghaym, D., Butler, M.: Class-diagrams for abstract data types. In: Van Hung, D., Deepak, K. (eds.) International Colloquium on Theoretical Aspects of Computing–ICTAC 2017. LNCS, pp. 100–117. Springer, Cham (2017). doi:10.1007/978-3-319-67729-3_7
10. Jackson, M.A.: System Development. Prentice-Hall, Englewood Cliffs (1983)
11. James, P., Moller, F., Nguyen, H.N., Roggenbach, M., Schneider, S.A., Treharne, H.: On modelling and verifying railway interlockings: Tracking train lengths. Sci. Comput. Program **96**, 315–336 (2014)
12. Leuschel, M., Butler, M.: ProB: An automated analysis toolset for the B method. Softw. Tools Technol. Transf. (STTT) **10**(2), 185–203 (2008)
13. Oliveira, M., Cavalcanti, A., Woodcock, J.: A UTP semantics for circus. Formal Aspects Comput. **21**(1–2), 3–32 (2009)
14. Reichl, K.: RailGround model on github (2016). https://github.com/klar42/railground/. Accessed 20 Apr 2017
15. Said, M.Y., Butler, M., Snook, C.: A method of refinement in UML-B. Softw. Syst. Model **14**(4), 1557–1580 (2015)
16. Schneider, S., Treharne, H.: CSP theorems for communicating B machines. Formal Aspects Comput. **17**(4), 390–422 (2005)
17. Schneider, S., Treharne, H., Wehrheim, H.: A CSP approach to control in event-B. In: Méry, D., Merz, S. (eds.) IFM 2010. LNCS, vol. 6396, pp. 260–274. Springer, Heidelberg (2010). doi:10.1007/978-3-642-16265-7_19
18. Snook, C.: iUML-B state-machines. In: Proceedings of the Rodin Workshop 2014, Toulouse, France, pp. 29–30 (2014). http://eprints.soton.ac.uk/365301/
19. Snook, C., Butler, M.: UML-B: Formal modeling and design aided by UML. ACM Trans. Softw. Eng. Methodol. **15**(1), 92–122 (2006)
20. Vu, L.H., Haxthausen, A.E., Peleska, J.: Formal modelling and verification of interlocking systems featuring sequential release. Sci. Comput. Program. **133**, 91–115 (2017)
21. Woodcock, J., Cavalcanti, A.: The semantics of *Circus*. In: Bert, D., Bowen, J.P., Henson, M.C., Robinson, K. (eds.) ZB 2002. LNCS, vol. 2272, pp. 184–203. Springer, Heidelberg (2002). doi:10.1007/3-540-45648-1_10

OVADO

Enhancing Data Validation for Safety-Critical Railway Systems

Manel Fredj, Sven Leger, Abderrahmane Feliachi[✉], and Julien Ordioni

RATP, ING/STF/QS, 54 rue Roger Salengro, 94724 Fontenay-sous-Bois, France
{manel.fredj,sven.leger,abderrahmane.feliachi,
julien.ordioni}@ratp.fr

Abstract. The safe behavior of railway software systems depends undeniably on the correctness of all data used by its components. Formal verification methods are nowadays successfully applied for the assessment of safety-critical systems in order to avoid inconsistencies, ambiguities or incompleteness. Unfortunately, these methods are rarely used by data validation tools, although they seem well-suited for this purpose. In this regard, RATP designed OVADO, a generic formal data-validation tool, which has been used in several projects covering a variety of data.

This paper gives an overview of the past, present and future developments, applications and improvements of OVADO. It emphasizes how OVADO allowed RATP to be more efficient in its data validation process and how new enhancements will improve its usability, reliability and efficiency. OVADO's ease-of-use is, thereby, improved through the development of the B-OVADO editor. Additionally, the process is optimized with the definition of a common library for CBTC applications.

Keywords: OVADO · Data validation · Formal methods · Safety-critical railway systems

1 Introduction

Railway systems contain safety-critical components, the failure or malfunction of which may cause economical loss, environmental damages, severe injuries and even human life loss. These components come under heavy scrutiny in RATP's[1] safety assessment labs as passengers safety is at the heart of its commitments. Furthermore, taking as an example the RER[2] line A in Paris used by over 300 million passengers each year, RATP operates one of the world's busiest networks. Thus, any system failure or malfunction may have considerable consequences.

Having this in mind, the safe behavior of safety-critical software components of a railway system must be scrupulously validated. This safety assessment

---

[1] *Régie Autonome des Transports Parisiens* is a public transport operator headquartered in Paris, France.

[2] RER: Paris suburban railway lines.

© Springer International Publishing AG 2017
A. Fantechi et al. (Eds.): RSSRail 2017, LNCS 10598, pp. 87–98, 2017.
https://doi.org/10.1007/978-3-319-68499-4_6

depends undeniably on the correctness of all the data used by this system, which are assessed during data validation activities. These activities may rely on formal methods which are mathematically based languages, techniques and tools. Formal methods [9,11] typically allow for better detection of inconsistencies, ambiguities and incompleteness that might otherwise go unrevealed.

Adopted and promoted by RATP, formal methods, such as the B method, have been successfully used in the transportation industry on many occasions. For instance, over 115 000 lines of B models were written during the development of METEOR [4], an automatic train operating system deployed in 1998 on the metro line 14, the first driver-less metro line in Paris. No bug has been detected since then on this system.

In this paper, addressing the issue of safety-critical data validation, we introduce OVADO[3], a generic and extensible tool designed by RATP for formal data validation activities. The motivations that led to its development and its successful applications in various railway projects are detailed as well. Finally, recent enhancements brought to OVADO or to the overall data validation methodology relying on OVADO are highlighted.

In the world of data validation, many project-specific or supplier-specific tools have been developed. As we explain throughout this paper, OVADO is meant to be generic and applicable for different types of projects. One other specificity of OVADO is the use of formal methods which is not always the case for the other tools, providing, thereby, all counter-examples for each falsified property to help the analysis of the potential errors. In the same tradition of OVADO, some generic formal data validation tools have been developed to fill the gap. We highlight mainly the tools by Clearsy [12] and SafeRiver [2] where, the former uses the B formal method, while the latter uses a synchronous formal language for data and software verification. In the family of B-based formal data validation tools, we note also the ProB model checker [10] used in some railway industrial projects.

2   OVADO - Background and Learned Lessons

2.1   Origins and Genesis

In 1977, SACEM[4] has been developed with new methods for safe computer-based application, including rigorous development model, and implemented in MODULA-2 code ($\geq$ 60000 lines of code). However, it was not sufficient as, in 1989, 20 unsafe scenarios have been discovered by applying a retro-modeling of the system using the Z formal method. Since then, RATP has made the decision to develop and systematize the use of formal methods for safety-critical systems. This led to the development of the first automatic driver-less metro line in Paris (Line 14) in the METEOR project operating since 1998. The development of

---

[3] OVADO stands for *Outil de VAlidation des DOnnées*, meaning data validation tool.
[4] SACEM is equivalent to the Automatic Train Protection system for the RER A suburban railway in Paris.

this system, realized by an external supplier, was entirely based on the formal B method.

After these successful applications of formal methods in the safety assessment of critical software, RATP highly recommend its suppliers to use formal methods to develop or verify railway critical software. In addition, RATP developed its own *a posteriori* verification technique called PERF [5] which intended to be applicable independently of the supplier's implementation choices.

A considerable effort was invested in the application of formal methods on the software components of safety-critical systems, leading to the development of methodologies, *e.g.* Scade, B. However, data validation was not afforded the same way of investment. Indeed, different data validation tools were developed for each project. However, these project-specific tools have been found to be hardly maintainable, barely extensible and not reusable from one project to another.

As an anticipation of new RATP's projects with heterogeneous suppliers processes, the problem of safety-critical data validation became palpable in 2009. The need to pool the efforts and to establish a generalized data validation process applicable to all projects emerges. The answer to this requirement relies inevitably on the development of a generic and extensible data validation tool. This was the starting point for the development of the OVADO tool [1,3] that eases the verification of safety requirements on configuration data.

OVADO is classified T2⁵ according to the CENELEC EN50128 Standard [6]. OVADO offers a rich integrated environment for properties [7] checking and counter examples analysis. Concretely, OVADO uses a subset of the B formal language (covering B expressions and predicates), named *B Predicate*, as a source language for the formalization of safety properties. Data and parameters can be integrated to the tool as B constant values, sets or relations. A screenshot of OVADO is given in Fig. 2.

The use of a formal language allows for a clear, unambiguous definition of the safety requirements as B properties. However, the use of a formal language does not necessarily imply a correct formalization of the safety properties. Thus, specific measures have to be taken in order to reduce the risk of incorrect formalization, like cross-checking for instance. Proof engines are used to check the correctness of the properties or, if not, to produce a set of counter examples. The advantage of using proof engines is their exhaustive exploration of the verified data space, giving a complete coverage of the targeted data. In the context of this T2 tool, in addition to the V & V activities, two independent proof engines are used in order to reduce the risk of errors in the proof task. The first proof engine is developed within OVADO while the second one is based on ProB.

As aforementioned, the prime needs that motivated the development of the OVADO tool are the genericity, reusability, extensibility and maintainability. In order to address all these concerns, the tool was designed following a plugin-

---

⁵ Type 2 tools support the test or verification of the design or executable code. Errors in these tools can fail to reveal defects but cannot directly create errors in the executable software.

oriented architecture, with a central kernel orchestrating the different extensions. The kernel ensures the interaction with the proof engine by providing a number of interfaces that have to be implemented by the different plugins. In order to support multiple data format for instance, an interface that maps data source definitions to B expressions is provided. With such configuration, the extensibility and the genericity of OVADO are guaranteed and the maintenance efforts are reduced since not all the tool is concerned but only a part of the plugins.

2.2   Use Cases and Learned Lessons

Since its first deployment in 2010–2011, OVADO has been extensively used to validate system and software data in numerous projects. As illustrated in Fig. 1, OVADO is used in 3 application types for data validation: (1) system data validation, (2) validation of the transformation of system data into embedded data and (3) embedded data validation. We call *system data* high-level information related to the track, for instance, track configuration, topology, beacons, signals and alike. We call *embedded data*, all data computed from system data using a set of transformations in order to be consumed directly by the software.

1. System data validation: It consists of validating safety constraints related to the system design (only if step 2 is considered). At this step, we verify whether the constraints that ensure system safety are compatible with the data collected from the track. For the validation, we use "System B predicates", a set of properties that are formalized in B language, to check the truthfulness of the predicates modeling the safety constraints to be applied on system data.
2. Software data transformation: It consists of validating the representativeness of the software embedded data with respect to system data. At this step,

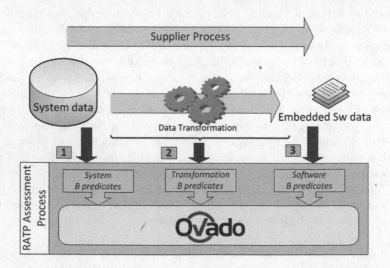

Fig. 1. Data assessment process

we check, using "Transformation B predicates", whether software embedded data are consistent with system data (verified in step 1), meaning that the supplier transformation process has not introduced errors when generating software embedded data.

3 Software embedded data validation: It consists of verifying the safety constraints on embedded data. These constraints may result from an additional safety analysis or emerge from the software implementation as exported constraints. OVADO uses "Software B predicates" to check the truthfulness of the predicates modeling the safety constraints to be applied on "software data".

OVADO has been used in several projects, namely in L13, L1, L3, L5 and L9, which are mainly Communication Based Train Control (CBTC) [8,13] software systems. Still, we are planning to use it for future CBTC systems and hybrid interlocking systems such as PHPI. For the 5 cases of CBTC, the 3 above-mentioned validation types are performed. In the following, we summarize the metrics, giving a range of values for the number of OVADO properties that are implemented for each step. We emphasize on specific metrics for Line 5, as it is the most recent data validation project and it includes the know-how developed throughout the previous safety assessments.

For system data validation, OVADO provides around 80% coverage of the system safety constraints. The remaining 20% of the constraints are manually validated, mainly due to data format incompatibility. For instance, data in track layout are not automatically processible, thus the related constraints need to be validated manually. Approximately, to model 80% of the system safety constraints, the number of OVADO properties is 1.3 times of the number of safety constraints. The latter is in the range of 120 to 200 constraints. For instance, system safety constraints are 123 for Line 13, 172 for Line 5 and 184 for Line 9. Interestingly, one-shot constraints formalization and their automatic verification may require more time and effort than a manual validation. However, OVADO turns out to be more effort-efficient when used for successive versions as the validation is performed automatically for the new versions with a minimal human intervention.

Regarding software embedded data and data transformation, OVADO enables to check up to 100% of the software constraints and the data transformation ones. As system data are assessed in step 1, all format issues are removed. In general, for software data transformation (i.e. step 2), the number of safety constraints are in the range of 150 to 200 constraints. Safety team implement the same number of OVADO properties as the number of software safety constraints. For instance, regarding the data transformation properties for Line 5, there are 3 kinds of equipments: an in/out module, a wayside controller and an on-board controller, which required to implement respectively 130, 58 and 143 OVADO properties for data transformation.

For embedded data validation, OVADO checks the validity of software constraints and/or additional safety constraints on the software data level. The safety constraints are in the range of 0 to 1000, requiring simple properties, essentially for ensuring typing compliance. For instance, in defensive programming the set of embedded data properties is almost empty.

The number of properties is not representative of the effort required for the data validation. OVADO is able to process more than a thousand of properties in few minutes, *e.g.* in Line 5, safety team implemented more than 1800 properties (including typing, right-construction of the database and additional control properties) that have been processed in 2 min on an 8-core Intel Xeon E5 processor with 2.60 GHz and 4 GB of RAM memory.

In fine, OVADO reduces drastically the time allocated for data validation, once the initial formalization of properties is completed as explained earlier. Consequently, once properties are implemented, data set changes require only to re-run the verification of the properties without any modification. Hence, the data validator can focus more on counter-examples analysis. Properties are revisited only when fundamental changes are performed on the database or on the safety constraints. Thus, in some projects, the entire validation activity was performed in less than one workday by a single person while the same activity used to last for several workdays and involved more than one person.

Still, throughout the use of OVADO on multiple projects, several needs have emerged to ease data validation process. In this paper, we focus and detail three of them in the following section.

2.3   Emerging New Needs

Need for easing edition. OVADO offers a large panel of data validation facilities and functionalities. The data and properties are fed to OVADO through B expressions and predicates presented in XML files. In order to gain in organization, performance and rapidity, a need for an appropriate editor emerges from the limitations of the current configuration. In addition, editing B expressions externally can be tedious, needing thereby to run numerous and complex scripts to manage XML entry files. Besides, the use of external scripts adds more complexity with regard to syntactic and semantic errors handling. For instance, in order to overcome syntactic errors, the user has first to generate the project on the OVADO Platform, then load the generated files and afterwards, eventually detect syntactic or semantic errors. For heavy models, a precious time is wasted in syntactic reviewing and type correction for the models, while this time may be used for properties formalization and validation.

Hence, from the need for an ergonomic and intuitive editing facilities, the B-OVADO editor was born. Section 3.1 details the way the editor is integrated in OVADO and the user facilities it offers.

Needs for sharing. Validating a single data set, using OVADO, is straightforward: (1) transform the data so that they can be provided as input to OVADO (if necessary), (2) identify the properties these data must comply with, (3) write these properties in the B language then (4) run OVADO and analyze its output. However, validating several data sets in a multi-project context where different team members are involved is arguably a bit trickier. The fact that there is no import mechanism in OVADO is one factor. Thus, some versatile definitions or properties tend to be manually copied from one project to another over time.

Obviously, reusing a definition or a property is not a bad practice. Nevertheless, as illustrated below, it must be done properly in order to avoid any deleterious consequence. Assume that a definition has been manually copied from one project to another, that the copy relation is not formalized in any way (with a comment, for instance) and that a semantic error with potentially severe consequences is identified and corrected on the copy. It is very likely that the correction will never be fed back to the original definition.

Therefore, definitions and properties which can be of interest to different projects might be grouped together, much like a library in software programming. This library can be imported by any project, using, for instance, symbolic links (a file-system functionality). Hence, errors found on definitions and properties inside the library will be corrected and these corrections will be more easily extended to every project that uses them.

Needs for guidelines. A property or a definition will surely be named, formalized and even indented differently by two different persons. Obviously, the fact that the B language is formal does not imply that there is a single way to write a property or a definition. Nonetheless, there are good practices that should be disseminated and bad practices that should be avoided. For instance, using meaningful names for definitions, properties and local variables is a good practice as it will help readers to understand their usage. On the contrary, having a very long file containing numerous definitions and properties can be a bad practice as it will be harder to find a specific definition or property.

Therefore, publishing a writing guide, similar to a programming guide in software programming, helps validators, especially the least experienced ones, to avoid some common pitfalls and improve the quality and maintainability of their work. This guide helps validators to better understand each other as well. As such, it is the first step toward the implementation of a shared library.

3   Enhancing OVADO

In order to overcome the different limitations and to fulfill the emerging needs, some developments have been started to extend OVADO with new functionalities. This resulted in the definition of three major enhancements for OVADO and more generally for the data validation process. The first enhancement is the extension of OVADO with an rich sophisticated editor. The second enhancement is more oriented to the data validation activity for railway applications, which is the definition of a common OVADO library for railway projects. The third enhancement is to provide good practice rules, to standardize properties and definitions writing. These enhancements are detailed in the following.

3.1   B-OVADO Editor

One major enhancement of OVADO is the recent development of the B-OVADO rich editor. The main purpose of the editor is to help and assist users in the development of definitions and properties. In the tradition of integrated development environment, the editor is meant to some several functionalities that ease the usage of OVADO. The first functionality is the syntactic control and auto-completion, based on the expressions and predicates syntax of the B language. The editor offers a Javadoc-like documentation, easy navigation using object linking and some basic quick fixing support.

In the semantic level, the editor supports very well nested scoping which can be very helpful when writing complex expressions. Another important semantic support is the sophisticated type inference and control system that have been integrated to the editor. This type system is based on the B typing rules for expressions and predicates with an additional notion of generic types. The typing is performed by assigning generic types to the parsed elements then refining these types following the full expression using type unification. Type errors are directly shown in the editor to avoid feeding OVADO with ill-typed constructs.

The editor is developed in an independent yet integrated way. It is independent from OVADO because it is developed as an additional plugin that does not interfere with the internal functioning of OVADO. The integration of the editor is transparent, the generation of all internal OVADO files is not visible to the user. The B-OVADO editor was immediately embraced by all internal OVADO users since its development, and provided important efficiency improvement. This improvement cannot be quantified since the use of the editor was only recently generalized. More enhancements are currently under study to provide more functionalities to the editor like semantic-oriented typing for instance.

3.2   Common Library

Data validation is quite often a time-consuming process and, arguably, one that tends to be underestimated. Nevertheless, data from different projects may present some similarities that have to be identified in order to speed up the process, using a technique inspired by modular programming. Obviously, the stronger the similarities are, the better the gain might be.

Modular programming is a pervasive software design technique which consist in separating the functionality of a program into independent modules. This technique seems to present a number of benefits, among which is reusability, as modules may be reused between different projects. Surely, identifying how to split a program in order to maximize reusability might be difficult as it requires a good knowledge of the current projects and those to come as well, which denotes a high level of maturity.

With OVADO, definitions are equivalent to modules in modular programming, which are named and reusable expressions. Note that definitions may use literals, constants (corresponding to the validated data) and call other definitions, again, like modules in modular programming. However, definitions do not have parameters like functions or procedures in programming languages, meaning that names used to access the data fed to OVADO or other definitions are static. Without rewriting a definition before importing it from one project to another, the validator may have to write few additional definitions to rename some constants or definitions before using it.

Nevertheless, building a library of, rather basic but well tested or even proved to be correct, definitions that will be shared among different projects is a key-concept to speed up and improve the overall quality of data validations activities conducted for these projects. Future projects will greatly benefit from this library as well as they won't have to start from scratch, which usually requires a lot of time and effort and might be considered the riskiest phase in the validation process.

Such library has been initiated for the purpose of validating safety-critical data consumed by the software components of the CBTC systems, known as OCTYS, which currently equip the lines 3, 5 and 9 of the Parisian metro, given their strong similarities (as a matter of fact, metro lines 5 and 9 share some generic software components which are instantiated with different sets of data). So far, this library has been used for several validation campaigns and is currently being deployed on other projects, such as SACEM (RER A) and SAET L14.

The aforementioned library contains a number of basic functions to define and manipulate points and zones on a model of a rail track, such as a metro line. For instance, one of these functions is used to define a zone from on a point on track, a direction and a distance, while another one is used to compute the intersection of two zones. Furthermore, these two functions can be used together to check if two points on track are at least a certain distance afar.

Obviously, projects must conform to the underlying topological choices this library has been built upon in order to use it. Accordingly, depending on the available data, it may be necessary to set up an abstraction layer. Nevertheless, it is proved according to our experience to be far easier than starting from scratch. Moreover, functions contained in the library have been carefully written by experienced validators to be efficient and are well tested. Therefore, less experienced validators greatly benefit from using them.

An example of a topological choice is described in the following. The rail track must be described with a set of non-overlapping continuous segments. Each segment has a name, a length and 0, 1 or 2 attached segments on each of its possible extremities. One of these extremities is the beginning of the segment while the other is its end. As such, a segment is always oriented.

3.3   Guidelines

Regarding properties and definitions naming, indentation, structure, etc., several good practices have been identified over time. They have been explicitly written down and centralized to be more easily disseminated, especially to the least experienced validators. Furthermore, for these practices to be easily understandable and more useful, the motivations behind them have been be exposed and examples were given to illustrate their purpose. These practices have been applied to the shared library introduced earlier and applied on several occasions.

3.4   Feedback

Since the deployment of the B-OVADO editor for internal data validation projects and by the more recent integration of the common railway data library, a drastic increase in the efficiency of the data validation activity is observed, be it on the required workload or on the whole process time. In addition to all the improvements brought by OVADO, the new enhancements presented herein make the data validation easily manageable. Even though proof and analysis times are not substantially improved by the new enhancements, preparation and formalization tasks, which are usually very time-consuming at the beginning of a project, can be reduced to less than the half as observed on current data validation activities conducted for the SACEM and SAET L14 projects.

Moreover, the new enhancements made OVADO more easy-to-use and user-friendly, which makes it very simple to train new team members. Consequently, more internal applications and projects are now gladly using OVADO for different purposes, which contribute to the enrichment of OVADO with new extensions and more feedback.

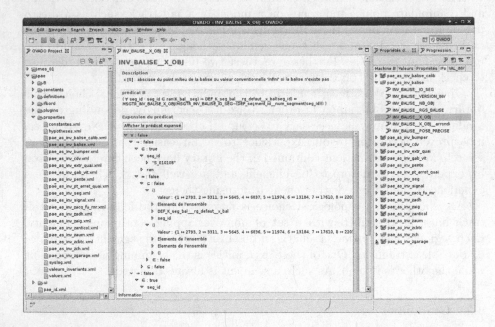

Fig. 2. A screenshot of OVADO

4   Conclusion

Data validation is a key activity in safety assessment of critical systems. For this purpose, RATP developed and used a formal tool called OVADO for the validation of system or software data used in its applications. One of the main strengths of this tool is being generic which makes it usable for different project types without considerable adjustments. Another strength is the use of formal methods for the expression of safety properties and for exhaustive data exploration which reduces the risk of any potential bias.

Over the different applications of OVADO for critical data validation, a number of new needs were identified to improve the overall validation process. In order to fulfill these needs, some enhancements were introduced and are now part of the whole process. The first improvement is the development of a rich editor for B expressions and predicates which simplifies the usability of the tool. The second improvement is the definition of a common library for railway applications capitalizing the know-how and easing the application of OVADO for new projects. The last enhancement is the definition of a number of coding rules making OVADO projects more readable, homogeneous and maintainable.

With this experience and expertise, OVADO and its associated data validation process can be considered as a generic mature industrial solution. Its application is planned to be generalized for all data validation projects at RATP using B-OVADO and the common library. The use of OVADO will also be generalized to other applications than CBTC, like signaling for instance. New libraries might be defined for these new applications if needed.

References

1. Ovado website. http://www.ovado.net/fr/index.html
2. Saferiver website. http://www.saferiver.fr/index.php?id=plateformes
3. Abo, R., Voisin, L.: Formal implementation of data validation for railway safety-related systems with OVADO. In: Counsell, S., Núñez, M. (eds.) SEFM 2013. LNCS, vol. 8368, pp. 221–236. Springer, Cham (2014). doi:10.1007/978-3-319-05032-4_17
4. Behm, P., Benoit, P., Faivre, A., Meynadier, J.-M.: Météor: a successful application of B in a large project. In: Wing, J.M., Woodcock, J., Davies, J. (eds.) FM 1999. LNCS, vol. 1708, pp. 369–387. Springer, Heidelberg (1999). doi:10.1007/3-540-48119-2_22
5. Benaissa, N., Bonvoisin, D., Feliachi, A., Ordioni, J.: The PERF approach for formal verification. In: Lecomte, T., Pinger, R., Romanovsky, A. (eds.) RSSRail 2016. LNCS, vol. 9707, pp. 203–214. Springer, Cham (2016). doi:10.1007/978-3-319-33951-1_15
6. CENELEC: Railway applications - communication, signalling and processing systems - software for railway control and protection systems (en50128) (2011)
7. Clabaut, M., Metaye, C., Morand, E.: Formal data validation - formal techniques applied to verification of data properties. In: ERTS 2010. SIA/3AF/SEE (2010)
8. Rail Transit Vehicle Interface Standards Committee: IEEE Standard for Communications-based Train Control (CBTC) Performance and Functional Requirements. IEEE (2005)
9. Fantechi, A., Flammini, F., Gnesi, S.: Formal methods for railway control systems. Int. J. Softw. Tools Technol. Transf. 16(6), 643–646 (2014)

10. Hansen, D., Schneider, D., Leuschel, M.: Using B and ProB for data validation projects. In: Butler, M., Schewe, K.-D., Mashkoor, A., Biro, M. (eds.) ABZ 2016. LNCS, vol. 9675, pp. 167–182. Springer, Cham (2016). doi:10.1007/978-3-319-33600-8_10
11. Haxthausen, A.E.: An introduction to formal methods for the development of safety-critical applications (2010)
12. Lecomte, T., Mottin, E.: Formal data validation in the railways. In: Developing Safe Systems, SSS 2016, February 2016
13. Pascoe, R.D., Eichorn, T.N.: What is communication-based train control? IEEE Veh. Technol. Mag. 4(4), 16–21 (2009)

A Domain-Specific Language for Generic Interlocking Models and Their Properties

Linh H. Vu[1], Anne E. Haxthausen[1], and Jan Peleska[2]

[1] DTU Compute, Technical University of Denmark, Kongens Lyngby, Denmark
{lvho,aeha}@dtu.dk
[2] Department of Mathematics and Computer Science, University of Bremen,
Bremen, Germany
jp@cs.uni-bremen.de

Abstract. State-of-the-art railway interlocking systems typically adhere to the product line paradigm, where each individual system is obtained by instantiating a generic system with configuration data. In this paper, we present a domain-specific language, **IDL**, for specifying generic behavioural models and generic properties of interlocking systems. An IDL specification of a generic model consists of generic variable declarations and generic transition rules, and generic properties are generic state invariants. Generic models and generic properties can be instantiated with configuration data. This results in concrete models and concrete properties that can be used as input for a model checker to formally verify that the system model satisfies desired state invariants. The language and a configuration data instantiator based on the semantics have been implemented as components of the **RobustRailS** tool set for formal specification and verification of interlocking systems. They have successfully been applied to (1) define a generic model and generic safety properties for the new Danish interlocking systems and to (2) instantiate these generic artefacts for real-world stations and lines in Denmark. A novelty of this work is to provide a domain-specific language for generic models and an instantiator tool taking not only configuration data but also a generic model as input instead of using a hard-coded generator for instantiating only one fixed generic model and its properties with configuration data.

Keywords: Railway interlocking systems · Domain-specific languages · Formal methods · Formal models · Formal verification

1 Introduction

This paper describes a domain-specific language, IDL, for defining generic models and properties of interlocking systems.

L.H. Vu and A.E. Haxthausen research has been funded by the RobustRailS project granted by Innovation Fund Denmark.

© Springer International Publishing AG 2017
A. Fantechi et al. (Eds.): RSSRail 2017, LNCS 10598, pp. 99–115, 2017.
https://doi.org/10.1007/978-3-319-68499-4_7

Context. Over the next 5–6 years, new signalling systems compatible with the standardised European Train Control System (ETCS) Level 2 [3] will be deployed on all long-distance lines in Denmark. A key component of these systems are the *interlocking systems* which are responsible for the safe routing of trains trough the railway network. In Europe, the development of software for railway control systems, including interlocking systems, must adhere to the CENELEC 50128 standard [2] which strongly recommends the use of formal methods for such safety-critical systems. The objective of using formal methods is to ensure that potential safety breaches can be identified systematically and efficiently.

Therefore, in the RobustRailS research project[1], accompanying the Danish re-signalling programme on a scientific level, a formal method with tools support for automated, formal verification of such interlocking systems has been developed [7,14–17]. The tools are centred around two inter-related DSLs (domain-specific languages):

- IDL (Interlocking Dynamic Language) for specifying (1) *generic, behavioural, formal models* of interlocking systems and their environment, and (2) *generic properties*, and
- ICL (Interlocking Configuration Language) for specifying *configuration data* that can be used to instantiate the generic artefacts.

This paper focuses on the first of these two languages (IDL), while the other language (ICL) has been described in the paper [14].

Contribution and Related Work. The main novelty of our method is to introduce the IDL in addition to the ICL: former approaches to tool-based interlocking system verification usually applied a hard coded model generator for creating models describing the concrete behaviour of an interlocking system and of trains passing through the network for each configuration data set. Hence, the tool could only be used for one single product line of interlocking systems based on the same generic behavioural rules. With the IDL at hand and a tool that besides the configuration data also takes an IDL generic model as input, it is now possible to create behavioural models for different product lines without changing the verification tool core.

Domain-specific languages, e.g. RailML, have been well-adopted to hide the use of formal methods in the formal development and verification of railway interlocking systems. For examples of this, see [1,4,6,8–10,12,18]. In all these cases, there is a DSL for specifying the configuration data, but no DSL for generic behavioural models and generic properties. Instead, these are specified in a GPL (general-purpose-language) like RSL, CASL, or ASM by formal methods experts, and configuration data specified in the DSL by domain experts has to be translated (by a tool) into a representation in the GPL, such that the generic models and properties can be instantiated. A drawback of this approach is the understanding gap between the formal methods experts and domain experts. The

---

[1] http://robustrails.man.dtu.dk.

former need to acquire reasonably deep understanding of the domain in order to encode the generic models and properties. The latter need to understand, review, and provide feedback on GPL specifications. Therefore, GPL specifications are not the most efficient and concise communication medium, and consequently may be error-prone.

The IDL presented in this paper is an appropriate formalism to bridge this understanding gap:

– *Ease to write and change generic models.* As will be explained in the next sections, the movement of trains through different railway networks may follow different behavioural rules, and this depends on (1) the granularity of the modelling paradigm which may depend on the verification objectives, and (2) on the operational rules applicable for the interlocking domain. Therefore, it is of considerable advantage to have a DSL for specifying generic behavioural models, instead of having to code new versions of the model generator, each time these rules change.
– *Readability.* DSL specifications of generic artefacts are easier for domain experts to understand as they use some dedicated language constructs based on intuitive and familiar terms and concepts of the railway domain. A corresponding GPL specification would typically be longer, using technically complicated GPL expressions.

Overview. The paper is organised as follows: First Sect. 2 gives a brief introduction to the railway domain as well as the RobustRailS tool set and its mathematical foundations. Then Sect. 3 informally describes the domain-specific language and its semantics. Finally, a conclusion is given in Sect. 4.

2   Background

This section gives a short introduction to the new Danish interlocking systems, an overview of the RobustRailS method, and mathematical preliminaries, in order to give the context of the IDL domain-specific language.

2.1   Interlocking Systems

Complete ETCS signalling systems consist of a multitude of components, such as interlocking systems, radio block centres, track elements (e.g. points, balises, axle counters), and on-board equipment (e.g. the *European Vital Computer (EVC)* performing automated train protection according to the ETCS protocols). An interlocking system has the task to control track side elements (e.g. points) in a railway network and to set safe train routes through this network according to traffic control requests. In the old signalling systems, interlocking systems also controlled signals placed along the tracks. In the new signalling systems, there are no signals installed along the tracks, but only *marker boards* to show the start and end of routes. The interlocking systems now have a *virtual signal* associated with each marker board. A virtual signal can be OPEN or CLOSED, allowing or disallowing trains to pass the associated marker board. Based on the state of the virtual signals, *movement authorities* (permissions to proceed) are sent via radio block centres to the on-board units in the trains.

For the specification of an interlocking system instance of a product line of interlocking systems, the railway signalling engineers use two documents: a *network diagram* describing the network under control and an *interlocking table* as described below. From these documents the configuration data for the generic control software is derived. In a similar way we will use these documents to derive configuration data for our generic models and properties.

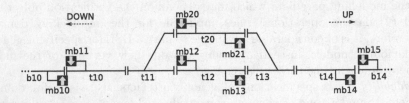

Fig. 1. An example railway network.

Network Diagrams. A network diagram outlines the geographical arrangement of the tracks and track-side equipment. Figure 1 shows an example of a network diagram for a typical smaller station. From the diagram it can be seen that the station has six linear sections (b10,t10,t12,t14,t20,b14), two points (t11,t13), and eight marker boards (mb10,...,mb21). Linear sections and points are collectively called *(train detection) sections*, as they are each provided with train detection equipment which the interlocking system uses to determine whether the section is occupied by a train or not. Along each section, up to two marker boards (one for each direction) can be installed. A marker board can only be seen in one direction and is used as reference location (for start and end of routes) for trains going in that direction. For instance, mb13 in Fig. 1 is installed along section t12, and it is intended for travel direction up.

Interlocking Tables. An interlocking table specifies the routes in a given network and the conditions (to be used by the interlocking system) for setting these routes. A *route* is a path from a *source* markerboard to a *destination* markerboard in the given railway network. In railway signalling terminology, *setting* a route denotes the process of allocating the resources (i.e. linear sections, points, and virtual signals) for the route, and then locking the route exclusively for only one train.

An interlocking table has one row for each route r. For an example, see Table 1. Each row has the following fields. Field **id** contains the route identification r, field **source** states its source marker board $\mathbf{src}(r)$, field **dst** states its destination marker board $\mathbf{dst}(r)$, and field **path** specifies the sequence

Table 1. Excerpt of the interlocking table for the network layout in Fig. 1.

id	src	dst	path	points	signals	conflicts
1a	mb10	mb13	t10;t11;t12	t11:p;t13:m	mb11;mb12;mb20	1b;2a;2b;3;4;5a;5b;6b;7
..	...	...	...	...	...	...
7	mb20	mb11	t11;t10	t11:m	mb10;mb12	1a;1b;2a;2b;3;5b;6a

The overlap column is omitted as it is empty for all of the routes.
Position 'p' means PLUS/straight/normal, 'm' means MINUS/diverging/reverse.

path(r) of track sections associated with r. Field **points** describes the set **points**(r) of points associated with the route. This includes points in the path and overlap, and points used for flank and front protection. For each point p associated with r, its required position **req**(r, p) to be enforced when allocating r is specified. The table field **signals** specifies the set **signals**(r) of virtual signals that must be CLOSED for flank or front protection of the route. The field **conflicts** describes the set **conflicts**(r) of routes *conflicting* with r: if two routes require the same point to be in different positions, or if the routes overlap such that concurrent use could lead to train collisions, they are considered to be conflicting. Function **next**(r, e) returns the next section after e on the route r. For the last section of a route, the function returns the first section of the consecutive route. Functions **first**(r) and **last**(r) may be used to return the route's first and last section, respectively.

2.2   The RobustRailS Method

This section gives a short overview of the RobustRailS method and core tools for formal verification of interlocking systems. More details can be found in [7, 14–17].

Two Domain-Specific Languages. As mentioned in the introduction, the method and tools are centred around two inter-related DSLs (domain-specific languages):

- **IDL** for specifying (1) *generic, formal behavioural models* of interlocking systems and their environment, and (2) *generic properties*, and
- **ICL** for specifying *configuration data* that can be used to instantiate the generic artefacts of IDL. The configuration data consists of a network description and an interlocking table.

The idea is that for a specific product line of interlocking systems the generic artefacts are specified once-and-for-all, while the configuration data is defined for each network to be controlled by an interlocking system.

Method Steps. For a given product line, the method consists of the following steps as illustrated in Fig. 2.

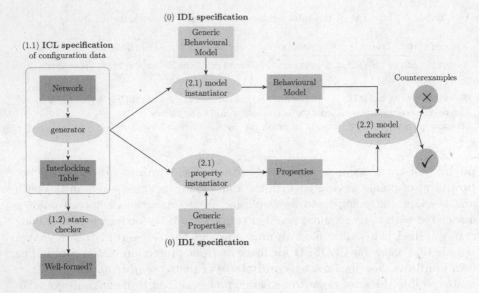

Fig. 2. Verification method and the associated toolchain.

(0) Initially a generic model and generic properties (which are common for all interlocking systems of the product line) are expressed in the domain-specific language IDL as explained in Sect. 3.

Then for each interlocking system to be verified, the following activities should be performed:

(1) First, (1.1) the configuration data should be specified in the domain-specific language ICL [14,16,17] as described in Sect. 2.1 and (1.2) the resulting specification should be validated by means of a static checker. The interlocking table may optionally be generated from the network diagram.
(2) Next, (2.1) instantiator tools should be applied to instantiate the generic model and the generic properties, respectively, with the specification of configuration data to produce a model M of the control system and its physical environment and the required properties ϕ. Finally, (2.2) a bounded model checker is applied to automatically check the validity of ϕ in M by means of k-induction.

Generated Models and Properties. A model generated by the tools is represented by a Kripke structure with an initial state and a transition relation, both expressed as first order predicates as explained in Sect. 2.3. Properties are given as state invariants, i.e., state predicates that must hold in all reachable states of the Kripke structure.

Tool Components. The toolchain associated with the method has been implemented in C++ using the RT-Tester framework [11,13].

2.3   Mathematical Foundations

Behavioural Models. The behavioural models generated by the tools are representations of Kripke structures that can be parsed and processed by model checkers or model-based testing tools.

A *Kripke structure* K is a five-tuple (S, s_0, R, L, AP) with state space S, initial state $s_0 \in S$, a total transition relation $R \subseteq S \times S$, and labelling function $L : S \to 2^{AP}$, where AP is a set of atomic propositions and 2^{AP} is the power set of AP. The labelling function L maps a state s to the set $L(s)$ of atomic propositions that hold in s.

In the considered models, the states of a Kripke structure are represented by valuation functions $s : V \to D$ over a finite set V of variables, where each variable $v \in V$ has an associated finite domain D_v. The range of a state s is $D = \bigcup_{v \in V} D_v$. The whole state space S is the set of all valuation functions $s : V \to D$ for which $s(v) \in D_v$ for all $v \in V$.

The initial state s_0 is represented by the following predicate I over free variables in V:

$$\bigwedge_{v \in V} v = i_v \tag{1}$$

where $i_v \in D_v$, called the initial value of v, is chosen such that $s_0(v) = i_v$.

Similarly, the transition relation $R \subseteq S \times S$ is represented by a first order expression Φ_R over free variables in $V \cup V'$ such that

$$R = \{(s, s') \in S \times S \mid \Phi_R(s, s')\}, \tag{2}$$

where $V' = \{v' \mid v \in V\}$ is a duplicate of V used to representing the next state, and $\Phi_R(s, s')$ is the predicate Φ_R with every occurrence of $v \in V$ replaced by the value $s(v)$, and every occurrence of $v' \in V'$ replaced by the value $s'(v)$.

The set of atomic propositions AP is the set $\mathcal{A}(V)$ of (type-correct) atomic propositions with free variables in V built from value literals, variable names $v \in V$, arithmetic operators $(+, -, *, /)$, bitwise operators $(\&, \oplus, \ll, \gg)$, and relational operators $(=, \neq, <, \leq, >, \geq)$. For example, $v = d$ with $v \in V$ and $d \in D_v$ and $v_1 < v_2 + 1$ with $v_1, v_2 \in V$ with numerical domains are elements of $\mathcal{A}(V)$.

The labelling function L is derived in a natural way by

$$\forall s \in S : L(s) = \{p \in AP \mid s \models p\}$$

where $s \models p$ (*"s is a model of p"*) means that proposition p, after replacing every free variable occurrence v by its valuation $s(v)$, evaluates to *true*.

3   Interlocking Dynamic Language, IDL

3.1   Overview

An IDL specification consists of a generic behavioural model specification and a collection of generic properties. The generic model behaviour is expressed by IDL encodings (generic variable declarations) and an IDL generic transition relation specification. Genericity is reflected by generic *encodings*, to be instantiated as concrete variables with associated types, by built-in generic *domain-specific functions* facilitating the reference to specific element-related data, and by quantifications over generic sets of elements. When instantiating the generic model and its properties, the encodings, function applications, and generic sets are instantiated with variables and constant data that are specified using the ICL. The generic transition relation is instantiated to a concrete one, specifying how the interlocking system behaves and how trains move in a controlled way through the concrete railway network managed by the interlocking system.

IDL specifications $\mathcal{S}$ have a *transformational semantics* formally defined in the thesis [16]: the meaning of $\mathcal{S}$ is a function mapping each admissible set of configuration data to a concrete Kripke structure K and associated concrete properties (obtained by instantiating the generic model and the generic properties, respectively). Hence, the meaning of two different generic models, may, when applied to the same configuration data, lead to different Kripke models. Each K is equipped with a concrete variable set and a state space consisting of variable valuation functions, and its behaviour is specified by a transition relation represented as a first order predicate over variable pre-states and post-states.

We emphasise again that the motivation for introducing the IDL is given by the fact that many different generic models have to be created for interlocking systems: (1) each set of new – often country-dependent – operational rules for interlocking induces a new generic specification, and (2) different levels of abstraction to be used in varying verification goals give rise to new – more or less abstract – parameters, encodings, and transition relations.

3.2   Accompanying Example

To illustrate the definition of the IDL and its instantiation rules, we use a toy example that suffices to highlight important IDL aspects. Readers are referred to [16,17] for far more complex IDL specifications applicable to real-world interlocking systems and their verification by model checking.

The toy example considers interlocking systems with conventional block section logic: blocks are specified by all the track elements connecting an entry signal to an exit signal. At most one train may reside in a block at a time. Routes always lead from the entry signal of a block to its exit signal. Blocks sharing one or more track elements are in conflict and may not be allocated at the same time. Routes have a life cycle, where they transit through several modes: Initially, they are FREE. When a route is requested it becomes DISPATCHED, and then the interlocking checks that no conflicting routes are allocated. If this is the case, it commands signals and points to their required aspects and positions (as stated for the route in the interlocking table) and turns into the ALLOCATING mode. When the signals and points have reached their commanded states, the interlocking commands the entry signal of the route to open, and the route enters the LOCKED mode. When a train enters the route, the route commands the entry signal to close and enters the OCCUPIED mode. Finally, when the train leaves the route, the route goes back to FREE.

We use a very coarse grained level of abstraction for modelling how trains move along sequences of track elements: either the train covers the element, or it does not; therefore it suffices to associate each element with a counter indicating how many trains cover the element. For safe operation, the counter may only be zero or 1. This concept is further simplified by the (unrealistic) assumption that the train only covers one track element at a time. Similarly, we make the simplifying assumption that points can change position from plus to minus (or vice verse) without first going through an intermediate state. Such coarse grained level of abstractions can be useful, for example, for very fast, preliminary verification of concrete models, before using the more refined and more realistic ones. As long as safety violations are still found in the coarse-grained model, there is no need to perform more refined, and therefore more time-intensive, checks.

3.3   IDL Definition

Encodings. In IDL, so-called *encodings* provide generic variable declarations. An encoding is a blueprint of the set of variables that should be used to represent the state of any interlocking-related element.[2] An encoding takes the form:

encoding
  elem−ty ::
    var−decl$_1$
    ...
    var−decl$_n$

where `elem-ty` $\in$ {**Linear, Point, Section, Signal, Route**} states the *element type* and each `var-decl`$_i$ is a generic variable declaration of the form

  v$_i$ → [role$_i$,ty$_i$,ival$_i$,min$_i$,max$_i$]   (∗)

In this variable declaration, v$_i$ is the identifier of the variable, ty$_i$ its type (only integers or Booleans are allowed here), min$_i$ and max$_i$ are a minimum and a maximum value, respectively, ival$_i$ is the initial value of v$_i$, and role$_i$ $\in$ {**INPUT, OUTPUT, LOCAL**} is the role of the variable as seen from the interlocking system.

Example 1. For the toy example introduced above, the following encodings are used for linear sections, points, signals, and routes (recall that sections are just the union of linear sections and points).

encoding
  Linear::
    CNT → [**INPUT**,"unsigned int",0,0,2]   /∗ occupied counter ∗/

---

[2] Encodings are similar to classes in object-oriented languages, but only allow for the declaration of variables (fields). Moreover, the variables can only be specified for a pre-defined set `elem-ty` of interlocking-related elements (objects).

Point::
   CNT → [**INPUT**,"unsigned int",0,0,2]   /* occupied counter */
   POS → [**INPUT**,"unsigned int",0,0,1] /* Actual position PLUS(0)/MINUS(1) */
   CMD → [**OUTPUT**,"unsigned int",0,0,1]   /* commanded position */
Signal::
   ACT → [**INPUT**,"unsigned int",0,0,1] /* actual aspect CLOSED(0) or OPEN(1) */
   CMD → [**OUTPUT**,"unsigned int",0,0,1]   /* commanded aspect */
Route ::
   MODE → [**LOCAL**,"unsigned int",0,0,4]   /* current mode FREE(0), ... */

The variables CNT for linear sections and points indicate the number of trains residing in the section. For every train entering the section, the counter is incremented, with a maximum value 2. Below, a safety condition will be specified stating that the counter must always be 0 or 1, so that 2 represents a safety violation. The variables POS for points and ACT for signals represent the actual position and the actual aspect of the point and the signal, respectively, while the variables CMD represent the last commanded position and aspect, respectively, requested by the interlocking system. The variables MODE for routes keeps track of the current mode of the route.   □

Instantiation Rules for Encodings. When instantiated with configuration data, an encoding of element type `elem-ty` gives rise to a set of variables for each concrete element e of type `elem-ty`. For this e, the instantiated variables are named $e.\mathtt{v}_1, \ldots, e.\mathtt{v}_n$, and they are specified according to the generic declaration of each $\mathtt{v}_1$ given in (∗).

Example 2. For the concrete railway network shown in Fig. 1, the encoding of linear sections gives rise to variables `t10.CNT`, `t12.CNT`, ..., `t20.CNT`. The point-related variables are `t11.CNT`, `t11.POS`, `t11.CMD` and `t13.CNT`, `t13.POS`, `t13.CMD`. The signal-related variables are `mb10.ACT`, `mb10.CMD`, ..., `mb20.ACT`, `mb20.CMD`. For routes, the interlocking table shown in Table 1 gives rise to route variables `r1a.MODE`, ..., `r7.MODE`.   □

Instantiation of the Initial Condition. For a concrete interlocking system, the initial state is given by the conjunction of initialisation expressions for all concrete model elements. This conjunction can be directly derived from the generic encodings, as soon as the concrete sets of elements of the types **Linear**, **Point**, **Section**, **Signal**, and **Route** are known for the specific interlocking system. Below, for simplicity, we re-use these type names also to denote their respective sets of concrete elements of the configuration data.

Then each encoding gives rise to the following predicate, representing the initial state of all the concrete elements of type `elem-ty`:

$$I_E \equiv \bigwedge_{e \in E} (e.v_1 = ival_1) \wedge \ldots \wedge (e.v_n = ival_n), \tag{3}$$

where E is the set of concrete element identifiers of type `elem-ty` in the configuration data and $ival_i$ is the initial value of variable v_i defined in the encoding for elements of type `elem-ty`. The complete initial condition is then specified as the conjunction

$$I_{\text{Linear}} \wedge \cdots \wedge I_{\text{Route}}$$

Example 3. For our example, the encodings specified in Example 1 give rise to the following initial condition.

$$
\begin{aligned}
I \equiv\ & \mathtt{t10.CNT} = 0 \wedge \cdots \wedge \mathtt{t20.CNT} = 0 \wedge \\
& \mathtt{t11.CNT} = 0 \wedge \mathtt{t11.POS} = 0 \wedge \mathtt{t11.CMD} = 0 \wedge \cdots \wedge \\
& \mathtt{mb10.ACT} = 0 \wedge \mathtt{mb10.CMD} = 0 \wedge \cdots \wedge \\
& \mathtt{r1a.MODE} = 0 \wedge \cdots \wedge \mathtt{r7.MODE} = 0
\end{aligned}
$$

□

Macro Declarations. Similar to C pre-processor declarations, the IDL allows for macro definitions.

Example 4. For specifying the mode of routes, the values of the following macro definition are used.

macro
 def FREE = 0, **def** DISPATCHED = 1, ..., **def** OCCUPIED = 4

With these macros, the last line of the formula in Example 3 could be written:

$$\mathtt{r1a.MODE} = \text{FREE} \wedge \cdots \wedge \mathtt{r7.MODE} = \text{FREE}$$

More complex macros are parameterised and use expressions; the parameters and expressions are instantiated using term replacement according to the given concrete ICL specifications.   □

Built-In Domain-Specific Functions. The IDL provides pre-defined functions for referring to various element-related data. For instance,

$$\text{src} : \textbf{Route} \longrightarrow \textbf{Signal}$$

is a generic function mapping routes to their entry signals. When instantiated, expressions **src(r)** are replaced by the identifier of the entry signal obtained for concrete route r from the interlocking table. Similarly, the other functions **dst(r)**, **conflicts(r)**, ... introduced in Sect. 2.1 are provided as built-in functions of the IDL.

Generic Logical Expressions. Generic logical IDL expressions are used in the specification of the generic transition relation and generic properties. We will see below, that neither the former, nor the latter may contain free variables. Therefore, every reference from a logical IDL expression to a variable v specified by an encoding must carry an element identifier e referring to a section, a signal, or a route. This identifier will be bound to a quantifier when the expression is used in the transition relation or in a property specification. Logical expressions are built according to the following rules.

1. Atomic propositions may refer to constants and variables of the form `id.v`, where `id` is an identifier and `v` a variable specified in an encoding for linear sections, points, signals, or routes. The identifier `id` is then interpreted as an element of the respective encoding type. Macros and built-in domain-specific functions may also be applied to represent constants and element identifiers. As operators connecting constants and variables, the usual arithmetic and comparison operators may be applied, so that this results in a Boolean expression.
2. Every atomic proposition is a generic logical expression.
3. If φ_1, φ_2 are valid generic logical expressions then $\neg\varphi_1$, $\varphi_1 \wedge \varphi_2$, $\varphi_1 \vee \varphi_2$, $\varphi_1 \Rightarrow \varphi_2$ are valid expressions as well.
4. If φ is a valid generic logical expression and `id.v` a variable occurring free in φ and interpreted by element type `elem-ty` $\in \{\mathbf{Linear}, \ldots, \mathbf{Route}\}$, then

   $$(\text{quantifier } id : \text{elem−ty} \bullet \varphi)$$

   is a valid generic IDL expression, where the quantifier is one of $\forall, \exists$.

Instantiation of Generic Logical Expressions. Generic logical expressions – whether occurring in the transition relation or in a property – are instantiated for a concrete interlocking system by first instantiating any subexpression which is a quantified expression, as will be explained below. If the result contains applications of built-in domain-specific functions these must then be instantiated as explained above. Any quantified generic logical expression

$$(\forall id : \text{elem−ty} \bullet \varphi)$$

is instantiated by

$$\bigwedge_{e \in \text{elem−ty}} \varphi[e/id]$$

The generic expression is turned into a conjunction containing one conjunct per concrete element e in the instantiation of set `elem-ty`. In the conjunct associated with e, the bound element identifier id is replaced by e. Here we have assumed that φ is quantifier free. If this is not the case, the instantiation rule above is applied repetitively. For

$$(\exists id : \text{elem−ty} \bullet \varphi)$$

the instantiation rule is

$$\bigvee_{e \in \text{elem−ty}} \varphi[e/id]$$

Examples for this instantiation technique will be given below for a safety property.

Generic Transition Relation Definition. A transition relation definition takes the following form

    transrel te

where **te** is a generic transition relation expression. These expressions are basically generic logical IDL expressions as introduced above, but some additional syntax is used to structure large logical expressions. Moreover, the concept of variable pre-states and post-states needs to be introduced, so that the transition between states can be specified. Finally, additional operators are provided to express choice.

Specifying updates: pre-states and post-states. In transition relation expressions, all references `id.v` which are based on encoding variables `v` are complemented by primed references `id.v'`. The former denote the pre-state of an encoding variable bound to `id`, while the latter denotes its post state.

An *atomic transition expression* specifies the condition and the effect of a valuation change for some referenced generic variables `id.v`. It takes the general form

    [name] guard $\longrightarrow$ update

where *name* is a unique identification of this transition relation sub-expression, *guard* is a generic logical IDL expression over unprimed variables only, and *update* is a generic logical expression where – apart from unprimed variable references – at least one primed variable reference occurs. Note that, as motivated above, atomic transition expressions need to be bound to quantifiers in order to become valid IDL expressions.

Example 5. For our example, the following atomic transition expression specifies how a point switches to a new position, when commanded by the interlocking controller.

    [switch_point] p.CMD $\neq$ p.POS $\longrightarrow$ p.POS$'$ = p.CMD

The next atomic transition expression explains how trains move on routes in our simple model: the train entering a new section **next**(r, e) on its route r is expressed by incrementing the counter of **next**(r, e), and leaving the previous section e is modelled by decrementing its counter. When incrementing, the upper bound 2 of the counter needs to be taken into account. Since two trains on the same section already represent a safety violation, a higher value is not required.

    [move_along_route] r.OCCUPIED $\wedge$ e $\in$ **path**(r) $\wedge$ e $\neq$ **last**(r) $\wedge$ e.CNT > 0 $\longrightarrow$
        next(r,e).CNT$'$ = min(2,**next**(r,e).CNT+1) $\wedge$ e.CNT$'$ = e.CNT $- 1$

The following expression describes that a new route can be entered when its marker board (the same as the signal at the end of the current route) signals OPEN. Recall from Sect. 2.1 that in this situation, **next**(r, e) denotes the first element of the next route.[3]

---

[3] Here it is assumed that the last element of route r is not a point, so that the next element is uniquely determined. This assumption is realistic for real interlocking systems.

[enter_next_route] e = **last**(r) $\wedge$ **dst**(r).ACT = OPEN $\wedge$ e.CNT > 0 $\longrightarrow$
    next(r,e).CNT$'$ = min(2,**next**(r,e).CNT+1) $\wedge$ e.CNT$'$ = e.CNT $-$ 1

Additional rules describe how trains can enter the network and how virtual signals .and the interlocking system behave. Binding atomic transition expressions to quantifiers will be illustrated in the next example.   □

Quantification by Nondeterministic Choice. When expressing that one atomic transition relation expression out of several enabled ones may "fire", this is expressed by the nondeterministic choice operator [=] which can be used like a quantifier:

([=] id : elem−ty • [name_id] te)

specifies that the effect of te may become visible, if its guard condition evaluates to true for the specific variable reference id. If the guard evaluates to true for several id, then one of them is chosen nondeterministically.

Example 6. If several points are commanded to switch their position and our behavioural model should act according to an interleaving semantics, only one of the points changes its position per transition step. This is expressed as

([=] p : **Point** • [switch_point] p.CMD $\neq$ p.POS $\longrightarrow$ p.POS$'$ = p.CMD)   □

Composition of transition relations. Quantified transition expressions can be combined by

- te_1 [=] te_2: nondeterministic choice between te_1 and te_2, if both are enabled.
- te_1 [>] te_2: if te_1 is enabled, its effect will become visible, otherwise the effect of te_2 will become visible, if the latter is enabled (prioritised choice).[4]

Instantiation of Transition Relations. Any transition relation expression can be instantiated according to the following rules.

1. An atomic transition expression guard$\longrightarrow$update is instantiated to $\phi_g \wedge \phi_u \wedge \phi$, where ϕ_g and ϕ_u are the instantiations of the sub-expressions guard and update, respectively, and ϕ is a predicate expressing that all variables that do not occur as primed variable references in update remain unchanged.
2. A quantified transition expression ([=] id : elem-ty • [name_id] te) is instantiated by $\bigvee_{e \in \text{elem-ty}} \varphi_e$, where φ_e is the instantiations of te[e/id].
3. The expression te_1[=]te_2 is instantiated by disjunction $\varphi_1 \vee \varphi_2$, where φ_i are the instantiations of the generic transition relation sub-expressions te_i.
4. The expression te_1[>]te_2 is instantiated by prioritised disjunction $\varphi_1 \vee (\neg g_1 \wedge \varphi_2)$, where φ_i are the instantiations of the te_i, and g_1 is a predicate expressing that at least one of the transition expressions in φ_1 may fire.

---

[4] This priority operator was invented by Hansen in [5].

Example 7. Instantiating the transition rule for points shown in Example 6 with data from the network diagram in Fig. 1 yields the first order predicate:

$$(t11.CMD \neq t11.POS \land t11.POS' = t11.CMD \land \phi_{t11.POS}) \lor$$
$$(t13.CMD \neq t13.POS \land t13.POS' = t13.CMD \land \phi_{t13.POS})$$

where $\phi_{id.v}$ is a formula expressing that all variable instances except $id.v$ remain unchanged by the transition.   □

Generic Properties. Generic properties are specified by generic logical expressions representing state invariants. Typically, these are used to specify safety properties. A property specification takes the form

invariant
  [id] prop

where **prop** is a generic logical IDL expression, such that all element references are bound to quantifiers. The instantiation of properties is performed according to the rules for instantiating generic logical IDL expressions described above.

Example 8. For our example, the following property specifies that no collisions should happen anywhere. It refers to the counter variable CNT associated with linear sections and points we have specified for the encodings of this example.

invariant
  [no_collision] $(\forall s : \textbf{Section} \bullet s.CNT < 2)$

Following the usual recipe, this is instantiated for the interlocking system from Fig. 1 to the first order predicate

$$no\_collision \equiv t10.CNT < 2 \land \cdots \land t20.CNT < 2 \land t11.CNT < 2 \land t13.CNT < 2.$$

                                                                □

4   Conclusion

This paper presented a domain-specific language IDL for generic behavioural interlocking models and their properties. The language and configuration data instantiators based on the semantics have been implemented in the RobustRailS environment and have successfully been applied to model and verify interlocking systems of the Danish Signalling Programme. The language turned out to be easy to use with its facilities for writing *generic constructs* like generic transition rules and generic properties, and its *built-in domain-specific constructions* making the specifications shorter to write and also easier to understand for domain experts than they would have been if a typical GPL had been used. The language was also powerful enough for specifying the behaviour of the Danish systems.

  The language was designed for the purpose of being used in the process of specifying the future Danish ERTMS/ETCS level 2 compatible interlocking systems. For this practical application, the IDL parsers and the instantiator tools (shown in Fig. 2) have been implemented as components of the **RobustRailS** tool set. The tool set uses the framework of the RT-Tester model-based testing tool which provides an efficient bounded model checker for Linear Temporal Logic LTL [11].

The generic models and generic safety properties used for the verification task are far too big to be shown in this paper, but they can be found in [16] and http://www.imm.dtu.dk/~aeha/RobustRailS/data/casestudy/generic_models, and a general description can be found in [16,17]. These documents also provide examples for which the generic model and properties have been instantiated, and they provide verification metrics for the model checking of the resulting concrete models and concrete properties.

Acknowledgements. The authors would like to thank Ross Edwin Gammon and Nikhil Mohan Pande from Banedanmark (Railnet Denmark) and Jan Bertelsen from Thales for helping us with their expertise about Danish interlocking systems; and Dr.-Ing. Uwe Schulze and Florian Lapschies from University of Bremen for their help with the implementation in the RT-Tester tool-chain.

References

1. Cao, Y., Xu, T., Tang, T., Wang, H., Zhao, L.: Automatic generation and verification of interlocking tables based on domain specific language for computer based interlocking systems (dsl-cbi). In: Proceedings of the IEEE International Conference on Computer Science and Automation Engineering (CSAE 2011), pp. 511–515. IEEE (2011)
2. CENELEC European Committee for Electrotechnical Standardization: EN 50128: 2011 - Railway applications - Communications, signalling and processing systems - Software for railway control and protection systems (2011)
3. European Railway Agency: Annex A for ETCS Baseline 3 and GSM-R Baseline 0, April 2012. http://www.era.europa.eu/Document-Register/Pages/New-Annex-A-for-ETCS-Baseline-3-and-GSM-R-Baseline-0.aspx
4. Hansen, H.H., Ketema, J., Luttik, B., Mousavi, M.R., van de Pol, J.: Towards model checking executable UML specifications in mCRL2. Innovations Syst. Softw. Eng. **6**(1), 83–90 (2010)
5. Hansen, J.B.: A formal specification language for generic railway control systems. Master's thesis, Technical University of Denmark, DTU Compute (2015)
6. Haxthausen, A.E.: Automated generation of formal safety conditions from railway interlocking tables. Int. J. Softw. Tools Technol. Transfer (STTT) **16**(6), 713–726 (2014). Special Issue on Formal Methods for Railway Control Systems
7. Haxthausen, A.E., Østergaard, P.H.: On the use of static checking in the verification of interlocking systems. In: Margaria, T., Steffen, B. (eds.) ISoLA 2016. LNCS, vol. 9953, pp. 266–278. Springer, Cham (2016). doi:10.1007/978-3-319-47169-3_19
8. James, P., Roggenbach, M.: Encapsulating formal methods within domain specific languages: a solution for verifying railway scheme plans. Math. Comput. Sci. **8**(1), 11–38 (2014)

9. Luteberget, B., Johansen, C., Feyling, C., Steffen, M.: Rule-based incremental verification tools applied to railway designs and regulations. In: Fitzgerald, J., Heitmeyer, C., Gnesi, S., Philippou, A. (eds.) FM 2016. LNCS, vol. 9995, pp. 772–778. Springer, Cham (2016). doi:10.1007/978-3-319-48989-6_49

10. Mewes, K.: Domain-specific Modelling of Railway Control Systems with Integrated Verification and Validation. Verlag Dr. Hut, München (2010)

11. Peleska, J.: Industrial-strength model-based testing - state of the art and current challenges. In: Petrenko, A.K., Schlingloff, H. (eds.) Proceedings 8th Workshop on Model-Based Testing, Rome, Italy. Electronic Proceedings in Theoretical Computer Science, vol. 111, pp. 3–28. Open Publishing Association (2013)

12. Peleska, J., Baer, A., Haxthausen, A.E.: Towards domain-specific formal specification languages for railway control systems. In: Schnieder, E., Becker, U. (eds.) Proceedings of the 9th IFAC Symposium on Control in Transportation Systems 2000, 13–15 June 2000, Braunschweig, Germany, pp. 147–152 (2000)

13. Verified Systems International GmbH: RT-Tester Model-Based Test Case and Test Data Generator - RTT-MBT - User Manual (2013). http://www.verified.de

14. Vu, L.H., Haxthausen, A.E., Peleska, J.: A domain-specific language for railway interlocking systems. In: Schnieder, E., Tarnai, G. (eds.) FORMS/FORMAT 2014 – 10th Symposium on Formal Methods for Automation and Safety in Railway and Automotive Systems, pp. 200–209. Technische Universität Braunschweig, Institute for Traffic Safety and Automation Engineering (2014)

15. Vu, L.H., Haxthausen, A.E., Peleska, J.: Formal modeling and verification of interlocking systems featuring sequential release. In: Artho, C., Ölveczky, P.C. (eds.) FTSCS 2014. CCIS, vol. 476, pp. 223–238. Springer, Cham (2015). doi:10.1007/978-3-319-17581-2_15

16. Vu, L.H.: Formal development and verification of railway control systems - in the context of ERTMS/ETCS Level 2. Ph.D. thesis, Technical University of Denmark, DTU Compute (2015)

17. Vu, L.H., Haxthausen, A.E., Peleska, J.: Formal modelling and verification of interlocking systems featuring sequential release. Sci. Comput. Program. 133(Part 2), 91–115 (2017). http://dx.doi.org/10.1016/j.scico.2016.05.010

18. Winter, K., Robinson, N.J.: Modelling large railway interlockings and model checking small ones. In: Proceedings of the 26th Australasian Computer Science Conference, ACSC 2003, vol. 16, pp. 309–316. Australian Computer Society, Inc., Darlinghurst (2003)

Bayesian Network Modeling Applied on Railway Level Crossing Safety

Ci Liang[1,2,5](✉), Mohamed Ghazel[1,2,5], Olivier Cazier[1,3], Laurent Bouillaut[4], and El-Miloudi El-Koursi[1,2,5]

[1] FCS Railenium, Valenciennes, France
ci.liang@railenium.eu
[2] IFSTTAR-COSYS/ESTAS, 20 Rue Élisée Reclus, BP 70317,
59666 Lille, Villeneuve d'Ascq, France
[3] SNCF Réseau, Paris, France
[4] IFSTTAR-COSYS/GRETTIA, Paris, Marne-la-Vallée, France
[5] University Lille 1, Lille, Villeneuve d'Ascq, France

Abstract. Nowadays, railway operation is characterized by increasingly high speed and large transport capacity. Safety is the core issue in railway operation, and as witnessed by accident/incident statistics, railway level crossing (LX) safety is one of the most critical points in railways. In the present paper, the causal reasoning analysis of LX accidents is carried out based on Bayesian risk model. The causal reasoning analysis aims to investigate various influential factors which may cause LX accidents, and quantify the contribution of these factors so as to identify the crucial factors which contribute most to the accidents at LXs. A detailed statistical analysis is firstly carried out based on the accident/incident data. Then, a Bayesian risk model is established according to the causal relationships and statistical results. Based on the Bayesian risk model, the prediction of LX accident can be made through forward inference. Moreover, accident cause identification and influential factor evaluation can be performed through reverse inference. The main outputs of our study allow for providing improvement measures to reduce risk and lessen consequences related to LX accidents.

Keywords: Bayesian network modeling · Level crossing safety · Train-car collision · Risk assessment · Statistical analysis

1 Introduction

Railway Level crossings (LXs) are potentially hazardous locations where trains, road vehicles and pedestrians move in close proximity to one another. LX safety remains one of the most critical issues for railways despite an ever-increasing focus on improving design and application practices [1, 2]. Accidents at European LXs account for about one-third of the entire railway accidents and result in more than 300 deaths every year in Europe [2]. In France, the railway network shows more than 18,000 LXs for 30,000 km of railway lines, which are crossed

A. Fantechi et al. (Eds.): RSSRail 2017, LNCS 10598, pp. 116–130, 2017.
https://doi.org/10.1007/978-3-319-68499-4_8

daily by 16 million vehicles on average, and around 13,000 LXs show heavy road and railway traffic [3]. Despite numerous measures already taken to improve the LX safety, SNCF Réseau (the French national railway infrastructure manager) counted 100 collisions at LXs leading to 25 deaths in 2014. This number was half the total number of collisions per year at LXs a decade ago, but still too large [4]. In order to significantly reduce the accidents and lessen their related consequences at LXs, an effective risk assessment means is needed urgently.

Many available studies dealing with LX safety have tended to take a qualitative approach to understand the potential factors causing accidents at LXs. These works employ surveys [5], interviews [6], focus group methods [7] or driving simulators [8], rather than collecting real field data. For example, Lenné et al. [9] examined the effect of installing active controls, flashing lights and traffic signals on vehicle driver behavior. This study was achieved through adopting the driving simulation. Tey et al. [10] conducted an experiment to measure vehicle driver response to LXs equipped with stop signs (passive), flashing lights and half barriers with flashing lights (active), respectively. In this study, both a field survey and a driving simulator have been utilized. Although those aforementioned approaches are beneficial to explore the potential factors causing accidents, they still show some limits. For instance, they do not allow for quantifying the contribution degree of these factors. In addition, the reaction of vehicle drivers in simulation scenarios could differ from that in reality, due to the different levels of feeling of danger. Therefore, quantitative approaches based on real field data are indispensable if we want to understand the impacting factors thoroughly and enable the identification of practical design and improvement recommendations to prevent accidents at LXs.

Nowadays, risk analysis approaches are required to deal with increasingly complex systems with a large number of configuration parameters. Therefore, such approaches should satisfy the following requirements:

- Strong modeling ability;
- Easy to specify a risk scenario or a system;
- High computational efficiency.

In the domain of risk assessment, various approaches are adopted for the modeling and analyzing process. Due to the combination of qualitative and quantitative analysis, the Fault Tree Analysis (FTA) developed by H.A. Watson at Bell Laboratories [11] has been widely used for risk analysis in various contexts. FTA is a deductive and top-down method which aims at analyzing the effects of initiating faults and events on a complex system and offering the designer an intuitive high-level abstraction of the system. Compared with the Failure Mode and Effects Analysis (FMEA), which is an inductive and bottom-up analysis method aimed at analyzing the effects of single component or function failures on equipment or subsystems, FTA is more useful in showing how resistant a system is to single or multiple initiating faults. However, one obvious disadvantage of FTA is that it is not clear on failure mechanism, since the causal relationship between events is not a simple YES or NO (1 or 0). Therefore, FTA is prone to missing the possible initiating faults. In addition, traditional static fault trees cannot handle the sequential interaction and functional dependencies between components. Consequently, it is necessary to employ dynamic methodologies to overcome these weaknesses. Markov Chains (MCs) and their extensions have been mainly used for modeling complex dynamic system behavior and dependability analysis of dynamic systems. Two-state Markov switching multinomial logit models are introduced by [12] to explain unpredictable, unidentified or unobservable risk factors in road safety. Although MCs can elaborate the statistical state transition of different variables, they cannot formalize causal relationships between the various events.

Afterward, risk analysis based on formal modeling expanded. In order to compare the effectiveness of two main Automatic Protection Systems (APSs) at LXs: two-half-barrier APS and four-half-barrier APS, Generalized Stochastic Petri Nets (GSPNs) were used in [13] to analyze the aleatory fluctuations of various parameters involved in the dynamics within the LX area. Over the last few years, Bayesian network (BN), a method of reasoning using probabilities, has been an increasingly popular method used for risk analysis of safety-critical systems or large and complex dynamic systems [14]. In order to obtain proper and effective risk control, risk planning should be performed based on risk causality, which can provide more information for decision making. In this context, a model using BNs with causality constraints (BNCC) for risk analysis was proposed in [15]. In [16], Bouillaut et al. discussed the development of a decision tool realized by hierarchical Dynamic BNs (DBNs), which is dedicated to the maintenance of metro lines in Paris. This modeling work has comprehensively described the rail degradation process, the different diagnosis actors (devices and staff) and the maintenance actions decision. In [17], Langseth and Portinal introduced the applicability of BNs for reliability analysis and offered an instance of BNs application for preventive maintenance. The advantages behind BNs were discussed in this article: (a) BNs constitute a modeling framework, which is particularly easy to use for interaction with domain experts; (b) the sound mathematical formulation has been utilized in BNs to generate efficient learning methods; and (c) BNs are equipped with an efficient calculation scheme which often makes BNs preferable to traditional tools like Fault Trees (FTs). To sum up, the BN technique offers interesting features: the flexibility of modeling, strong modeling power, high computational efficiency and, most importantly, the outstanding advantages involving causality analysis based on both forward inference and reverse inference [18] and the conjunction of domain expertise.

Therefore, based on the above investigation of risk analysis, an approach of Causal Reasoning Analysis based on Bayesian risk model (CRAB) is presented in this paper to deal with the risk assessment at LXs. Namely, a thorough statistical analysis based on the accident/incident data pertaining to French LXs is firstly performed, and the statistical results are used as the import sources of BN risk model. Then, the BN risk model is developed according to the causal relationships between the accidents and various influential parameters considered. Through the BN risk model, one can quantify the risk level impacted by various potential factors and identify the factors which contribute most to the accidents at LXs, as well as their combined impact on LX safety.

2   Preliminary Introduction of Bayesian Belief Networks

In railways, potential hazards including equipment failures, human errors and some non-deterministic factors, such as environment aspects, may lead to accidents. In fact, causalities between accidents and these impacting factors exist, as shown in Fig. 1. Identifying such causality relationships is a crucial issue in the process of reasoning. In particular, a functional intelligent identification model should have the ability of making reasoning based on the causal knowledge.

The Bayesian belief network (BN) employed to model causality is a graphical model that can be characterized by its structure and a set of parameters [19]. $BN = (P, G)$, where P represents the parameters of prior probabilities that quantify the arcs, while G defines the model structure. $G = (V, A)$, which is a Directed Acyclic Graph (DAG), is comprised by a finite set of nodes (V) linked by directed arcs (A). The nodes represent random variables (V_i) and directed arcs (A_i) between pairs of nodes represent dependencies between the variables [19].

In our study, the BN works based on the theory of probability for discrete distributions. Assume that there is a set of mutually exclusive events: B_1, B_2, ...,B_n and a given event A, such that, $P(A)$ can be expressed as follows:

$$P(A) = \sum_{i=1}^{n} P(B_i) P(A|B_i) \tag{1}$$

According to Bayes' formula:

$$P(B_i|A) = \frac{P(B_i)P(A|B_i)}{\sum_{j=1}^{n} P(B_j)P(A|B_j)} \tag{2}$$

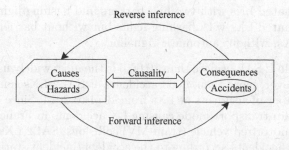

Fig. 1. Reasoning between hazards and accidents.

Equation (2) can be converted into:

$$P(B_i|A) = \frac{P(B_i)P(A|B_i)}{P(A)} \tag{3}$$

where $P(B_i)$ is the prior probability, $P(B_i|A)$ is the posterior probability.

For any set of random variables in a BN, the joint distribution can be computed through conditional probabilities using the chain rule as shown in Eq. (4):

$$P(X_1 = x_1, \ldots, X_n = x_n) = \prod_{v=1}^{n} P(X_v = x_v | X_{v+1} = x_{v+1}, \ldots, X_n = x_n) \tag{4}$$

Due to the conditional independence, X_v only relates to its parent node $Pa(X_v)$ and is independent of the other nodes. Hence, Eq. (4) can be rewritten as follows:

$$P(X_1 = x_1, \ldots, X_n = x_n) = \prod_{v=1}^{n} P(X_v = x_v | Pa(X_v)) \tag{5}$$

For more details about BN, the reader can refer to the tutorial book on Bayesian networks edited by [20].

3   Methodology

As mentioned before, the present study aims to perform risk assessment at French LXs. The CRAB approach is illustrated to assist our risk assessment based on the accident/incident data collected by SNCF Réseau. Namely, it is applied to assessing the risk level with regard to various impacting factors taken into account and evaluating the contribution degree of these factors. Thus, we pave the way towards identifying the important factors which contribute most to the overall risk.

There are 4 LX types in France [21]:

– SAL4: Automated LXs with four half barriers and flashing lights;
– SAL2: Automated LXs with two half barriers and flashing lights;
– SAL0: Automated LXs with flashing lights but without barriers;
– Crossbuck LXs, without automatic signaling.

As shown in Table 1, SAL2 (more than 10,000) is the most widely used type of LX in France. Moreover, more than 4,000 accidents at SAL2 LXs contributed most to the total number of accidents at LXs from 1974 to 2014. Since the motorized vehicle is the main transport mode causing LX accidents in France [22], considering the train/motorized vehicle (train-MV) collisions, SAL2 LXs also have the most part of LX accidents according to the accident/incident statistics as shown in Fig. 2. Moreover, according to the SNCF statistics, these accidents can be considered as the most representative for LX accidents in general. For all these reasons, our analysis will focus on train-MV accidents occurring at SAL2 LXs.

Table 1. Accidents at different types of LXs in France from 1974 to 2014

Type of LX	Number	#Accident
SAL4	>600	>600
SAL2	>10,000	>4,200
SAL0	>60	>50
Crossbuck LX	>3,500	>700

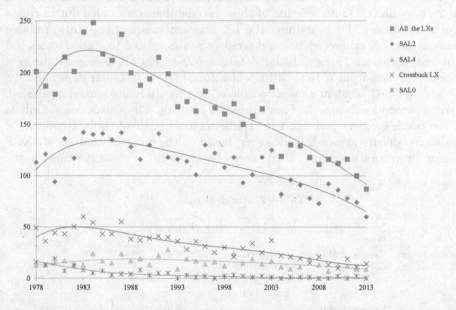

Fig. 2. The number of train-MV collisions at different types of LX from 1978 to 2013

3.1 Data Collection

SNCF Réseau has recorded the detailed elements of each LX accident, including various attributes of LX accidents/incidents, surrounding characteristics of LXs and accident causes, and provides two accident/incident databases to support our study. The first database (D1) records the accident/incident data that cover SAL2 LXs in mainland France from 1990 to 2013.

From D1, the subdataset (SD1) including the data ranging in the decade from 2004 to 2013 is selected, which provides reliable and sufficient information about both LX accidents and static railway, roadway and LX characteristics. Namely, the selected LX inventory presents the LX identification number, the railway line involved, the LX kilometer point, the LX accident timestamp, the average daily railway traffic, the average daily road traffic, the rail speed limit, the LX length and width, the profile and alignment of the entered road and geographic region involved. There are 8,332 public SAL2 LXs included in SD1.

According to the statistics of SNCF Réseau, the majority of train-MV accidents at LXs are caused by motorist violations. Due to the lack of accident causes in SD1, causal relationship analysis cannot be performed with regard to the static factors and motorist behavior. Therefore, we seek another database which records detailed accident causes. Fortunately, the second database (D2) contains the information about SAL2 LX accidents from 2010 to 2013, the LX identification number, the railway line involved and detailed accident causes (including static factors and inappropriate motorist behavior). Thus, using the LX ID and the railway line ID, data merging of these two databases is carried out to create a new database (ND) containing the LX accident information, static railway, roadway and LX characteristics and accident causes related to static factors and motorist behavior. This combined database ND covers LX accidents during a period of 4 years from 2010 to 2013, which forms the basis of our present study.

The detailed accident causes considered in this study are shown in Table 2. Here, a second-level cause is given: corrected moment. The conventional formula of the traffic moment is defined as: Traffic moment = Road traffic frequency × Railway traffic frequency [22]. However, based on the previous analysis of SNCF Réseau, we adopt a variant called "corrected moment" instead (CM for short).

Table 2. Accident causes

Primary causes	Second-level causes	Third-level causes	Explanation
Static factors	Corrected Moment (CM)	Average daily railway traffic (T)	$CM = V^{0.354} \times T^{0.646}$;
		Average daily road traffic (V)	
	Railway speed limit		The maximum permission speed of train within the LX section;
	Alignment		Horizontal road alignment shape: "straight", "curve" or "S";
	Profile		Vertical road profile shape: "normal" or "hump or cavity";
	Width		The width of LX;
	Length		The length of LX that road vehicles need to cross;
	Region risk		Region Risk factor, highlighting the general LX-accident-prone region: *The number of SAL2 accidents over the observation period in the region considered/The number of SAL2 LXs in the region considered*;
Inappropriate motorist behavior	Stall on LX	Blocked on LX	A vehicle is blocked on the SAL2 LX by the external environment;
		Stop on LX	A motorist intentionally stops the vehicle on the SAL2 LX;
	Zigzag violation		A vehicle skirts the half barriers to cross the SAL2 LX;

$CM = V^a \times T^b$, where $b = 1 - a$ and the best value of a in terms of fitting is computed to be $a = 0.354$ according to the statistical analysis performed by SNCF Réseau [23], since railway traffic has a more marked impact on LX accidents than road traffic. Therefore, $(V^{0.354} \times T^{0.646})$ is considered as an integrated parameter that reflects the combined exposure frequency of both railway and road traffic.

3.2 Bayesian Risk Model Establishment

Variable Definition. Based on the combined database ND, the statistical results are organized as input sources which will be imported to the BN risk model. Data discretization is applied on continuous variables. Namely, the continuous variables, i.e., "Average Daily Road Traffic", "Average Daily Railway Traffic", "Railway Speed Limit", "Width", "Length" and "Corrected Moment", are divided into 3 groups and each group has the similar number of samples. As for the "Region Risk" factors corresponding to 21 regions in mainland France, they are divided into 3 groups as well, ranked according to the risk level in descending order, and each group contains 7 region risk factors. As for the finite discrete variables, i.e., "Alignment", "Profile", "Stall on LX", "Zigzag Violation", "Blocked on LX" and "Stop on LX", we allocate an individual state to each value of the variable. The consequence severity of SAL2 accidents [24] is defined according to the number of fatalities and injuries in an SAL2 accident. The definition of consequence severity pertaining to an SAL2 accident is shown in Table 3. Five levels of consequence severity are set according to the number of fatalities, severe injuries and minor injuries caused by the accident, respectively. The consequence severity increases progressively from level 1 to 5. Thus, a summary of states of each node in the BN risk model is offered in Table 4.

Table 3. Consequence severity definition

Consequence severity	Level 1	Level 2	Level 3	Level 4	Level 5
$0 \leq$ fatalities < 5, $0 \leq$ severe injuries < 5, $0 \leq$ minor injuries < 20;	×	–	–	–	–
$0 \leq$ fatalities < 5, $0 \leq$ severe injuries < 5, $20 \leq$ minor injuries;	–	×	–	–	–
$0 \leq$ fatalities < 5, $5 \leq$ severe injuries, $0 \leq$ minor injuries < 20;	–	–	×	–	–
$0 \leq$ fatalities < 5, $5 \leq$ severe injuries, $20 \leq$ minor injuries;	–	–	×	–	–
$5 \leq$ fatalities, $0 \leq$ severe injuries < 5, $0 \leq$ minor injuries < 20;	–	–	–	×	–
$5 \leq$ fatalities, $0 \leq$ severe injuries < 5, $20 \leq$ minor injuries;	–	–	–	×	–
$5 \leq$ fatalities, $5 \leq$ severe injuries, $0 \leq$ minor injuries < 20;	–	–	–	–	×
$5 \leq$ fatalities, $5 \leq$ severe injuries, $20 \leq$ minor injuries;	–	–	–	–	×

Table 4. States of nodes in the BN risk model

Node name	Node property	Node state
Corrected Moment (CM)	Chance node	CM_below_19 ($0 \leq$ CM < 19),
		CM_19_49 ($19 \leq$ CM < 49),
		CM_49_up ($49 \leq$ CM);
Average Daily Railway Traffic (ADRT)	Chance node	ADRT_below_9 ($0 \leq$ ADRT < 9),
		ADRT_9_25 ($9 \leq$ ADRT < 25),
		ADRT_25_up ($25 \leq$ ADRT);
Average Daily Road Vehicle (ADRV)	Chance node	ADRV_below_72 ($0 \leq$ ADRV < 72),
		ADRV_72_403 ($72 \leq$ ADRV < 403),
		ADRV_403_up ($403 \leq$ ADRV);
Railway Speed Limit (RLS)	Chance node	RLS_below_70 ($0\,$km/h $\leq$ RLS $< 70\,$km/h),
		RLS_70_110 ($70\,$km/h $\leq$ RLS $< 110\,$km/h),
		RLS_110_up ($110\,$km/h $\leq$ RLS);
Alignment	Chance node	Straight, C_shape, S_shape;
Profile	Chance node	Normal, Hump_cavity;
Width (W)	Chance node	W_below_5 ($0\,$m $\leq$ W $< 5\,$m),
		W_5_6 ($5\,$m $\leq$ W $< 6\,$m),
		W_6_up ($6\,$m $\leq$ W);
Length (L)	Chance node	L_below_7 ($0\,$m $\leq$ L $< 7\,$m),
		L_7_11 ($7\,$m $\leq$ L $< 11\,$m),
		L_11_up ($11\,$m $\leq$ L);
Region Risk (R)	Chance node	R_low (region with low risk level),
		R_medial (region with medial risk level),
		R_high (region with high risk level);
Stall on LX	Chance node	True, False;
Blocked on LX	Chance node	True, False;
Stop on LX	Chance node	True, False;
Zigzag Violation	Chance node	True, False;
Motorist Behavior Accident	Chance node	True, False;
Static Factor Accident	Chance node	True, False;
SAL2 MV Accident	Chance node	True, False;
Fatalities (F)	Chance node	F_0_5 ($0 \leq$ F < 5), F_5_up ($5 \leq$ F);
Severe Injuries (S)	Chance node	S_0_5 ($0 \leq$ S < 5), S_5_up ($5 \leq$ S);
Minor Injuries (M)	Chance node	M_0_20 ($0 \leq$ M < 20), M_20_up ($20 \leq$ M);
Consequence Severity	Deterministic node	Level_1, Level_2, Level_3, Level_4, Level_5;

Model Structure. Artificial restrictions are adopted to build the model structure, which means the model structure is defined according to the causal relationships between accident occurrence and influential variables based on expert proposes, instead of using general structure learning methods, since the general structure learning methods suggest us unreasonable model structures which

Table 5. Spearman correlation checking

Static factors Motorist behavior	Railway speed limit	Length	Width	Corrected moment	Alignment	Profile	Region risk factor
Blocked on LX	-0.0444	0.0031	-0.0341	-0.0525	-0.1769	-0.0352	-0.0432
Stop on LX	0.0179	-0.0668	-0.1138	-0.0402	-0.0329	-0.0307	-0.0420
Zigzag violation	0.0347	0.0374	0.1143	0.2118	-0.0462	-0.0221	0.1238

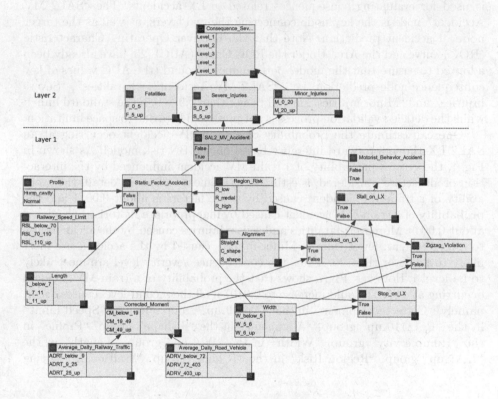

Fig. 3. BN risk model

are inconsistent with the causal relationships in reality and impede identification of important accident causes. It is worth noticing that there are still some potential connections between static factors and motorist behavior. The Spearman correlation checking is adopted to explore important connections and filter off negligible connections between these two kinds of variables. As shown in Table 5, the absolute values of correlation bigger than 0.05 are highlighted (Red color highlights negative values and green color highlights positive values). Their corresponding connections will be considered in our model. Conditional probability parameters are generated based on the real field accident/incident data.

The final model is developed as shown in Fig. 3, which contains 3,132 conditional probabilities.

4   Analysis and Discussion

As shown in Fig. 3, the risk model contains two layers: (1) **Layer 1** is used for predicting accident occurrence and diagnosing influential factors; (2) **Layer 2** is used for evaluating consequences related to LX accidents. The "SAL2 MV Accident" node is the key node connecting the two layers, as well as the target node of accident prediction. Note that the Receiver Operating Characteristic (ROC) curve and the Area Under the ROC Curve (AUC) [25] have already been adopted to ensure that the model performance is sound (the AUC values of key consequence node prediction, i.e., "SAL2 MV Accident", "Fatalities", "Severe injuries" and "Minor injuries", are all bigger than $0.9 > 0.5$: the standard limit); while the detailed validation process is not presented here due to space limitation.

One can estimate the probability of a train-MV accident occurring at an SAL2 LX through forward inference based on the BN risk model. As shown in Fig. 4, the general probability of a train-MV accident influenced by the interaction of all factors considered, is estimated as almost 0.0061. In detail, the probability of a train-MV accident caused by static factors is about 0.0011 and the probability of a train-MV accident caused by inappropriate motorist behavior is about 0.0049. Moreover, fatalities and severe injuries caused by the accident are, to a large extent, fewer than 5. Minor injuries caused by the accident are most likely to be fewer than 20. Thus, the consequence severity level are most likely to be level 1. However, Fig. 5 shows that the probability of a train-MV accident occurring at a SAL2 would increase to 0.0107 if all the second-level causes occur, namely, "Corrected Moment" in the "CM_49_up" group, "Railway Speed Limit" in the "RSL_110_up" group, "Alignment" in the "S_shape" group, "Profile" in the "Hump_cavity" group, "Width" in the "W_6_up" group, "Length" in the "L_11_up" group, "Region Risk" in the "R_high" group, "Stall on LX" being

SAL2_MV_Accident		Static_Factor_Accident		Motorist_Behavior_Accident	
▇ False	0.99390817	▇ False	0.99894278	▇ False	0.99511565
☐ True	0.0060918269	☐ True	0.0010572159	☐ True	0.0048843469

Fatalities		Severe_Injuries		Minor_Injuries	
▇ F_0_5	0.99999427	▇ S_0_5	0.99999323	▇ M_0_20	0.99998072
☐ F_5_up	5.7331767e-006	☐ S_5_up	6.7722109e-006	☐ M_20_up	1.9277586e-005

Consequence_Severity	
Level_1	0.99996826
Level_2	1.9238033e-005
Level_3	6.7658374e-006
Level_4	5.7268032e-006
Level_5	6.3735037e-009

Fig. 4. General prediction results

SAL2_MV_Accident		Static_Factor_Accident		Motorist_Behavior_Accident	
False	0.98928112	False	0.99107373	False	0.99834918
True	0.01071888	True	0.008926271	True	0.001650816

Fatalities		Severe_Injuries		Minor_Injuries	
F_0_5	0.99998991	S_0_5	0.99998808	M_0_20	0.99996608
F_5_up	1.0087817e-005	S_5_up	1.1916051e-005	M_20_up	3.3919897e-005

Consequence_Severity	
Level_1	0.99994416
Level_2	3.3850301e-005
Level_3	1.1904836e-005
Level_4	1.0076603e-005
Level_5	1.1214505e-008

Fig. 5. Prediction results when second-level causes occur

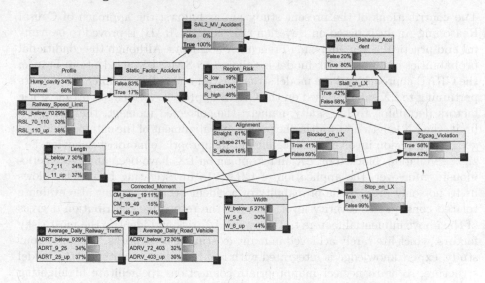

Fig. 6. Cause diagnosis when a train-MV accident occurs

true and "Zigzag Violation" being true. The related consequences are likely to be severer as well.

Subsequently, the "SAL2 MV Accident = True" state is configured as the targeted state. In this way, one can assess the contribution degree of each influential factor to train-MV accident occurrence through reverse inference. Detailed results are given in Fig. 6. It is worth noticing that accidents caused by inappropriate motorist behavior contribute 80% to the entire train-MV accidents at SAL2 LXs, while accidents caused by static factors contribute only 17%. As for inappropriate motorist behavior, "Zigzag violation" is more significant than "Stall on LX" in terms of causing train-MV accidents, due to the contribution of 58% (compared with 42% contribution of "Stall on LX"). On the other hand, in terms of static factors, when a train-MV accident occurs at a SAL2 LX, this LX has the probabilities of 74%, 38%, 44%, 37% and 46% respectively involved in the most risky situations that "Corrected Moment" in the "CM_49_up" group, "Railway Speed Limit" in the "RSL_110_up" group, "Width" in the "W_6_up" group, "Length" in the "L_11_up" group and "Region Risk" in the "R_high" group. These results indicates that more attention needs to be paid to LXs having the above risky static characteristics. Moreover, technical solutions need to be implemented to prevent motorist zigzag violations, for example, transforming SAL2 LXs into SAL4 LXs (Four-half barrier systems) or SAL2F (two-full barrier LXs) or installing median separators between opposing lanes of road traffic in front of SAL2 LXs.

5   Conclusions

The contributions of the present study are as follows: the approach of Causal Reasoning Analysis based on Bayesian risk model (CRAB) is proved to be fruitful and practical when analyzing French LX accidents. Although the conditional probabilities of our BN risk model is tailored to SAL2 LX accidents in France, the CRAB approach and the model structure can be applied to different contexts pertaining to LX safety. Based on the CRAB approach, various important static factors pertaining to LX safety, namely, the corrected moment, the rail speed limit, the LX length and width, the profile and alignment of the entered road and geographic region involved, and significant inappropriate motorist behavior, i.e., zigzag violation, blocked on LX and stopping on LX, have been analyzed meticulously. Moreover, the application of CRAB to investigating LX safety allows us to not only predict the probability of accident occurrence, but also evaluate related consequence severity level, quantify the respective contribution degrees of the above influential factors to the overall LX risk and identify the most risky factors, which are rarely achieved in many existing related works. Besides, in our study, expert knowledge is integrated with real field data to optimize the model structure, so as to neglect inappropriate connections to facilitate highlighting the main causes.

In summary, the outcomes of the BN risk model offer a significant perspective on potential parameters causing LX accidents and pave the way for identifying practical design measures and improvement recommendations to prevent accidents at LXs. In future works, a thorough analysis on inappropriate motorist behavior will be carried out due to its significant contribution to LX accident occurrence. In addition, practical solutions will be proposed to improve LX safety according to the analysis results of the BN risk model and the effectiveness of these solutions (e.g., transforming SAL2 LXs into SAL4 LXs or SAL2F or installing median separators) will be investigated.

Acknowledgements. This work has been conducted in the framework of "MORI-PAN project: MOdèle de RIsque pour les PAssages à Niveau" within the Railenium Technological Research Institute, in partnership with the National Society of French Railway Networks (SNCF Réseau) and the French Institute of Science and Technology for Transport, Development and Networks (IFSTTAR).

References

1. Ghazel, M.: Using stochastic Petri nets for level-crossing collision risk assessment. IEEE Trans. Intell. Transp. Syst. **10**(4), 668–677 (2009)
2. Liu, B., Ghazel, M., Toguyeni, A.: Model-based diagnosis of multi-track level crossing plants. IEEE Trans. Intell. Transp. Syst. **17**(2), 546–556 (2016)
3. SNCF Réseau World Conference of Road Safety at Level Crossings (Journée Mondiale de Sécurité Routière aux Passages à Niveau), France (2011). http://www.planetoscope.com/automobile/1271-nombre-de-collisions-aux-passages-a-niveau-en-france.html
4. SNCF Réseau: 8th National Conference of Road Safety at Level Crossings (8ème Journée Nationale de Sécurité Routière aux Passages à Niveau), France (2015). http://www.sncf-reseau.fr/fr/dossier-de-presse-8eme-journee-nationale-de-securite-routiere-aux-passages-a-niveau
5. Wigglesworth, E.C.: A human factors commentary on innovations at railroadhighway. J. Saf. Res. **32**(3), 309–321 (2001)
6. Read, G.J., Salmon, P.M., Lenné, M.G., Stanton, N.A.: Walking the line: understanding pedestrian behaviour and risk at rail level crossings with cognitive work analysis. Appl. Ergon. **53**, 209–227 (2016)
7. Stefanova, T., Burkhardt, J.-M., Filtness, A., Wullems, C., Rakotonirainy, A., Delhomme, P.: Systems-based approach to investigate unsafe pedestrian behaviour at level crossings. Accid. Anal. Prev. **81**, 167–186 (2015)
8. Larue, G.S., Rakotonirainy, A., Haworth, N.L., Darvell, M.: Assessing driver acceptance of intelligent transport systems in the context of railway level crossings. Transp. Res. Part F Traffic Psychol. Behav. **30**, 1–13 (2015)
9. Lenné, M.G., Rudin-Brown, C.M., Navarro, J., Edquist, J., Trotter, M., Tomasevic, N.: Driver behaviour at rail level crossings: responses to flashing lights, traffic signals and stop signs in simulated rural driving. Appl. Ergon. **42**(4), 548–554 (2011)
10. Tey, L.S., Ferreira, L., Wallace, A.: Measuring driver responses at railway level crossings. Accid. Anal. Prev. **43**(6), 2134–2141 (2011)
11. Ericson, C.A., Li, C.: Fault tree analysis. In: Proceedings of 17th International Systems Safety Conference, Orlando, Florida, pp. 1–9 (1999)
12. Malyshkina, N.V., Mannering, F.L.: Markov switching multinomial logit model: an application to accident-injury severities. Accid. Anal. Prev. **41**(4), 829–838 (2009)
13. Ghazel, M., El-Koursi, E.-M.: Two-half-barrier level crossings versus four-half-barrier level crossings: a comparative risk analysis study. IEEE Trans. Intell. Transp. Syst. **15**(3), 1123–1133 (2014)
14. Chemweno, P., Pintelon, L., Van Horenbeek, A., Muchiri, P.: Development of a risk assessment selection methodology for asset maintenance decision making: an analytic network process (ANP) approach. Int. J. Prod. Econ. **170**, 663–676 (2015)
15. Hu, Y., Zhang, X., Ngai, E.W.T., Cai, R., Liu, M.: Software project risk analysis using Bayesian networks with causality constraints. Decis. Support Syst. **56**, 439–449 (2013)
16. Bouillaut, L., Francois, O., Dubois, S.: A Bayesian network to evaluate underground rails maintenance strategies in an automation context. Proc. Inst. Mech. Eng. Part O J. Risk Reliab. **227**(4), 411–424 (2013)
17. Langseth, H., Portinale, L.: Bayesian networks in reliability. Reliab. Eng. Syst. Saf. **92**, 92–108 (2007)

18. Weber, P., Medina-Oliva, G., Simon, C., Iung, B.: Overview on Bayesian networks applications for dependability, risk analysis and maintenance areas. Eng. Appl. Artif. Intell. **25**(4), 671–682 (2012)
19. Jensen, F.V.: An Introduction to Bayesian Networks, vol. 210. UCL Press, London (1996)
20. Pourret, O., Naim, P., Marcot, B.: Bayesian Networks: A Practical Guide to Applications. Wiley, Hoboken (2008)
21. SNCF: Research on the material of level crossing in 2014, France (2015)
22. Liang, C., Ghazel, M., Cazier, O., El Koursi, E.M.: Risk analysis on level crossings using a causal Bayesian network based approach. Transp. Res. Procedia **25**, 2172–2186 (2017)
23. SNCF Réseau: Statistical analysis of accidents at LXs, France (2010)
24. EN 50126: Railway applications-The specification and demonstration of Reliability, Availability, Maintainability and Safety (RAMS), British Standards Institution (1999)
25. Hanley, J.A., McNeil, B.J.: The meaning and use of the area under a receiver operating characteristic (ROC) curve. Radiology **143**(1), 29–36 (1982)

Deductive Verification of Railway Operations

Eduard Kamburjan[(✉)] and Reiner Hähnle

Department of Computer Science, Technische Universität Darmstadt,
Darmstadt, Germany
{kamburjan,haehnle}@cs.tu-darmstadt.de

Abstract. We use deductive verification to show safety properties for
the railway operations of Deutsche Bahn. We formalize and verify safety
properties for a precise, comprehensive model of operational procedures
as specified in the rule books, *independently* of the shape and size of the
actual network layout and the number or schedule of trains. We decompose a global safety property into local properties as well as composition-
ality and well-formedness assumptions. Then we map local state-based
safety properties into history-based properties that can be proven with
a high degree of automation using deductive verification. We illustrate
our methodology with the proof that for any well-formed infrastructure
operating according to the regulations of Deutsche Bahn the following
safety property holds: whenever a train leaves a station, the next section
is free and no other train on the same line runs in the opposite direction.

1 Introduction

In the paper [14] we reported on our ongoing effort to create a formal and highly
comprehensive model of the regulations described in the rulebooks [4,5] that
govern railway operations of Deutsche Bahn. This executable model is expressed
in terms of the Abstract Behavioral Specification (ABS) language [12], a formal,
concurrent modeling language that follows the active objects paradigm. ABS is
equipped with a program logic that supports specification and verification of
properties expressed over first-order event histories. The program verification
system KeY-ABS [6] allows users to perform mechanical proofs of safety properties for ABS models by means of deductive verification [1]. In [14] we gave a
proof-of-concept that deductive verification of safety properties for our ABS railway model is possible. The main contribution of the present paper is to extend
that approach into a full-fledged *verification methodology* for railway operations.

Rulebooks are long and complex documents that—at their core—describe
those communication protocols between train drivers, controllers, track elements,
etc., that are supposed to guarantee safe operation. Their complexity stems
mainly from the requirement to ensure continuing and safe train operation even
in the case of failure of individual components. Moreover, at any time the system
must guarantee that any safety-critical action cannot be inadvertently revoked or
compromised. Changing a rulebook and having it re-certified is a complex, time-
consuming, and expensive procedure, for which at the moment only minimal tool
support and no formal analysis is available. For this reason, a methodology for

© Springer International Publishing AG 2017
A. Fantechi et al. (Eds.): RSSRail 2017, LNCS 10598, pp. 131–147, 2017.
https://doi.org/10.1007/978-3-319-68499-4_9

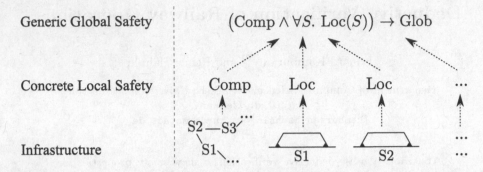

Fig. 1. Decomposition of global safety properties. Loc are local guarantees, Comp composition guarantees, Glob a global safety property. Si are stations.

the formalization and tool-supported verification of safety properties pertaining to rulebooks is highly desirable.

Rulebooks of railway operators state operational rules that are valid for *any* track layout that satisfies certain regulations [5], *well-formed infrastructures*, as we call them. The rules are also valid independent of the number of trains or schedules, as long as these satisfy a valid initial state (for example, not more than one train is placed in each segment). This means that model checking is ruled out as a technique for verification of *global*, system-wide properties. Instead, we use deductive verification in the program logic of ABS, as outlined in Fig. 1.

Assume we want to prove that a global safety property Glob holds in a given ABS model for any well-formed infrastructure, any number of trains and any number of stations S. First, we decompose the proof of this property into proofs for a local guarantee Loc at each station and composition guarantees Comp. For local composition guarantees (for example, aspects of the interlocking system), established model checking techniques may be used. Our approach is not intended to replace established and well-working verification technology, but to *extend* it so as to be able to prove *global* properties of a highly *precise* model. Local guarantees Loc only hold under assumption of a well-formed infrastructure, expressed in Comp.

In this paper we make two contributions: first, a systematic methodological approach to decompose global system properties for any well-formed infrastructure into local guarantees that are then proven by a combination of deductive verification and model checking. As detailed in Sect. 5.1, we prove state-based global properties expressed over actions by transforming them into history-based properties of processes. The latter can then be expressed and proved as local method invariants in KeY-ABS. Second, we demonstrate the viability of our approach with an ABS model of a part of the actual Deutsche Bahn rulebooks and a typical safety property. Contrary to prior work [14] we prove (1) the procedures used in current operations and (2) show a global safety property, rather than only one of its fractions.

The paper is organized as follows: In Sect. 2 we explain very briefly those elements of the ABS language needed to understand the paper. In Sect. 3 we give a short account of the program logic of ABS. Section 4 explains how we modeled railway operations and rules in ABS. Section 5 is the core of the paper where we explain our methodology in detail and sketch the proof of one of the safety properties. We conclude, and give related as well as future work, in Sect. 6.

2   The Abstract Behavioral Specification Language (ABS)

We give a very brief introduction to the Abstract Behavioral Specification language (ABS), for a full account and the formal semantics we refer to [10, 12].

ABS is a modeling language for distributed systems, which has been designed with a focus on analyzability. Its syntax and semantics are similar to Java to maximize usability. We list the main language features (slightly simplified) and the statements associated with them.

Strictly encapsulated objects. Communication between different objects is only possible via method calls. All fields of an object are private and inaccessible even to other instances of the same class and there are no static fields. This ensures that the heap of an object is only accessed by its own processes.

Asynchronous communication with futures. Asynchronous calls are dispatched with the statement Fut<T> f = o!m(e), where method m is called on the object stored in o with parameters e. Upon making this call, the caller obtains the *future* f and continues execution without interrupt. A future is a handle to the called process and may be passed around. Once the called process terminates, its return value may be accessed via the associated future. To read a value from a future, the statement T i = f.get; is used.

Cooperative scheduling. In ABS at most one process is active per object. Running processes cannot be preempted, but give up control only when they suspend or terminate. Hence the ABS modeler has explicit control over interleaving. The active process suspends itself by waiting for a guard. A guard can be a future—then the suspension statement has the form await f?; and the process may become active again once f was resolved (i.e., its process terminated). Otherwise, a guard can be a side-effect-free Boolean expression—then the suspension statement has the form await e; and the process may become active again if e evaluates to true. If a future is accessed with f.get before it was resolved, then the whole object blocks until f is resolved. When blocked, an object may still receive method calls, but it will not execute them.

Cooperative scheduling enables one to reason about code between the start and end of a method, as well as suspension statements, as if it were executed sequentially, because the process is guaranteed to have exclusive access to the memory of its object. ABS is not completely object-oriented, as the enforced asynchronous communication leads to overhead for simple look-up operations. To avoid the overhead, ABS uses Algebraic Data Types (ADT) to abstract from data values which have no internal state. Figure 4 shows an ABS class using the ADT SignalState.

3   The ABS Program Logic

The calculus used for reasoning about concurrency in ABS uses a *history* of *communication events* [6,7], modeled as finite first-order sequences. A communication event is an action on a future: either an *invocation* event modeling an asynchronous method call, an *invocation reaction* event, modeling the start of the corresponding process, a *completion* event modeling the termination of a process, and a *completion reaction* event modeling the read access to a future.

Definition 1 (Events). *Let o, o' range over object IDs, f over futures, e over values and m over method names. The symbol e^* denotes a possibly empty sequence of values and represents the parameters of a method call. Events* Ev *are defined by the following grammar:*

$$
\begin{aligned}
\text{Ev} ::= \quad &\text{invEv}(o, o', m, f, e^*) && (\textit{Invocation Event})\\
\mid \; &\text{invREv}(o, o', m, f, e^*) && (\textit{Invocation Reaction Event})\\
\mid \; &\text{futEv}(o', m, f, e) && (\textit{Completion Event})\\
\mid \; &\text{futREv}(o, f, e) && (\textit{Completion Reaction Event})
\end{aligned}
$$

Histories are used for a compact representation and specification of communication behavior. They abstract away from computations and allow to reason directly about communication on futures.

Figure 2 illustrates the connection of events to processes and futures. Every history h, which an ABS system produces is *well-formed*, satisfying certain conditions on the ordering of events. For example, if there is an $i \in \mathbb{N}$ with $h[i] = \text{invREv}(o, o', f, m, e^*)$, then there must be a $j < i$ with $h[j] = \text{invEv}(o, o', f, m, e^*)$. This condition expresses that every process starts its execution only after it was called. The well-formedness conditions for all event types are listed in [7].

ABS uses invariant reasoning: Safety and consistency properties are formulated as first-order formulas and are shown to hold at the beginning of each method execution and at every suspension point. First-order properties are expressed in the ABS Dynamic Logic (ABSDL) [6], a program logic over statements from the ABS language. Matching the ABS concurrency model, formulas can only access the fields of a single class, hence only reason about a single object. Heap memory is modeled with a dedicated program variable *heap*, which can be accessed and changed with **select** and **store** functions, respectively. While every object has its own heap, multiple heap may be used for technical reasons, e.g., to refer to the state before the method starts.

Example 1. The following formula ϕ expresses that the field 1 on an object **self** is a list containing only positive values:

$$\phi \equiv \forall \, \text{Int} \; k. \; \big(0 \leq k < length(select(heap, \mathbf{self}, 1)) \to select(heap, \mathbf{self}, 1)[k] > 0\big)$$

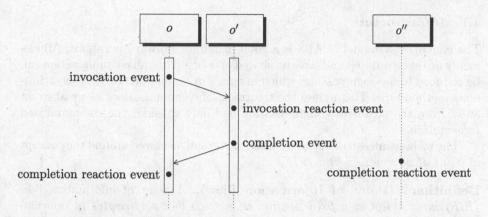

Fig. 2. Events on futures, diagram taken from [6].

ABSDL formulas may reference the history visible to the object in question. Whether an ABSDL formula is an invariant for the methods declared in a class can be mechanically checked with the KeY-ABS theorem prover [6].

Example 2. The following ABSDL formula expresses that if the last element of the history h is a completion event on m, then ϕ holds

$$\forall\, \mathsf{Fut}\ f.\ \forall\, \mathsf{Object}\ e.\ last(h) \doteq \mathsf{futEv}(\mathbf{self}, \mathsf{m}, f, e) \rightarrow \phi$$

ABSDL formulas are inherently local. To specify global properties we use an extension of ABSDL, called ABSDL*, that lifts the restriction to reason about only one object. Therefore, KeY-ABS cannot be used to reason about ABSDL* formulas. To express that the state σ of an object o satisfies the formula ψ at the moment when the i-th event was added to the history we use the notation $\sigma[i](o) \models \psi$.

Example 3. The following ABSDL* formula expresses that whenever object o reads from a future f, then its field k is positive:

$$\forall\, \mathsf{Object}\ o.\ \forall m, f, e, i.\ \Big(h[i] = \mathsf{futREv}(o, f, e) \rightarrow \big(\sigma[i](o) \models select(heap, o, k) > 0\big)\Big)$$

4   Modeling Railway Operations

We give a brief summary of our ABS model for railway operations. Here we are concerned with communication between stations, so we introduce only the most important concepts needed for our safety analysis. In particular, we refrain from describing our train model. The description of the full ABS model is in [14].

4.1   Infrastructure

The concurrency model of ABS is a good match for railway operations: All elements are encapsulated and have no shared memory. Thus all communication can be reduced to message passing, which in turn can be mapped to ABS asynchronous method calls. This unifies the treatment of communication, as we abstract away from the *means* of communication and only consider the communicated *information*.

The railway infrastructure is modeled as a graph, centered around the concept of *point of information flow (PIF)*.

Definition 2 (Point of Information Flow). *A* point of information flow *(PIF) is an object at a fixed position on a track that participates in information flow, if one of the following criteria applies:*

- *It is a structural element allowing a train to receive information, for example, a signal or a data transmission point of a train protection system.*
- *It has a critical distance before another PIF, where its information is transmitted at the latest. E.g., at the point where a signal is seen at the latest.*
- *It is a structural element allowing a train to send information, for example, a track clearance detection device (axle counter), or the endpoints of switches that may transfer information when passed over.*

A PIF is a position at a track and an object that describes the information to be transmitted or relayed. Instead of modeling all features of a PIF in one object, we use a model of four layers to organize and separate its structure:

1. **Graph Layer.** The lowest layer is an undirected graph, where edges correspond to tracks and nodes correspond to the *position* on a track of a PIF. We refer to the set of tracks between two signals as a *section* and to the set of sections between the exit signal of one station and the entry signal of another as a *line*. There may be multiple lines between two stations.
2. **Physical Element Layer.** The second layer corresponds to track elements. Each track element is either a physical device that allows information flow either from or to a *virtual element* that is responsible to model information flow at a specific distance from a physical element. Each element of this layer is assigned to one node of the graph layer. In case several devices are at the same position, a node at the graph layer has multiple track elements assigned.
3. **Logical Element Layer.** The third layer groups physical elements from the second layer, e.g., a pre-signal and a main signal (an exhaustive list of physical elements belonging to a logical object is in [14]). Each physical element can be assigned to multiple logical elements, e.g., a pre-signal can be assigned to two logical signals with two different main signals, or to no logical element, if the physical element never changes its state.
4. **Interlocking Layer.** This layer models the interlocking logic and the communication between stations. Each logical element is assigned to one station.

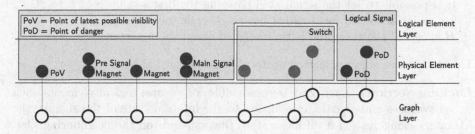

Fig. 3. Illustration of the lower three layers of a station entry in the layer model.

```
1  class SignalImpl(...) implements Signal {
2    SignalState state = STOP;
3    ...
4    Train observedBy = null;
5    Unit triggered() { if (resp != null) resp!triggered(this); }
6    Unit setObserver(Train obs) { observedBy = obs; }
7    Unit setGo() {
8      // ... notify physical elements
9      state = FAHRT;
10     if (observedBy != null) { observedBy!notify(Info(FAHRT),now()); }
11   }
12 }
```

Fig. 4. Simplified implementation of a logical signal.

The lower three layers of a station entry are illustrated in Fig. 3. The (simplified) implementation of a logical signal is shown in Fig. 4.

The lower three layers only communicate up or down. This means that logical objects only communicate to assigned physical objects and to the assigned station at the interlocking layer. Every global property is established by communication on the interlocking layer.

4.2 Communication

The German railway system has different modes of operation for driving trains outside and inside of stations. Here, we focus on operation outside of stations and do not model, e.g., intermediate signals inside of a station. The rulebooks differentiate between two kinds of stations: *Blockstellen* which operate block signals and only divide a track line into two parts to increase the possible number of trains on the line and *Zugmeldestellen* (Zmst) which are able to "store" trains and rearrange their sequence. The generalization of both is *Zugfolgestelle* (Zfst). In the following, we use the term "station" for Zmst.

A Zfst is responsible for safety on the next section, a Zmst is additionally responsible for establishing safety on a whole line. To let a train drive from Zmst A to Zmst B on a line L, the following conditions must be fulfilled:

– It is possible to set the signal at A covering the first section S of L to "Go", i.e., S is not locked by A and A has the permit token for S.
– B accepted the train and is thus notified about its departure.

There are three communication protocols that ensure safety:

Locking sections. Each Zfst is responsible for several logical elements such as switches and signals. In addition to the internal state of the signals, the interlocking system itself has a state that depends on the neighboring Zfst. Each section has an additional Boolean state *locked*. Consider a signal covering a section leading out of the Zfst. After a signal is set to "Go" and a train passes it, the section it covers is automatically *locked* and the electronic message *"preblock"* is sent to the subsequent signal. A signal cannot be set to "Go" again, as long as the section it covers is locked. It must be unlocked by receiving the *"backlock"* message from the subsequent signal. That signal in turn can only send *"backlock"* after the train passed.

Permit token. For each line there is exactly one token that allows a station to admit trains on this line. Without the token the signal that covers the track cannot be set to "Go".

Accepting and reporting back trains. Before a train leaves a station A with destination B, A *offers* the train and waits for B to accept. This ensures that B has (or will have) a track to park the train. Before the train departs, the departure is *announced* to B. The offering, announcement and acceptance of trains are modeled as methods—the current state of a Zmst is not encoded only in its fields, but also in the currently active (but possible suspended) processes.

4.3   Well-Formedness

The interlocking layer in Sect. 4.1 only communicates to logical objects, it has neither direct control nor knowledge about the layers below it. Every Zmst is assuming that its knowledge about the train network is correct and that its fields reflect its state correctly. Consider, e.g., an entrance signal: A station is only notified that the train detection device covering the danger point of this signal was triggered. It relies on the guarantees that (1) the train detection device is set up at the correct position and in the correct direction, (2) the train detection device is assigned to the correct signal and (3) the line covered by the signal is indeed the one which is listed as covered inside the station. The most critical point for this to work is the correct encoding of tracks: The `other` field must realize the mapping between the endparts of a line correctly and the line must correspond to a path in the graph layer.

Definition 3 (Well-Formed Infrastructure). *We say that an ABS railway model is* well-formed, *when its initialization block fulfills the following conditions:*

Correct Encoding of Lines. *Every line corresponds to a path through the graph of the lowest layer and is partitioned correctly into sections according to* *the intermediate signals. The* other *field of the Zmst implementation realizes lines correctly: If a line L has starting sections S, S' then for the neighbouring stations map the section on each other: $S = $ other(S') and $S' = $ other(S). Formally, if L is a line between two stations A and B with starting sections S, S' then the following holds:*

$$S = A.\text{other}(S') = B.\text{other}(S') \qquad S' = A.\text{other}(S) = B.\text{other}(S)$$
$$A.\text{other}(S'') = S \rightarrow S'' = S' \qquad B.\text{other}(S'') = S \rightarrow S'' = S'$$
$$A.\text{other}(S'') = S' \rightarrow S'' = S \qquad B.\text{other}(S'') = S' \rightarrow S'' = S$$

Additionally, for each line L, the method forcePermit, *which initializes the permit token, is called exactly once.*

Correct Encoding of Zfst. *For each section S bordering a Zfst, the field* next *encodes sections correctly. I.e.,* next*(S) is the signal at the end of S. For each signal S', we denote its covered section with S'.covers.*

This definition of well-formedness is suitable for our verification methodology and can be extended. For example, we do not reason about safety inside the stations here, but a fitting well-formedness condition would be the classical notion of safety for interlocking systems. Well-formedness is decidable, but here we are not concerned with checking an initialization block for well-formedness.

5 Deductive Verification

5.1 Methodology

Safety properties in technical documents, e.g. [18] are given as informal descriptions. A system state is considered safe if it fulfills a property. ABS is verified with invariants, which state that the history, i.e., the *past* states have a certain property. To express safety properties of railways we connect *state* invariants with *history* invariants. As described in Sect. 4, we map railway concepts partly to methods instead of fields. E.g., the dispatching of a train is modeled by the method process. In a well-formed infrastructure, we can connect events of methods with the state of the whole system. To model informally stated safety notions in ABSDL we use the following schema:

1. We formulate the safety notion *informally* as a property of the global state.
2. We reformulate the safety notion *informally* as a property of *past actions*.
3. Using the model in Sect. 4, we map actions to methods and states to fields, thus deriving a formal, global invariant of histories in ABSDL*.
4. Finally, we prove the global invariant by splitting it into local invariants by using well-formedness of histories and infrastructure. To connect histories and state, we formulate and prove local invariants with KeY-ABS.

Well-formedness of the infrastructure is needed at two points: In step 3 it is used to connect model and reality: E.g., only in a well-formed infrastructure we can assume that the termination of `process(t)` models a dispatch of train `t` and does not set the route and signal for some other train: we need well-formedness to translate the informal property *"A train t was dispatched."* to *"Method `process(t)` terminated."*. In step 4 well-formedness is used to reason about consistency of the model: E.g., only in a well-formed infrastructure we can assume that a signal `S` covering line `L` is indeed unlocked by the signal at the end of `L`.

We illustrate deductive reasoning with two safety properties. Each of the property establishes (partial) safety on one of the described layers for train departure: The first property establishes that the permit token is exchanged correctly and the second property establishes that a signal is set to "Go" only when the covered section is free. Together with the obvious property that for every line at any given point in time only one station has the token [1], we regard these properties as the safety notion for departure of trains from A to B: the next section is free and the whole line is free of trains going from B to A. For presentation's sake, we only present the proof of the first property in detail.

5.2   Permission

Recall the description of the permit token from Sect. 4: Each line L has an associated token. This token models the permission to dispatch trains on this line. The token is implemented as a field `permit` in the Zmst class that maps the first section of the line to a Boolean value modeling the token. A Zmst has the token for a section st if `permit`[st] is set to `True`. When a station plans to dispatch a train, it must first acquire the token for line L. The exchange is not only secured by the station having the token, but also by the station requesting it: The requesting station knows which trains are on the line in its direction, as all the trains are announced and saved as expected. It only requests the token if it is known that no trains are on the line in its direction. The station having the token only checks that the token is not locked, i.e., it is not in the process of dispatching a train using this token.

We examined the case where only the station having the token secures it in [14], however, that protocol is not in use in modern railway operations of Deutsche Bahn. Here we show the following, more complex, property. This property corresponds to Step 1 in the verification scheme.

> *"If station A acquires the permit token for line L from station B, then there is no train on L with arrival station A."*

Station A acquires the permit token when the call on B.`rqPerm` from method `setPreconditions` terminates. If we assume that all stations are connected correctly, the condition that there are no trains on L with arrival station A can be expressed as A.`expectIn`[st] == `Nil`, where st is the first section of L from A.

---

[1] We do not give a proof for this, as this property follows directly from well-formed infrastructure and that the adding of the token at one end is synchronized to happen after its removal at the other end.

We can rewrite the above property into the following property. This property corresponds to Step 2 in the verification scheme.

"If station A reads from the future for B.rqPerm, then at this moment the following holds: A.expectIn$[st]$ == Nil."

The formulations differ, as the first condition describes a *state*, but the second one additionally the *history*. We can now formalize the property in ABSDL. This property corresponds to Step 3 in the verification scheme. Step 4 is performed in the proof itself.

Lemma 1. *The following formula holds for all histories generated by the model in Sect. 4 with a well-formed infrastructure. Let A be a Zmst and L a line bordering A with st being the first section of L from A and A.other(st) the last.*

$$\phi_1(A, st) \equiv$$
$$\forall i, f.\ h[i] = \mathsf{futREv}(A, \mathtt{rqPerm}, f, [\mathtt{True}, st]) \rightarrow$$
$$\sigma[i](A) \models \mathtt{expectIn}(A.\mathtt{other}(st)) = \mathtt{Nil}$$

Proof. To show that claim expectIn(A.other(st)) = Nil holds at the point where rqPerm is read it must be shown that expectIn is not extended while the process executing setPreconditions is suspended. The method that can do so is offer. So we have to show that between calling and reading True from rqPerm, no process that is executing offer terminates. We distinguish two cases:

1. rqPerm is scheduled after offer is called. In this case the station having the token has locked its token—rqPerm would return False.
2. rqPerm is scheduled before offer is called. In this case the station requesting the token has locked acceptance—offer will not terminate.

The cases correspond to two, intuitively wrong, situations: (1) the token is released by B while it is in the process of dispatching a train (2) a train is accepted by A while it is in the process of requesting the token.

The formal argument is as follows (we mark all properties that were proven mechanically with KeY-ABS with $\mathcal{K}$).[2] First, by the well-formedness axioms there are indices i''', i'', i' with $i' < i'' < i''' < i$ and

$$h[i'] = \mathsf{invEv}(A, B, \mathtt{rqPerm}, f, [A, st])$$
$$h[i''] = \mathsf{invREv}(A, B, \mathtt{rqPerm}, f, [A, st])$$
$$h[i'''] = \mathsf{futEv}(B, \mathtt{rqPerm}, f, [\mathtt{True}, B.\mathtt{other}(st)])$$

Position i' corresponds to a call on rqPerm: the only call is in setPreconditions at line 458. We have the following property, because the statement directly before the call has this condition as its guard.

$$\sigma[i'](A) \models \mathtt{expectIn}(st) = \mathtt{Nil} \land \mathtt{allowed}[st] = \mathtt{False}$$

---

[2] The model, invariants and KeY-ABS and instructions to compile are available under http://formbar.raillab.de/en/publications-and-tools/latest/.

It remains to show that `expectIn` is not modified between the read and the mentioned guard at line 460. The only method adding to `expectIn` is `offer`. I.e, we show that there is no position k with $i' < k < i$ and

$$h[k] = \mathsf{futEv}(B, A, \mathtt{offer}, f', [T, st]))$$

for any `Train` T. Assume there is such a k. Then, by the well-formedness axioms, there are indices k'', k' with $k'' < k'$ and

$$h[k'] = \mathsf{invEv}(B, A, \mathtt{offer}, f', [T, st, B])$$
$$h[k''] = \mathsf{invREv}(B, A, \mathtt{offer}, f', [T, st, B])$$

We have $k' < k'' < k < i$ and make a case distinction

- **Case 1:** $i' < k''$, i.e. the process for `offer` is scheduled after the call on `rqPerm` is made. However, when $A.\mathtt{offer}$ terminates, $A.\mathtt{allowed}[A.\mathtt{other}(st)]$ is set to `True`. This is proven by the following invariant in KeY-ABS:

    $$\forall\, \mathtt{Train}\ T.\ \forall\, \mathtt{Section}\ st. \hspace{3cm} (\mathcal{K})$$

    $$last(h) = \mathsf{futEv}(\mathbf{self}, \mathtt{offer}, f, [T, st]) \to \mathbf{self}.\mathtt{allowed}[st] = \mathtt{True}$$

    Thus $\sigma[k](A) \models \mathtt{allowed}[st] = \mathtt{True}$. But as $\sigma[i'](A) \models \mathtt{allowed}[st] = \mathtt{False}$ holds, it must be set to `True` at some point between i' and k'. The only method setting any key of `allowed` to `True` is `setPreconditions`. Only one such process is active at any one time, thus there cannot be such a modification, and hence no such k' or i'.
- **Case 2:** $k'' < i'$, i.e. the process for `offer` is scheduled before the call on `rqPerm` is made. In this case we cannot rely on the `allowed` field of A. But, $B.\mathtt{unlocked}[st]$ is set to `False` at the moment the call is made, i.e.,

    $$\sigma[k'](B) \models \mathtt{unlocked}[st] = \mathtt{False}$$

    This is proven by the following invariant in KeY-ABS:

    $$\forall\, \mathtt{Train}\ T.\ \forall\, \mathtt{Section}\ st.\ \forall\, \mathtt{Station}\ B. \hspace{2cm} (\mathcal{K})$$

    $$last(h) = \mathsf{invEv}(\mathbf{self}, B, \mathtt{offer}, f, [T, st, \mathbf{self}]) \to \mathbf{self}.\mathtt{unlocked}[st] = \mathtt{False}$$

    But when `rqPerm` terminates and returns `True`, then the line must be unlocked. This is proven by the following invariant in KeY-ABS:

    $$\forall\, \mathtt{Section}\ st. \hspace{4cm} (\mathcal{K})$$

    $$last(h) = \mathsf{futEv}(\mathbf{self}, \mathtt{rqPerm}, f, [\mathtt{True}, st]) \to \mathbf{self}.\mathtt{unlocked}[st] = \mathtt{True}$$

    Thus there cannot be such k' or i'. $\hspace{6cm} \square$

5.3   Train Involvement

Railway signals are managed by interlocking systems, but are not detached from the actual movement of the trains: *Zugmitwirkung* ("Train Involvement") is an

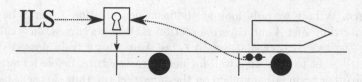

Fig. 5. *Zugmitwirkung* ("Train Involvement"): The train has to trigger the second signal before the first can be set to "Go" again.

established concept in German railway operations and states that certain actions of the dispatcher are linked to actions of the train and their detection by the infrastructure. We show the following property, taken from [18]: A signal can only be set to "Go", if the train that passed it the last time has left the covered track. To ensure this, when a signal is set to "Halt", after a train passed it, the used line is *locked*. A signal can no longer be set to "Go" when the route is set to the line while the signal is locked. A signal can only be unlocked when the signal *at the end of the covered section* sends a *backlock* message. Figure 5 illustrates the situation. The desired property, expressed as a statement over states (Step 1 in the verification scheme):

> "If a non-entry signal S is set to "Go", then the covered section is free of trains going away from it."

Given the procedure described above, we can again rephrase this into a history-oriented version. For presentation's sake, we do not consider the case that a signal may cover multiple sections. Especially we do not deal with the special requirements for entry signals (Step 2 in the verification scheme).

> "If a signal S is set to "Go" twice, then a train triggered the point of danger of the next signal at some time in between."

Using our assumption of well-formed infrastructure (in particular that the **next** field encodes the lines correctly), we can rephrase it more formally with methods and fields as:

> "If there are two position i, j with $j < i$, such that $h[i]$ and $h[j]$ are invocation reaction events on **setGo** on some Signal S covering section S', then there is a k with $j < k < i$ such that $h[k]$ is an invocation reaction event on **trigger** on **next** (S')."

We can now formalize the property in ABSDL as an invariant (Step 3 in the verification scheme, Step 4 is again performed in the proof):

Lemma 2. *The following formula holds for all histories generated by the model in Sect. 4 with a well-formed infrastructure. Let A be a Zmst and S a signal.*

$$\phi_2(A,S) \equiv \forall i. \left(h[i] = \mathsf{invREv}(A, S, \mathsf{setGo}, f, []) \rightarrow \right.$$

$$\forall j. \left(j < i \wedge h[j] = \mathsf{invREv}(A, S, \mathsf{setGo}, f', []) \rightarrow \right.$$

$$\left. \left. \exists\, \mathtt{DangerPt}\; P. \exists k.\; j{<}k{<}i \wedge h[k]{=}\mathsf{invREv}(P, \mathsf{next}(S.covers), \mathtt{trigger}, f'', []) \right) \right)$$

Proof sketch. W.l.o.g we only look at the last such position j. Let S be an exit signal managed by Zfst A and covering section st. Whenever S.setGo is called, the managing Zfst has outLocked[st] set to False. But after a train passed signal S, outLocked[st] is set to True. In a well-formed infrastructure, before a train passed a signal, no other train is dispatched on the same section, thus outLocked[st] must have been set to False. The only such method is backlock which is only called by the next Zfst once a signal has been triggered. In a well-formed infrastructure, this can only be S.next.   □

5.4   Discussion

We have shown the following (informal) theorem:

Theorem 1. *Every train departure is safe: when the exit signal S in station A is set to "Go" for train T on a line L to station B, then the first section of L is free, no train is on L in direction of A.*

Formally, this theorem states that the following is an invariant for all histories produced by the model when executed on a well-formed infrastructure.

$$\forall\, \text{Zmst } A.\ \forall\, \text{Section } st.\ (\phi_1(A, st) \wedge \forall \text{Signal } S.\ \phi_2(A, S))$$

As Lemma 2 also reasons about block signals, we can also state the following:

Corollary 1. *Every train run from station A to station B is safe: during the run, no train will enter the line in the direction of A and whenever a signal is set to "Go", the next section is free.*

Proof sketch. Induction on n, the number of Zfst between A and B.

- Case $n = 0$: In this case this is Theorem 1.
- Case $n = n' + 1$: By induction hypothesis, the train passed the first n' Zfst. By Lemma 1 the permit token cannot be exchanged when the next signal is set to "Go", as the train is still on the line. By Lemma 2 the next section is free, as a Zfst has no entry signals.   □

Formally, Corollary 1 states that the following is an invariant for all histories produced by the model when executed on a well-formed infrastructure.

$$\forall\, \text{Zmst } A.\ \forall\, \text{Section } st.\ \phi_1(A, st) \wedge \forall\, \text{Zfst } Z.\ \forall \text{Signal } S.\ \phi_2(Z, S)$$

We do not discuss entry signal and entrance into stations. German regulations differ between rules inside and outside of stations and in this work we only reason about the outside rules. The shown properties involve multiple communicating parties. More simple properties can be verified directly by reformulation in ABSDL.

Lemma 3. *If a station A accepts a train t, then there is a track reserved for t. I.e., the following is an ABSDL invariant for the ZugMelde class:*

$$\forall\, \text{Train } T.\ \forall\, \text{Section } st.\ \forall\, \text{Station } B. \tag{$\mathcal{K}$}$$

$$last(h) = \text{futEv}(\text{self}, B, \text{offer}, f, [T, st, B]) \to \exists\, \text{Signal } S.\ \text{self.reserved}[S] = T$$

6   Conclusion

Following the feasibility study [14], the present work is the first time deductive verification is applied to railway operations. Prior verification approaches concentrated on single *components*, not on the *communication structure*, and they mainly used model checking. Our method is not intended to replace model checking of interlocking tables and of consistency properties of the infrastructure. On the contrary, we rely on those results by assuming a *well-formed* infrastructure while reasoning about safety at a higher abstraction level. This allows us to reason globally about systems, however, at the cost of full automation.

Our schema for verifying safety properties with active objects and deductive verification is not limited to the safety properties discussed above. It is as well applicable to other domains than railways, as long as state changes can be associated with events visible in the history. The proofs presented here are a combination of mechanized and pen-and-paper proofs. It would have been possible to formalize and mechanize the whole theory and all proofs. The reasons for the decision to refrain from doing so are twofold: (1) the pen-and-paper approach allows to relate the structure of the proof to informal concepts from the modeled domain, for example, the case distinction in Lemma 1. This strengthens confidence in the model. (2) While the theory of local histories is formalized in KeY-ABS, arguments on the level of multiple objects require a more general logic. KeY-ABS was designed and optimized with the verification of single methods in mind—we conjecture that a formalization of stateful *global* histories is possible, but the required amount of effort does not correlate with the benefits of having more confidence in the proof.

Possibly, an other approach than a purely logical approach to compositional reasoning may be a better fit, however, we do not know of any. The automation of decomposition and localization of safety properties in distributed systems is an open research question.

6.1   Related Work

This is the first full-fledged case study on deductive verification of railway operations, but verification of other aspects of railways has a long tradition which is surveyed in [8].

Verifying railway operations so far has been mostly based on model checking, where the state explosion problem prohibits the reasoning about microscopic models with a large number of participants. To mitigate state explosion, several approaches were proposed. Macedo et al. [16,17] describe a topological decomposition that allows to check the monolithic model of the whole network by checking sub-models. They propose two different cuts to split the monolithic model and corresponding criteria for stations, that ensure that composition is sound. Similarly to our approach, composition guarantees are shown outside of the tool. However, they are still restricted to checking scenarios with a fixed number of model elements, no general infrastructure. Their approach has tool support for OCRA [3,15], a refinement-based approach which models component-based infrastructure with LTL contracts. Cappart et al. [2] verify by simulating the most likely runs in a train station. However, their approach is not exhaustive.

A systematic comparison of the differences between our *modeling* of railway operations and previous approaches to model components can be found in [14].

6.2 Future Work

The split of global invariants into local invariants was performed manually. We plan to formulate safety properties as session types [11], which were recently extended to the ABS concurrency model [13]. This will further automate the verification, while the additional structure of session types allows to relate the strucutre of the proof to real world concepts. We are also interested in the verification of non-functional safety properties, especially deadlock-freedom. We plan to extend the DECO tool [9] with all features needed to handle our model. Furthermore, we plan to model all faults described in [4], fully formalizing and verifying the notion of safety provided there and in related technical documents.

Acknowledgments. We thank the anonymous reviewers for their constructive and valuable feedback. This work is supported by FormbaR, "Formalisierung von betrieblichen und anderen Regelwerken", part of AG Signalling/DB RailLab in the Innovation Alliance of Deutsche Bahn AG and TU Darmstadt.

References

1. Beckert, B., Hähnle, R.: Reasoning and verification. IEEE Intell. Syst. **29**(1), 20–29 (2014)
2. Cappart, Q., Limbrée, C., Schaus, P., Legay, A.: Verification by discrete simulation of interlocking systems. In: 29th Annual European Simulation and Modelling Conference ESM, pp. 402–409 (2015)
3. Cimatti, A., Dorigatti, M., Tonetta, S.: OCRA: a tool for checking the refinement of temporal contracts. In: 28th IEEE/ACM International Conference on Automated Software Engineering (ASE), pp. 702–705 (2013)
4. DB Netz AG, Frankfurt, Germany: Richtlinie 408, Fahrdienstvorschrift (2017)
5. DB Netz AG, Frankfurt, Germany: Richtlinie 819, LST-Anlagen planen (2017)
6. Din, C.C., Bubel, R., Hähnle, R.: KeY-ABS: a deductive verification tool for the concurrent modelling language ABS. In: Felty, A.P., Middeldorp, A. (eds.) CADE 2015. LNCS, vol. 9195, pp. 517–526. Springer, Cham (2015). doi:10.1007/978-3-319-21401-6_35
7. Din, C.C., Owe, O.: Compositional reasoning about active objects with shared futures. Formal Aspects Comput. **27**(3), 551–572 (2015)
8. Fantechi, A., Flammini, F., Gnesi, S.: Formal methods for railway control systems. STTT **16**(6), 643–646 (2014)
9. Flores-Montoya, A.E., Albert, E., Genaim, S.: May-Happen-in-Parallel based deadlock analysis for concurrent objects. In: Beyer, D., Boreale, M. (eds.) FMOODS/FORTE -2013. LNCS, vol. 7892, pp. 273–288. Springer, Heidelberg (2013). doi:10.1007/978-3-642-38592-6_19

10. Hähnle, R.: The abstract behavioral specification language: a tutorial introduction. In: Giachino, E., Hähnle, R., de Boer, F.S., Bonsangue, M.M. (eds.) FMCO 2012. LNCS, vol. 7866, pp. 1–37. Springer, Heidelberg (2013). doi:10.1007/978-3-642-40615-7_1

11. Honda, K., Yoshida, N., Carbone, M.: Multiparty asynchronous session types. SIGPLAN Not. **43**(1), 273–284 (2008)

12. Johnsen, E.B., Hähnle, R., Schäfer, J., Schlatte, R., Steffen, M.: ABS: a core language for abstract behavioral specification. In: Aichernig, B.K., de Boer, F.S., Bonsangue, M.M. (eds.) FMCO 2010. LNCS, vol. 6957, pp. 142–164. Springer, Heidelberg (2011). doi:10.1007/978-3-642-25271-6_8

13. Kamburjan, E., Din, C.C., Chen, T.-C.: Session-based compositional analysis for actor-based languages using futures. In: Ogata, K., Lawford, M., Liu, S. (eds.) ICFEM 2016. LNCS, vol. 10009, pp. 296–312. Springer, Cham (2016). doi:10.1007/978-3-319-47846-3_19

14. Kamburjan, E., Hähnle, R.: Uniform modeling of railway operations. In: Artho, C., Ölveczky, P.C. (eds.) FTSCS 2016. CCIS, vol. 694, pp. 55–71. Springer, Cham (2017). doi:10.1007/978-3-319-53946-1_4

15. Limbrée, C., Cappart, Q., Pecheur, C., Tonetta, S.: Verification of railway interlocking - compositional approach with OCRA. In: Lecomte, T., Pinger, R., Romanovsky, A. (eds.) RSSRail 2016. LNCS, vol. 9707, pp. 134–149. Springer, Cham (2016). doi:10.1007/978-3-319-33951-1_10

16. Macedo, H.D., Fantechi, A., Haxthausen, A.E.: Compositional verification of multi-station interlocking systems. In: Margaria, T., Steffen, B. (eds.) ISoLA 2016. LNCS, vol. 9953, pp. 279–293. Springer, Cham (2016). doi:10.1007/978-3-319-47169-3_20

17. Macedo, H.D., Fantechi, A., Haxthausen, A.E.: Compositional model checking of interlocking systems for lines with multiple stations. In: Barrett, C., Davies, M., Kahsai, T. (eds.) NFM 2017. LNCS, vol. 10227, pp. 146–162. Springer, Cham (2017). doi:10.1007/978-3-319-57288-8_11

18. Pachl, J.: Systemtechnik des Schienenverkehrs: Bahnbetrieb Planen, Steuern und Sichern. Springer Vieweg, Berlin (2008)

Safety Analysis of a CBTC System: A Rigorous Approach with Event-B

Mathieu Comptier[1], David Deharbe[1(✉)], Julien Molinero Perez[1],
Louis Mussat[2], Thibaut Pierre[3], and Denis Sabatier[1]

[1] ClearSy System Engineering, Aix-en-Provence, France
{mathieu.comptier,david.deharbe,
julienmolinero.perez,denis.sabatier}@clearsy.com
[2] RATP, Paris, France
louis.mussat@ratp.fr
[3] ClearSy System Engineering, Paris, France
thibaut.pierre@clearsy.com

Abstract. This paper describes a safety analysis effort on RATP's communication-based train control (CBTC) system Octys. This CBTC is designed for multi-sourcing and brownfield deployment on an existing interlocking infrastructure. Octys is already in operation on several metro lines in Paris, and RATP plans its deployment on several other lines in the forthcoming years. Besides the size and complexity of the system, the main technical challenges of the analysis are to handle the existing interlocking functionalities without interfering with its design and to clearly identify the responsibilities of each subsystem supplier. The distinguishing aspect of this analysis is the emphasis put on intellectual rigor, this rigor being achieved by using formal proofs to structure arguments, then using the Atelier B tool to mechanically verify such proofs, encoded in the Event-B notation.

With this approach, we obtain a rigorous mathematical proof of the safety at system level—a level that is usually covered by informal reasoning and domain expert knowledge only. Such proof is thus feasible and it brings to light and precisely records the knowledge and know-how of the domain experts that have designed the system.

1 Introduction

Formal proof, instrumented with a formal method such as Event-B [1] and the accompanying software Atelier B, has been shown to be a powerful tool to perform rigorous safety analysis at the system level [5,6].

Paris metro operator RATP has mandated ClearSy to perform a safety analysis of an existing CBTC system, named Octys. The aim is to prove that the system meets the safety goals: absence of collisions and derailments caused by uncontrolled switches, no over-speeding, and passenger safety. The Octys CBTC system is an assembly of subsystems, including for instance wayside and carborne computers, also linked to external subsystems such as the wayside interlocking. ClearSy's task is to mathematically assert the safety by proving the above safety

A. Fantechi et al. (Eds.): RSSRail 2017, LNCS 10598, pp. 148–159, 2017.
https://doi.org/10.1007/978-3-319-68499-4_10

goals, based on the detailed specifications of these subsystems. We bring out the reasoning ensuring these goals, first in an informal but completely rigorous way, then we turn these reasonings into Event-B models proven with the Atelier-B tool. The role assigned to each subsystem has to be based only on what we find in the subsystems requirements, possibly with addenda or precisions if some requirements turn out to be ambiguous or incomplete.

The Octys CBTC system is particularly fit for this, being the standard system for the automation of existing RATP lines, carried out by a brownfield migration to Grade of Automation level 3 (GoA 3), i.e. train operation is mostly automatic, with a human pilot responsible for starting the train and taking over driving in case of emergencies. Octys is defined through a set of interoperability specifications allowing the use of subsystems from different independent suppliers. Every global function has been carefully split into precise roles for each subsystem, and the resulting requirements have gone through a considerable work, to ensure that each subsystem can be seamlessly purchased from any compliant vendor. This implies in particular very detailed interface specifications. Conversely, this carefully defined decomposition constitutes a system level design that has a paramount global impact, including on the safety. So it would be possible, and undesirable, that all subsystems match their Octys requirements, but that safety issues still remain at the system level. Such pitfalls are difficult to detect and solve, and, in case of failure, the responsibilities would likely be that of the system integrator, namely RATP. This motivates the system level mathematical proof presented here.

In this proof-oriented approach, we produce not only Event-B models and Atelier B proofs, but more importantly textual documents, at least for the sake of usability by users unfamiliar with Event-B. These documents identify the set of requirements from the original subsystem specifications used to perform the proof: because the proof was possible, we know that this set is at least sufficient. All the needed precisions, complements or disambiguations are also listed and explained. What if some requirements from the Octys specifications are not in this set, in particular if they are marked as safety critical? In such cases their role for the safety has to be carefully reviewed: either they are not needed, or something has been missed.

In this paper, we first present details about Octys. Then we describe the organization needed to perform such a proof. To give the reader an insight into how such a proof works, we expose some example mechanisms involved in the safety of Octys and how their rigorous proof is possible. We will also explain a key point: how it is possible to insert the existing interlocking in such a proof, without a detailed knowledge of its legacy design, considering its paramount role in the safety for such brownfield CBTCs. Finally, we discuss the benefits of this approach and the use of the results.

2   The CBTC System Octys

RATP (Paris Transport Authority) is undertaking a vast project to gradually upgrade their subway lines with driver. Accordingly, a *Communication Based*

Train Control (CBTC) solution [3,7] named Octys, for *Open Control of Train Interchangeable and Integrated System,* has been deployed since 2010. As a CBTC system, its main goals are to improve throughput and safety by ensuring continuous train speed control, to participate in ensuring the safety of passenger transfers through the train and platform screen doors, to diminish the headway and to reduce wayside signaling requirements. Also, Octys relies on multi-sourcing and interchangeability. Indeed, the system is split in different sub-parts that are to be developed by different suppliers and interchangeable as any compliant sub-part, whatever its supplier, shall fit seamlessly in the system. Octys has been deployed successively on Paris lines 3, 5 and 9; two other lines are scheduled to be equipped in the near future. Since service should not be disrupted during the migration, a key challenge is to maintain a good level of line availability.

The CBTC has four different subsystems: the train controllers, the zone controllers, the data communication system and the I/O modules (Fig. 1). The train controller is an on-board equipment that estimates the position of the train on the line, according to the cartography, signals from beacons installed along the track, and on-board odometric sensors. This calculated position is communicated to the zone controller subsystem. The second main function of the train controller is to continuously calculate and control the maximum speed authorized for the train depending on movement authority sent by the zone controller. The zone controller uses the train localizations and the interlocking system informations (track circuits, spot detectors, ...) to compute a track occupation mapping. This track occupation is then used to compute movement authority limits for each automatic train. These limits are calculated to avoid train-to-train collisions and derailments over uncontrolled switches. The I/O modules interface zone controllers with the interlocking for data such as track circuits occupation states or signal states. While the communication with the zone controllers is message-based, the interface with interlocking is analog. Finally, the data communication subsystem provides the communication infrastructure between the other equipments.

The specificity of the Octys CBTC is its adaptation to the RATP signaling system: in Octys, the interlocking remains a separated system with a legacy

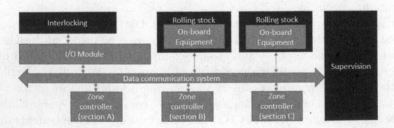

Fig. 1. Octys decomposition into subsystems. The blue blocks represent the wayside CBTC systems, the carborne CBTC systems and the data communication system between the wayside and carborne CBTC systems. The black boxes represent the existing sub-parts to be renewed to operate with the CBTC solution. (Color figure online)

design. Octys functions are tailored so that they fit with this existing design, introducing groups of automated trains in spaces already protected by the interlocking. Indeed, Octys mainly relies on the interlocking to guarantee that trains will not encounter unlocked switches, face-to-face collisions or side collisions over switches (in particular, the Octys CBTC does not move the switches, they remain under the sole control of the interlocking). This close interaction has an important impact on our system level proof as we want it to be independent from the legacy interlocking design; we had to carefully formulate the safety ensured by the interlocking before addition of the CBTC and check that all the modifications involved by the CBTC indeed preserve the system safety. Two examples are presented in Sect. 4.

3 Methodology

3.1 Organization

This project involves three partners: the operator of the system, the safety analysis team, and a solution expert. The system operator is *RATP* and involves experts in both formal methods and railway systems. These experts also have access to the configuration of the existing lines where Octys is deployed and are able to answer clarification requests with respect to the system requirements. The analysis team is from *ClearSy* and initially started with three persons. It gradually built up to a group of five engineers (not all of them working full time on the project), with different technical background, but all with a strong knowledge of formal methods. The solution expert partner is *Siemens* and has a deep knowledge of Octys.

The main input for the analysis consists essentially of a dozen documents in PDF format, on the following subjects: functional and technical system specification describing the overall architecture, the top-level requirements and the main functionalities; specification of each subsystem with the specific hypotheses and requirements; interfaces and communication protocols between the different subsystems; interface between Octys and interlocking; system parameters; the system data base; and the rationale for some (but not all) design choices for the interface between Octys and interlocking. Each such source document is mainly textual, with illustrative diagrams and a few tables.

The partners have monthly meetings where the agenda consists mainly of presentations by the safety analysis team members. Such presentations typically revolve around a specific property: the corresponding Octys mechanism is introduced, illustrated with different scenarios and the draft of the proof mechanism is presented. This serves several purposes: to obtain clarifications and to verify that there is no misunderstanding with respect to the input documents, to validate argument hypotheses, to present proof mechanisms. Also, partners interact regularly by phone or by email, on an on-demand basis, mostly to provide to the safety analysis team the elements they need to conduct their work. Within the safety analysis team, informal discussions over technical issues occur routinely.

3.2 Approach

The goal is to produce a well-founded argument readable by anyone familiar with the main mechanisms of a CBTC, where safety appears as a logical consequence of a set of verified hypotheses. The absence of collision and of derailment derives from precise properties that hold for every possible event. This allows to conclude safety with a network topology that is neither known nor static. In a nutshell, we associate to every train a so called *train protection zone* where it is guaranteed to stay by its own braking forces, if nothing but the train changes on the track. If such zones are safe from collision and derailment, then we may conclude globally. An approach would be to study the evolution of the train protection zones caused by the interlocking and the CBTC functions. However only the CBTC functions are known and documented, whereas the sole hypothesis for interlocking is its safety when no CBTC is added. The key is to prove that each CBTC function leaves train protection zones safe, under the assumption that all the mechanisms of interlocking, that may occur concurrently, are safe.

Initially, some, but not all members of the safety analysis teams, had a strong background in CBTC systems. Of course none of them had previous knowledge of the specifics of Octys. Therefore the initial stage consisted in leveling the domain expertise across the team and in understanding the system. This was achieved by reading the source documents, and by producing so-called *exploratory scenarios*, i.e. simulating the system functionalities according to their understanding of the specification. Such scenarios are validated by the solution expert.

The safety analysis follows a hierarchical decomposition, guided by a top-level analysis of the different levels of protection zones and the impact of the different functions of Octys on these protections. The result is a collection of related safety arguments, each addressing a different target property. When expressing properties, our formal approach proves beneficiary as it demands an unambiguous and meaningful statement. A safety argument is a rigorous demonstration demanding a global understanding of the system. Such demonstration is based on hypotheses, which are justified with unsafe scenarios that would happen in case they do not hold. In some cases, hypotheses are considered as terminal, if close enough to a realistic truth (i.e. it is stated in the input document, is a physical property, or is submitted to validation). Otherwise, an additional demonstration is needed (see examples in Sect. 4).

For each analyzed property, a specific Word document is produced, according to the following template: a *front matter* identifying the document, its author(s) and history; an *introduction* describing the property, the corresponding mechanism, its role in Octys, and a list of reference documents; a statement of the *target property*, with an exposition of the technical aspects of Octys related to this property; a compendium of all *hypotheses* needed to argue that the property stands; the *rigorous demonstration* of the target property under the given hypotheses; the *formalization in B* of this demonstration, given as a set of formal models that have been mechanically verified with the Atelier B tool; a lexicon of *frequently used notions* useful to simplify explanations.

Hypotheses. There are three kinds of hypotheses. Firstly, an hypothesis may be a pointer to a requirement, or set of requirements, found in the source documentation. This is the most common kind of hypotheses, and may come together with a request to change the wording of the requirement. Secondly an hypothesis may be an implicit assumption that needs to be made explicit. It must be submitted to the validation by an authority in the corresponding field. Thirdly, an hypothesis may be a new property about some mechanism of the CBTC. In that case, a proof of the property is necessary and a new document needs to be produced.

Demonstration. It is in textual form, and is sometimes illustrated with pictures. For clarity, entities may be represented by identifiers and conditions stated in mathematical form, yet the argument is presented in a such way that it can be read, followed and verified by an engineer without expertise in Event-B.

Formalization. The Event-B models formalizing the demonstration are included in the document, together with comments. Event-B is a text-based formalism to model systems by both specifying their properties, using classical logic, and describing their behavior, as event-based state machines [1]. Although Event-B is application domain-agnostic, its language includes simple mathematical entities useful for system modeling: integers, sets, relations, sequences to mention but a few. Event-B enforces that the user verify the behavior is consistent with the properties, by including a systematic generation of so-called proof obligations that the user must discharge, with the help of certified automatic and interactive theorem provers. The Event-B models that this project produces are usually of a small to moderate size and little effort is required from the user to discharge the proof obligations. The reason is that each model captures the essence of an argument establishing a specific property and nothing else, this argument has been established beforehand. In some cases, this formalization uncovers a corner case that has been omitted in the original argument. It usually requires little work to rectify the argument and the corresponding Event-B model.

How do we ensure that Event-B models do not miss a technical detail, rendering the proof irrelevant? Imagine for instance some kind of back-door functionality requested in a remote part of a document, that would bypass the proven mechanisms. There is obviously no other method to avoid this than to go through all the source documents. We do this exhaustive coverage in a traced way; for each document section we verify that it *does not contradict* what was modeled. Indeed, as we model only what is needed to ensure the target safety properties, functional and performance related mechanisms are not detailed. To give a rough example, we model that a train will stop before its movement authority limit but we do not model anything predictive about how it could accelerate. Nevertheless we do model that, when not braking in emergency, the train may accelerate at any time, so all functionalities linked to starting train movements (while not braking in emergency) in the source documents do not contradict the models. So we have to check this for all models and all the source documents—a demanding task, but the grouping of source documents by topics is of great help here. If a requirement was given in the wrong source document regarding this topic splitting, it would not be applicable correctly anyway.

4   Illustrative Examples

4.1   Track Circuits Backup Example

As stated in Sect. 2, railway interlocking systems use sensor devices, such as track circuits, to detect trains. For instance, interlocking maintains a switch locked as long as occupation of the track portion containing this switch holds, ensuring protection against derailment on an uncontrolled switch (a top-level safety property).

When a track circuit (TC) fails, it falls back to the occupied state. For interlocking, this means that this track portion is potentially unsafe and that trains should be prevented from entering it. Consequently, this fall-back behavior preserves safety, but at the expense of availability. To improve throughput, Octys has a function to back up TC occupancy, based on a logical tracking of trains done by the zone controller. When Octys TC backup is enabled, interlocking sees the track portion free if one of the sensor state and the output of this backup function is free.

The backup modifies the timing between the detection of a train by a TC and the acquisition of the information by interlocking. The traditional path corresponds to the relay drop time (approximatively 200 ms). With backup, the path requires additional time due to communication and processing. Therefore, safety cannot be guaranteed without a careful analysis.

Without hypotheses on maximum train speed, minimal train length or minimal TC size, this new "occupation delay" may be so large that a train could have left the TC area when it is seen occupied by interlocking. In theory, this consideration exists already with the legacy system, but with a maximum delay of 200 ms, it is clearly not an issue in practice. This is no longer the case when the backup interfere, so a detailed analysis to prove that, when TC backup is enabled, interlocking still ensures protection against derailment has been performed. Essentially this analysis boils down to show whether the new delay is small enough to ensure that interlocking will always follow train progression based on TC information. This provides us the following *target property* (see also Fig. 3).

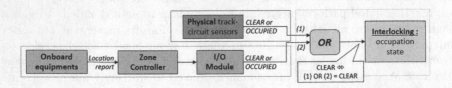

Fig. 2. Flow of information for the track circuit backup.

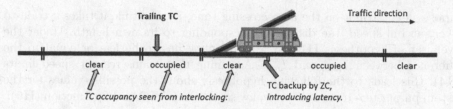

Fig. 3. Trailing TC.

When a train circulates on an oriented track portion, covered by a set of TCs $N_0, N_1, \ldots, N_k$, there exists continuously a so-called "trailing track circuit" having the following properties:

- interlocking sees it as occupied;
- the tail of the train is downstream the area covered by this TC.

The existence of such trailing TC ensures that interlocking maintains locked the switches not yet crossed by the train and consequently protects the train progression, as it did originally with TC sensors (see Fig. 2).

The *proof* of this property uses induction and consists in showing that, assuming N_0 is a trailing TC at time t_0, then there exists a t_1 such that $t_0 \leq t_1$ and both N_0 and N_1 are trailing TCs. A simplified version of this argument follows. Let us introduce a few notations: N being a TC,

- $T_i(N)$: the time the train enters the area covered by N;
- $T_o(N)$: the time the rear of the train leaves the area covered by N;
- $T_{occ}(N)$: the time interlocking starts seeing N occupied;
- $T_{fre}(N)$: the time interlocking starts seeing N free again.

This notation being set, we claim that:

$$T_{occ}(N_1) \leq T_{fre}(N_0) \tag{1}$$

The argument to establish those properties is based on the following hypotheses:

H1. Once a train has occupied a TC N, this TC takes a minimum delay $T_{min} \geq 0$ before it is freed upon the train leaving completely the area covered by this sensor: $T_o(N) + T_{min} \leq T_{fre}(N)$. *Explanation:* This is essentially equivalent to say that a TC cannot become free while under a train. Note that, otherwise, the legacy system would not have been safe.

H2. After a train gets on a TC N, this TC will eventually be seen occupied by interlocking before a maximum delay T_{max}: $T_{occ}(N) \leq T_i(N) + T_{max}$. *Explanation:* This is the same as stating that a train cannot "jump over" a TC. Again, otherwise the legacy system would not have been safe.

By applying **H1** to N_0 and **H2** to N_1, and assuming TCs are contiguous (**H3**), the additional hypothesis $T_{max} - T_{min} \leq T_o(N_0) - T_i(N_1)$ establishes inequality 1. This condition is sufficient to establish the proof. Essentially, it imposes a constraint on the auto-crossing time, i.e. the time it takes a train to cover, at full speed, the distance corresponding to its own length. Under the given set of hypotheses **H1**–**H3**, this quantity has to be less or equal to the difference between $T_{\max}$ and $T_{\min}$. Assuming that trains respect speed limits (**H4**), this leads to the following hypothesis about the possible values for the system parameters to be able to deploy safely Octys' TC backup function (**H5**):

$$T_{\max} - T_{\min} \leq \frac{\text{MinLength}}{\text{MaxSpeed}}$$

Comments. The actual proof of the property takes into account other system parameters, namely the gap of shunt between consecutive TCs and the non-shunting dimensions at the ends of the trains. The existence and the value of $T_{\min}$ and $T_{\max}$ must be verified by another study which needs to consider other functionalities of the CBTC. We have verified that the values of the system parameters in Octys are such that hypothesis **H5** is indeed fulfilled, even though neither the hypothesis nor its argument are explicit in the source document. The analysis has been coded as an Event-B model and validated with Atelier B, guaranteeing the correctness of the reasoning presented with no possible contest.

Our analysis based on formal proofs aims to uncover such arguments, done during the design phase, and to explicit all necessary hypotheses. For the backup function, we exhibited an hypothesis that constrains the possible values of the system parameters and demonstrated that it is necessary to fulfill it to avoid sequences of events leading to the derailment of a train over uncontrolled switches.

4.2   Emergency Cancellation/Nominal Crossing Example

In railway interlocking, setting a route reserves a space for a train, where it can progress with the guarantee that it is protected against collisions and derailments on uncontrolled switches. When an emergency cancellation is requested, the route signal turns red so that no train can enter it. But the route signal also turns red as soon as a train occupies the first TC of that route. In Octys, signal status is an input to several functions of the ZC. For automated Octys trains, localization uncertainties difficult identifying the cause of the signal change by the ZC. If the ZC wrongly identifies the cause of the signal change, it may either force an unnecessary emergency brake of the train or authorize it to progress on an unprotected route, as explained below.

First, consider a localized automated train K that crosses a signal S that turns red because K occupies the first TC after S. The new aspect of S is communicated to the zone controller (ZC). Also, K being localized, its position is calculated by the on-board calculator then transmitted to the ZC. Note that this position is tainted with two uncertainties: the measurement, transmitted as well and known by the ZC; and the flight time of the messages. For the ZC, K has been localized some seconds ago between two extreme positions. In this scenario, the last position of K received by the ZC does not allow it to conclude that the train has occupied the first TC. Assessing the situation, the ZC cannot exclude the possibility that K is still approaching S, which could have turned red due to a cancellation. This uncertainty occurs nominally, and commanding the train to brake here would impair seriously availability. So the CBTC shall avoid stopping a train on a red signal if there is a doubt that this red signal may be caused by the progression of K.

Second, consider again a train K approaching a signal S, but now an emergency cancellation occurs, causing S to turn red. As in the previous scenario, the new aspect of S is communicated to the ZC, and due to the uncertainty in the localization information, the ZC may see the head position of K downstream S. Since the ZC cannot exclude the possibility that K has crossed the signal, it cannot command to brake immediately. If nothing is done though, K may cross S after the moment when the emergency destruction was executed. K would risk either derailing on a moving switch or colliding against another train engaged in a conflicting route set later.

The solution to this uncertainty is to delay braking after the signal turned red. Nevertheless, this delay shall imperatively end soon enough to ensure that K will be stopped before the route cancellation delay expires. As far as formalism is concerned, the proof consists in exhibiting the reason why K is safe, either if it is stopped soon enough, or if it crosses the signal before the deadline.

Synthesis. On the one hand, a supplier wishing to implement the ZC subsystem should obey rigorously the safety demand and command the train to brake before it is too late, on the other hand, it should also optimize the functionality for its system, by providing the widest possible window for the train to cross the signal. In order to meet both criteria, an unambiguous description of the last moment at which the ZC should command the braking is needed. Conveniently, one corollary result of the formal argument we developed for this case is the valuation of the maximum delay before a ZC commands the braking.

5   Discussion and Lessons Learnt

As presented before, for each target property we analyze the mechanisms and we find the "reason why it always holds" *before* writing Event-B models. However we discovered that the reasoning is far from being complete until the corresponding Event-B models are written and proved. It appears that it is very difficult, or nearly impossible, to obtain the expected rigor without formulating in some kind of mathematical language; Event-B and the Atelier B tool serve here as a test of rigor. Of course, we have to ensure that all aspects of the reasoning are correctly captured in the B models: this is done by verifying that if we remove any required hypotheses according to the informal reasoning, the proof in the B model actually becomes impossible.

With this process we isolate a set of hypotheses sufficient to ensure each property; these hypotheses have to be requirements found in the input documents, sub-properties proved afterwards, or agreed precisions to be added. Our output documents detail these requirements and precisions: this is probably the most important benefit of this work, as it allows the identification of possible pitfalls and the improvement of the source documents. One interesting case is when some requirements marked as safety critical are not used in our reasoning. Then the topic must be carefully examined with the domain experts to find out what those requirements were meant for. This can be difficult as Octys is based on the design of existing CBTCs that were developed over a long period of time.

Anyway, the interaction maintained with the domain experts is of paramount importance. This is not an easy topic: the proof team in this effort arrives after the design, as a kind of independent assessment in an already multi-supplier context, and the proof directly deals with the know-how and the know-why of this design. Any pitfall or needed precision that we find will be correctly taken into account only if the involved domain experts have enough time to carefully check these findings and are convinced. Then this contribution is perceived as a benefit, not a burden.

The ideal solution would be that the proof team be present with the design team from the time of what we could call the "prospective design ready" phase, i.e. when the design exists but is not yet finalized. There the notions found by the proof team could be directly used by the design, with benefits in obtaining the system level safety as well as in optimizing the subsystem requirements, potentially leading to an easier development of subsystems. We think that the proof team shall remain separated from the design team, as proof as well as design are demanding tasks that deserve a full dedication and because the proof team shall remain neutral regarding the choice of design solutions. A frequent and trusted interaction between the teams, although not necessary, would make the approach even more efficient and beneficial.

In the case of a multi-supplier interoperability specification like Octys, the interaction between design and proof is more complicated: the system level design is stabilized and the subsystems' design is the responsibility of suppliers, either existing or future. In this context the subsystem properties used as assumptions in our proofs could become target proof goals for the design of these parts. RATP uses formal methods to assert the correctness of such subsystems' design, particularly at software level by verifying the software source code of the supplier. So the output proof assertions from the system level proof could be used as target properties for this software formal verification. This is not yet done but certainly forecasted.

6   Conclusion

We have presented an on-going effort to analyze the safety of a CBTC system designed for deployment on existing interlocking using a rigorous approach. This approach consists in expressing properties key to the system safety, both in natural language and mathematical notation, and in constructing formal proofs that these properties hold. During the construction of these proofs, all necessary hypotheses are identified, be they explicitly stated in the specification of the system, physical laws, or requirements appearing to be missing from the specification.

While this effort is yet unfinished, it is now clear that such system level proof is feasible for a system like the Octys CBTC, with the appropriate level of independence with the intricate but out of scope interlocking. The findings are discussed in an on-going basis and already provide their benefits. In addition, the output results are expected to be used as input properties for subsystem formal analysis performed by RATP [2].

We forecast that the future Octys instantiations will put into light the benefits of this proof, through the presence of well established, strong safety related reasonings and the absence of system level pitfalls or doubts. We believe that this work will stimulate the application of this kind of system level proof for industrial projects.

References

1. Abrial, J.R.: Modeling in Event-B: System and Software Engineering. Cambridge University Press, Cambridge (2010)
2. Bonvoisin, D.: 25 years of formal methods at RATP. From manual approach for proof of programs to instrumented demonstration of railway systems safety (2016)
3. Forioni, S.: An Innovative Approach and An Adventure in Rail Safety. Computer Engineering Series. Wiley, New York (2014)
4. Lecomte, T., Pinger, R., Romanovsky, A. (eds.): RSSRail 2016. LNCS, vol. 9707. Springer, Cham (2016). doi:10.1007/978-3-319-33951-1
5. Sabatier, D.: Using formal proof and B method at system level for industrial projects. In: Lecomte, T., et al. [4], pp. 20–31. doi:10.1007/978-3-319-33951-1_2
6. Sabatier, D., Burdy, L., Requet, A., Guéry, J.: Formal proofs for the NYCT Line 7 (Flushing) modernization project. In: Derrick, J., Fitzgerald, J., Gnesi, S., Khurshid, S., Leuschel, M., Reeves, S., Riccobene, E. (eds.) ABZ 2012. LNCS, vol. 7316, pp. 369–372. Springer, Heidelberg (2012). doi:10.1007/978-3-642-30885-7_34
7. Tremblin, C., Lesoille, P., Rezzoug, O.: Use of Formal Proof for CBTC (Octys). Computer Engineering Series. Wiley, New York (2014)

B-PERFect

Applying the PERF Approach to B Based System Developments

Alexandra Halchin[1,2]([✉]), Abderrahmane Feliachi[1], Neeraj Kumar Singh[2],
Yamine Ait-Ameur[2], and Julien Ordioni[1]

[1] RATP, ING/STF/QS, 54 Rue Roger Salengro, 94724 Fontenay-sous-Bois, France
{alexandra.halchin,abderrahmane.feliachi,julien.ordioni}@ratp.fr
[2] INPT-ENSEEIHT/IRIT, 2 Rue Charles Camichel, 31071 Toulouse, France
{Alexandra.Halchin,nsingh,yamine}@enseeiht.fr

Abstract. An independent safety assessment of railway software systems
is performed by RATP (Régie Autonome des Transports Parisiens) for all
safety-critical systems before their deployment in its network. Whenever
possible, this activity is performed using the PERF approach (Proof Executed over a Retro-engineered Formal model). PERF is a methodology
which handles formal verification of already developed software. This approach is applied to a variety of software systems, developed using languages
such as SCADE, Ada or C. It provides an alternative verification that can
be applied for the independent safety assessment of critical systems used by
RATP. In this paper, we propose the B-PERFect method to generalize the
application of the PERF approach for critical systems which are based on
the B method. In particular, this paper focuses on transformation strategy
from B language to the pivot language of PERF: HLL. HLL is a synchronous data-flow language equipped with formal verification techniques. The
differences between B and HLL are pointed out and the translation process
is presented in this regard.

Keywords: PERF · B method · HLL · Safety assessment · Translation

1 Introduction

For several years, RATP has been involved in the application of formal verification techniques to assess the safety level of railway systems. RATP pays
a lot of attention to the safety of its deployed systems. This safety regime is
implemented through a mandatory internal independent safety assessment of all
safety-critical railway systems. It gave birth to a formal verification methodology
called PERF [3]. It is an independent assessment that helps to double-check the
safety of the developed software in addition to the verification performed by the
software supplier.

PERF was designed to be applicable to any software system independently
of their development processes and languages. By taking the source code of
the developed software as the target of the verification, it ensures a complete

© Springer International Publishing AG 2017
A. Fantechi et al. (Eds.): RSSRail 2017, LNCS 10598, pp. 160–172, 2017.
https://doi.org/10.1007/978-3-319-68499-4_11

language-agnostic and non-interference with the software supplier which drastically reduces any possible bias. It also allows for applying formal verification techniques to the safety assessment activity, which is not always achieved by the software supplier in its safety verification.

In order to support the different solutions of all RATP's suppliers, a number of translators were developed and integrated into PERF. These translators give a formal representation of the targeted source code in the PERF's pivot language HLL, a synchronous data-flow language, similar to Lustre, allowing to express, in the same formalism, the system behavior as well as safety requirements. The role of the translators is to give a semantics-preserving formalization of the software to be analyzed in HLL. Currently, translators for SCADE, Ada and C languages are integrated in the PERF tool chain.

In a similar vein, the B-PERFect project was initiated in order to investigate the applicability of PERF on software systems developed using the B method [1]. Software systems developed using B are valid by construction with respect to safety requirements. The idea behind the B-PERFect project is not to replace the formal verification process of B but to propose a verification alternative to be used for the internal independent safety assessment. This will not question the proof process of B. However, it may eventually reveal any error in the initial formalization of safety requirements.

This paper describes a new approach for software safety verification and gives an overview of a translation process from B0 (a subset of B language close to imperative programs) to HLL, the pivot language of PERF. Moreover, it shows the general architecture of the code generation process, including technical challenges related to tool development. Section 2 introduces the context of this work and motivates the proposed approach. The required background related to the B method and HLL is described in Sect. 3. Section 4 presents the general translation strategy. In Sect. 5, we present some related works. Finally, Sect. 6 concludes our work along with future directions.

2   Context

RATP operates one of the most complex urban multi-modal public transportation networks in the world. In the Parisian region, its network includes 16 metro lines, 2 RER (intercity trains) lines, 7 tramway lines and more than 300 bus lines; transporting not less than 10 Million passengers each day. RATP has built, throughout the years, a rich expertise not only in operating transportation networks, but also in the engineering of railway transportation systems. This expertise made RATP one of the world pioneers in metro automation and one of the experts in automating existing lines.

The growing demand of transportation capacity coupled with continuous advances in computer technology accelerates the obsolescence of existing systems. These factors, added to the improvement and modernization desires, have led RATP to upgrade its network by adopting integrated and upgradeable solutions, through partially or fully automated transportation systems. The coexistence of these different systems brings additional difficulties, particularly related to the safety assessment of the railway systems which depend on the automation level of these systems. One major concern of RATP is to ensure the safety of any deployed system on the network during all the project phases.

In order to guarantee a better and more extensive safety analysis, RATP's engineering department (ING) relies, whenever possible, on rigorous verification methodologies based on formal methods. One of the first application of formal methods in an RATP project goes back to the late eighties were the Z method revealed a number of safety critical bugs for the SACEM system (RER A) which already passed the tests campaign. This successful application of formal methods led RATP to require their use by all safety-critical software systems suppliers. As a consequence, the development of the first driverless metro line in Paris (Line 14) in 1998 was realized using the B formal method. The safety of the system was proven by the construction which helped to remove all testing phases while guaranteeing a complete coverage.

The use of formal methods cannot be required by RATP anymore because, according to the regulations, this would promote some suppliers over the others. However, the use of a formal development method is still highly recommended by RATP to all its suppliers. In addition, an independent safety assessment is performed internally by RATP. RATP's opinion is that using formal methods independently of the supplier reveals usually more bugs than the simple verification of the supplier's testing campaign. Since the 2000s, RATP is working with different suppliers, using different development methods and languages. This heterogeneity requires RATP to master all its supplier methods and languages, which introduced a skill management difficulty with regards to the assessment process. The solution was to use a unified verification approach, pointed as an "ex post facto" proof, for the different projects which allows for the application of formal verification independently of the supplier's development language or method.

This situation was the starting point of the PERF (Proof Executed over a Retro engineered Formal model) methodology and its supporting team. The technique has been successfully used on Thales, Ansaldo and Alstom (ex-Areva TA) products, in charge of the Computer Based Interlocking Lines 1, 4, 8 & 12, the wayside and the on-board equipment of CBTC (Communication Based Train Control) Line 3, 5, 9 & 13 projects. PERF is now applied in every project, whenever possible, meaning essentially when the source language of the software is supported. This is currently the case for projects developed using C, Ada or Scade languages. The general workflow of the PERF methodology is given in Fig. 1. The real strength of PERF is its supporting tool chain, composed of translators, counter-example analyzers and SAT-based proof engines [17].

A number of projects keep using the B method for the development of safety-critical systems. In this case, the independent assessment is a bit more complicated and might be intrusive in some situations. Even though the formal verification performed by the B proof engines can be trusted, the validation of the safety properties can only be performed by cross-reading which, besides being a tedious task, may not be very effective. The idea of the B-PERFect project is to provide an independent alternative for the verification of the safety

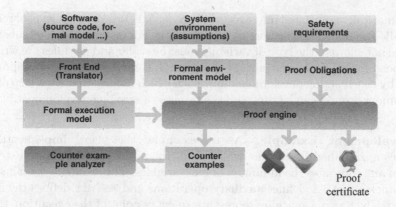

Fig. 1. The PERF verification workflow

properties on systems developed using the B method. The B code is transformed in a HLL formal execution model. To this model, the safety requirements targeted by the verification are added and the entire model is passed to the prover. By doing so, one can prove initial system properties which are expressed in natural language. The idea behind this is not to prove again the existent B code but to check if safety properties were modeled correctly in the initial code. The PERF approach makes this verification non intrusive and also supports the verification of the code generation process if needed. It will also help, in the context of heterogeneous systems, to apply a unified verification to all system components.

3   Background

B Method. The B method is a formal method based on first-order logic and set theory. It can handle a complete critical-software development process from specification to code [1]. The B development process is layered. Each layer corresponds to an abstraction level and the refinement provides the relation between layers. This method has proven its feasibility for large-scale industrial applications, particularly in railway domain [2].

Models are represented in B as machines. A machine contains state variables, instances of other machines, a state invariant, an initialization clause and operations acting on the defined variables. Generally, B project models represent a state transition system in which the initialization clause sets the initial values of variables and the operation clause specifies how variables are modified from one state to another. The invariant describes the safety properties of the model and is specified using predicate logic. The highest level of abstraction is the specification, a representation of functional requirements and the lowest one corresponds to the implementation where only programming-like constructs are allowed [7]. The refinement is the process of transformation from an abstract model into a concrete model specified in a subset of the B language: the B0 language, which can be automatically translated into executable code [5,14,18,19]. Last level of refinement called implementation must be deterministic. For instance, parallel substitutions are not allowed, the type of variables must be scalar and modules are written in a procedural style. The advantage of using the B method is that it supports a correct by construction development approach which implies that each step of the development process can be proved if the target is a zero bug development.

B Development Example. As an example, the below implementation describes a simplified B machine which reads the input values from an external machine and computes the minimum of two variables. This example contains two B machines: Utils_i defines auxiliary operations and Main_i defines the main program. The Main_i machine represents an entry point of the execution. Main is an operation to select an order of the execution using defined operations in the imported machine. In the example, firstly, the operation computeSum is called that changes the state of the machine Utils_i as a side effect. The variable xx is initialized using the output of the operation readVar. This operation returns the value of a variable which is modified when computeSum is called. Finally, the minimum of two variables is computed using the operation minimum.

```
1  IMPLEMENTATION Main_i REFINES Main IMPORTS Utils
2  CONCRETE_VARIABLES xx,yy,rr
3  INVARIANT xx ∈ NAT ∧ yy ∈ NAT ∧ rr ∈ NAT
4  INITIALISATION xx:= 0 ; yy:= 0 ; rr:= 0
5  OPERATIONS
6    Main =
7     computeSum; xx <-- readVar; rr <-- minimum (xx , yy)
8    END
9  END
```

Listing 1. Main Implementation of B Machine

```
1  IMPLEMENTATION Utils_i REFINES Utils
2  CONCRETE_VARIABLES sum
3  INVARIANT sum ∈ NAT
4  INITIALISATION sum:= 0
5  OPERATIONS
6   rr <-- minimum (aa, bb) =
7     IF aa >= bb THEN rr:= bb ELSE rr:= aa END;
8   computeSum  =
9    VAR ii IN ii:= 0;
10       WHILE ii < 2 DO
11          ii:= ii + 1; sum:= sum + ii;
12       INVARIANT ii ∈ NAT ∧ ii ≤ 2
13       VARIANT 2 - ii
14       END
15    END;
16   rr <-- readVar =
17       rr:= sum
18  END
```

Listing 2. Utils Implementation of B Machine

HLL, the Pivot Language of PERF. The PERF approach is built around HLL (High Level Language), a formal declarative and synchronous data flow language in the tradition of LUSTRE [11]. Models are defined by typed streams that can be composed using either temporal or data operators. Temporal operators can be used to describe clock-dependent expressions. The data operators, such as arithmetic, logical and array operators, are used to manipulate streams values. The declarative nature of the language makes it suitable for the definition of formal models as well as safety properties.

An HLL model is described by a number of sections containing type definitions, constant definitions, stream declarations and definitions, proof obligations, constraints and namespaces definitions. Streams can have integer or boolean values and they are interpreted in the mathematical sense, without any notion of side effects. The notion of sequentiality is absent, which means that the order of the items does not affect the meaning of the HLL model. A HLL project is organized in *namespaces* sections. Streams are declared in *declarations* blocks with type checking information, and their values are given in the *definitions* blocks. The *proof obligations* block contains a set of properties related to streams for verification purpose. *Constraints* expressions are used to reduce the domain definition of unbound input streams.

HLL Development Example. This section describes the HLL model that would result from translating the B example given above. The produced HLL model contains two namespaces, one corresponding to the translation of the Main_i machine and another for the translation of the imported machine Utils_i. For each B operation, a corresponding HLL namespace section is created, such as "Main" which contains the translation of the B operation Main.

```
1   Namespaces: "Main_i"{ // B: Main_i implementation
2   Declarations:
3   int "xx"; int "yy"; int "rr"; int "xx<0>"; int "yy<0>";int "rr
    <0>";
4   Definitions:   "xx<0>" := 0; "yy<0>" := 0; "rr<0>" := 0;
5   "xx" := "Main"::"xx<1>"; // B: xx <-- readVar;
6   "yy" := "Main"::"yy<0>";
7   "rr" := "Main"::"rr<1>"; // B: rr <-- minimum(xx,yy)
8   Namespaces: "Main"{ // B: Main operation
9   Declarations: int "xx<0>"; int "yy<0>"; int "rr<0>";
10  Definitions:
11  "xx<0>" := "Main_i"::"xx<0>"; // Maps the initial values of
    variables
12  "yy<0>" := "Main_i"::"yy<0>";
13  "rr<0>" := "Main_i"::"rr<0>";
14  "xx<1>" := "Utils_i<0>"::"readVar<0>"::"rr"; // Operation call
15  "rr<1>" := "Utils_i<0>"::"minimum<0>"::"rr"; // Operation call
16  }}
```

Listing 3. HLL Translation of Main Machine

HLL is an SSA language (Single State Assignment) since, in a model, a stream can be assigned only once. As stated in [8], when converting from a programming language to SSA form, assignments of a program variable are replaced with assignments to new versions of the variable. Each B assignment will thus be translated to an HLL assignment with a new version of the modified variable. The value of the original variable is replaced by the value of the last known version of this variable.

```
17   Namespaces: "Utils_i<0>"{ // B:Utils_i implementation
18   Declarations: int "sum<0>";  int "sum<1>";
19   Definitions:  "sum<0>" := 0;
20   "sum<1>" := "computeSum<0>"::"sum";
21   Namespaces: "computeSum<0>"{ // First call of B: computeSum
     operation
22   Declarations:
23   int "sum<0>"; int "ii<0>"; int "ii<1>"; int "ii<2>"; int "sum";
24   Definitions:
25   "sum<0>" := "Utils_i<0>"::"sum<0>"; "ii<0>" := 0;
26   // While Loop - iter 0
27   "ii<1>" := "ii<0>" + 1;
28   "sum<1>":= "sum<0>" + "ii<1>";
29   "ii<2>" := if "ii<0>" < 2 then "ii<1>" else "ii<0>";
30   "sum<2>" := if "ii<0>" < 2 then "sum<1>" else "sum<0>";
31   //... Repeat the loop code with new index
32   "sum" := "sum<4>";
33   }
34   "readVar<0>"{ // First call of B: readVar operation
35   Declarations: int "rr";
36   Definitions: "rr":= "Utils_i<0>"::"sum<1>";
37   }
38   "minimum<0>"{ // First call of B: minimum operation
39   Declarations:
40   int "aa<0>";int "bb<0>";int "rr";int "rr<0>";int "rr<1>";int"rr
     <2>";
41   Definitions:
42   "aa<0>" := "Main_i":":"Main"::"xx<1>"; //Mapping of input
     parameters
43   "bb<0>" := "Main_i"::"Main"::"yy<0>";
44   "rr<0>" := "bb<0>"; // IF block substitution
45   "rr<1>" := "aa<0>"; // ELSE block substitution
46   "rr<2>" := if "aa<0>" >= "bb<0>" then "rr<0>" else "rr<1>";//IF
     block
47   "rr" := "rr<2>";
48   }}
```

Listing 4. HLL Translation of Utils Machine

Line 3 defines the variables used for the translation of the machine Main_i with their corresponding type. Line 4 and lines 8–16 represent the computation done in blocks INITIALISATION and OPERATIONS of the B machine, respectively. In line 14, the output of the operation readVar is assigned to the local variable "xx<1>". Note that state variables are necessary to memorize the final values of variables after the execution of the operation Main (lines 5–7). As the operation call computeSum, does not modify the state of variables in the machine Main_i, its translation is not present in the Main namespace. Lines 21–35 represent the translation of the first call of computeSum.

4   Translation Principles

Our work consists in translating concrete formal models based on B0 language in HLL. We propose a transformation strategy, allowing to obtain an equivalent HLL code which is further used for verification purposes. The goal of this work is to obtain HLL models which are behaviorally equivalent to B modules.

The semantic-preserving translation from B to HLL is not straightforward. The first issue to handle is the semantic mismatch between the two paradigms. Thus, a particular attention has to be given to several notions like variable values evolution and updates or loops behaviors. An example of such problems is illustrated in Listing 1. There, a B machine may have operations with side-effects, implicitly affecting the state of another B machine. For *Main_i* machine, the changes that occur to the variables in order to compute the value of the sum are transparent and not explicit. If the translation process does not follow the correct sequence of the variable changes, the generated HLL model may be erroneous. This kind of scenarios is very tricky to handle. It leads to incorrect HLL models and may hide problems related to safety. Figure 2 illustrates the general translation process made of three main steps: B parsing, preprocessing and code generation. In this paper, we focus on the code generation phase.

The first step of our approach generates an intermediate tree representation AST (Abstract Syntax Tree) of an input code by analyzing it syntactically and semantically. B0 is close to an imperative programming language and handles deterministic B instructions: concrete data (variables and constants), *SEES*, *USES* and *IMPORTS* clauses, and operation calls. Due to the semantics of the HLL language, the preprocessing step annotates the abstract syntax tree with additional information useful for variables evolution or loop transformation. This annotation defines an environment used and updated on the fly by each application of a translation rule. The last part of the process is the HLL code generation. Below, we give the relevant elements related to the code generation process we have set up. We have limited this description due to space limitation.

General Concepts. At the present time, we are interested in translating the IMPLEMENTATION module, the lowest level of a B project, in HLL. Since HLL proposes constructs to divide models in small units and to avoid naming conflicts, the initial B component structure can be preserved in the translation.

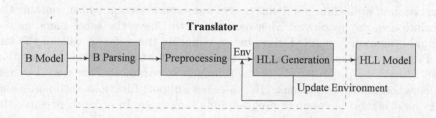

Fig. 2. Translation Workflow from B to HLL

Therefore, we propose to model B machines as HLL namespaces because both have a notion of variable scoping and structuring facilities which lead to a certain data encapsulation. Dependent machines obtained from IMPORTS, USES and SEES clauses must also be translated into HLL namespaces.

The language used in B expressions is essentially predicate logic and set theory. A B arithmetic expression is a mathematical formula that can contains constants, variables and operators. The supported arithmetic operators are: $+, -, \times, \div$. A predicate expression is evaluated to be true or false in B0 as branching conditions of *if substitutions* or in *while loops*. Except for division, the translation of B expressions and B predicates is straightforward because HLL provides the same quantifiers as B [15].

Sequence. In B0, a sequence represents an action which leads to the next action in a predetermined order. All B variables are translated in HLL variables with equivalent types. The link between B0 variables and HLL variables is very crucial for semantics preservation of the translation. This link is not very obvious. In B, variables may evolve during the execution of operations, whereas, in HLL, they correspond to data streams without memory and having a unique value during a cycle. However, our goal is to maintain memory state consistency between B and HLL representation. The HLL equivalent representation of a B variable xx is "xx<i>" for each occurrence i of this variable in left-hand side of an assignment. A new HLL variable is defined by the concatenation of the B variable name and its state evaluated in the translation context. While applying this renaming process, the following properties must be preserved: (i) all value changes of a variable shall be traced and (ii) generated code shall preserve the semantics of the B language. Therefore, the context in which a variable modification occurs is stored and associated to a variable.

Operations. In B language, the dynamic parts of the components are modeled by substitutions, which allow the modification of the data space of a model. Substitutions are used in INITIALISATION and OPERATIONS clauses of a B machine. The proposed transformation of B0 substitutions is based on the understanding of the semantic differences between HLL and B. The general form of an operation is: $out \leftarrow op\_name(in)$ where *in* and *out* can be variables or lists of variables representing the parameters of the operation *op_name*. Each B operation is translated in HLL as follows: inside the namespace associated to the translation of a machine we define a new namespace section which contains the translation of an operation. This namespace will have the same name as the original operation appended to an index, counting the different calls of the latter. Parameter passing is one of the crucial points for the semantics preservation when translating programs [4]. In the B language, parameters are passed by reference when calling operations. HLL does not support functions with non scalar types as it is used in common programming languages. In order to preserve the B semantics when transforming to HLL, the translation of B operation call is realized in two steps by separating the operation body substitutions translation and the parameter mapping translation. Extra assignments are introduced in order to map the effective input parameters to formal input ones in an operation call namespace. This situation is illustrated in Listing 4, lines 42–43 where variables "aa<0>","bb<0>" have the role of formal input parameters of the namespace. The operation output it is transformed in a new assignment as shown in Listing 3, line 15.

If Conditions. Both languages provide *IF* construction with the difference that in HLL it is an expression where in B language it is a statement. In order to merge the information issued from different control flow branches, the translation is performed in two steps. First, the blocks of instructions of each branch are translated (Listing 4, lines 44–45), second, extra conditional HLL assignments are introduced taking into account the condition evaluated initially and the previous substitutions. In the example of minimum operation, this corresponds to line 46 of Listing 4.

While Loops. Unlike the B language, HLL does not support loop structures. Therefore, B loops should be flattened in the HLL model. The general form of a loop construct in B0 is WHILE C DO S INVARIANT I VARIANT V END, where S is a substitution, C is a boolean expression, I is a loop invariant and V is a variant that guarantees the loop termination. In B, while loop is a shorthand for writing the same block of instructions many times. A while loop must end after a finite number of iterations a variant is required. We propose to translate while loop as HLL if expressions repeated as many times as the maximum number of iterations needed to exit the loop. This information is extracted using the VARIANT clause. The substitution S is translated using HLL constructs. The translation of invariant is not explicitly required in the HLL code, but it could be modeled as HLL Proof Obligations or Constraints. In the example presented in Listing 2 the maximum number of iterations of the loop is 2, so the HLL translation process repeats according to it. In Listing 4, lines 26–30 show the translation of the first loop iteration. The fact that variables are expressed in function of condition and their previous value guarantees the correctness of the translation by value propagation even if the number of iterations is an over-approximation.

5   State of the Art

There are several works [4,18,19] focusing on code generation in many programming languages (i.e. C, Ada and Java) from B specifications. In [13], the authors present a set of translation rules from B to Java/SQL studied in the database domain. To increase the use of formal methods, a tool B2Jml [6] was developed to produce JML specifications from B models. Bonichon et al. [5]

have developed LLVM-based code generator that provides llvm executable code for B specification. Moreover, they have also developed a tool b2llvm to automate the code generation process. Furst et al. [10] proposed a code generator to produce C code from Event-B models. In Singh et al. [14], a tool supported code generator, namely EB2ALL, producing source code in many programming languages from verified Event-B specifications is described. Following similar principles, Ge et al. [15] have proposed an approach for translating Event-B models into HLL models. In fact, the main objective of this work is to produce C code from Event-B specification using an intermediate HLL representation. To our knowledge, the proposed translation approach from Event-B to HLL is not automated yet. Similarly, Petit-Doche et al. [16] reported an a posteriori approach for applying formal methods on the developed software, in which a translation strategy is proposed to transform SCADE code to HLL code. In [12], the authors present an approach based on the synchronous language SIGNAL [9] to validate system designs. SIGNAL formal models are generated from C/C++ programs using an SSA intermediate representation. Moreover, translators from C, ADA to HLL already exist. The used translation strategy is not a direct one. An intermediate imperative language is used as a pivot language. There, the goal is to avoid multiple translation steps and to master the whole translation process. It is important to observe that our approach is in similar vein in order to increase confidence in the generated code and promote the use of formal methods in industrial practices. In our work, we propose a translation strategy to produce HLL code from B specification covering the whole B project. Moreover, our approach also highlights the process of translation from a tool development point of view.

6   Conclusion

We study the applicability of PERF, an industrial toolset which allows the formal verification of systems independently of their development process, on software developed in B. This paper presents our approach to generate verifiable HLL code from an implementation described as B0 code. We focus on the core concepts to ensure semantics preservation when translating B0 implementations to HLL data-flow language. The semantic differences between the two studied languages are pointed out and a general translation scheme is proposed. We describe a translation process as well as a set of translation principles for the constructs that require a particular attention. Our initial ideas are already under development on a prototype tool for automatic translation. In this perspective, we have investigated the existing B parsers and BCompiler[1], an open source tool that offers complex parsing features for syntactical and semantical analysis.

Our future work consists in providing a formalization of the translation rules which shall cover the whole B components and constructs. The correctness of

---

[1] https://sourceforge.net/projects/bcomp/.

the translation is not studied in this paper. A possible starting point could be the definition of the semantics of both B and HLL in a unified framework and then check semantics preservation. Another possible extension of this work is to handle higher abstraction levels of the B developments in order to enrich the HLL model with lemmas or hints that might help the proof of properties.

References

1. Abrial, J.R.: The B-book: Assigning Programs to Meanings. Cambridge University Press, New York (1996)
2. Behm, P., Benoit, P., Faivre, A., Meynadier, J.-M.: Météor: a successful application of B in a large project. In: Wing, J.M., Woodcock, J., Davies, J. (eds.) FM 1999. LNCS, vol. 1708, pp. 369–387. Springer, Heidelberg (1999). doi:10.1007/3-540-48119-2_22
3. Benaissa, N., Bonvoisin, D., Feliachi, A., Ordioni, J.: The PERF approach for formal verification. In: Lecomte, T., Pinger, R., Romanovsky, A. (eds.) RSSRail 2016. LNCS, vol. 9707, pp. 203–214. Springer, Cham (2016). doi:10.1007/978-3-319-33951-1_15
4. Bert, D., Boulmé, S., Potet, M.-L., Requet, A., Voisin, L.: Adaptable translator of B specifications to embedded C programs. In: Araki, K., Gnesi, S., Mandrioli, D. (eds.) FME 2003. LNCS, vol. 2805, pp. 94–113. Springer, Heidelberg (2003). doi:10.1007/978-3-540-45236-2_7
5. Bonichon, R., Déharbe, D., Lecomte, T., Medeiros, V.: LLVM-based code generation for B. In: Braga, C., Martí-Oliet, N. (eds.) SBMF 2014. LNCS, vol. 8941, pp. 1–16. Springer, Cham (2015). doi:10.1007/978-3-319-15075-8_1
6. Cataño, N., Wahls, T., Rueda, C., Rivera, V., Yu, D.: Translating B machines to JML specifications. In: SAC 2012, pp. 1271–1277. ACM (2012)
7. ClearSy: Atelier B user manual version 4.0 (2009)
8. Cytron, R., Ferrante, J., Rosen, B.K., Wegman, M.N., Zadeck, F.K.: Efficiently computing static single assignment form and the control dependence graph. ACM Trans. Program. Lang. Syst. **13**(4), 451–490 (1991)
9. Espresso: Polychrony tool. http://www.irisa.fr/espresso/Polychrony
10. Fürst, A., Hoang, T.S., Basin, D., Desai, K., Sato, N., Miyazaki, K.: Code generation for Event-B. In: Albert, E., Sekerinski, E. (eds.) IFM 2014. LNCS, vol. 8739, pp. 323–338. Springer, Cham (2014). doi:10.1007/978-3-319-10181-1_20
11. Halbwachs, N., Caspi, P., Raymond, P., Pilaud, D.: The synchronous data flow programming language LUSTRE. Proc. IEEE **79**(9), 1305–1320 (1991)
12. Kalla, H., Talpin, J.P., Berner, D., Besnard, L.: Automated translation of C/C++ models into a synchronous formalism. In: ECBS 2006. pp. 9–436, March 2006
13. Mammar, A., Laleau, R.: From a B formal specification to an executable code: application to the relational database domain. Info. Soft. Technol. **48**(4), 253–279 (2006)
14. Méry, D., Singh, N.K.: Automatic code generation from EVENT-B models. In: SoICT 2011, pp. 179–188. ACM (2011)
15. Ge, N., Dieumegard, A., Jenn, E., Voisin, L.: Correct-by-construction specification to verified code. Ada-Europe 2017 (2017)
16. Petit-Doche, M., Breton, N., Courbis, R., Fonteneau, Y., Güdemann, M.: Formal verification of industrial critical software. In: Núñez, M., Güdemann, M. (eds.) FMICS 2015. LNCS, vol. 9128, pp. 1–11. Springer, Cham (2015). doi:10.1007/978-3-319-19458-5_1

17. Prasad, M.R., Biere, A., Gupta, A.: A survey of recent advances in SAT-based formal verification. Int. J. Softw. Tools Technol. Transf. **7**(2), 156–173 (2005)
18. Storey, A.C., Haughton, H.P.: A strategy for the production of verifiable code using the B Method. In: Naftalin, M., Denvir, T., Bertran, M. (eds.) FME 1994. LNCS, vol. 873, pp. 346–365. Springer, Heidelberg (1994). doi:10.1007/3-540-58555-9_104
19. Tatibouët, B., Requet, A., Voisinet, J.-C., Hammad, A.: Java card code generation from B specifications. In: Dong, J.S., Woodcock, J. (eds.) ICFEM 2003. LNCS, vol. 2885, pp. 306–318. Springer, Heidelberg (2003). doi:10.1007/978-3-540-39893-6_18

Formal Verification of Train Control
with Air Pressure Brakes

Stefan Mitsch[1(✉)], Marco Gario[2], Christof J. Budnik[2], Michael Golm[2],
and André Platzer[1]

[1] Computer Science Department, Carnegie Mellon University,
Pittsburgh, PA 15213, USA
{smitsch,aplatzer}@cs.cmu.edu
[2] Siemens Corporate Technology, Princeton, NJ, USA
{marco.gario,christof.budnik,michael.golm}@siemens.com

Abstract. Train control technology enhances the safety and efficiency of railroad operation by safeguarding the motion of trains to prevent them from leaving designated areas of operation and colliding with other trains. It is crucial for safety that the trains engage their brakes early enough in order to make sure they never leave the safe part of the track. Efficiency considerations, however, also require that the train does not brake too soon, which would limit operational suitability. It is surprisingly subtle to reach the right tradeoffs and identify the right control conditions that guarantee safe motion without being overly conservative.

In pursuit of an answer, we develop a *hybrid system* model with *discrete control decisions* for acceleration, brakes, and with *continuous differential equations* for their physical effects on the motion of the train. The resulting hybrid system model is systematically derived from the Federal Railway Administration model for flat terrain by *conservatively* neglecting minor forces.

The main contribution of this paper is the identification of a controller with control constraints that we formally verify to always guarantee collision freedom in the FRA model. The safe braking behavior of a train is influenced not only by the train configuration (e.g., train length and mass), but also by physical characteristics (e.g., brake pressure propagation and reaction time). We formalize train control safety properties in differential dynamic logic and prove the correctness of the train control models in the theorem prover KeYmaera X.

1 Introduction

Train control (TC) technology is meant to safeguard the control of trains such that they cannot collide with other trains, cannot move into unauthorized track segments, and cannot derail because of excessive speed. While they do not prevent accidents caused by mechanical failures like axle breakage, train protection systems are the major safety technology controlling the safety of the motion of trains.

This material is based upon work supported by Siemens Corporate Technology.

Train protection systems monitor the motion and the operator's control decisions and take infrastructure information into account to stop the train before reaching the position of other trains or otherwise moving into unauthorized track segments. Of course, TC needs to initiate the brakes early enough in order to make sure the train finally comes to a stop safely (or below the speed limit) before the unsafe track position. At the same time, railway operation would be disrupted substantially if an automatic train protection system were to frequently cause a train to brake unnecessarily.

Consequently, it is useful to find out how late the train brakes can still be applied without losing guaranteed stopping capabilities of the train. More generally, the challenge is to identify a maximally permissive train protection controller that gives the operator and other train controllers maximal degrees of freedom in operating the train, while still always ensuring that the train brakes will automatically be applied early enough so that the train will come to a stop before reaching any unsafe track positions.

Trains can perform different types of braking, e.g., through traction of the motors in the locomotive, and magnetic or pneumatic brake shoes on the train's cars. Combined with various ways of triggering the brakes (e.g., electronically or through air pressure pipes), we get a range of available brake forces and durations until full braking force is available. For example, air pressure propagation along the train causes the effective braking force to change and ramp up slowly over time. This complicates the safety analysis and requires safe TC controllers to be aware of the worst-case influence of the various train parameters on the guaranteed safe stopping distance. Some parameters (e.g., train length) have significant influence on the pressure propagation and in turn on the stopping distance, while others (e.g., aerodynamic drag) can be approximated by either their upper or lower bound, depending on the direction of their influence.

Approach. In order to discover the right safety constraints and justify their safety with mathematical rigor, we develop a controller for a mathematical model based on the physics of the *Federal Railway Administration* (FRA) model [6]. This results in a *hybrid systems* model, because it includes differential equations for the continuous physical effects of motion and the discrete control decisions of when to accelerate, when to apply moderate braking in normal operation, and when to begin or stop applying maximum brakes. The model considers train length and mass, reaction times, brake pressure propagation, penalty brake force, service brake force, and acceleration force. Unlike the FRA model, we ignore roll resistance, air resistance, and curve resistance, because these are negligible for freight trains and only make the train stop earlier (so the controller is safer). As a first step, we simplify the model to consider flat terrain only, leaving more complex terrain profiles as future work.

We formalize safety of the TC controller as a formula in differential dynamic logic d$\mathcal{L}$ [19–22], which is the logic for hybrid systems. Besides the identification of the safety conditions for the TC controller, our main contribution is its rigorous mathematical justification by providing a proof in the d$\mathcal{L}$ theorem prover KeYmaera X [13]. Formalizing and proving motion and controller together in a

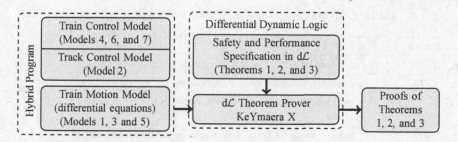

Fig. 1. Overview of formal verification process in dℒ and artifacts

hybrid systems model has the additional benefit of *identifying constraints* on the decisions that a controller has to make *ahead of time for any subtle combination of system state and control choice.* Fig. 1 summarizes our formal verification approach and the artifacts of this paper. These findings are part of an ongoing effort to rigorously formalize the safety of train controllers.

2   Preliminaries: Differential Dynamic Logic

We use *differential dynamic logic* dℒ [19–22] to verify safe braking behavior. Differential dynamic logic has a notation for hybrid systems as *hybrid programs*, which use differential equations as program statements to describe continuous behavior in addition to discrete computations.

One of the challenges of developing a safe braking controller is to analyze its safety over a broad range of possible control decisions that were taken prior to braking, where a train should be allowed to speed up or slow down in any appropriate way. In addition to programming constructs familiar from other languages (e.g., assignments and conditional statements), hybrid programs provide nondeterministic operators that allow us to describe such unknown prior behavior concisely. Nondeterminism has the additional benefit that later optimization (e.g., use better sensors or implement a faster algorithm) may be possible without re-verification as variations are already covered.

Table 1 summarizes the syntax of hybrid programs together with an informal semantics. We briefly describe each operator with an example. Sequential composition $\alpha;\beta$ says that program β starts after α finishes (e.g., first determine track grade, then let the train choose acceleration). The nondeterministic choice $\alpha \cup \beta$ follows either α or β (e.g., the train may be in normal operation or in braking mode). The nondeterministic repetition operator α^* repeats α zero or more times (e.g., the train's target speed may be revised over and over again, but we do not know exactly how often). Assignment $x := \theta$ instantaneously assigns the value of the term θ to variable x (e.g., let the train choose maximum braking). Instead $x := *$ assigns an arbitrary value to x (e.g., the track grade may change arbitrarily, we do not know which value exactly). $x' = \theta \;\&\; F$ describes a continuous evolution of x along the differential equation $x' = \theta$ of arbitrary duration (even zero time). The evolution domain F can be used to restrict the

Table 1. Hybrid program representations of hybrid systems

Statement	Effect
$\alpha; \ \beta$	sequential composition, first run program α, then β
$\alpha \cup \beta$	nondeterministic choice, following either program α or β
α^*	nondeterministic repetition, repeats program α any $n \geq 0$ times
$x := \theta$	assign value of term θ to variable x (discrete jump)
$x := *$	assign any arbitrary real number to variable x nondeterministically
$?F$	check that formula F holds at the current state, and abort if it does not
$\{x'_1 = \theta_1, \ldots, x'_n = \theta_n \& F\}$	evolve x_i along differential equation system $x'_i = \theta_i$ restricted to maximum evolution domain F for any duration $r \in \mathbb{R}$

continuous evolution to a certain region in space-time (e.g., restrict duration to at most $5s$). The test $?F$ checks that a particular condition F holds and aborts if it does not (e.g., continue accelerating only when the distance to the track position limit is large enough). Execution of hybrid programs with backtracking is a good intuition, since other nondeterministic choices may still be possible if one run fails. A typical pattern that involves assignment and tests is to limit the assignment of arbitrary values by their bounds (e.g., limit acceleration to the normal operation conditions, as in $f_a := *; \ ? - F_{sb} \leq f_a \leq A$, which assigns to f_a any value between the service brake force $-F_{sb}$ and acceleration force A).

The set of d$\mathcal{L}$ formulas is generated by the following grammar ($\sim$ is any operator in $\{<, \leq, =, \neq, \geq, >\}$, θ_1, θ_2 are arithmetic expressions in $+, -, \cdot, /$ over the reals):

$$\phi ::= \theta_1 \sim \theta_2 \mid \neg\phi \mid \phi \wedge \psi \mid \phi \vee \psi \mid \phi \rightarrow \psi \mid \phi \leftrightarrow \psi \mid \forall x\, \phi \mid \exists x\, \phi \mid [\alpha]\phi \mid \langle\alpha\rangle\phi$$

To specify the desired correctness properties of hybrid programs, a d$\mathcal{L}$ formula $F \rightarrow [\alpha]G$ means that if started at an initial state in which formula F is true, then all executions of the hybrid program α only lead to states in which formula G is true. Differential dynamic logic comes with a formal verification technique to prove these and other correctness properties. We did all our proofs in the verification tool KeYmaera X [13], which implements the d$\mathcal{L}$ verification technique [19, 21, 22]. The d$\mathcal{L}$ verification technique is sound, which means that a formula that has a proof is *valid*, i.e., true in all states. For high confidence, the d$\mathcal{L}$ verification technique has been cross-verified [3] in the Isabelle and Coq theorem provers. This gives d$\mathcal{L}$-based verification results an extraordinarily strong degree of reliability for high confidence safety assurance cases.

3   Train Control Models

In normal operation, trains may speed up or slow down at will. The brakes are then typically operated with moderate braking force, referred to as *service braking*. When a train is about to violate the track position limit or speed limit in normal operation, the goal of TC is to ensure safety by switching to *penalty braking* with maximum brake force. The air pressure brakes on a train exert strong braking force but require some time to build up maximum brake force by propagating air pressure along the train. For fail-safety reasons, air brakes along a train apply pressure brakes in proportion to how the air pressure from the locomotive is lost instead of increased, but they are, nevertheless, subject to slow propagation and build-up of braking force along the train.

Figure 2 illustrates the behavior that we model. In free driving—i.e., when the train respects the speed limit and is at a safe distance from the track position limit e—the train may speed up or slow down at will (e.g., according to the train driver's decisions or those of other optimizing controllers). At time $t = 1$, the train receives a speed limit $d_1 = 1$ that is in place from e_1 onwards, so it engages its service brakes $-F_{sb}$ and afterwards decides to coast to respect the speed limit. Later, the speed limit changes to a full stop $d_2 = 0$ at e_2. The remaining distance to e_2 is too small to stop safely just using the service brakes. Therefore, at time $t = 2$ the train engages its penalty brakes, which, however, need time t_{appl} until they are operational at full force $-F_{pb}$. The train then continues braking with full brake force $-F_{pb}$ until it is fully stopped. This scenario includes the following model components (detailed subsequently):

- A track controller may repeatedly issue new speed limits d that are in place from a position e onwards. Limit $d = 0$ means stop at e. It should not demand physically impossible maneuvers (e.g., ask a freight train traveling at 60 mph to stop in 3ft).
- A train controller decides between free driving (using arbitrary engine acceleration and the service brakes) and penalty braking using maximum brake

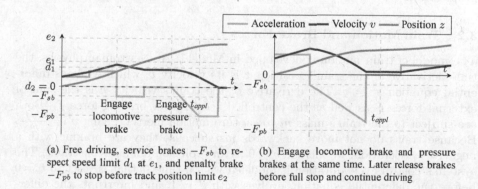

(a) Free driving, service brakes $-F_{sb}$ to respect speed limit d_1 at e_1, and penalty brake $-F_{pb}$ to stop before track position limit e_2

(b) Engage locomotive brake and pressure brakes at the same time. Later release brakes before full stop and continue driving

Fig. 2. Braking with instantaneous service brakes and air pressure penalty brakes

force. The decision is based on the resulting slowdown/stopping distance from its current speed v to speed limit d and the remaining safety distance to track position e.

– The safety margins follow from a motion model of the train, whose behavior depends on train parameters (e.g., length) and external conditions (e.g., track grade).

– Acceleration and service brake via the train's engine have immediate but limited effect. Penalty brakes provide higher overall braking force at the cost of pressure propagation time along the individual freight or passenger cars of the train.

3.1   Safety and Performance Considerations

The main safety objective in train control is to respect speed and track position limits [6]. Predicting the stopping distance is therefore key to a safe and effective controller. Errors in the prediction may let a train run past the track position limit (overshoot), stop unnecessarily early (undershoot), or brake unnecessarily, resulting in undesired effects on the overall railway network operation. The FRA characterizes safety by limiting overshoots, i.e., with 99.9995% probability trains must not overshoot the track position limit [6]. Usually one overestimates the stopping distance by some safe factor. While this can improve the overall safety of the system, it might be detrimental to system performance: trains significantly underperform when train length and weight are not considered in the braking decision [24], and braking frequently or significantly earlier than needed has negative impacts both on energy considerations as well as on the overall throughput of the network. An orthogonal performance objective, therefore, limits undershoots to 500 ft for trains at less than 30mph, and 1000 ft above 30 mph [6].

To find a suitable safety and performance trade-off, we need to consider more realistic (and therefore complex) models of the dynamics to which the train is subject. We compare a simpler model that considers only the delay of brake pressure propagation with a more accurate model of gradual pressure propagation.

3.2   Train Motion and Brake Forces

The model of train motion is developed in Model 1. By Newtonian physics, the time-derivative of the train's position z is its velocity v, which explains differential equation $z' = v$. The derivative of the train's velocity v is the sum of external forces F as well as the controlled acceleration/braking force f_a. Both are subject to the train's mass m to capture motion inertia, giving $v' = \frac{F+f_a}{m}$. Because trains do not move backwards just because they are braking with a negative acceleration, we include $v \geq 0$ as an evolution domain constraint. The system's control cycle duration is modeled with a timer t that is reset to $t := 0$ before the differential equation, evolves with $t' = 1$, and interrupts the differential equation after at most ε time due to the evolution domain $t \leq \varepsilon$. This ensures that the motion will "stop" to give the subsequent controllers a chance

Model 1. Train Motion Model

$$motion \equiv t := 0; \ \{z' = v, \ v' = \frac{F + f_a}{m}, \ t' = 1 \ \& \ v \geq 0 \land t \leq \varepsilon\} \tag{1}$$

Model 2. Track Control

$$tc \equiv e := *; \ d := *; \ ? \left(d \geq 0 \land (v^2 - d^2)m \leq 2F_{sb}(e - z)\right) \tag{2}$$

to run at the latest after ε time again. The initial values of position z and speed v are unknown.

The forces that act on the train are its own braking force F_b and locomotive traction F_l, as well as the track grade force F_g (incline or decline), the track curvature force F_c, and the bearing, rolling, and aerodynamic resistive forces F_r [6, p. 57]. Model 1 uses f_a to summarize the train's braking force F_b and locomotive tractive effort F_l, so $F = -(F_g + F_r + F_c)$ in (1). The train's acceleration will be limited by a maximum braking force $-F_{pb}$ and a maximum acceleration force A. An important characteristic of air pressure brakes is the time t_{appl} that it takes from initiating braking until the full braking force F_{pb} is available [6]. The time t_{appl} depends on the length l of the train with constants $c_1^{t_{appl}}$ to $c_3^{t_{appl}}$ as follows: $t_{appl} = c_1^{t_{appl}} + c_2^{t_{appl}} l + c_3^{t_{appl}} l^2$ by [6, p. 57].

The resistive forces F_r can be estimated from the train's speed v, weight $W = mg$ with gravity constant $g > 0$, number of cars N and axles n with constants c_1^r to c_4^r using $F_r = c_1^r W + c_2^r n + c_3^r W v + c_4^r N v^2$ [6]. The track curvature force F_c depends on the train's weight W and the average curvature C under the train $F_c = c_1^c C W$ [6]. Since both resistive force and track curvature force oppose forward motion (i.e., improve braking), we can neglect them for safety analysis purposes by assuming $c_i^r = c_i^c = 0$. The track grade force F_g depends on the train's weight and average track grade G under the train by $F_g - c_1^g G W$, so $F_g = 0$ for flat tracks. Additional detail on the external forces acting on trains is in [2]. We take a first step by assuming external forces $F = -(F_g + F_r + F_c) = 0$ to focus solely on the effect of brake pressure propagation on f_a in flat terrain (forces F_r and F_c improve braking, so make our controllers safer).

3.3 Track Control

The central track controller tc in Model 2 can update speed limits d and track position limit e at any time, as long as it does not demand the train moves backwards (so $d \geq 0$) and the remaining distance between the train's position z and the track position limit e allows the train to respect the speed limit safely within the limits of physics. For a reasonable system design, the track controller should also only choose d and e such that the train can safely follow by just using the service brakes $-F_{sb}$.

Crucially, the condition (2) characterizes the relationship between the train's current speed v and position z, and the speed limit d and track position limit e.

Condition (2) can be discovered in KeYmaera X by proving a simplified hybrid program (3) that uses the service brakes $f_a := -F_{sb}$ and neglects other model details (external force $F = 0$):

$$F = 0 \wedge F_{sb} > 0 \wedge m > 0 \rightarrow [f_a := -F_{sb}; \; motion](z \leq e \rightarrow v \leq d) \quad (3)$$

Formula (3) is not valid but still true in some states, which allows KeYmaera X to find conditions on e and z that make it provable. These conditions can be explained as follows: from $v' = \frac{F + f_a}{m}$ in *motion* we see that, with service brakes, the train needs $\frac{(v-d)m}{F_{sb}}$ time to overcome the difference between its current speed v and speed limit d. The differential equation in *motion* is solvable, so its solution gives the slowdown distance $\int_0^{\frac{(v-d)m}{F_{sb}}} \left(v - \frac{F_{sb}}{m}t\right) dt$, implying $\frac{(v^2 - d^2)m}{2F_{sb}}$ as minimum distance between the track position limit e and the train z, see equivalent condition in (2).

3.4 Train Control

The primary safety question in train controller design is finding conditions under which it is safe to drive freely, and when it is necessary to engage the brakes as a last resort safety action. The major safety argument for the controller has to justify why the train will always respect the target speed at the track position limit.

For traceability purposes and for managing the analytic complexity it is beneficial to develop these conditions in increasingly realistic brake pressure propagation models. We first consider a conservative approximation delaying the whole effect of brakes for the entire propagation time (Sect. 3.5). Then we follow the FRA model that gradually increases the effect of the air pressure brakes with a constant jerk or jolt (Sect. 3.6).

Keeping acceleration constant between decisions significantly simplifies the task of finding the safety distances. The effects of changing accelerations manifest in position constraints: with gradual increase j in braking force we need to solve $z''' = j$. With delayed brake onset $z'' = f_a$ is enough. Figure 3 illustrates the conservative approximation in comparison to a gradual increase in brake force. Both models behave the same in free driving. When engaging the pressure brakes,

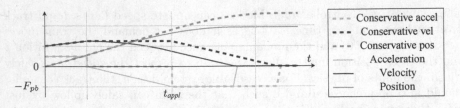

Fig. 3. Delayed brake onset conservatively approximates brake pressure propagation. The train length determines how long (t_{appl}) it takes to reach full braking force $-F_{pb}$.

the conservative approximation coasts for the entire brake pressure propagation time, while gradual braking force already decelerates the train with limited force while the brake force builds up. Since we prove the safety of both controllers, we can subsequently compare the loss in performance for the more simplistic model compared to the more accurate FRA model with jerk.

3.5   Delayed Braking

The simpler train model that conservatively takes the effect of gradual pressure brake build-up into account simply pretends the pressure brakes would have no effect at all until they finally have full effect after the pressure propagated along the train. This is counterfactual with reality but a conservative approximation, because some braking force already takes effect in the middle of the process of building up braking force from the pressure brakes. Pretending this deceleration would be 0 is inaccurate but only makes the real train brake quicker than the model, so safer.

The train motion in Model 3 follows the motion of Model 1 with changes highlighted in bold. The pressure brake build-up delay is modeled with a timer c with $c' = s$ that can be enabled or disabled by setting its slope s either to 1 (enabled) or to 0 (disabled), but it never exceeds the brake delay ($c \leq t_{appl}$), which is only relevant if $s \neq 0$.

The train controller for delayed brake onset that we develop in Model 4 can (nondeterministically) choose to either *drive* or *brake* (5). The choice is nondeterministic in order to maximize flexibility of the train controller and, thus, also maximize how many concrete train controller implementations are covered by our single safety proof.

When driving freely, in (6) any choice between the train's service brake force $-F_{sb}$ and maximum acceleration force A is allowed by a nondeterministic assignment $f_a := *$ followed by a subsequent test to check that $-F_{sb} < f_a < A$ is true. The choice of f_a is nondeterministic in order to cover a large variety of concrete controllers under the safety argument (imagine controllers optimizing secondary objectives such as energy consumption or decisions by train conductors that determine the concrete choice of f_a during each execution of *drive*). The brake delay timer c is reset ($c := 0$) and turned off ($s := 0$) in (7), because the penalty brakes are not activated when driving freely.

Of course, driving freely or accelerating is not always safe. KeYmaera X points us to the worst possible scenario of this control decision: acceleration with full force A for the maximum allowed time ε and postponing braking for the maximum allowed delay t_{appl}. Condition (8) checks whether or not the remaining

---

Model 3. Train Motion Model with Delayed Brake Onset, extends Model 1

$$motion \equiv t := 0; \; \{z' = v, \; v' = \frac{F + f_a}{m}, \; t' = 1, \; \boldsymbol{c' = s} \; \& \; v \geq 0 \wedge t \leq \varepsilon \wedge \boldsymbol{c \leq t_{appl}}\} \quad (4)$$

Model 4. Train Controller for Delayed Brake Onset

$$ctrl_z \equiv drive \cup brake \tag{5}$$

$$drive \equiv f_a := *; \ ?(-F_{sb} \le f_a \le A); \tag{6}$$

$$c := 0; \ s := 0; \tag{7}$$

$$?(e - z \ge margin) \tag{8}$$

$$margin = \frac{(v^2 - d^2)m}{2F_{pb}} + \left(\frac{A}{F_{pb}} + 1\right)\left(\frac{A}{2m}\varepsilon^2 + \varepsilon v\right) + \left(v + \frac{A}{m}\varepsilon\right)t_{appl} \tag{9}$$

$$brake \equiv \begin{cases} \text{if } \left(e - z \ge \frac{(v^2 - d^2)m}{2F_{sb}}\right) & f_a := -F_{sb}; \ c := 0; \ s := 0 \\ \text{else if } (c \ge t_{appl}) & f_a := -F_{pb}; \ s := 0 \\ \text{else if } (c > 0) & f_a := f_a \\ \text{else} & f_a := 0; \ s := 1 \end{cases} \tag{10}$$

distance $e - z$ on the track is large enough to handle this worst-case scenario, i.e., defer braking for yet another control cycle duration ε. If it is large enough, the chosen acceleration force f_a will be made operational. Otherwise (i.e., if (8) does not hold), the controller falls back to executing *brake* as the only remaining option in nondeterministic control choice (5). When introducing brake pressure propagation we will see later that the condition (8) could be improved with separate conditions on braking and accelerating.

Braking is modeled along four increasingly critical cases in (10). The train prefers the service brake over the penalty brakes $f_a := -F_{sb}$ if the remaining distance to e is still enough for service brakes alone to ensure safety. Otherwise, the penalty brakes are used in the following way: If the brake delay has expired ($c \ge t_{appl}$), the full braking force is available with $f_a := -F_{pb}$. If the brake delay has not been reached yet but the train is already waiting for the brakes to activate ($c > 0$), then it just keeps waiting by keeping its current acceleration force $f_a := f_a$. Otherwise, the train turns the engine off to stop accelerating $f_a := 0$ and the brake delay timer is started with $s := 1$.

Theorem 1 (Train Controller with Delayed Brake Onset). *The braking controller for motion with delayed brake onset from Model 4 guarantees to observe a maximum speed $v \le d$ when the train passes the track position limit $z \ge e$. That is, the following dℒ formula is proved: assumptions $\rightarrow$ $[(tc \cup (ctrl_z;\ motion))^*](z \ge e \rightarrow v \le d)$.*

3.6 Brake Pressure Propagation

The FRA's dynamical model of trains with brake pressure propagation differs in subtle but substantial ways from the simplified delayed braking model. The key differences of the resulting Model 5, highlighted in boldface, are that the acceleration force f_a is increasing continuously over time along $f_a' = j$ with

Model 5. Train Motion Model with Brake Pressure Propagation

$$motion \equiv t := 0; \; \{z' = v, \; v' = \frac{F + f_a}{m_z}, \; \boldsymbol{f_a' = j}, \; t' = 1 \; \& \; v \geq 0 \wedge \boldsymbol{-F_{pb} \leq f_a} \wedge t \leq \varepsilon\}$$

(11)

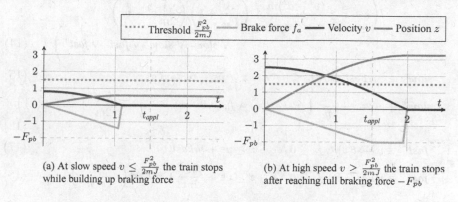

(a) At slow speed $v \leq \frac{F_{pb}^2}{2mJ}$ the train stops while building up braking force

(b) At high speed $v > \frac{F_{pb}^2}{2mJ}$ the train stops after reaching full braking force $-F_{pb}$

Fig. 4. Brake force and stopping distance

the jerk j from the pressure brake propagation. The effective force of penalty braking is limited by $-F_{pb}$, reflected in an additional evolution domain constraint $-F_{pb} \leq f_a$, beyond which the subsequently developed physics controller will deactivate jerk and keep constant acceleration force.

Our train controller for brake pressure propagation in Model 6 follows the same basic setup as the controller for brake delay; differences are highlighted in bold. The main difference is condition (13)–(14) and its components (15)–(21) that allow driving with any acceleration, and the control decisions on the brake jerk j in the braking cases. In mode *drive*, penalty braking is deactivated $j := 0$ and the train controller chooses any acceleration between service braking with force $-F_{sb}$ and full acceleration force A. This is safe if service braking later ensures that the train will still always respect the speed limit d (13), or if penalty braking to a full stop with the pressure brakes will later always keep the train inside the track position limit (14). The pressure propagation along the train increases the available brake force over time up to the maximum braking force F_{pb}. As a result, the distance margin for stopping safely splits into two cases, as pointed out by KeYmaera X during the proof: slow trains will stop while the braking force is still ramping up (see Fig. 4a), fast trains will stop after reaching the maximum braking force (see Fig. 4b). In each case, the margin additionally depends on whether the train controller presently wants to slow down $f_a \leq 0$ (*slow⁻* (15) and *fast⁻* (17)) or speed up $f_a \geq 0$ (*slow⁺* (16) and *fast⁺* (18)). KeYmaera X points to a subtle combination of the worst-case bounds in margins (20) and (21). Per condition (16), a slow train may accelerate with current force f_a for the maximum allowed duration ε, if the safety margin $e - z$ is large enough for the future higher speed $u = v + \frac{f_a \varepsilon}{m}$. In the converse scenario (17), however,

Model 6. Train Controller for Brake Pressure Propagation

$$ctrl_z \equiv drive \cup brake \tag{12}$$

$$drive \equiv j := 0; \; f_a := *; \; ? - F_{sb} \leq f_a \leq A; \tag{13}$$

$$? \Bigg(e - z \geq \frac{(v^2 - d^2)m}{2F_{sb}} + \left(\frac{A}{F_{sb}} + 1 \right) \left(\frac{A}{2m} \varepsilon^2 + v\varepsilon \right)$$
$$\vee \, slow^- \vee slow^+ \vee fast^- \vee fast^+ \Bigg) \tag{14}$$

$$slow^- \equiv \neg isFast(v) \wedge f_a \leq 0 \wedge e - z \geq v\varepsilon + mSlow(v) \tag{15}$$

$$slow^+ \equiv [u := v + \frac{f_a\varepsilon}{m}] \left(\neg isFast(u) \wedge f_a \geq 0 \wedge e - z \geq v\varepsilon + \frac{f_a\varepsilon^2}{2m} + mSlow(u) \right) \tag{16}$$

$$fast^- \equiv isFast(v) \wedge f_a \leq 0 \wedge e - z \geq v\varepsilon + mFast(v) \tag{17}$$

$$fast^+ \equiv isFast(v) \wedge f_a \geq 0 \wedge e - z \geq v\varepsilon + \frac{f_a\varepsilon^2}{2m} + mFast\left(v + \frac{f_a\varepsilon}{m} \right) \tag{18}$$

$$isFast(v) \equiv v \geq \frac{F_{pb}^2}{2mJ} \tag{19}$$

$$mSlow(v) = \frac{2}{3} v\sqrt{2mv/J} \tag{20}$$

$$mFast(v) = \frac{mv^2}{2F_{pb}} + \frac{vF_{pb}}{2J} - \frac{F_{pb}^3}{24mJ^2} \tag{21}$$

$$brake \equiv \begin{cases} \text{if } \left(e - z \geq \frac{(v^2 - d^2)m}{2F_{sb}} \right) & f_a := -F_{sb} \\ \text{else if } (v \leq d) & j := 0; \; f_a := *; \; ? -F_{sb} \leq f_a \leq 0 \\ \text{else if } (f_a \leq -F_{pb}) & j := 0 \\ \text{else} & j := -J; \; f_a := \min(f_a, 0) \end{cases} \tag{22}$$

KeYmaera X reveals with a counterexample that using the future speed $v + \frac{f_a\varepsilon}{m}$ is unsafe, because all intermediate speeds up to ε time require a larger safety margin (i.e., the current speed v determines the worst-case bound).

Akin to Model 4, braking is structured into increasingly critical cases: the train's main preference is to use service braking $f_a := -F_{sb}$ if the remaining distance is sufficient ($e - z \geq \frac{(v^2-d^2)m}{2F_{sb}}$). If the train is slow enough already ($v \leq d$), then penalty braking is disabled $j := 0$ and any level of service braking or coasting is used instead (in the force range $-F_{sb}$ to 0); If the brake pressure propagation is finished, meaning that the brakes are fully engaged ($f_a \leq -F_{pb}$), then there will be no further increase in braking force ($j := 0$). Otherwise, the train did not yet build up sufficient braking force, but at least keeps increasing braking force with jerk $j := -J$ and $J = \frac{F_{pb}}{t_{appl}}$ from its current deceleration ($f_a := \min(f_a, 0)$). Note that $\min(f_a, 0)$ also models that the train stops acceleration through its locomotive when it starts the brake pressure propagation. The term

$\min(f_a, 0)$ in (22) also covers the case where the train already uses service braking in *drive* but decides to switch to the stronger penalty braking for safety reasons.

Theorem 2 (Train Controller with Brake Pressure Propagation is Safe). *Model 6 with brake pressure propagation stays within a maximum speed $v \leq d$ beyond track position limit $z \geq e$. That is, the following dℒ formula is proved in KeYmaera X:*

$$assumptions \rightarrow [(tc \cup (ctrl_z;\ motion))^*](z \geq e \rightarrow v \leq d).$$

4   Performance Analysis

The safety analysis proved train control is safe both with delayed braking (Model 4) and with pressure brake propagation models (Model 6). While the former was much easier to design and prove safe, its controller suffers an additional safety margin because it neglects that real brakes already have partial effect while pressure is still propagating along the train. Model 6 is certainly the more realistic model while Model 4 is further away from the FRA model. It might still be a better tradeoff to settle for a conservative overapproximation that is easier to analyze than a full-blown realistic model.

To analyze this tradeoff we use the FRA performance objective [6] of not stopping too early (but still before a certain critical point). The performance objective can be analyzed in the following ways. *(i)* Comparing the performance objective of motion models Models 3 and 5 through simulation of some scenarios, e.g., as illustrated in Fig. 3. *(ii)* More systematic characterization by comparing the symbolic safety margins of the models, see Sect. 5. *(iii)* Full formal guarantees for *all* permitted behaviors when proving a lower bound on the stopping point of the train, dual to the upper bounds from the safety proofs (this section). Intuitively, a train controller has a good performance if it does not stop "too early" but without ever endangering safety.

For proving performance it is important to only engage penalty braking when it is absolutely necessary to avoid overshoot, i.e., when (8) is no longer satisfied, but not earlier. Braking for any other reason at any earlier point is detrimental to proving performance bounds, but allowed in Model 4 for flexibility, so that train operators can do so to react to other unforeseen events along the track or to simply stop at a station. For a performance proof, Model 7 adapts Model 4 to favor free driving over braking by making the nondeterministic choice $drive \cup brake$ deterministic (23). This deterministic choice implies that, at the start of the braking maneuver, the safety margin to the track position limit e is at most $\frac{(v^2 - d^2)m}{2F_{pb}} + accMargin(v)$, cf. (26). The model keeps track of this margin by remembering the initial speed v_0 at the beginning of the brake maneuver.

For safety reasons, the train assumes all aspects in *accMargin* might be disadvantageous for the train (e.g., just a split-second later accelerating may no longer be safe). As a result, if all aspects in *accMargin* turn out in favor of the train (e.g., if the train could still have accelerated almost the full ε time later),

---

Model 7. Train Controller for Late Braking

$$ctrl_z \equiv \text{if } (e - z \geq \textbf{\textit{margin}}) \; \{\textbf{\textit{drive}}\} \text{ else } \{\textbf{\textit{brake}}\} \tag{23}$$

$$\textbf{\textit{drive}} \equiv f_a := *; \; ?(-F_{sb} \leq f_a \leq A); \; c := 0; \; s := 0 \tag{24}$$

$$accMargin(v) = \left(\frac{A}{F_{pb}} + 1\right)\left(\frac{A}{2m}\varepsilon^2 + \varepsilon v\right) + \left(v + \frac{A}{m}\varepsilon\right) t_{appl} \tag{25}$$

$$margin = (v^2 - d^2)m/(2F_{pb}) + accMargin(v) \tag{26}$$

$$brake \equiv \begin{cases} \text{if } \left(e - z \geq \frac{(v^2 - d^2)m}{2F_{sb}}\right) & f_a := -F_{sb}; \; c := 0; \; s := 0 \\ \text{else if } (c \geq t_{appl}) & f_a := -F_{pb}; \; s := 0 \\ \text{else if } (c > 0) & f_a := f_a \\ \text{else} & f_a := 0; \; s := 1; \; v_0 := v \end{cases} \tag{27}$$

---

the train will stop with $accMargin(v_0)$ distance to the track position limit e. Theorem 3 formalizes this intuition. Note that we neglect track control tc here, since it issues stopping points for the service brakes.

Theorem 3 (Late Braking of Train Controller with Brake Delay). *Model 7 ensures that the train stops no earlier than point $e - accMargin(v_0)$ when it uses pressure brakes. The following formula is proved in KeYmaera X:*

$$assumptions \rightarrow [(ctrl_z; \; motion)^*]\Big(\underbrace{c > 0}_{\text{Pressure brake engaged}} \wedge \underbrace{v \leq d}_{\text{Braking finished}} \rightarrow z \geq \underbrace{e - accMargin(v_0)}_{\text{Earliest stopping point}}\Big).$$

5   Experimental Results

Simulation (Fig. 3) of the motion models suggests that, for safety reasons, the symbolic safety margin (9) of the brake delay model (Model 4) needs to be more conservative than the margins (15)–(18) of the pressure propagation model (Model 6). The difference in safety margins to the latest stopping point is characterized by this brake performance:

$$margin - \begin{cases} v\varepsilon + mSlow(v) & \text{if } \neg isFast(v) \wedge f_a \leq 0 \\ v\varepsilon + \frac{f_a\varepsilon^2}{2m} + mSlow\left(v + \frac{f_a\varepsilon}{m}\right) & \text{if } \neg isFast(v) \wedge f_a \geq 0 \\ v\varepsilon + mFast(v) & \text{if } isFast(v) \wedge f_a \leq 0 \\ v\varepsilon + \frac{f_a\varepsilon^2}{2m} + mFast\left(v + \frac{f_a\varepsilon}{m}\right) & \text{if } isFast(v) \wedge f_a \geq 0 \end{cases} \tag{28}$$

We use formula (28) to compare the performance of Models 4 to 6 on parameters chosen according to standard configurations [6], see Table 2. Using these parameters, the net stopping distance with full braking force $-F_{pb}$ when neglecting brake pressure propagation is $\frac{v^2 m}{2F_{pb}}$ (e.g., 8 682 ft for a fast, long, loaded train,

Table 2. Experiment parameter choices (in FRA standard units)

Parameter		Value	Description	Source
l_z	Short	753ft	10 cars	[6, Fig. 20]
	Medium	2 345ft	40 cars	[6, Fig. 20]
	Long	5 531ft	100 cars	[6, Fig. 20]
m	Loaded	$263\frac{\text{klb}}{\text{car}}$	e.g., medium train 10 520klb	[6, Table 2]
	Empty	$64\frac{\text{klb}}{\text{car}}$	e.g., medium train 2 560klb	[6, Table 2]
v	Slow, Fast	10, 60mph		[6, Table 2]
F_{pb}	Loaded	$35\,750\frac{\text{lbf}}{\text{car}}$	e.g., medium train 1 430klbf	[6, p. 22]
	Empty	$10\,575\frac{\text{lbf}}{\text{car}}$	e.g., medium train 423klbf	[6, p. 22]
	Unknown	$23\,338\frac{\text{lbf}}{\text{car}}$	e.g., medium train 933.5klbf	[6, p. 22]
t_{appl}			$12.22 + 0.0156 l_z + 0.000000278 l_z^2$	[6, Fig. 20]
A		$5\frac{\text{mph}}{\text{min}}$	Force by $\frac{0.44704A}{60}m$, e.g., medium train 391.91klbf	[6, Fig. 27]
f_a		$1.75\frac{\text{mph}}{\text{min}}$	e.g., medium train 136.76klbf	[6, Fig. 27]
ε		100ms		

which is close to the stopping distances in [6, Fig. 10]). With brake pressure propagation, the proofs of Theorems 1 and 2 show that an additional safety margin is needed to avoid overshoot. The resulting stopping distances including these safety margins are summarized for various configurations in Table 3. Note that F_{pb} in [6] is approximated with $23\,338\frac{\text{lbf}}{\text{car}}$ for unknown load, i.e., when trains are not equipped with sensors to determine whether or not their cars are empty. This approximation "improves" the brakes of empty cars, so in Table 3 empty trains with $F_{pb} = 23\,338\frac{\text{lbf}}{\text{car}}$ for unknown load stop sooner than those with $F_{pb} = 10\,575\frac{\text{lbf}}{\text{car}}$ for known load. The brake pressure propagation time t_{appl} is much larger than control cycle time ε, so the additional safety margin of the

Table 3. Stopping distance with brake pressure propagation (in ft, lower is better); bold differences exceed the performance objective of [6] (slow: 500ft, fast: 1000ft)

Cars	Slow						Fast					
	Loaded			Empty			Loaded			Empty		
	10	40	100	10	40	100	10	40	100	10	40	100
Brake force for unknown load $F_{pb} = 23\,338\frac{\text{lbf}}{\text{car}}$												
Model 4	726	1,110	1,942	446	830	1,662	15,436	17,742	22,730	5,369	7,676	12,664
Model 6	541	710	1,017	239	345	503	14,364	15,494	17,880	4,278	5,334	7,383
Difference	185	400	**925**	207	485	**1,161**	**1,072**	**2,248**	**4,850**	**1,091**	**2,342**	**5,281**
Brake force for known load, loaded: $F_{pb} = 35\,750\frac{\text{lbf}}{\text{car}}$, empty: $F_{pb} = 10\,575\frac{\text{lbf}}{\text{car}}$												
Model 4	597	982	1,814	554	939	1,771	10,817	13,123	18,111	9,277	11,583	16,571
Model 6	409	565	822	364	512	746	9,743	10,859	13,188	8,200	9,309	11,602
Difference	188	417	**992**	190	427	**1,025**	**1,074**	**2,264**	**4,923**	**1,077**	**2,274**	**4,969**

conservative model is dominated by the train's speed and the brake pressure propagation time. After all, the delay term $(v + \frac{A}{m}\varepsilon)t_{appl}$ implies that the train controller assumes it might be driving with its current speed for the entire brake propagation time t_{appl}. The effect is even more pronounced for empty trains, because a larger fraction of the entire braking process occurs while pressure is still propagating. The remaining improvements of Model 6 over Model 4 target effects during the control cycle time (e.g., distinguish between accelerating and braking, account for the actual chosen acceleration instead of worst-case acceleration), so could be neglected without much impact on the performance for the specific values of our experiments. The cases highlighted in bold indicate cases where just the additional error incurred by the delay model exceeds the FRA's performance objective goal. This indicates the potential for using more advanced control algorithms.

Proof Effort. From an engineering viewpoint, more realistic models are certainly desirable. However, higher modeling fidelity often results in higher proof complexity, especially in the resulting arithmetic. Proofs in KeYmaera X consist of three main aspects: (i) find invariants for loops and differential equations, (ii) symbolically execute programs to determine their effect (results in formulas in real arithmetic), and finally (iii) verify the resulting real arithmetic with external solvers. High modeling fidelity becomes expensive in the arithmetic parts of the proof, since real arithmetic is decidable but of high complexity. As a result, proofs of high-fidelity models may require arithmetic simplifications (e.g., reduce the number of variables by abbreviating complicated terms, or by hiding irrelevant facts) before calling external solvers. The proof process in KeYmaera X can be scripted with tactics to provide human guidance when necessary.

The main insights of doing the proofs are reflected in the model in terms of the control constraints that switch between driving and braking. We illustrated how to obtain such constraints systematically from the motion model of the train when designing the track control. Further guidance provided in the proof tactics of Theorems 1 and 2 are related to arithmetic simplifications, deferred case splitting to avoid duplicate proof effort, and to speed up rerunning proofs over automated tactics.

The proof of Model 4 was mostly automated with minor case-splits. The tactics nevertheless script differential equation handling to speed up rerunning the proofs. Model 6, in contrast, required arithmetic simplifications to become tractable, and even then resulted in significantly lower proof performance. Table 4 summarizes the proof statistics.

6   Related Work

Train interlocking systems check that trains are not *scheduled to share* route sections at the same time. Formal verification techniques was used in academia [8,16] and industry [5]. Formal methods provide an effective way to satisfy certification requirements such as CENELEC EN-50126 [7]. The properties are

Table 4. Proof statistics

Main tactic purpose	Tactic size		Proof steps	Time [s]	Performance [$\frac{Steps}{s}$]
	LOC	Steps			
Theorem 1 Case-splitting (loop invariant max)	107	200	35,740	100	357
Theorem 2 Arithmetic simplifications	216	624	59,998	270	222

phrased as safety properties in temporal logic, and analyzed by model checking, e.g., in SystemC [14], or Simulink [4,12]. High-level safety specifications can also be linked to interlocking rules represented in lookup tables through assurance case arguments [17]. At industrial scale, discrete aspects of train control were formally specified and with the B method [1] preserved along refinements to implementations, e.g., in the Paris METEOR project and the New York City Canarsie line [10], or for analyzing railway network topology [11]. Safety of approaching and passing railroad crossings was analyzed with timed automata (e.g., [15,18]), with motion represented, if at all, as jumps at discrete time steps. These approaches provide guarantees on the discrete train coordination but not the motion.

We analyze the complementary question whether the physical motion of trains respects the instructions issued by a correct route interlocking protocol. The combination of both answers is required for safe control. The job of interlocking approaches is to guarantee that disjoint movement authorities are issued to trains. Our results guarantee that the train controllers with their continuous dynamics ensure that the trains never move outside these permitted areas, without which the system would not be safe.

ETCS verification [20,23] formally verifies collision freedom between trains when following the movement authorities issued by a radio-block controller. The protocol is modeled as a hybrid systems model, including motion of the train. The ETCS proofs were the basis for a case study on the Chinese train control system [25]. Similar motion models were used for safety verification of railroad crossings with hybrid automata [9].

Here, we focus on significantly more detailed physical models for train braking, which are the gold standard by the Federal Railway Authority. Their additional considerations of mass, length of the train, their effect on pressure brake propagation, and resulting jerk on the dynamics leads to a more realistic yet also more challenging verification result. We analyze the models both for safety and performance objectives.

7 Conclusion

We analyzed the safety of train control by formalizing hybrid systems models of control decisions and their physical effect in terms of stopping distance under two braking models. We studied a lower-fidelity braking model that conservatively approximates pressure propagation with delayed brake onset, and a higher-fidelity braking model with gradual braking force increase during pressure propagation. Our proofs in the hybrid systems prover KeYmaera X show that safety is achievable in both braking models with appropriate control constraints that indicate when free driving is safe and when braking is required for safety. We developed these constraints alongside the proof.

Conservative approximation in braking controllers may degrade performance and engage brakes unnecessarily early, but more complex controller designs and physics models may increase verification/implementation complexity and runtime resource consumption. We analyzed the trade-off between modeling fidelity and verification complexity: the performance comparison between the two models indicates a significantly better performance (i.e., lower stopping distance) in the higher-fidelity model. However, in this case higher modeling fidelity also results in higher proof complexity, especially in the resulting arithmetic. KeYmaera X provides support for scripting proofs with tactics to provide the necessary human guidance in a machine-repeatable way.

References

1. Abrial, J.: The B-book - Assigning Programs to Meanings. Cambridge University Press, New York (2005)
2. Ahmad, H.A.: Dynamic braking control for accurate train braking distance estimation under different operating conditions (2013)
3. Bohrer, B., Rahli, V., Vukotic, I., Völp, M., Platzer, A.: Formally verified differential dynamic logic. In: Bertot, Y., Vafeiadis, V. (eds.) Certified Programs and Proofs - 6th ACM SIGPLAN Conference, Cp. 2017, Paris, France, January 16–17, 2017, pp. 208–221. ACM (2017)
4. Bonacchi, A., Fantechi, A., Bacherini, S., Tempestini, M., Cipriani, L.: Validation of railway interlocking systems by formal verification, a case study. In: Counsell, S., Núñez, M. (eds.) SEFM 2013. LNCS, vol. 8368, pp. 237–252. Springer, Cham (2014). doi:10.1007/978-3-319-05032-4_18
5. Borälv, A.: Case study: Formal verification of a computerized railway interlocking. Formal Aspects Comput. 10(4), 338–360 (1998)
6. Brossaeu, J., Ede, B.M.: Development of an adaptive predictive braking enforcement algorithm. Technical report FRA/DOT/ORD-9/13, Federal Railroad Administration (2009)
7. Cimatti, A., Corvino, R., Lazzaro, A., Narasamdya, I., Rizzo, T., Roveri, M., Sanseviero, A., Tchaltsev, A.: Formal verification and validation of ERTMS industrial railway train spacing system. In: Madhusudan, P., Seshia, S.A. (eds.) CAV 2012. LNCS, vol. 7358, pp. 378–393. Springer, Heidelberg (2012). doi:10.1007/978-3-642-31424-7_29
8. Cimatti, A., Giunchiglia, F., Mongardi, G., Romano, D., Torielli, F., Traverso, P.: Model checking safety critical software with spin: an application to a railway interlocking system. In: Ehrenberger, W. (ed.) SAFECOMP 1998. LNCS, vol. 1516, pp. 284–293. Springer, Heidelberg (1998). doi:10.1007/3-540-49646-7_22

9. Damm, W., Hungar, H., Olderog, E.-R.: On the verification of cooperating traffic agents. In: Boer, F.S., Bonsangue, M.M., Graf, S., Roever, W.-P. (eds.) FMCO 2003. LNCS, vol. 3188, pp. 77–110. Springer, Heidelberg (2004). doi:10.1007/978-3-540-30101-1_4

10. Essamé, D., Dollé, D.: B in large-scale projects: the Canarsie line CBTC experience. In: Julliand, J., Kouchnarenko, O. (eds.) B 2007. LNCS, vol. 4355, pp. 252–254. Springer, Heidelberg (2006). doi:10.1007/11955757_21

11. Falampin, J., Le-Dang, H., Leuschel, M., Mokrani, M., Plagge, D.: Improving railway data validation with ProB. In: Romanovsky, A., Thomas, M. (eds.) Industrial Deployment of System Engineering Methods, pp. 27–43. Springer, Berlin (2013)

12. Ferrari, A., Fantechi, A., Magnani, G., Grasso, D., Tempestini, M.: The Metrô Rio case study. Sci. Comput. Program. **78**(7), 828–842 (2013)

13. Fulton, N., Mitsch, S., Quesel, J.-D., Völp, M., Platzer, A.: KeYmaera X: an axiomatic tactical theorem prover for hybrid systems. In: Felty, A.P., Middeldorp, A. (eds.) CADE 2015. LNCS, vol. 9195, pp. 527–538. Springer, Cham (2015). doi:10.1007/978-3-319-21401-6_36

14. Haxthausen, A.E., Peleska, J., Kinder, S.: A formal approach for the construction and verification of railway control systems. Formal Asp. Comput. **23**(2), 191–219 (2011)

15. Heitmeyer, C.L., Lynch, N.A.: The generalized railroad crossing: a case study in formal verification of real-time systems. In: RTSS, pp. 120–131. IEEE Computer Society (1994)

16. Hong, L.V., Haxthausen, A.E., Peleska, J.: Formal modelling and verification of interlocking systems featuring sequential release. Sci. Comput. Program. **133**, 91–115 (2017)

17. Iliasov, A., Romanovsky, A.: Formal analysis of railway signalling data. In: HASE 2016, pp. 70–77. IEEE Computer Society (2016)

18. Ortmeier, F., Reif, W., Schellhorn, G.: Formal safety analysis of a radio-based railroad crossing using deductive cause-consequence analysis (DCCA). In: Cin, M., Kaâniche, M., Pataricza, A. (eds.) EDCC 2005. LNCS, vol. 3463, pp. 210–224. Springer, Heidelberg (2005). doi:10.1007/11408901_15

19. Platzer, A.: Differential dynamic logic for hybrid systems. J. Autom. Reas. **41**(2), 143–189 (2008)

20. Platzer, A.: Logical Analysis of Hybrid Systems: Proving Theorems for Complex Dynamics. Springer, Heidelberg (2010)

21. Platzer, A.: Logics of dynamical systems. In: LICS, pp. 13–24. IEEE (2012)

22. Platzer, A.: A complete uniform substitution calculus for differential dynamic logic. J. Autom. Reas. **59**(2), 219–265 (2017)

23. Platzer, A., Quesel, J.-D.: European train control system: a case study in formal verification. In: Breitman, K., Cavalcanti, A. (eds.) ICFEM 2009. LNCS, vol. 5885, pp. 246–265. Springer, Heidelberg (2009). doi:10.1007/978-3-642-10373-5_13

24. Polivka, A., Ede, B.M., Drapa, J.: North american joint positive train control project. Technical report DOT/FRA/ORD-09/04 (2009)

25. Zou, L., Lv, J., Wang, S., Zhan, N., Tang, T., Yuan, L., Liu, Y.: Verifying chinese train control system under a combined scenario by theorem proving. In: Cohen, E., Rybalchenko, A. (eds.) VSTTE 2013. LNCS, vol. 8164, pp. 262–280. Springer, Heidelberg (2014). doi:10.1007/978-3-642-54108-7_14

Light Rail and Urban Transit

An Efficient Evaluation Scheme for KPIs in Regulated Urban Train Systems

Bruno Adeline[1], Pierre Dersin[1], Éric Fabre[2], Loïc Hélouët[2(✉)], and Karim Kecir[1,2]

[1] ALSTOM, Saint-Ouen, France
{bruno.adeline,pierre.dersin}@alstom.com
[2] INRIA Rennes, Rennes, France
{eric.fabre,loic.helouet,karim.kecir}@inria.fr

Abstract. This paper considers evaluation of Key Performance Indicators (KPIs) for urban train systems equipped with regulation algorithms. We describe an efficient simulation model that can represent a network, animate metros, and integrate existing regulation schemes as black boxes. This macroscopic model allows efficient simulation of several hours of networks operations within a few seconds. We demonstrate the capacities of this simulation scheme on a case study and show how statistics can be derived during simulation campaigns. We then discuss possible improvements to increase accuracy of models.

Keywords: Key Performance Indicators · Metro networks · Regulation · Simulation

1 Introduction

Urban train systems are subject to performance requirements originating from customers, operators or local authorities. These requirements (or Key Performance Indicators) can focus on punctuality of metros, regularity of service, passengers comfort... Recent indicators also address energy consumption. Usually, trains follow optimized schedules (a.k.a. *timetables*) that allow, if realized as expected, to meet quality requirements. In a perfect world, trains arrive at stations and leave at the exact dates prescribed by a timetable or by a service rate. However, in everyday life, perturbations arise, and schedules are rarely satisfied.

Indeed, urban train systems are subject to random perturbations originating from weather conditions, passengers misbehavior, or failures. To recover from small delays, metro systems are equipped with *regulation* mechanisms, that give advice to train drivers (or to automated systems embedded in trains, if the line is driverless). Advice can be, for example, to reduce/increase dwell time or change commercial speed for a while to resume to the original timetable or to meet a regular service rate. Regulation mechanisms are hence a key element for metros performance. They should be seen as an important part of the design of a metro line, and be considered at early design stages. Several standard regulation techniques appear in the literature: the simplest ones try to stick to a

© Springer International Publishing AG 2017
A. Fantechi et al. (Eds.): RSSRail 2017, LNCS 10598, pp. 195–211, 2017.
https://doi.org/10.1007/978-3-319-68499-4_13

prescribed timetable, but complex proprietary regulation algorithms are also in use. One can however notice that there is no consensual mechanism considered as the best regulation technique: efficiency of a regulation scheme depends on frequency of delays, passengers behaviors, metro lines topology, and many other contextual features. Considering regulation and evaluating its performance at early design stages has several advantages. First, it allows to decide which regulation technique is adapted to particularities (inter-station length, maximal commercial speed of trains, number of trains, passenger behaviors...) of the line under construction. Second, it allows to build timetables and to estimate achievable performance.

Several tools have been used to evaluate performance of mainline railway systems. Following the classification in [8], one can define these tools as macroscopic or microscopic simulation tools. Macroscopic approaches abstract away details (fine modeling of trains acceleration, adherence to tracks...) and do not usually consider trains particularities for simulation; they usually lead to optimistic results. An example of such macroscopic model is the NEMO tool [6]. This tool uses abstract network graphs to compute timetables and detect possible bottlenecks. Microscopic approaches consider trains details, and many parameters such as weather conditions and up to passenger flows. Usually, these approaches consider how trains influence one another at runtime. They use synchronous techniques, i.e., repeatedly evaluate evolution of a network during user-defined time steps (for instance one second). OpenTrack is an example of such simulation framework (see for instance a description in [8]). Synchronous simulation is time consuming, and many steps simulated by the tools are simply useless, as no interaction between trains (forcing one of them to brake, for instance) nor change to a train's behavior (excepted for their positions) occur during most of time steps. OpenTrack and NEMO, as well as commercial softwares such as RailSys target main lines, where delays between departures and arrivals are quite long, and where small local perturbations have little influence on service performance. Challenges for these models are to design timetables, that are quite stable, and in case of failure in a network, find alternative paths for trains (see [3] for an introduction to the timetabling problem and associated tools). Computation of best alternative routes can take a few minutes without affecting too much traffic. In metro networks, paradigms change: trains are really close, minor disturbances may affect service quality, and advice has to be computed as fast as possible to be usable. Hence, corrective mechanisms are quite reactive, and the computed solutions to recover from a delay are applied as soon as possible. Models such as those proposed in the SimMETRO tool [7] address performance of metro systems in a microscopic (and stochastic) setting.

This paper describes a macroscopic performance evaluation scheme for regulated metro systems, that can be used at early design stages. Metro networks are modeled as a variant of Stochastic Time Petri Nets [5]. Dwell and trip times are modeled as sojourn times in places, perturbations are modeled as random variations for these durations. In addition to the network dynamics, the system integrates a timetable and a regulation algorithm. The regulation algorithm is used as a black box that sends departure orders to trains and recomputes the timetable. We consider a fixed block policy: the metro network is divided into zones that can be entered by a single train. The distributions governing trip and dwell durations are defined using expolynomial distributions. Indeed, as delays are more likely than advances the repartition of trip durations have particular asymmetric shapes that cannot be captured by standard uniform, exponential or Gaussian distributions. Distributions are hence defined on an interval in which durations with the highest probabilities are concentrated around several nominal values (nominal dwell or running times). Simulation of traffic is performed using an efficient technique that advances time to the date of the next event(s) (departures and arrivals), hence avoiding useless steps of standard synchronous simulation approaches. The proposed model is abstract enough to allow efficient simulation (many characteristics of trains, tracks and so on are abstracted away), but yet accurate enough to derive useful performance measures. We show that KPIs can be easily evaluated from our model, and demonstrate its practical interest on a real case study, namely line 1 on Santiago's metro. The paper is organized as follows: Sect. 2 introduces our simulation model. Section 3 introduces KPIs and shows statistics obtained from a simulation of 4 h of exploitation on our case study. Section 4 discusses our design choices, and possible improvements of the model, before conclusion.

2   Modeling

Urban train networks are composed of tracks, trains, safety and regulation mechanisms. Tracks can be decomposed in stations, rails and platforms, depots and turn back areas. Trains follow paths expressed as a succession of trips from departure to arrival terminuses and turn back maneuvers. The trip plans are usually detailed in a prebuilt timetable for a day or part of a day of exploitation. Timetables give a desired ideal schedule of trains departures and arrivals. They are an idealized representation of behaviors of trains, that is never perfectly met because of random delays due to incidents, weather conditions, etc. To leverage the effects of these disturbances, urban train systems are equipped with traffic regulation mechanisms that observe delays and compute orders and reschedulings to help the system get back to the ideal timetable.

We propose to model urban train systems with a variant of Stochastic Time Petri Nets as defined by Horváth et al. [5]. As we will show later in this section, this graphical model is particularly adapted to represent a network topology, and to manipulate durations subject to random perturbations. In the rest of the section, we only give an informal presentation of the model and refer to [4] for a complete presentation of the model and of its semantics.

Definition 1 (Stochastic Time Petri Net). *A Stochastic Time Petri Net (STPN for short) is a tuple* $\mathcal{N} = \langle P, T, {}^{\bullet}(), ()^{\bullet}, m_0, \mathsf{eft}, \mathsf{lft}, \mathcal{F} \rangle$ *where P is a finite set of places; T is a finite set of transitions;* ${}^{\bullet}() : T \to 2^P$ *and* $()^{\bullet} : T \to 2^P$ *are pre and post conditions depicting from which places transitions consume tokens, and to which places they output produced tokens;* $m_0 : P \to \{0, 1\}$ *is the initial*

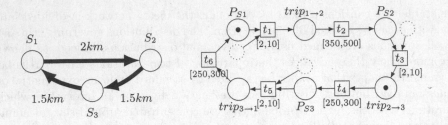

Fig. 1. An example STPN, symbolizing a simple ring topology with two trains.

marking of the net; eft $: T \to \mathbb{Q}_{\geq 0}$ *and* lft $: T \to \mathbb{Q}_{\geq 0} \cup \{+\infty\}$ *respectively specify the minimum and maximum time-to-fire that can be sampled for each transition; and* $\mathcal{F} : T \to \Sigma_{\mathsf{pdf}}$ *associates a probability distribution to each transition.*

Intuitively, places of a net represent either a track segment, a station, or a boolean condition allowing departure of trains. Transitions represent actions, i.e., departures or arrivals of trains. Intervals associated to transitions symbolize the range of possible dwell and trip times, and the distributions attached to transitions the probability distribution for each of these durations.

We denote by f_t the distribution $\mathcal{F}(t)$. To be consistent, we assume that for every $t \in T$, the support of f_t is $[\mathsf{eft}(t), \mathsf{lft}(t)]$. For a given transition $t \in P \cup T$, ${}^{\bullet}t$ will be called the preset of t, and $t^{\bullet}$ the postset of t. Transitions represent departures or arrivals of trains. The preset of an arrival transition has a single place representing the track portion arriving to the station. A departure transition has two places in its preset: a place representing a station, and a place representing an order from the regulation system allowing departures (we will come back to these places later in this section). Consider for instance the drawing at the left of Fig. 1. This is a toy ring topology with 3 stations (S_1, S_2, S_3). The distance between S_1 and S_2 is 2 km, and the distance between S_2 and S_3 is equal to the distance between S_3 and S_1 and is equal to 1.5 km. The commercial speed of train is 20 km/h, and the ring contains 2 trains. This simple topology can be depicted by the STPN at the right of the figure. The places labeled by P_{S_i} symbolize station S_i, and places labeled by $trip_{i \to j}$ the track portion between station S_i and station S_j. Transitions t_1, t_3, t_5 symbolize departures, and t_2, t_4, t_6 arrivals of trains. The intervals associated with transitions represent possible ranges of dwell and running times. In the represented net, places P_{S_1} and $trip_{2 \to 3}$ contain tokens, which represents a situation where a train is stopped at station S_1 and another one is moving from station S_2 to station S_3.

This syntax of STPNs is similar to the one in [5], but we need to adapt their semantics to represent metro systems: for safety reasons, trains in a metro network have to preserve a *safety headway*. A way to address this safety requirement is to decompose a network into *blocks*, and allow a train to enter a block only when no other train uses it. This policy is called *fixed block* policy. Standard semantics of transitions firing in Petri nets consume tokens from the preset of a transition and produce tokens in its postset regardless of the contents of a place.

In the standard setting, places can contain more that one token. To implement a fixed block policy, we define a blocking semantics that requires, in addition to standard rules, that places in $^\bullet t$ that receive tokens when firing a transition t are empty.

The semantics of STPNs is defined in terms of sequences of discrete transition firings, and timed moves. We will say that a transition t is *enabled* by a marking m iff $\forall p \in {}^\bullet t, m(p) = 1$. For a given marking m and a set of places P', we will denote by $m - P'$ the marking that assigns $m(p)$ tokens to each place $p \in P \setminus P'$, and $m(p) - 1$ tokens to each place $p \in P'$. Similarly, we will denote by $m + P'$ the marking that assigns $m(p)$ tokens to each place $p \in P \setminus P'$, and $m(p) + 1$ tokens to each place $p \in P'$. Firing a transition t is done in two steps and consists in: (1) consuming tokens from $^\bullet t$, leading to a *temporary* marking $m_{\text{tmp}} = m - {}^\bullet t$, then (2) producing tokens in $t^\bullet$, leading to a marking $m' = m_{\text{tmp}} + t^\bullet$.

The blocking semantics of an STPN can be informally described as follows. A variable τ_t is attached to each transition t of the STPN. If a transition t represents an arrival at a station S, when $^\bullet t$ is marked, this means that there is a train on its way to station S. If t represents a departure from a station S, when $^\bullet t$ is marked this means that a train is stationed at station S, and has received an authorization to leave. As soon as a transition t is enabled, τ_t is set to a random value ζ_t (called the *time-to-fire* of t, or TTF for short) sampled from $[\text{eft}(t), \text{lft}(t)]$ according to f_t. Intuitively, this TTF represents a duration that *must* elapse before firing t once t is enabled. The value of τ_t then decreases as time elapses but cannot reach negative values. When the TTF of a transition t reaches 0, then if $t^\bullet$ is empty t becomes *urgent* and has to fire unless another transition with TTF 0 and empty postset fires; otherwise (if $t^\bullet$ is not empty), t becomes *blocked*: its TTF stops decreasing and keeps value 0, and its firing is delayed until the postset of t becomes empty; in the meantime, t can be disabled by the firing of another transition. The semantics of STPNs is *urgent*: time can elapse by durations that do not exceed the minimal remaining TTF of enabled transitions that are not blocked. At a given moment, one can consider all remaining time to fire of enabled transitions, and compute the delay that has to elapse before some transition firing will occur. This allows to avoid synchronous approaches and perform *macro* time steps between two discrete events.

Let us say a few words about distributions attached to transitions. In our model, transitions symbolize departures and arrivals of trains. Places symbolize a station, or a track portion between two stations. A departure occurs a certain amount of time after arrival of the train at the considered station, and similarly, going from one station to another one takes time. Distributions describe the probability of durations for dwell and running times. If one wants to obtain realistic models and accurate enough performance measures, these distributions have to be realistic enough. Distributions can be discrete (i.e., a list of possible values with associated weight), but for precision reasons, it is preferable to use continuous distributions. An usual way to model continuous distributions is to use Gaussian distributions, i.e., of the form $f(x) = \frac{1}{\sqrt{2\pi\sigma^2}}.e^{\frac{(x-\mu)^2}{2\sigma^2}}$, where μ and σ are parameters of the distribution. Such distributions describe a bell shaped curve, centered around the most probable value. In the setting of durations for dwell times or trips, delays are more likely than advance, and in general our distributions are not that symmetric. We hence use asymmetric distributions, modeled with expolynomial functions.

Definition 2. *A truncated expolynomial function over domain $[u, v]$ is a function of the form* $f(x) = \begin{cases} \sum_0^K c_k.x^{a_k} e^{-\lambda_k.x} & \text{if } x \in [u, v] \\ 0 & \text{otherwise} \end{cases}$ *where u, v and c_k, a_k, λ_k for every $k \in \{0, 1, \ldots, K\}$ are rational values.*

$f(x)$ is an expolynomial probability density function iff $\int_u^v f(x) = 1$.

During simulations of our Petri net model, dwell and trip durations are sampled according to distributions attached to transitions. Sampling from continuous distributions can be done using inverse transform techniques (see for instance [11]). Let us denote by F_t the cumulative distribution function (CDF) associated with f_t, i.e., $F_t(x) = \int_0^x f_t$. We will assume that every CDF F_t is strictly increasing on $[\mathsf{eft}(t), \mathsf{lft}(t)]$, which allows for *inverse transform sampling*. Then sampling a value for a distribution defined by f_t amounts to sampling a value v from the standard uniform distribution in the interval $[0, 1]$, compute the value x such that $F_t(x) = v$, and take x as the random duration sampled from law f_t.

For efficiency reasons, one can also approximate truncated expolynomial functions with areas defined by zones, which greatly simplifies sampling for an acceptable precision loss. Figure 2 shows a Gaussian distribution $g(x) = \frac{1}{\sqrt{2\pi}}.e^{-\frac{(x-4)^2}{2}}$ (i.e., with parameters $\mu = 4$ and $\sigma = 1$), an expolynomial distribution $f(x) = 0.58.x^2.e^{-1.7x} + 0.29.x^3.e^{-1.2x}$ defined over $[0.5, 6]$, and an approximation of this function on the same domain by an area delimited by two affine functions. On this figure, one can notice that a Gaussian distribution is centered around a pivot value: $g(x)$ describes a distribution in which the most probable values lay around 4 time units, but where the probability density of values before and after 4 is exactly 0.5. Conversely, the expolynomial distribution $f(x)$ has its most probable values centered around 2 time units, but the probability mass of values greater than 2 (0.67) is larger than that of values

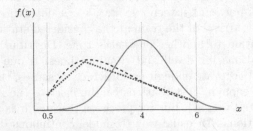

Fig. 2. A Gaussian distribution (plain line), an expolynomial function (dashed line), and its area approximation (dotted line).

smaller than 2 (0.33). This can be interpreted as: the most probable value for a delay is 2, and the probability to be delayed is higher than the probability to be in advance.

Now, STPNs only describe the dynamics of trains, i.e., how they move from one track portion to another, and the time needed to move from one part of the network to another. As already mentioned, unwanted delays are recovered using regulation techniques that should hence be considered when evaluating the overall dynamics and performance on an urban train network. The overall behavior of our model is hence provided by a combination of a Petri net, and of a regulation algorithm. The Petri net part of our simulator simulates train moves, dwell and running times and random delays for these durations. Firing a transition in this net means a departure or an arrival of a train at a given date. The regulation part of the model reads arrival and departure dates of trains (i.e., firing dates of transitions of the Petri net), and allows departures at dates prescribed by a timetable. Upon delay, the regulation algorithm recomputes a new timetable according to a regulation policy. Regulation algorithms usually recompute future departure or arrival dates of trains, which amounts to change dwell time or commercial speed (through the reduction of running and dwell times) upon observation of a delay. These techniques usually allow to catch up delays within a few stations. However, more involved regulation algorithms can redefine trains paths, allow overtaking of trains, insert/extract trains, etc.

Our simulation framework integrates regulation as follows: places of the Petri net represent stations or track portions. Transitions of the net represent departures or arrivals of trains. Some places in the preset of a departure transition (dotted places in Fig. 3) represent orders given by the regulation algorithm. When all places of $^\bullet t$ are filled and in particular the dotted place, the departure is allowed. This way, regulation algorithms can allow departures at a precise date, or impose a direction to a train leaving a station, in order to follow a plan. Consider the example of Fig. 3. Place P_{S_1} contains a token. This token was put in the place by transition t_1. The occurrence date of t_1 can be recorded and compared by the regulation algorithm to detect whether this event (a train arrival) was late. If this is the case, then the time table attached to the system can be updated. As soon as the regulation part fills place C_1, a value from $[12, 20]$ can be sampled, and the train will leave as soon as this TTF reaches 0. Place P_{S_2} also contains a token, but the place has several transitions consuming tokens from it. According to the mission of the next train leaving station S_2, the regulation module will fill either place C_2, allowing firing of t_4 between 20 and 25 s later, or $C3$, allowing firing of t_5 between 18 and 25 s later.

This way, our simulator is an abstract representation of trains moves, but integrates a real regulation policy. Regulation algorithms are written as a set of rules applicable following a triggering event such as the delayed arrival of a train. They can be simple rules of the form "if a train arrives late by more than x time units then reduce dwell time to minimum allowed dwell time for the station". They can also be intricate rules choosing a decision to perform according to a set of thresholds... The framework proposed above has the advantage of integrating

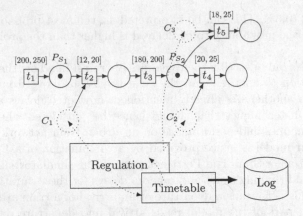

Fig. 3. The SIMSTORS simulation framework

a real regulation policy. The same network and train fleets can be tested with different regulation algorithms without changing the whole model. However, this modularity and the expressiveness allowed in regulation has a cost: it is very hard to formalize and analyze the effect of regulation on the overall behavior of the model, that is hence more adapted to statistical analysis of performance via simulation. The first results obtained are quite promising: the structure of the net mimics the topology of the specified network, and the behavior of trains and the corrections brought by regulation are very similar to those usually observed.

In the modeled setting, we consider that regulation is a deterministic process: for a given delay detected at departure or arrival of a train, the changes to the schedule computed by the regulation algorithm is always the same. Though our simulation framework uses regulation as a black box, i.e., imposes no constraint of the type of regulation used by the system, this assumption seems sensible. An advantage of this assumption is that randomness comes exclusively from the part of the system represented by the stochastic time Petri net. An access to the current state of the schedule and to the times to fire of all transitions suffices to know the date of the next event that will occur in the system (a departure order given by the regulation, an effective departure, or an arrival of a train). As a consequence, one needs not discretize time according to a fixed sampling rate, and can consider only dates at which events occur. This is called *event-based simulation*, and allows for fast simulation of long runs of metro systems.

We have used this model to represent Line 1 of Santiago's metro [1]. This line is a complex ring topology: two intertwined rings connecting 24 stations. The Petri net built for this line is a net with 102 dwell places, 147 trip places, 147 control places, 147 departure transitions and 147 arrival transitions. The model contains depots and turn back zones in addition to stations and their interconnections. With this Petri net, we can simulate 4 h of operations of Santiago's metro with 50 trains and random perturbations in 40 s on an average laptop.

3   KPIs and Simulation Campaign Results

Urban train networks are driven by operators that have commitments with local authorities to meet quality criteria. These criteria are standardized by the UITP [9], and known as Key Performance Indicators (KPIs for short). Failing to meet fixed performance objectives can result in financial penalties for operators. KPIs address several criteria: punctuality, regularity of service, number of failures, ratios of successful missions completed, but also more subjective measures such as passengers comfort... Usually, KPI measures are obtained by computing statistics from logs of train operations. Of course, these statistics make sense only if logs are recorded for a sufficiently long duration (day, week or month). Statistics are derived from a set of complete trips (travel from one terminus of a line to another endpoint of a line). In what follows, we assume that a sufficiently large set of effectively realized trips T is recorded. For each trip, departure and arrival dates at all stations have been recorded. We also assume that reference timetables are provided, indicating expected dates of departures and arrivals of trains when no perturbation arises.

Given this set T, the **punctuality** KPI is defined as "the ratio of train trips delayed by less than x minutes over the total number of trips" [9]. As formalized by UITP, this KPI only considers ending dates of trips. Formally speaking, this KPI is defined as

$$P_{\text{KPI}} \triangleq \left| \{t \in T \mid \dot{d}(t) - d(t) < x\} \right| / |T|$$

$\dot{d}(t)$ is the occurrence date of the last event of trip t, $d(t)$ the scheduled date of the last event of t, and x is a given threshold (in minutes).

The **regularity** KPI is defined by UITP as "the ratio of train departures at specified stations complying with planned headways within x minutes over the total number of departures from the specified stations". More formally, we assume a selection of stations $S = \{s_1, s_2, \ldots, s_m\}$ of interest where regularity is important. For each station $s_j \in S$, we denote by $Ed_j = \{ed_{1,j}, ed_{2,j}, \ldots, ed_{k,j}\}$ the ordered set of departures from station s_j. We also denote by $\dot{h}(ed_{i+1,j})$ the effective headway between departure event ed_{i+1} and its predecessor ed_i, and by $h(ed_{i+1,j})$ the reference headway (for instance the headway planned for these trips in a reference timetable). The regularity KPI is then formally defined as:

$$R_{\text{KPI}} \triangleq \sum_{j=1}^{m} \left| \{ed_{i+1,j} \in Ed_j \mid 1 < i \le k \wedge \dot{h}(ed_{i+1,j}) - h(ed_{i+1,j}) < x\} \right| / \sum_{j=1}^{m} |Ed_j|$$

x is a given threshold.

We have performed a simulation campaign for Santiago's metro based on the model of line 1 mentioned in Sect. 2. We have simulated the first 4 h of operation of the line, with 50 trains operating on the line[1]. The system was equipped with

---

[1] Traffic is not immediately maximal but increases progressively as trains are inserted in the network.

a regulation algorithm trying to stick as much as possible to a precomputed ideal timetable TT^{id}. The regulation plays on dwell times to recover from unexpected delays, and maintains a feasible timetable that associates to departures and arrivals their earliest possible occurrence date. This 4 h simulation has been performed 100 times to record arrival and departure dates at all stations. During each simulation, dwell and running times for each event are randomly sampled from their respective distributions. The distributions attached to transitions were discretization of asymmetric bell shaped curves (i.e., close to a discretization of an expolynomial function).

At the end of the simulation campaign, the obtained data were a succession of departure and arrival dates corresponding to 100 simulations, each simulation providing departure and arrival dates for all steps of realized trips. From these data, we have computed statistics and derived a KPI, namely the mean deviation w.r.t. desired departure headways. Overall, the campaign took around 1 h.

Figure 4 depicts the mean deviations computed for each individual simulation. Abscissa indicate the simulation number (ranging from 1 to 100). The different curves on the picture represent the mean deviation with respect to the ideal timetable TT^{id} at each station (1 curve per station). The dark curve represents one particular station, namely Pajaritos, in running direction 1. Note that we slightly abuse the term "station", as for each physical location of line 1, we have a station number for each running direction. (There are two possible directions: direction 1 from station "San Pablo" to "Los Dominicos" and direction 2 the converse way.) From these recorded mean deviations w.r.t. TT^{id}, one can observe the randomness of the simulation, as for each run, the results are different.

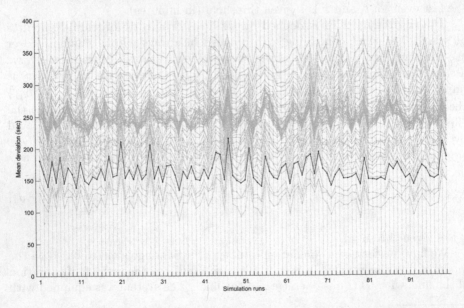

Fig. 4. Mean deviations from reference timetable for $n = 100$ runs

Let n be the number of simulations performed during a campaign (in our case $n = 100$), and let r_j with $j = 1, 2, \ldots, n$ denote the jth simulation (also called a *run* hereafter). Let m be the number of stations, and let us denote by s_k with $k = 1, 2, \ldots, m$ the kth station on the line. Events occurring at a given station s_k in a run r_j are denoted $e_{i,j,k}$ with $i = 1, 2, \ldots, q_k$. Note that, during our simulation campaign, the number of events per station was the same from a run to another. Considering the idealized timetable TT^{id}, one can easily find the ith event (departure or arrival) at station k, and hence obtain its planned occurrence date. We denote by $d(e_{i,j,k})$ the *reference date* for the occurrence of event $e_{i,j,k}$, which is the ideal occurrence date. Note that as $d(e_{i,j,k})$ is the same for all runs, we can simply write it as $d_{i,k}$. We denote by $\dot{d}_{i,j,k}$ the *effective occurrence date* of event $e_{i,j,k}$ in run r_j at station s_k. The *deviation* (w.r.t. the reference timetable dates) for an event $e_{i,j,k}$ is the difference $\delta_{i,j,k} = \dot{d}_{i,j,k} - d_{i,k}$ between its effective date of occurrence and its desired occurrence date. Consider Fig. 5. This graphics represent data collected during a single run of our simulation. Each curve represents the evolution of deviations for a particular station. Abscissa represent time elapsing, and ordinates give the deviations $\delta_{1,1,k}, \delta_{2,1,k}, \ldots, \delta_{q_k,1,k}$. It might seem surprising that deviations grow but this is due to the chosen parameters for the simulation: we have deliberately selected high values of perturbations, to be able to observe the impact of regulation. One can see that, in the beginning of the simulation, the regulation is able to recover, more or less, from the perturbations but, as time progresses, the system becomes unstable. This is due to the fact that more and more trains are inserted into the network. As a consequence, it becomes harder for regulation algorithms to recover from consequent delays, and bunching phenomena appear.

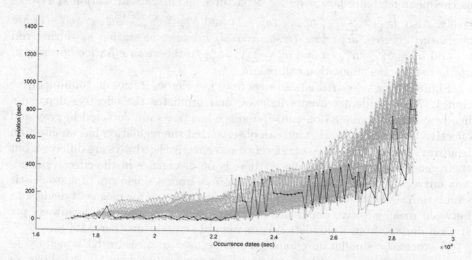

Fig. 5. Progress of deviations from reference timetable for station Pajaritos, direction 1

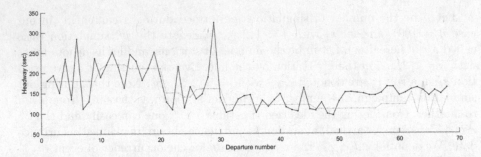

Fig. 6. Effective and reference headways for station Los Héroes, dir. 1 for one simulation

Instead of reasoning in terms of occurrence dates and deviations, one can also consider **headways**, as they give a better measure of traffic regularity. For headways to be relevant, they have to be measured only between events of the same type (i.e., departures or arrivals). We hence denote by $e_{i,j,k}^d$ (resp. $e_{i,j,k}^a$) the ith departure (resp. arrival) at station s_k in run r_j. Similarly, we denote by q_k^d (resp. q_k^a) the total number of departures (resp. arrivals) at station k (one need not differentiate between runs). We then denote by $h_{i,k}^d \triangleq d(e_{i+1,k}^d) - d(e_{i,k}^d)$ the reference headway at departure $i+1$ and by $h_{i,k}^a \triangleq d(e_{i+1,k}^a) - d(e_{i,k}^a)$ the reference headway at arrival $i+1$ at station s_k. We denote by $\dot{h}_{i,j,k}^d \triangleq \dot{d}(e_{i+1,j,k}^d) - \dot{d}(e_{i,j,k}^d)$ the effective headway at departure $i+1$ in run r_j and $\dot{h}_{i,j,k}^a \triangleq \dot{d}(e_{i+1,j,k}^a) - \dot{d}(e_{i,j,k}^a)$ the reference headway at arrival $i + 1$ at station s_k.

We can then define $\overline{h}_k^d \triangleq \sum_{i=1}^{q_k^d-1} h_{i,k}^d / \left(q_k^d - 1\right)$ and $\overline{h}_k^a \triangleq \sum_{i=1}^{q_k^a-1} h_{i,k}^a / \left(q_k^a - 1\right)$ as the mean reference headways for departures and arrivals at station s_k respectively. Also, $\tilde{h}_{j,k}^d \triangleq \sum_{ix=1}^{q_k^d-1} \dot{h}_{i,j,k}^d / \left(q_k^d - 1\right)$ and $\tilde{h}_{j,k}^a \triangleq \sum_{i=1}^{q_k^a-1} \dot{h}_{i,j,k}^a / \left(q_k^a - 1\right)$ are the *mean effective departure (resp. arrival) headway* at station s_k during run r_j, and $\tilde{h}_k^d \triangleq \sum_{j=1}^n \dot{h}_{j,k}^d / n$ and $\tilde{h}_k^a \triangleq \sum_{j=1}^n \dot{h}_{j,k}^a / n$ the *mean effective headway at station s_k* for the simulation campaign.

Figure 6 shows departure headways from Los Héroes station in running direction 1. Abscissa depict events indexes, and ordinates the effective departure headways for one simulation run. Reference headways are depicted in gray and effective headways in black. One can observe that the regulation has an effect on headways. Indeed the curves of reference and effective headways are different, but their general profile remains close (there is no divergence in the effective headway curve). Now, one cannot draw conclusions from a single run of a stochastic simulation. In what follows, we give confidence intervals for means of deviations between mean effective departure headways and mean reference headways per station derived from a simulation campaign of several runs (here, 100).

A stochastic simulation campaign can be used to measure KPIs defined as mean value of some quantity ζ_i measured for each sampled run r_i. It is however interesting to know how the computed value approaches the theoretical mean μ for this KPI. Such a confidence can be quantified through **confidence intervals**. We call $M \triangleq \frac{1}{n} \sum_{i=1}^n \zeta_i$ the *sample mean* obtained from ζ_i's, and σ the

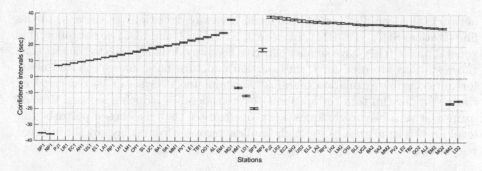

Fig. 7. 99.9% confidence intervals for means of deviations between mean effective departure headways and mean reference headways per station

corresponding *estimated standard deviation*. According to the law of large numbers, M approaches μ only when the number of samples n is sufficiently large. To increase confidence in the computed value, a standard approach is to set a confidence level α, and compute a confidence interval I from M. I is the confidence interval for μ at confidence level $1 - \alpha$, i.e., the probability that μ belongs to I is $1 - \alpha$. Given n, M, σ and α, the confidence interval is defined as:

$$I \triangleq \left[M - \gamma_\alpha \frac{\sigma}{\sqrt{n}}, M + \gamma_\alpha \frac{\sigma}{\sqrt{n}} \right] \tag{1}$$

where γ_α is a value depending only on α called the *z-score*.[2]

Let us now consider a KPI measuring the mean deviation w.r.t. reference departure headways for a station. The *headway deviation* (difference between the effective headway and the reference headway) for event i, in run r_j at station s_k is defined as $\theta_{i,j,k} = \dot{h}^d_{i,j,k} - h^d_{i,k}$. The *mean headway deviation in a run r_j at station s_k* is given by $\overline{\theta}_{j,k} \triangleq \sum_{i=1}^{q^d_k - 1} \theta_{i,j,k} / (q^d_k - 1)$. Finally, the *mean headway deviation at station s_k for a simulation campaign of n runs* is $\overline{\theta}_k \triangleq \sum_{j=1}^{n} \overline{\theta}_{j,k} / n$. The *standard deviation* of $\overline{\theta}_k$ in a simulation campaign of n runs is $\sigma_k \triangleq \sqrt{\sum_{j=1}^{n} \left(\overline{\theta}_k - \overline{\theta}_{j,k} \right)^2 / (n - 1)}$.

Figure 7 shows the confidence intervals computed for headway deviations at each station. The parameters of the simulation are $n = 100$ runs, and the intervals are computed for a confidence $1 - \alpha = 99.9\%$. In this Figure, the horizontal axis carries station names, and the ordinates represent values of mean deviations. For each station, the graphics contain an interval around the sample mean value computed from the simulation campaign. One can notice that headway deviations grow progressively from station Pajaritos direction 1 to Manquehue direction 1 and from Manquehue direction 2 to Pajaritos direction 2. This is explained by an accumulation of delays due to bottlenecks at both ends of the

---

[2] This value is the real value such that $\mathbb{P}\left[|N| \leq \gamma_\alpha\right] = 1 - \alpha$, where N is a variable following a normal law $\mathcal{N}(0, 1)$. This value is not easily computable, but all statistical tools provide means to obtain γ_α, for instance using precalculated *z-tables*.

network. One can also notice that mean headway deviations at the ends of the line (stations SP1, NP1, HM1, LD1, SP2, NP2, HM2, and LD2) do not follow this general profile (they have smaller effective headways). This is due to the fact that these stations are used for train insertion and turn back maneuvers and allow for more flexible regulation margins. Accumulated delays can be recovered at these stations (up to a certain limit) by considerably reducing sojourn time or using fast turn back techniques. Last, one can see that the chosen perturbation level for this simulation is too high to allow recovery from delays by the selected regulation.

4   Discussion and Improvements

The model proposed in this paper has been tested on a real case study; namely, the Line 1 of Santiago's Metro, with a hold-on regulation policy that tries to stick as much as possible to a predetermined timetable. This first experimentation allows to obtain simulation results within a reasonable time (a few seconds for 4 h of operation of a real network, i.e., a real topology with its actual train fleet). This shows feasibility of a simulation approach to evaluate performance of regulation algorithms. Now, this simulation framework can be improved along several directions. First of all, distributions for delays were designed from an a priori knowledge of normal dwell and running times between two stations. To guarantee that these distributions are accurate enough, one could observe trains and passengers behaviors over a long enough period, and derive distributions from the collected data.

A second issue regarding distributions is that the delays are modeled as Markovian noise. In this setting, every delay is sampled independently from the others. In urban train networks, latencies are correlated. For instance, if a train gets late, more passengers will enter the train, which will increase the chances of delay. Similarly, if a train is delayed due to bad weather between two stations, all trains of the network are likely to be delayed on the same part of the network. This means that sampling in our simulator should consider a context, and that distributions should be conditional distributions of the form $p(x \mid c_1, c_2, \ldots, c_k)$ where x is a delay, and $c_1, c_2, \ldots, c_k$ are variables representing the context (station, weather, day of the week, time of the day, etc.) in which delay x is sampled. This change does not require much effort to be integrated to our simulation model. However, it does require a lot of effort from designers to evaluate the impact of an environmental factor on the distributions.

Train fleets: A second issue that should be considered is the impact of fleet composition on computed metrics. In the simulation that we have performed, we have considered regulation techniques that cannot change composition of fleets to meet their objectives. The number of running trains changes according to the period of the day, but follow planned insertions and removals of trains: It would be interesting to consider regulation techniques that can recommend to insert or remove trains to meet a desired KPI. In a similar way, we have considered uniform fleets. This is however not the case that all trains have the same speed, same capacities, etc. One can easily integrate to distributions (and to the context as described above) the type of each train when sampling a dwell or running duration. As for all environmental factors, this difference between trains can be defined using conditional distributions, but with an increased design cost.

Moving block: In this paper, all experiments have been conducted assuming that the line was operated with a fixed block policy, forbidding trains to enter an already occupied track section (block). However, in reality, trains can also follow a moving block policy [10]. The moving block policy as described by Pearson states that *"A train is continuously supplied with accurate information of the position of the nearest obstacle on the track ahead of it [...] it may be a preceding train, which itself may be moving or stationary. The speed of the train is constantly checked and adjusted [...] so that it is always possible for the train to be brought to rest without colliding with the obstacle."* In this setting, several trains can enter a track portion as long as they adapt their speed to their predecessors. Changing the Petri net setting to adapt to this change needs to consider running times as constrained delays attached to trains and not as time to fire attached to transitions. This change to the model is currently under study.

Distributions: Currently, the sampling technique for running and dwell times represented by an expolynomial probability density function f with domain $[u, v]$ uses a discretization of the cumulative distribution function $F(x) = \int_0^x f(y)$. That is we obtain a set of values $x_1, \ldots x_K$, where K in the number of slices for our cumulative function and $x_i = (v - u) \cdot i/K$. Then after sampling a value η from the uniform distribution, we select the discrete value $z = x_i$ such that η lays within $[F(x_i), F(x_{i+1})]$. This raises two issues. First of all these distributions are designed from a priori knowledge of Santiago's network, and in particular the commercial speeds on the network, and from an abstraction of the behavior of metro users resulting in bounded delays. These distributions can be improved through a fine observation of delays and using learning algorithms once a network is operational. Second, the sampling technique can result in a loss of accuracy if the probability density function is too roughly discretized, or in a loss of performance if the sampling technique consumes too much time.

Regulation: The regulation considered in this paper is a simple policy that tries to stick to a predetermined timetable. The architecture of our tool uses regulation algorithms as a particular module and replacing the current regulation by another one is quite simple. Currently, what our regulation does is: first receive an arrival date for a train, then compare it with the expected date in a timetable. Last it propagates the delays and taken decisions to the yet unexecuted part of the timetable. Changing this regulation for another one (for instance, one that tries to maintain headways between trains) within this architecture is an easy task, and other regulation techniques are currently under implementation.

Passengers flows: The last aspect that may improve accuracy of the model is to consider how passengers transfer from one line to another. Indeed, metro networks are often composed of several interconnected lines. A flow of passengers entering a line at an endpoint is likely to transfer to another line at a junction point of the network. This flow of passengers is often captured with Origin-Destination Matrices, in which entries indicate the proportion of passengers alighting at station i that leave a train at station j, or which proportion of passengers leaving at a junction station enter the next train of another line. In its current status, our model does not integrate flows nor address the number of passengers. As already mentioned, the number of passengers impacts the distribution of delays. However, integrating passengers flows to our model is likely to increase simulation time dramatically, as it requires counting (or at least quantizing) trains population, and remembering passengers alighting histories to guarantee faithful representation of passengers flows. An inspiration for this improvement of our model and of our simulation framework is the *multiphase fluid Petri nets* proposed in [2]. Another difficulty in flows representation is that Origin-Destination matrices are not known a priori. They are not available at early design stages. They have to be built once a metro network is operational, which usually requires observation of passenger habits for long periods of time.

5   Conclusion

In this paper, we have detailed a framework for performance evaluation of regulation algorithms on a particular metro line. This framework consists of a high-level model of the network and of train moves, with random perturbations, in which a regulation algorithm is inserted to correct these delays. The overall system allows for fast simulation, and hence for realization of simulation campaigns to obtain statistics on the efficiency of a regulation algorithm to meet KPI objectives.

The proposed framework allowed us to derive statistics for a case study, namely Line 1 of Santiago's Metro. A key question raised by our study is the tradeoff between abstraction (allowing efficiency of simulation) and accuracy of the statistics derived. Petri nets allow for an accurate modeling of network topologies, the key ingredient for our model is hence accuracy of running and dwell times. As explained in the paper, truncated expolynomial functions allow for precise modeling of distributions in which trains are more likely to be delayed than advanced. When sampling for such functions is too time consuming, these functions can be approximated with areas delimited by affine functions.

Now, a major challenge is to define these distributions. Of course, at early stages of design, one can rely on expected characteristics of the network and trains to design distributions a priori. For an existing system, when the challenge is not design but rather to adapt regulation train fleets and their paths to improve KPIs, one may want to work with accurate distributions, that consider elements from context: passengers, trains, but also regulation itself. In such a situation, collected logs can help learning parameters of a distribution for dwell or running time, but it remains a challenging task to estimate the contribution of passengers or regulation to a certain duration, as these parameters are usually not remembered in logs. As a future work, we plan to use our tool to compare regulation techniques, and to improve its accuracy by learning distributions.

References

1. Santiago's metro map. http://transitmap.net/post/18863388725/santiago
2. Haar, S., Theissing, S.: A hybrid-dynamical model for passenger-flow in transportation systems. In: ADHS'15, IFAC-PapersOnLine, vol. 48(27), pp. 236–241 (2015)
3. Hansen, I.A.: Railway network timetabling and dynamic traffic management. Int. J. Civil Eng. **8**(1), 19–32 (2010)
4. Hélouët, L., Kecir, K.: Realizability of schedules by stochastic time Petri nets with. In: Kordon, F., Moldt, D. (eds.) PETRI NETS 2016. LNCS, vol. 9698, pp. 155–175. Springer, Cham (2016)
5. Horváth, A., Paolieri, M., Ridi, L., Vicario, E.: Transient analysis of non-markovian models using stochastic state classes. Perform. Eval. **69**(7–8), 315–335 (2012)
6. Kettner, M., Sewcyk, B., Eickmann, C.: Integrating microscopic and macroscopic models for railway network evaluation. Association for European Transport (2003)
7. Koustopoulos, H.N., Wang, Z.: Simulation of urban rail operations: model and calibration methodology. In: Chung, E., Dumont, A.-G. (eds.) Transport Simulation, Beyond Traditional Approaches, pp. 153–169. EFPL Press, Lausanne (2009)
8. Nash, A., Huerlimann, D.: Railroad simulation using opentrack. In: Allan, J., Hill, R.J., Brebbia, C.A., Sciutto, G., Sone, S. (eds.) Computers in Railways IX, pp. 45–54. WIT Press, Southampton (2004)
9. UITP (International Association of Public Transports). Metro service performance indicators, a uitp information sheet (2011)
10. Pearson, L.V.: Moving Block Railway Signalling. Ph.D. thesis, Wiley (1973)
11. Rubinstein, R.Y., Kroese, D.P.: Simulation and the Monte Carlo Method, 2nd edn. Wiley, Hoboken (2008)

Redundant and Reliable Architecture Based on Open Source Tools for Light-Rail-Transit On-Board-Systems

Vincenzo Di Massa[1][⊠], Mirko Damiani[2], Maurizio Papini[1], and Gianluca Mandò[1]

[1] Thales Italia S.p.A., Florence, Italy
{vincenzo.dimassa,maurizio.papini,gianluca.mando}@thalesgroup.com
[2] Develer S.r.l., Campi Bisenzio, Italy
mirko.damiani@develer.com

Abstract. The LRT (Light Rail Transit) systems are a kind of urban transport that has aspects in common to both tramways and metros. This paper analyses the Thales LRT On-Board-Systems (OBS) architecture, which is designed to achieve a high level of availability. Such architecture is built on top of open source technologies and consolidated telecommunication standards. Architectural requirements are met also thanks to the used Open-Source foundations. In particular the Qt framework, the 0MQ and the ASN.1 to C compiler have been used to develop a micro-service oriented fault resistant system. Redundant services are spawned on replicated identical hardware units, one of which is the master, and are seamlessly and automatically kept in sync by the algorithms described in this paper. In case of a service failure on one of the replicated hardware boxes, a choice is made between two alternatives: (1) a full mastership changeover is performed and another redundant box becomes the new master (2) a micro-service is migrated to another redundant box in order to take control of the same non-faulty device. The described architecture is being actively used in both LRT and metro solutions, thus this work will describe the benefits on the field and the effectiveness of the architecture in terms of code quality and maintainability. Since the development of the mentioned projects has been carried on inside an Agile team, some considerations will be made about benefits, constraints and pitfalls of such kind of methodologies, on strictly regulated and safety related projects.

Keywords: On board systems · Light rail transit · Open source · Software architecture · Redundant system · Micro service · Agile

1 Introduction

The architecture this paper describes has been selected, implemented and operated on the field by the authors. This paper focuses on analyzing the benefits and trade-offs of the selected architecture in the context of LRT on board devices.

© Springer International Publishing AG 2017
A. Fantechi et al. (Eds.): RSSRail 2017, LNCS 10598, pp. 212–220, 2017.
https://doi.org/10.1007/978-3-319-68499-4_14

The techniques and the architecture described in the following chapters have been chosen in order to overcome the problems of the former implementation that can be summarized in: complexity of the software, high cost to test the software, difficulty in documenting the interfaces and changing system components. Because the reasoning behind the authors' choices is driven by their context, the reader must be warned that this paper will not address pitfalls this architecture could have in different contexts.

In order to understand the LRT environment, Sect. 2 will briefly describe the authors LRT context, Sect. 3 will explain the relevant design goals of the authors, Sect. 4 will provide an overview about the architecture, Sect. 5 will analyze the performance of the system and Sect. 6 will conclude highlighting the benefits and pitfalls.

2   The LRT Context

An LRT system is composed by different subsystems that offer different functionalities. All the subsystems consume and send data to both allow monitoring the LRT service by an Operational Control System (OCC) and to feed inputs and read outputs from the other subsystems. The physical distribution of the systems is conventionally classified into three different zones:

the OCC where operators monitor the service by reading the system generated events in real-time and can intervene by talking to drivers and on board personnel and by acting on the LRT subsystems (e.g. manual override);

the wayside (WS) is a distributed system that provides and distributes information about the LRT physical status and state like, e.g. status of the trains, current configuration of the signals and switches, passenger information and announces services (PIS/PAS), video disk recording (VDR);

the on board systems (OBS) are connected to train devices, sensors, displays speakers, radios (e.g. Tetra, 802.11abgn, LTE) and are able to collect, distribute and store service data that is used to both allow the train to: connect to wayside elements (e.g. when a train reaches a junction area it requests a route to the signaling system); to allow devices, personnel and passengers to communicate with the OCC and wayside (to receive and send service related data - e.g. PIS/PAS - while on board); to localize the train using e.g. GNSS and tag readers data.

The authors, and thus this paper, are focused on the non safety critical OBS. The on board systems can be split in two categories: safety critical (e.g. systems that are able to influence train position and speed) and non safety critical (e.g. train localization and PIS/PAS). Note that fleet safety critical decisions (signaling) is delegated to wayside units, thus, even if a train fails at communicating its status, the wayside units are designed to prevent incidents without train collaboration. Thus the authors context can be summarized as:

- No safety critical issues;
- Redundancy required with seamless switch of mastership;

- Embedded device environment;
- Many network interfaces devices and protocols (Tetra, LTE, Wifi);
- Processing of real time data;

In this context a monolithic application, as was implemented in previous versions of the same OBS, tends to be fragile. E.g. a single protocol handler for a low priority data source can crash an entire OBCU (on board control units, i.e. an embedded PC). This motivated the authors to investigate a distributed architecture.

3   Redundancy

An OBS malfunction can cause a system failure that can interrupt or damage the continuity of the LRT operation. For this reason the OBS use redundancy as a means to provide degraded modes of operation that can permit the normal LRT service to continue also in case of on board failures. In particular the described architecture allows the seamless migration of single services from instances of replicated devices. This is particularly useful for services that handle hardware components: in case of multiple failures the system can continue to work in degraded mode unless the failures take down all the same kind of resource among all the replicas. E.g. on a system that has two replicated OBCUs connected to both a Tetra radio and a tag reader each, this architecture allows a degraded mode to work even if both the tag reader of one OBCU and the radio of the other OBCU are in fault condition. Still, if only one OBCU fails, even though the failure completely prevents its operation, the system can gracefully degrade with the other OBCU as the new master.

All the mastership changes can happen at any time. For this reason the status of the slave systems/devices is always kept in sync: when a system failure happens the new candidate master devices already have their state ready and they can switch mode within an as little as possible time gap.

4   Architecture and the Problem of Distributed Applications

Shared state updates is necessary when the complexity of a project justifies its organization into separate software applications. The authors addressed this problem using the Open Source project ØMQ [1]. The following section will show what design decisions have been chosen in order to address the problems this approach poses in our context.

ØMQ is a communication library aimed at making messaging patterns simple. The connect of two software processes, is often implemented using *client-server* paradigm, where the *server* side provides some service to one or more *clients*. Actually client-server is a generic pattern because there are many ways for which a service can be provided. In fact client-server only defines which process is listening and which one is connecting. ØMQ tries to abstract away how the two parties are connected to each other, focusing instead on how messaging takes place. There are various types of sockets in order to exploit the basic messaging patterns. In the following we will motivate the authors' reasons to use an advanced messaging pattern such as the *Clone Pattern*.

4.1   Patterns for Interconnected of Applications

When implementing a distributed system, or separating the complex logic of a system into several separate processes, it must be considered that this approach often involves higher communication costs and system complexity, so it's not always convenient to follow this pattern, especially on small projects. However, the organization of the overall business logic into separate applications has some advantages including:

- A smaller application usually has a lower complexity than a larger one, so it is easier to maintain.
- Working in large teams is easier.
- Responsibility can be bound, in case of malfunctions.
- Parts of the system can be updated without turning down the entire service.
- The overall systems scales better, if properly organized.
- A possible crash doesn't affect other applications, but just the one showing the bug.
- Testing smaller applications that define clear interfaces is easier to automate.

Since the logic of the whole system is distributed over several applications, also the state turns out to be distributed. In fact, each application or component has its own state. Usually the most immediate solution is the direct connection between such components, as illustrated in Fig. 1a.

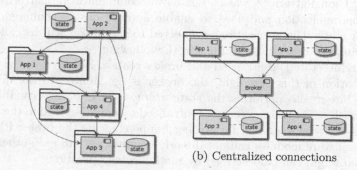

(a) Decentralized connections

(b) Centralized connections

Fig. 1. Interconnection of software applications

This decentralized architecture in Fig. 1a is very flexible because there are no constraints. However, this high degree of flexibility leads to higher complexity and maintenance costs. In fact, potentially each application could communicate with each peer independently, thus defining many per application state update policies and possibly endpoints.

A centralized architecture (in Fig. 1b) can be used to address the raise of complexity. In this case, a solution that uses a *broker* that manages both delivery and storage of distributed applications states is a well known pattern. The usage of a central component brings both advantages and potential pitfalls.

- Advantages:
  - A broker simplifies the discovery of network applications.
  - Each application is connected to the broker using the same protocol.
  - No need to define which one, in every possible couple of communicating applications, has to *bind* and which one has to *connect*.
  - The system scales better along with the number of applications in terms of number of connections, even though the broker's data traffic increases. For example, if the system is composed of 10 applications, the broker approach would need 10 connections, but the broker-less approach would potentially require 100 connection.
  - The addition of a new application does not always involve the modification of all the already present ones.
- Pitfalls:
  - The broker may be a bottleneck, thus the amount of traffic data must known and evaluated.
  - There may be some latency and jitter upon sending messages, according to the data traffic and system load.

4.2   Shared State and the ØMQ Clone Pattern

The ØMQ ClonePattern [2] was chosen as the communication pattern for inter process communication and used to enable applications to communicate and share their state. The applications connected to the broker will be called *clone nodes* or simply *nodes* or *applications* in the following.

This architecture is centralized and broker centric. However, in the author's implementation of this paradigm, the broker is not limited to the *delivery* of messages, but it also performs the state *storage*. Such storage capability is a variation with respect to the generic centralized model, described in the previous paragraph. State storage and forwarding happens inside the broker itself since the other software modules can not directly communicate to each others.

This paradigm can be described by the following operations:

1 **Synchronize** operation. Applications synchronize as soon as they connect to the Clone broker. During synchronization the application obtains from the broker the shared state it needs. Thanks to this, the application could e.g. be restarted from where it was before crashing or being stopped. Synchronization

is performed using a pair of Request-Reply [2] sockets. The broker always listens to state requests and whenever it receives one, it stops its normal operations work-flow in order to send its whole state back.

2 **Update** operation. Propagation of data within the network takes place through a couple of Publisher-Subscriber [2] sockets. The messages shared among nodes are key-value couples. The key is called *topic* while the value is the *payload*. Applications can *subscribe* to topics. When a subscription is established, the broker forwards to the application all the messages it receives with the subscribed topic, i.e. the application receives a topic *update*.

3 **Change** operation. Applications can *change* shared data by sending messages whose topic is recognized by the broker as a change topic. In particular, each module forwards its change through a pair of Pipeline [2] sockets. The broker serializes all changes that are received from applications, it updates its state and it republishes (update) the change. After any change, the shared state whose key is equal to the message topic's name will have a value equal to the message payload.

The Clone Pattern, and thus our implementation, defines how messages are exchanged between components, but it imposes no constraints on the payload format. In order to have well defined software interfaces, the payload can be defined by other formalisms like ASN.1 [3], MessagePack, JSON and others. But this decision is up to the business logic of the application.

The authors choice for the payload is to use the well proved and much used in telecoms ASN.1 format.

4.3   State Replication and Changeover

A hot spare mechanism (*hot-standby*) has been added to the centralized architecture described in Sect. 4.2 to increase its availability. In this context, the term *system* defines the set of all applications and the broker, running on the same machine. Two systems are instantiated and linked (see Fig. 2) together. In particular the two brokers are connected in a way that is described below. One of the two systems is the *Spare* the other is the *Active* system.

The broker system which assumes the role of hot spare (system B) subscribes to the entire state of the active system (system A), without any limitation. This means system B will get all updates and keeps its own state aligned with system A's. The broker does not need to be extended so that it can connect to another broker: a *federation-style* approach is used, rather than having ad-hoc communication channels (*peering* approach).

In Fig. 2 the implementation of this mechanism is shown. Two special applications, similar to normal nodes, bridge system A and system B. The special applications *OuterApp* and *InnerApp* are in charge of injecting messages from one system into the other. Note that *OuterApp* uses an ad-hoc connection to the *InnerApp*. As described above, every message sent to system A (e.g. from App1) is republished to every application connected to it: to prevent message loops *OuterApp* tags the messages it receives and filters out messages that have

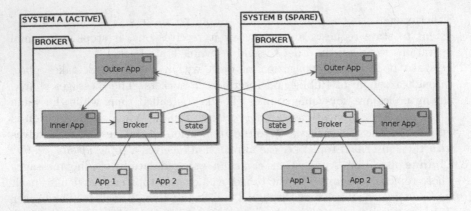

Fig. 2. Hot Redundancy

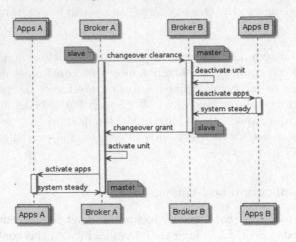

Fig. 3. Full changeover operation example

already been tagged by any *Outer App*. This mechanism is sufficient to keep nodes on both systems synchronized and to allow live migration of a single application form one system to the other.

4.4   Mastership Change

A full changeover operation may be initiated at any time by one of the participants. That is, any of the two systems may request to switch master-slave (Active-Spare) roles, as depicted by the sequence diagram in Fig. 3.

In this case the entire system gets activated or deactivated, causing every application to migrate from one system to another. This kind of synchronization is designed in order to prevent multiple copies of the same service from running simultaneously on different replicas.

5 Performance Considerations

We extensively tested our system on a quite recent embedded system, with a Intel Atom 1.6 GHz processor, 1 GiB of RAM and the Linux operating system. During the performance tests an OBCU was running in a production like environment with 35 running nodes. Table 1 shows the statistics of a 60 s temporal window.

Table 1. Statistics of the clone network

		Min	Max	Avg	Std
Round trip time	[ms]	0.91	74.41	5.30	9.21
Round trip jitter	[ms]	−56.07	71.32	0.68	14.29
Changeover time	[ms]	268	702	362.06	106.91
Update posts	[#/s]	4	83	29.13	19.29
Payload size	[B]	0	2736	279.93	470.61
Network data rate	[B/s]		8418		
Topics count	[#]		73		
Apps count	[#]		35		

The round trip time is very low on average, but we experienced also very few cases where this value increases up to 75 ms. The total number of applications is 35 and there are peaks of 83 updates per seconds over a range of 73 different data types. Exchanged payload size varies from a minimum of 0 bytes to a maximum of 2736 bytes. The total network data rate is about 8 KiB/s. Eventually changeover time is about 360 ms on average. These figures nicely fit a non safety-critical LTR on-board system.

6 Conclusion

Detecting the right time and circumstances to perform a full changeover is not straightforward and the possible triggers events can be undetectable or impossible to distinguish from events in which a changeover is not desirable.

In particular there some observations that could require context dependent reasoning before adapting this technique to other cases:

- We use a keep alive message to detect if the other system has stopped working. The timeout is a critical parameter.
- It would be desirable to have a dual channel of communication between the two brokers in order to avoid that a network fault can be mistaken for a malfunction of the active system.
- The two systems have to reach a consensus if both of them are spare, especially at boot up.

- Changeovers should be minimized because the service is shortly *down* during the change of mastership.
- Before activating the spare system, all modules in the active system must be properly deactivated.

From the authors' point of view the architecture proposed above has been a winning choice. The key benefits have been:

- Higher code quality because the small services can be tested in depth more easily.
- Improved task parallelization due to independence between services.
- Lowered the learning curve for new team members.
- Writing a small service fits well even into a two weeks SCRUM sprint.
- The system is easy to extend and to measure.
- Powerful and extensive logging capabilities. This point is really important for the described context. Having all the shared state available for easy inspection allows developing safety, security and debugging features with small development effort.

References

1. Sustrik, M.: ØMQ: The Theoretical Foundation (2011). http://250bpm.com/concepts
2. ØMQ The Guide. http://zguide.zeromq.org/page:all
3. ITU-T Recommendation X.680 (2002) – ISO/IEC 8824–1:2002, Information technology - Abstract Syntax Notation One (ASN.1): Specification of basic notation

Dependable Dynamic Routing for Urban Transport Systems Through Integer Linear Programming

Davide Basile[1,2(✉)], Felicita Di Giandomenico[1], and Stefania Gnesi[1]

[1] I.S.T.I "A.Faedo", CNR Pisa, Italy
davide.basile@isti.cnr.it
[2] Department of Information Engineering, University of Florence, Florence, Italy

Abstract. Highly automated transport systems play an important role in the transformation towards a digital society, and planning the optimal routes for a set of fleet vehicles has been proved useful for improving the delivered services. Traditionally, routes are planned beforehand. However, with the advent of autonomous urban transport systems (e.g. autonomous cars), possible obstructions of tracks due to traffic congestion or bad weather conditions need to be handled on the fly. In this paper we tackle the problem of dynamically computing routes of vehicles in urban lines in the presence of potential obstructions. The problem is formulated as an integer linear optimization problem. The proposed algorithm will assign routes to vehicles dynamically, considering the track segments that are no longer available and the positions of the vehicles in the urban area. The recomputed routes guarantee the minimal waiting time for passengers. Safety of the computed routes is also guaranteed.

1 Introduction

Nowadays, most of the research in the transport sector is devoted to build smart solutions for moving people within the cities, to reduce costs and improving sustainability while ensuring reliability and safety of the transport services. Highly automated transport systems play an important role in the transformation towards a digital society and technologies as driver-less transports are already adopted in metropolitan cities [17]. In particular, planning the optimal routes for a set of fleet vehicles has been proved useful for reducing costs and energy consumption of vehicles while improving user satisfiability in terms of waiting time.

This problem has been widely studied in the literature [15,16]. Traditionally, two-step approaches based on planning fixed routes and execute them have been studied and are adopted in the railway industry. These approaches rely on the availability of tracks, which is in general guaranteed for railway tracks but it is no longer possible in urban area, where events such as obstructions of tracks must be handled. More recently, newly dynamic routing applications are emerging, thanks to a number of technological advances. For example, the increasing hardware performances for data processing, together with accurate positioning

© Springer International Publishing AG 2017
A. Fantechi et al. (Eds.): RSSRail 2017, LNCS 10598, pp. 221–237, 2017.
https://doi.org/10.1007/978-3-319-68499-4_15

systems as Global Positioning Systems (GPS) and Geographic Information Systems (GIS) led to the development of Intelligent Transport Systems (ITS). These systems combine the above technologies and made possible to track fleet vehicles and to manage them in real time.

In particular, the possibility of dynamically computing new routes for vehicles opens new opportunities for reducing operational costs and environmental impact while improving customer services dependability. Indeed, especially in urban area it is often the case that itineraries may be temporarily unavailable due to obstructions. In this case, a mechanism can be adopted to recompute dynamically new routes for the affected vehicles, such that they are able to complete their missions. This aspect is of crucial importance for improving the overall dependability of these urban transport services and improving the user satisfiability.

In this paper we propose a routing algorithm for handling possible detected obstructions of tracks in urban area, by assigning new routes dynamically and by considering a set of tracks temporarily unavailable. The proposed algorithm takes in input a graph abstracting an urban map, where edges correspond to itineraries and nodes to points, the locations and destinations of vehicles in the urban area and the set of detected obstructed tracks. The output of the algorithm is the set of optimal routes for each vehicle, to be communicated to the vehicles until the obstructed tracks are restored to their normal operation. The optimal routes computed are safe by construction. In particular, it is guaranteed that no collisions among vehicles will ever occur both on itineraries and on points. Moreover, the computed routes guarantee progress of the overall network of vehicles: no deadlocks will ever occur, i.e. each vehicle eventually reaches its destination. Note that, although there are specific subsystems strongly tailored to assure safety (e.g., interlocking), also at the level of route planning safety can be considered by developing solutions that avoid potential train collisions, as we pursue in our study.

We modelled the dynamic vehicle routing as an optimization combinatorial problem, through a set of linear equations. In particular, the vehicle routes are modelled as flows in a graph such that the objective function minimises the arrival time of each vehicle to its destination. This in turns guarantees an improvement in user satisfiability by minimising the waiting time. Safety aspects are enforced by a set of constraints allowing only one vehicle in each itinerary and only one vehicle to traverse a point in a given time step.

The proposed model has been implemented in *A Mathematical Programming Language* [8] (AMPL). Preliminary experiments were performed showing the feasibility of the proposed approach. The implementation of the dynamic vehicle routing algorithm is open source. It can be downloaded at https://github.com/davidebasile/routingproblem, together with data and set-ups of experiments.

Structure of the paper. The paper starts with a description of the problem in Sect. 2. The proposed architecture of a dependable dynamic vehicle routing system is introduced in Sect. 3. Section 4 contains some background on Integer Linear Programming (ILP) and flow problems; and the proposed model for solving the routing problem is described in Sect. 5. The implementation of the algorithm and some experiments are, respectively, in Sect. 6 and Sect. 7. Finally, related work is in Sect. 8 while conclusion and future work are in Sect. 9.

2 Description of the Problem

Planning the time schedule and routing of vehicles (known as Dynamic Vehicle Routing Problem) is a problem that has been widely researched and nowadays several transport systems adopt automatic solutions for planning the routes of vehicles and for supervising their movements [9,15,16].

Recently, these systems have been extended from subway and train lines to comprehend other urban systems, as tramway lines. Tramway lines are generally less expensive than subway lines and automatic systems can be applied to optimize the time scheduling and energy consumption. Solutions as signals, priority management and traffic lights are adopted to regulate the circulation and ensure safety. While metropolitan lines widely adopt automated guidance systems, in tramway systems the driver is in charge of enforcing speed, braking and safety distances. Generally, signal entities are used to allow trams to occupy the specified route.

An important problem in urban scenarios is the presence of possible obstructions in the assigned routes. This can be due, for example, to other vehicles or to accidents. Generally technologies as, for example, radars and gps are used to detect these hazardous situations. Hence, implementing innovative dependable routing solutions while enforcing rail safety represents a challenge for the research community.

In particular when a specific route is no longer available due to obstructions of the path or other possible failures, the preassigned routes are no longer valid. It is important to recompute efficiently a new route from the location of each vehicle to its destination, to avoid obstructed tracks and potential deadlocks. Signalling systems are in charge of communicating to the drivers the newly assigned routes, set up the traffic lights, commute points, and set up the other devices composing the signalling system.

3 Dynamic Vehicle Routing

In Fig. 1 our proposed dynamic vehicle routing system is depicted. In particular, through the on-board equipment each vehicle can communicate its precise location thanks to GPS coordinates or similar systems. Moreover, communications with the control station are also handled. In case of possible obstructions in one of the assigned tracks (detected by sight or by automatic devices as, e.g. radar) the preassigned standard routes are no longer valid; and the blocked vehicle will communicate to the central control station its coordinates and will identify such obstructed track. In this scenario it is necessary to adopt alternative routes until the unavailable tracks are restored to their normal operation conditions. We assume that the unavailable tracks notified to the control station will remain so for an amount of time worthy of recomputing new routes. On the contrary,

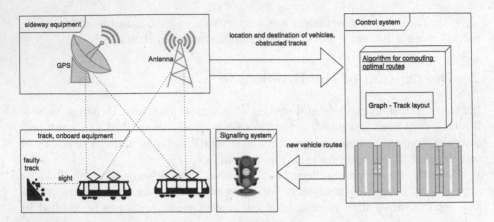

Fig. 1. The dependable dynamic vehicle routing system for urban lines

vehicles will wait until the obstructed tracks are restored to normal operation conditions.

Once the communication has been received by the control unit, the coordinates (also called locations) and the destinations of all vehicles in the urban area will be collected by the control unit. These data will be used by the control system to compute new routes for each vehicle dynamically, given its current location and its destination, and communicate them to the signalling system. In our framework destinations are, for example, next stops, i.e. we divide a round trip of a vehicle into a sequence of stops that are computed dynamically. Our proposed model will compute the optimal solution by minimising the overall time needed by all vehicles to arrive at their destination, that is optimising the user satisfiability in terms of minimal waiting time. Moreover, the model will ensure route safety, i.e. no collisions on tracks or points will ever occur.

The newly computed routes are communicated to the drivers and to the signalling system. Indeed, the problem of setting traffic lights, commutating points and other operations on the tracks useful to implementing the selected routes are managed by other systems. It is assumed that other systems are in charge of communicating to the drivers the assigned route and to implement the signalling system to allow each vehicle to move according to its selected route (see Sect. 2).

In the following sections the algorithm for computing new routes (right block in Fig. 1) is specified, implemented and tested. Note that the proposed algorithm is not tailored to a specific urban transport system, but can be reused in different scenarios such as, among the others, autonomous cars and tramway lines.

4   Network Flow Problem

In this section we introduce network flow problems and their formalisations. The dynamic vehicle routing problem will be formalised and solved as a network flow problem in the following section.

A flow network [6] (also known as a transportation network) is a directed graph where each edge has a capacity and each edge receives a flow. Let $G = (Q, T)$ be a graph with set of nodes Q and edges T, that are pair of nodes. Generally there are two types of special nodes: *source nodes*, that are generating flow, and *sink nodes*, that are consuming the flow. Given a node $q \in V$, the *forward star* $FS(q)$ is the set of outcoming edges of q, while the *backward star* $BS(q)$ is the set of incoming edges in the node q.

For each edge $t \in T$, the *flow variable* x_t represents the flow that is passing through the edge t. Generally, a maximum capacity a_t is assigned to each edge t, representing the maximum amount of flow allowed, and a cost c_t representing the cost of utilising the edge t. A network flow problem is a type of network optimization problem where the objective function requires to optimize a flow such that the solution respects the following constraints:

- the amount of flow on an edge cannot exceed the capacity of the edge (*capacity constraints*), written $\forall t \in T . x_t \leq a_t$;
- the amount of flow incoming into a node equals the amount of flow leaving it, unless it is a source, with only an outgoing flow d, or a sink, with only an incoming flow d (*flow conservation*), written:

$$\forall q \in Q . \sum_{t \in BS(q)} x_t - \sum_{t \in FS(q)} x_t = \begin{cases} -d & \text{if } q = q_s \\ 0 & \text{if } q \neq q_s, q_f \\ d & \text{if } q = q_f \end{cases}$$

- depending on the studied problem, it can be required that the computed flow must be an integer value (*integrity constraints*), written: $\forall t \in T . x_t \in \mathbb{N}$.

Examples of network flow problems are the *Maximum flow problem* [7] or the *Minimum-cost flow problem* [11]. The first problem consists in maximizing the amount of flow that can be sent from the source nodes to the sink nodes. The objective function is then $\max \ d$. In the second problem a cost is associated with each edge of the network, and the objective function is minimised in order to find the optimal cost for sending a given amount of flow from the source nodes to the sink nodes, that is $\min \ \sum_{t \in T} x_t c_t$.

These problems are solved by using *Integer Linear Programming* (ILP) [10,19]. Indeed, all constraints are represented by linear inequalities, and the objective function is linear. Several solvers are available for solving linear optimization problems automatically and efficiently, by using for example the simplex algorithm [8].

In the next section we will formalise the automatic route scheduling as a flow problem. The flow variables will be split into time steps $1, \ldots K$, where K will be the upperbound to the maximum number of edges that a route can traverse. The maximum capacity for each edge will be of one unit, that is only one vehicle can be on a specific track in a specific moment. Similarly, the flow d will be of one unit, that is each flow will be in correspondence with a single route. We will not consider costs for edges, which are left as future work (e.g. energy, performance).

Finally, the flow variables will be split into a set of binary variables $x_{u,k,t}$ where u identifies the vehicle, k identifies the discrete step considered in our analysis and t will identify the itinerary (i.e. edge). In particular, $x_{u,k,t} = 1$ if and only if vehicle u at moment k is in itinerary t. These flow variables will describe the optimal routes computed by our ILP model. The goal will be to minimise the overall routing time.

5   Description of the Model for the Vehicle Routing Problem

In this section we formalise the dynamic vehicle routing problem as a network flow problem. Similarly to [3,14,20], we abstract a generic urban tramway layout as a graph. At our level of abstraction, we are only interested in modelling the path that each vehicle must traverse in order to arrive at its destination. A destination could be the next stop that the vehicle needs to reach. Each edge of the graph will possibly represent a sequence of segments where a single vehicle is allowed (i.e. an itinerary), that must be traversed in order to move from one point to another. Nodes in the graph are in correspondence with points in the track. We assume that vehicles may only get stuck in points, and not while traversing itineraries. Indeed, unavailability of itineraries is ascertained in the nearest points.

We firstly introduce the notation used in this section. We assume a finite set of vehicles U, where each vehicle has one route, a finite set of itineraries (i.e. edges) T, a finite set of nodes Q. Trivially, no segment has the same point as source and destination. Indeed, we assume that no inner cycles are present in the graph, i.e. $\forall q \in Q.FS(q) \cap BS(q) = \emptyset$. This requirement can be imposed as a constraint in the model (see Eq. 13).

Moreover, let $|S|$ be the cardinality of a set S. Then $K = |U| * |T|$ is the upper bound to the maximum amount of time needed by each vehicle to reach its destination provided that at each discrete step $k \in 1 \ldots K$ at least one vehicle in U moves into an itinerary in T. In particular in the worst case $|U| * |T|$ only one vehicle moves at each step, all vehicles need to traverse all itineraries in the graph and each route traverses each itinerary at most one time (i.e. no loops). Moreover, given a vehicle $u \in U$, let $location(u), destination(u) \in Q$ be the location and destination of vehicle u. Finally, we assume the presence of a subset of itineraries $F \subset T$ that are temporarily unavailable and cannot be traversed. The output of the ILP model will be the new routes assigned to each vehicle.

Example 1. Before providing the details of the model we explain the formalisation with the help of an intuitive example. In Fig. 2 a graph representing a sub-portion of an urban area is depicted. Adjacent nodes are connected in both directions, to improve readability for each pair of connected nodes only

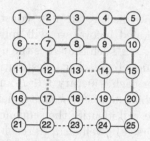

Fig. 2. The grid used for the experiments with the routes computed in Experiment 1 (thick edges) and obstructed itineraries (dotted edges)

one edge is reported in Fig. 2. In Sect. 7 this graph will be used for testing the proposed model. Assuming that the obstructed tracks are itineraries in $F = \{(1,2),(1,6),(2,1),(2,7),(6,1),(7,2),(10,2)\}$ and that two vehicles u_1 and u_2 are present such that $location(u_1) = 15$, $location(u_2) = 9$, $destination(u_1) = 12$, $destination(u_2) = 11$. The optimal route for u_1 is represented by the variables $x_{u_1,1,(15,14)} = 1, x_{u_1,2,(14,13)} = 1, x_{u_1,i,(13,12)} = 1$ where $i = 3,\ldots,K$ (all other variables $x_{u_1,k,t}$ having value zero). The optimal route for u_2 is represented by the variables $x_{u_2,1,(9,8)} = 1, x_{u_2,2,(8,7)} = 1, x_{u_2,3,(7,6)} = 1, x_{u_2,j,(6,11)} = 1$, where $j = 4,\ldots,K$ (all other variables $x_{u_2,k,t}$ having value zero). In particular, at step $k = 1$ we have that vehicle u_1 is on itinerary $(15,14)$ and vehicle u_2 on $(9,8)$; at step $k = 2$ vehicle u_1 has moved to the adjacent itinerary $(14,3)$ and u_2 to $(8,7)$, at step $k = 3$ vehicle u_1 has moved to $(13,12)$ (so reaching its destination) and u_2 to $(7,6)$. Finally at step $k = 4$ vehicle u_1 remains idle while u_2 reaches its destination $(6,11)$.

These $x_{u,k,t}$ variables are computed automatically by the ILP model described below, and are such that each vehicle reaches its destination in the shortest number of steps possible.

5.1   Integer Linear Programming Model

The ILP model is defined below.

Objective function. We start by defining the objective function:

$$\max \gamma \tag{1}$$

$$\gamma \geq 0 \tag{2}$$

The objective function maximises a threshold γ, which is constrained to be a positive integer. The parameter γ will represent the overall amount of time spent by vehicles in their destinations in terms of number of discrete steps (see Eq. 4), i.e. the earliest a vehicle reaches its destination the higher γ will be.

Flow Constraints. We now discuss the flow constraints used to model the routes of vehicles. As mentioned before, we will split the time window under analysis into discrete steps $1 \ldots K$ such that K is the upper bound to the number of steps needed by each vehicle to reach its destination. In particular, at each discrete step $k \in 1 \ldots K$, for each itinerary $t \in T$ and vehicle $u \in U$ a binary variable $x_{u,k,t}$ identifies if vehicle u at step k is in itinerary t. The set of variables $x_{u,1,t_1}, \ldots, x_{u,K,t_n}$ set to one will identify the sequence of itineraries (i.e. route) $t_1, \ldots, t_n$ that must be traversed be vehicle u to reach its destination t_n starting from its location t_1, and the discrete steps k that the vehicle must spent in these itineraries.

$$\forall k \in 1 \ldots K, \forall u \in U, \forall t \in T. \ x_{u,k,t} \in \{0,1\} \tag{3}$$

The following equation ensures that each vehicle u reaches its destination in the minimum possible amount of time. In particular, for all vehicles $u \in U$, steps $k \in K$, and for all itineraries $t \in T$ incoming into each vehicle destination ($t \in BS(destination(u))$, the sum of all variables $x_{u,k,t}$ must be greater or equal to γ.

Indeed, the objective function (1) maximises the threshold γ, and as a result the sum (left hand side term of Eq. 4) will be maximised: the earliest each vehicle u reaches its destination, the higher this sum will be (i.e. vehicles $u \in U$ will spend more time in itineraries $t \in BS(destination(u))$.

$$\sum_{u \in U, k \in K, t \in BS(destination(u))} x_{u,k,t} \geq \gamma \tag{4}$$

Note that constraint 4 also guarantees the problem to be bounded: in particular by constraint 4 it holds that $\gamma \leq |K| * |U|$.

The constraints ensuring that a set of variables $x_{u,1,t}, \ldots, x_{u,K,t}$ correctly identify one route are now discussed. The following equation constraints a vehicle u to be in only one itinerary t at each step k.

$$\forall u \in U, \forall k \in 1 \ldots K. \sum_{t \in T} x_{u,k,t} = 1 \tag{5}$$

The following equations ensure that each vehicle starts its trip from its current location and arrives at its destination (in the worst case it arrives at step K).

$$\forall u \in U. \sum_{t \in FS(location(u))} x_{u,1,t} = 1 \tag{6}$$

$$\forall u \in U. \sum_{t \in BS(destination(u))} x_{u,K,t} = 1 \tag{7}$$

The constraints below are necessary for ensuring that each vehicle only moves into a connected path or stays idle at each step k. In particular, fixing a vehicle u, for each node q, and step k such that vehicle u is incoming in q at step $k-1$ we require that the difference between the incoming itineraries in q at step $k-1$

and the sum of the incoming and outgoing itineraries at step k (for the same point q and vehicle u) must be equal to zero.

$$\forall q \in Q, \forall u \in U, \forall k \in 2 \dots K, \sum_{t \in BS(q)} x_{u,k-1,t} > 0.$$

$$\sum_{t \in BS(q)} x_{u,k-1,t} - \left(\sum_{t \in FS(q)} x_{u,k,t} + \sum_{t \in BS(q)} x_{u,k,t} \right) = 0 \qquad (8)$$

We further detail Eq. 8; recall that by Eq. 5 and the conditions on constraints 8 ($\sum_{t \in BS(q)} x_{u,k-1,t} > 0$, i.e. vehicle u at step $k-1$ is incoming into node q), it must be that at step k either u is still incoming (i.e. $\sum_{t \in BS(q)} x_{u,k,t} = 1$ and $\sum_{t \in FS(q)} x_{u,k,t} = 0$); or vice-versa (i.e. $\sum_{t \in BS(q)} x_{u,k,t} = 0$ and $\sum_{t \in FS(q)} x_{u,k,t} = 1$), that is u is outgoing from q. However, Eq. 8 does not prevent scenarios in which a vehicle moves from one incoming itinerary t in q at step $k-1$ to another incoming itinerary $t' \neq t$ in q at step k. The following constraints are used to avoid this scenario:

$$\forall q \in Q, \forall u \in U, \forall k \in 2 \dots K, \forall t_1, t_2 \in BS(q), t_1 \neq t_2 . x_{u,k-1,t_1} + x_{u,k,t_2} \leq 1 \quad (9)$$

Safety. The following constraints are those entailing safety of the computed routes. In particular, the proposed model will compute optimal routes such that no collisions will ever occur. Moreover, it is ensured that an obstructed itinerary will never be traversed by any vehicle. Note that the absence of deadlocks is entailed by constraints 7.

The constraints below are used to avoid possible collisions among vehicles. Firstly, only one vehicle is allowed in each itinerary t and step k:

$$\forall k \in 1 \dots K, \forall t \in T. \sum_{u \in U} x_{u,k,t} \leq 1 \qquad (10)$$

Moreover, in the presence of more vehicles approaching a point $q \in Q$, they cannot be served at the same step k. The constraints below guarantee that at most one vehicle can be served by a point q for each step k.

$$\forall q \in Q, \forall k \in 2 \dots K. \sum_{u \in U} \sum_{t \in BS(q)} x_{u,k-1,t} - 1$$

$$\leq \sum_{u \in U} \sum_{t \in BS(q)} x_{u,k-1,t} x_{u,k,t} \leq \sum_{u \in U} \sum_{t \in BS(q)} x_{u,k-1,t} \qquad (11)$$

Note that Eq. 11 contains a product of two binary variables. Recall that given two binary variables v_1 and v_2, their product $z = v_1 * v_2$ can be linearised through constraints: $z \leq v_1$; $z \leq v_2$; $z \geq v_1 + v_2 - 1$. For brevity, here we prefer to use this compact version than the linearised one.

In Eq. 11, the term $\sum_{u \in U} \sum_{t \in BS(q)} x_{u,k-1,t} x_{u,k,t}$ represents the number of vehicles approaching point q that have not moved between consecutive steps $k - 1$ and k. Indeed, vehicles that have approached q at step k but were not present at step $k - 1$ are ruled out (their product is zero), as well as those that were approaching q at step $k - 1$ and left at step k. This product is used for avoiding vehicles approaching u at step k but not present at step $k - 1$. Since at most one vehicle must be served by q between steps $k - 1$ and k, $\sum_{u \in U} \sum_{t \in BS(q)} x_{u,k-1,t} x_{u,k,t}$ must be equal to either:

- $\sum_{u \in U} \sum_{t \in BS(q)} x_{u,k-1,t}$, that is no vehicle has moved between steps $k - 1$ and k from q, or
- $\sum_{u \in U} \sum_{t \in BS(q)} x_{u,k-1,t} - 1$, in this case only one vehicle has been served by point q between steps $k - 1$ and k.

Finally, the last constraint ensures that no failed itinerary is ever traversed by any route computed by the ILP model.

$$\forall t \in F. \sum_{u \in U} \sum_{k \in 1 \ldots K} x_{u,k,t} = 0 \qquad (12)$$

Graph Structure. The constraints below are used to verify that the graph does not contain inner cycles. Note that these constraints are not necessary for solving the routing problem. They are used for preprocessing the user input and can be avoided provided that the input is verified. The equation below could sum up to 2 only if there exists an itinerary $t \in T$ such that $t \in FS(q) \cap BS(q)$, i.e. an inner cycle.

$$\forall q \in Q, \forall u \in U, \forall k \in 1 \ldots K, \forall t \in T. \sum_{t \in FS(q)} x_{u,k,t} + \sum_{t \in BS(q)} x_{u,k,t} \leq 1 \qquad (13)$$

Cyclic routes are also ruled out in our model. Indeed, a round trip of a vehicle will be split into two separate routes, the first into one direction and the other in the opposite one (note that this assumption is crucial for ensuring $K = |U| * |T|$).

Output. Recall that the output of the ILP model will be the set of routes U computed by our procedure. These routes will be communicated to the signalling system. Moreover, the routes of each vehicle u are described in terms of steps k and locations t, such that for each vehicle in correspondence with a variable $u \in U$ its route will be $\forall u \in U.Route(u) = \{x_{u,k,t} | x_{u,k,t} = 1, k \in 1 \ldots K, t \in T\}$, that is, we identify for each step the position of vehicle u.

6   Implementation

In Fig. 3 the implementation of the ILP model described in the previous section is displayed. This implementation is open source and can be downloaded

```
——————————————— routeplanning.mod ———————————————
param n; #points    param k; #discrete steps       param u; #vehicles        1
set Q := {1..n}; set K := {1..k}; set U := {1..u};                            2
param t{Q,Q}; #itineraries       param location{U}; param destination{U};     3
param F{Q,Q} binary; #constraint 2            var gamma >= 0 integer;         4
#constraints 3    var x{U,K,Q,Q} binary;                                      5
var uxu{U,K,Q,Q} binary; var uxu2{U,K,Q,Q,Q} binary;                          6
                                                                              7
#objective function, equation 1                                              8
maximize time: gamma;                                                         9
                                                                             10
# FLOW CONSTRAINTS                                                           11
#graph constraints: only itineraries can be traversed by vehicles            12
subject to graph{i in U, j in K, s in Q, d in Q}: x[i,j,s,d] <= t[s,d];      13
                                                                             14
#minimise waiting time                                                       15
subject to c4: (sum{i in U, s in Q, j in K, d in Q: d == destination[i]} x[i,j,s,d]) >= gamma;  16
                                                                             17
#only one itinerary per time                                                 18
subject to c5{i in U, j in K}: sum{s in Q, d in Q} x[i,j,s,d] = 1;           19
                                                                             20
#each vehicle starts from its location                                       21
subject to c6{i in U}: sum{s in Q, d in Q: s==location[i]} x[i,1,s,d] = 1;    22
                                                                             23
#all vehicles reach their destination eventually                             24
subject to c7{i in U}: sum{s in Q,d in Q: d==destination[i]} x[i,k,s,d] = 1;  25
                                                                             26
#constraints linearise 1,2,3 used to linearise  uxu[i,j,s,d] = x[i,j-1,s,d]*x[i,j,s,d]  27
subject to linearise1{i in U, j in {2..k}, s in Q, d in Q}:                   28
                 uxu[i,j,s,d]<= x[i,j-1,s,d];                                 29
subject to linearise2{i in U, j in {2..k}, s in Q, d in Q}:                   30
                 uxu[i,j,s,d]<= x[i,j,s,d];                                   31
subject to linearise3{i in U, j in {2..k}, s in Q, d in Q}:                   32
                 uxu[i,j,s,d]>= x[i,j-1,s,d] + x[i,j,s,d] - 1;                33
                                                                             34
#constraints linearise 4,5,6 used to linearise  uxu2[i,j,s,q,d] = x[i,j-1,s,q]*x[i,j,q,d]  35
subject to linearise4{i in U, j in {2..k}, s in Q, q in Q, d in Q}:           36
                 uxu2[i,j,s,q,d]<= x[i,j-1,s,q];                              37
subject to linearise5{i in U, j in {2..k}, s in Q, q in Q, d in Q}:           38
                 uxu2[i,j,s,q,d]<= x[i,j,q,d];                               39
subject to linearise6{i in U, j in {2..k}, s in Q,q in Q, d in Q}:            40
                 uxu2[i,j,s,q,d]>= x[i,j-1,s,q] + x[i,j,q,d] - 1;             41
                                                                             42
#flow constraints, for each k each vehicle  i stays idle or move into an adjacent itinerary  43
subject to c8{i in U, q in Q, j in {2..k}}:                                   44
(sum{s in Q:s!=q} x[i,j-1,s,q])   -                                           45
(sum{s in Q, d in Q:d!=q && s!=q} uxu2[i,j,s,q,d]  + sum{s in Q:s!=q} uxu[i,j,s,q]) = 0;  46
                                                                             47
#complement previous constraints: vehicles do not "jump"  itineraries        48
subject to c9{i in U, q in Q, j in {2..k}, s1 in Q, s2 in Q: s1!=s2}:         49
  x[i,j-1,s1,q]+x[i,j,s2,q] <= 1;                                            50
                                                                             51
# SAFETY                                                                     52
#no collisions on itineraries                                                53
subject to c10{j in K, s in Q, d in Q}: sum{i in U} x[i,j,s,d] <= 1;         54
                                                                             55
#no collisions on points                                                     56
subject to c11_1{q in Q, j in {2..k}}:                                        57
        sum{i in U, s in Q} x[i,j-1,s,q] - 1 <= sum{i in U, s in Q} uxu[i,j,s,q];  58
subject to c11_2{q in Q, j in {2..k}}:                                        59
        sum{i in U, s in Q} uxu[i,j,s,q] <= sum{i in U, s in Q} x[i,j-1,s,q];  60
                                                                             61
#routes must not pass through damaged itineraries                            62
subject to c12{s in Q, d in Q: F[s,d]==1}: sum{i in U,j in K} x[i,j,s,d]=0;  63
```

Fig. 3. The implementation in AMPL of the dynamic routing optimization problem.

at https://github.com/davidebasile/routingproblem. The ILP model has been implemented in *A Mathematical Programming Language* (AMPL) [8], a widely used language for describing and solving optimization problems. The model can be loaded and executed in AMPL through command line. In particular, script `routeplanning.run`, to be launched with the command `ampl`, is described below:

```
————————————— routeplanning.run ——————————————
option solver cplex; // use the simplex algorithm in C                    1
model routeplanning.mod; // select the route planning model               2
data routeplanning.dat;   // load the input data                          3
solve;   //apply the simplex algorithm                                    4
display {i in U,j in K, s in Q, d in Q:  x[i,j,s,d]>0} x[i,j,s,d];        5
//display the computed routes                                             6
```

Firstly the solver `cplex` is selected, that is the simplex method implemented in C. However it is possible to select other available solvers. The script loads the automaton from the file `routeplanning.dat`, displayed in Fig. 3. The input file provides the number of vehicles u and nodes n, and two binary matrix $Q \times Q$ called t and F. In this implementation edges are represented as pairs of nodes, i.e. source and target nodes of the corresponding edge. The first matrix is used for identifying the graph structure, in particular $t[n_1, n_2] = 1$ if there is an edge connecting node n_1 with node n_2, $t[n_1, n_2] = 0$ otherwise. Similarly, the second matrix F identifies the unavailable itineraries. Finally, two arrays *location* and *destination* are such that, for example, $location[u] = n$ if the location of vehicle u is n.

The implementation file `routeplanning.mod` in Fig. 3 follows the model described in Sect. 5, with few differences detailed in the following. The additional graph constraints $\forall i \in U, j \in K, s \in Q, d \in Q : x[i, j, s, d] <= t[s, d]$ (lines 12–13) are used to ensure that the flow variables x only use edges of the graph. Indeed, if $t[s, d] = 0$ then the flow $x[i, j, s, d]$ on edge (s, d) is forced to be zero.

Moreover constraints `linearise 1 ... 6` (lines 27–33) are used to linearise the products of Eqs. 8 and 11. In particular, for Eq. 8 it is not possible to specify the condition $\sum_{t \in BS(q)} x_{u,k-1,t} > 0$ directly in AMPL, hence the following constraints (lines 43–47) have been used in the implementation:

$$\forall q \in Q, \forall u \in U, \forall k \in 2 \ldots K.$$

$$\sum_{t \in BS(q)} x_{u,k-1,t} - \left(\sum_{t' \in FS(q), t \in BS(q)} x_{u,k,t'} x_{u,k-1,t} + \sum_{t \in BS(q)} x_{u,k,t} x_{u,k-1,t} \right) = 0$$

If $\sum_{t \in BS(q)} x_{u,k-1,t} = 0$ then the above term will sum up to zero. The binary variable $uxu[u, k, s, d]$ (line 6) identifies product $x[u, k, s, d]x[u, k - 1, s, d]$ (also used in Eq. 11, lines 56–60), while variable $uxu2[u, k, s, q, d]$ (line 6) identifies product $x[u, k, q, d]x[u, k - 1, s, q]$.

7   Experiments

In this section we report on preliminary experiments that have been performed for evaluating and validating the proposed model. Similarly to [20] we will use a grid 5×5 as graph to test the ILP model, displayed in Fig. 2, which may represent a sub-portion of an urban area. We will assume the presence of four vehicles in the grid. The script routeplanning.run has been enriched with the automatic generation of obstructed tracks, locations and destinations of vehicles. These data are randomly generated according to a uniform distribution. Three experiments have been carried on, where in each of them a round of the ILP model has been executed. In Sect. 9 we discuss future extensions to simulate a whole day, with several obstructions and computations.

The ILP model successfully computed the routes of each experiment. The results are displayed in Table 1. For each experiment the failed tracks are reported, together with location, destination and computed routes of each vehicle. When a vehicle reaches its destination, it is assumed that in the remaining steps the vehicle stays idle. In particular, concerning Experiment 1, locations and destinations of vehicles are the furthest possible and have been inserted

Table 1. For each experiment the computed routes are displayed, together with obstructed tracks, location and destination of each vehicle.

	Experiment 1
Obstructed tracks	(2,7) (6,7) (9,8) (11,6) (13,14) (17,12) (19,18) (22,23) (23,24)
Vehicle 1	Location = 1, destination = 24
	Route = (1,2) (2,3) (3,8) (8,9) (9,14) (14,15) (15,20) (20,25)
Vehicle 2	Location = 25, destination = 1
	Route = (25,20) (20,15) (15,10) (10,5) (5,4) (4,3) (3,2) (2,1)
Vehicle 3	Location = 5, destination = 21
	Route = (5,10) (10,9) (9,14) (14,13) (13,12) (12,17) (17,16) (16,21)
Vehicle 4	Location = 21, destination = 5
	Route = (21,16) (16,11) (11,12) (12,7) (7,8) (8,9) (9,4) (4,5)
	Experiment 2
Obstructed tracks	(1,6) (2,1) (2,7) (6,1) (6,7) (7,2) (9,8) (10,2) (10,15) (23,22)
Vehicle 1	Location = 14, destination = 11, route = (14,13)(13,12)(12,11)
Vehicle 2	Location = 8, destination = 10, route = (8,9)(9,10)
Vehicle 3	Location = 13, destination = 18, route = (13,18)
Vehicle 4	Location = 21, destination = 12, route = (21,16)(16,11)(11,12)
	Experiment 3
Obstructed tracks	(1,2) (1,6) (2,1) (2,7) (6,1) (7,2) (10,2)
Vehicle 1	Location = 15, destination = 12, route = (15,14)(14,13)(13,12)
Vehicle 2	Location = 9, destination = 11, route = (9,8)(8,7)(7,6)(6,11)
Vehicle 3	Location = 14, destination = 19, route = (14,19)
Vehicle 4	Location = 22, destination = 13, route = (22,17)(17,12)(12,13)

Table 2. Performances of experiments.

Experiment	Time (seconds)	Cumulative allocated memory (byte)	MIP simplex iterations
1	49.5	13315294784	5532
2	48.9531	13315330472	5438
3	44.9531	13315215272	6127

manually; the routes of the four vehicles are displayed in Fig. 2 with different colours.

In Table 2 for each experiment we report the time, memory consumption and iterations of the simplex algorithm. In particular, the memory consumption is displayed as the cumulative sum of the memory allocated in the different phases of the execution (i.e. compile, genmod, collect, presolve, solve). The performances are similar in all experiments, and are mainly due to the size of the input graph (in terms of number of nodes) and the number of vehicles. It has been used a machine with CPU Intel Core i5-4570 at 3.20 GHZ with 8 GB of RAM, running 64-bit Windows 10 and the CPLEX solver version 12.7.1.0.

8   Related Work

The dynamic vehicle routing problem (i.e. finding optimal routes for vehicles with minimum travel time) was firstly introduced by Dantzig and Ramser [4] as a generalization of the Traveling Salesman Problem introduced by Flood [5], and it has been surveyed in [15,16]. Different solutions have been proposed in the literature, for example by using neural networks [13], dynamic programming [1], mixed integer non-linear programming [2] and random search strategy [12].

Standard vehicle routing problems solutions are not suitable when the conditions of the traffic layout can change dynamically, due for example to traffic congestions, accidents or bad weather conditions. More recently, with the advent of automatic driving systems, as for example autonomous vehicles, the dynamic routing problem has been revived. Modern technology, for example global positioning system and geographic information systems, can be used to collect dynamically the traffic situation to allow the dynamic assignment of routes to vehicle, as proposed by our methodology.

The problem of vehicle routing in urban traffic network is discussed in [20]. A notion of critical node is used to identify the current position of vehicles in the network, and each vehicle has associated a set of customers that must be visited in minimal time. The route of each vehicle is computed locally. An approximate initial starting solution is computed through a genetic algorithm. By dividing the flow variables into discrete steps we are able to identify the current location of each vehicle in the urban network, instead of using special nodes that would augment the state space of the problem. Moreover, our approach does not need to generate an initial solution. Indeed, once a vehicle reaches a destination, its new destination will be updated and the new routes will be recomputed.

This is mainly due to the presence of possible faulty events in the tracks (e.g. obstructions), a condition not addressed in [20]. The routing solution is generated globally by considering routes of each vehicle in the network.

The problem of computing the train scheduling and routing in combination is addressed in [18]. A multi-objective function constituted by the minimum average travel time of all trains, the minimum energy consumption and the minimum delayed times is used. The train scheduling problem is solved through a simulation algorithm according to the train control strategies, and a genetic algorithm is used in case of large scale networks for the train routing problem. Compared to our work, in [18] faulty events are not considered, whilst we only focus on the vehicle routing problem and we abstract away from details of time schedule. Indeed, our ILP model should be executed to restore the system to a working state when obstructions in the tracks are detected, until normal operation conditions are established.

The routing problem for freight trains is studied in [3]. Similarly to our approach, the minimum time in terms of vehicles reaching their destination is computed globally, by taking into account all routes of vehicles. Moreover, the layout structure of the rail road track is abstracted as a graph, and the day partitioned into time steps. A fixed number of vehicles is allowed to enter a particular track segment throughout the whole day. An important difference with respect to our approach is that routes are statically assigned to vehicles and are not adapted dynamically, i.e. faults in tracks are not considered. We also enforce safety properties for avoiding possible collisions among vehicles.

In [14] an Automatic Train Supervision for preventing the occurrence of deadlocks in train routes is studied. Similarly to our solution, the track layout is abstracted as a graph. However, the proposed solution does not account for possible failures in tracks (i.e. dynamic vehicle routes). Indeed, each route of a train is fixed and it is an input parameter. Trains decide whether to move at a given discrete steps autonomously and according to their routes, whilst we dictate when vehicles move (i.e. steps). The algorithm takes in input also the graph layout and a set of areas (i.e. nodes in the graph) where only a given number of trains are allowed to enter. The absence of possible deadlocks is verified through model checking given the aforementioned data.

We conjecture that our model can be extended with minor changes to solve the deadlock problem. Indeed, it suffices to add to our model additional constraints to only allow a fixed number of vehicles to enter a predetermined area (modelled as set of transitions), and to fix a specific route to each vehicle as an input parameter. Moreover by using a bi-level objective function min max it is possible to determine if a configuration of routes into discrete steps exists such that vehicles are deadlocked.

9   Conclusion and Future Work

We presented a dependable dynamic vehicle routing system, focussing on the ILP model for computing new routes of vehicles given their actual location, destination and detected obstructed tracks. Similarly to [3,14,20], we abstracted the urban map as a graph such that edges and nodes are in correspondence, respectively, with itineraries and points of the urban area. The algorithm has been modelled as a flow problem, where each flow corresponds to a vehicle route. The newly computed routes are equipped with safety guarantees on the absence of deadlocks and possible collisions among vehicles, both in points and itineraries. The proposed solution has been implemented in *A Mathematical Programming Language* [8](AMPL) and preliminary experiments have been carried, on showing the effectiveness of the proposed solution; the implementation and all data are available at https://github.com/davidebasile/routingproblem.

Some possible future extensions of the proposed approach are discussed below. Whilst preliminary experiments showed the feasibility of our approach, we would like to apply the proposed solution to a real world urban scenario. Moreover, it would be valuable to extend the proposed model to include also aspects related to performances of vehicles (i.e. acceleration, speed, braking) and energy consumption (fuel, other energy dissipation). Indeed, it is possible to associate to each edge of the graph (i.e. itinerary) also a pair of cost and time for traversing the itinerary, which are inversely proportional. Different strategies could be adopted for synthesising the routes of vehicles, for example by minimising either the cost or time, or a linear combination of both. Concerning the experiments, we would like to include the proposed ILP model into a framework for simulating possible failures of tracks, to evaluate the ILP model in the presence of different conditions randomly generated and throughout a whole day. It would be then possible to measure the energy consumption and user satisfiability adopting different strategies for computing the routes, to select the best one.

Acknowledgements. This work has been partially supported by the Tuscany Region project POR FESR 2014–2020 SISTER and H2020 2017–2019 S2R-OC-IP2-01-2017 ASTRail.

References

1. Assad, A.: Analysis of rail classification policies. INFOR: Inf. Syst. Oper. Res. **21**(4), 293–314 (1983). doi:10.1080/03155986.1983.11731905
2. Bodin, L.D., Golden, B.L., Schuster, A.D., Romig, W.: A model for the blocking of trains. Transp. Res. Part B: Methodol. **14**(1), 115–120 (1980). http://www.sciencedirect.com/science/article/pii/0191261580900375
3. Borndörfer, R., Klug, T., Schlechte, T., Fügenschuh, A., Schang, T., Schülldorf, H.: The freight train routing problem for congested railway networks with mixed traffic. Transp. Sci. **50**(2), 408–423 (2016)
4. Dantzig, G.B., Ramser, J.H.: The truck dispatching problem. Manage. Sci. **6**, 80–91 (1959)
5. Flood, M.M.: The traveling-salesman problem. Oper. Res. **4**(1), 61–75 (1956)
6. Ford, D.R., Fulkerson, D.R.: Flows in Networks. Princeton University Press, Princeton (2010)
7. Ford, L.R., Fulkerson, D.R.: A simple algorithm for finding maximal network flows and an application to the hitchcock problem. Canadian J. Mathe, 210–218 (1957)

8. Fourer, R., Gay, D.M., Kernighan, B.W.: AMPL: a mathematical programming language. AT & T Bell Laboratories Murray Hill (1987)

9. Ghiani, G., Guerriero, F., Laporte, G., Musmanno, R.: Real-time vehicle routing: solution concepts, algorithms and parallel computing strategies. Eur. J. Oper. Res. **151**(1), 1–11 (2003)

10. Hemmecke, R., Koppe, M., Lee, J., Weismantel, R.: Nonlinear integer programming. In: Junger, M., Liebling, T.M., Naddef, D., Nemhauser, G.L., Pulleyblank, W.R., Reinelt, G., Rinaldi, G., Wolsey, L.A. (eds.) 50 Years of Integer Programming 1958–2008, pp. 561–618. Springer, Heidelberg (2010)

11. Klein, M.: A primal method for minimal cost flows, with applications to the assignment and transportation problems (1967)

12. Li, F., Gao, Z., Li, K., Yang, L.: Efficient scheduling of railway traffic based on global information of train. Transp. Res. Part B Methodol. **42**(10), 1008–1030 (2008). http://www.sciencedirect.com/science/article/pii/S0191261508000337

13. Martinelli, D.R., Teng, H.: Optimization of railway operations using neural networks. Transp. Res. Part C Emerg. Technol. **4**(1), 33–49 (1996). http://www.sciencedirect.com/science/article/pii/0968090X9500019F

14. Mazzanti, F., Ferrari, A., Spagnolo, G.O.: Experiments in formal modelling of a deadlock avoidance algorithm for a CBTC system. In: Margaria, T., Steffen, B. (eds.) ISoLA 2016. LNCS, vol. 9953, pp. 297–314. Springer, Cham (2016). doi:10.1007/978-3-319-47169-3_22

15. Pillac, V., Gendreau, M., Guéret, C., Medaglia, A.L.: A review of dynamic vehicle routing problems. Eur. J. Oper. Res. **225**(1), 1–11 (2013)

16. Psaraftis, H.N., Wen, M., Kontovas, C.A.: Dynamic vehicle routing problems: three decades and counting. Netw. **67**(1), 3–31 (2016)

17. Schoitsch, E.: Introduction to the special theme - autonomous vehicles. ERCIM News 2017 (109) (2017)

18. Sun, Y., Cao, C., Wu, C.: Multi-objective optimization of train routing problem combined with train scheduling on a high-speed railway network. Transp. Res. Part C Emerg. Technol. **44**, 1–20 (2014). http://www.sciencedirect.com/science/article/pii/S0968090X14000655

19. Wallace, S.W. (ed.): Algorithms and Model Formulations in Mathematical Programming. Springer, New York (1989)

20. Yanfeng, L., Ziyou, G., Jun, L.: Vehicle routing problem in dynamic urban traffic network. In: ICSSSM 2011, pp. 1–6 (2011)

Engineering Techniques and Standards

Theories, Techniques and Tools for Engineering Heterogeneous Railway Networks

Paulius Stankaitis$^{(\boxtimes)}$ and Alexei Iliasov

School of Computing Science, Newcastle University, Newcastle upon Tyne, UK
{p.stankaitis,alexei.iliasov}@ncl.ac.uk

Abstract. Modernising outdated national railway systems will be done gradually due to practical constraints thus creating network areas with different signalling systems. Formal methods have been successfully applied in the railway domain for years. Yet the latest railway challenges such as heterogeneous railway signalling will require novel modelling techniques and adequate verification tools support. In this research we aim to develop new theories, techniques and tools for modelling and verification of complex networks comprising areas with a mixed signalling. This student paper discusses the research problem, related work and presents the ongoing work.

Keywords: Distributed railway interlocking · Hybrid systems · Event-B method

1 Introduction

In the last few decades railway domain has proved to be a fruitful area for applying various formal methods. Yet the latest railway challenges will require novel modelling techniques and adequate formal verification tools support. Integrating modern railway signalling systems within an outdated national railway networks is currently one of the major challenges. Indeed a gradual railway modernisation process means that heterogeneous railway signalling networks will be inevitable due to practical constraints. In some situations mainline services must be integrated with urban networks which simply require different signalling solutions as high service availability can only be achieved with a moving block signalling solution[1]. To give an example Crossrail is a major ongoing railway project where mainline services will be integrated with a high performance urban railway system. This particular network will operate with three different signalling systems. In western and eastern branches of the network fixed block signalling systems will operate whereas the central area will be operated with a moving block principle. Novel signalling interfaces will be developed to ensure a smooth and safe rolling stock signalling transition. In short this PhD study aims to address the challenge of modelling and verification of railway networks with different signalling systems.

---

[1] To this date a moving block signalling solution only operates in urban networks.

© Springer International Publishing AG 2017
A. Fantechi et al. (Eds.): RSSRail 2017, LNCS 10598, pp. 241–250, 2017.
https://doi.org/10.1007/978-3-319-68499-4_16

The following section overviews key difficulties in formally modelling and verifying such systems which are in fact cyber-physical systems. Secondly we discuss more notable related work examples and present technical contributions this research aims to achieve. Last two sections discuss the current work on modelling and verification of a distributed railway network in the Event-B language and future research objectives.

2 Formal Methods in Railway Domain

Formal methods - a mathematical model driven methods provide a systematic approach for developing complex systems. They offer an approach to specify systems precisely via a mathematically defined syntax and semantics as well as formally validate them by using semi-automatic or automatic techniques. At the moment among the biggest challenges in the field is ensuring safety and correctness of cyber-physical systems.

For years formal methods have been successfully applied to the railway domain however yet a considerably little work has been done in including a cyber-physical nature of railway for a safety reasoning. Established railway operation principles did not require that so formal methods mainly focused on a static railway data verification - control table verification. However modern signalling systems were developed to reduce an overdesign and hence increase the capacity of railway networks. Railway operational principles have been rapidly moving towards a continuous agent communication and a more dynamic parameter (e.g. permitted speed profile) computation which are indeed two essential aspects of cyber-physical systems - communication and computation. Therefore to model and reason about safety of a modern signalling system we believe it is paramount to consider a cyber-physical nature of railway.

In general cyber-physical systems [30] have tight integration of communication, computation and control aspects and include discrete as well as continuous behaviours. Indeed the difficulty in modelling and verifying cyber-physical systems is a necessity to consider all these aspects together. To this date there exists no formal framework which could capture a tight integration of these systems aspects [18]. Furthermore for a lot of safety-critical system the dynamic nature of an environment has to be considered in the model as well. For instance a lossy communication aspect is particularly important when modelling modern-radio based railway signalling systems or railway systems with signalling transitions. Hybrid systems formal verification challenges arise mainly due to continuous variables with non-linear dynamics [3,31]. An algorithmic verification of hybrid systems with available model checking tools is limited even under severe restrictions whereas simulation tools coverage is not adequate for a safety reasoning. In spite of that system validation through simulation is still the most prevalent method used by railway industry today. Alternative methods such as a deductive verification method are not limited by the state space and combined with computer algebra systems can deal with non-linear dynamics though some problems for an automated deductive verification still have to be resolved [4].

Related work. Over the years formal methods were primarily applied only for a discrete safety reasoning of the railway systems. The literature review revealed that only a small fraction of all railway oriented research considered a cyber-physical nature of railway systems. The following paragraphs discuss a more notable related work on distributed dynamic railway systems which are a class of cyber-physical systems.

To authors knowledge the earliest attempt to formally analyse distributed railway solid-state interlocking systems was completed by Morley [23]. In this interesting work author developed a formal model of a protocol for a cross boundary route locking and releasing mechanism. By analysing temporal properties of the model he discovered that in certain scenarios safety properties can be violated. Few years later a paper by Cimatti et al. [10] presented an industrially driven formal methods study where authors formally modelled a communication protocol for safety-critical distributed systems including distributed railway interlocking systems. Their method used Statecharts diagrams to specify high level protocol properties and the OBJECTGEODE model checker for the protocol validation. In other work a different concept of distributed railway control system was introduced by Haxthausen and Peleska [14]. Their presented engineering concept of the control system relied on a radio based communication and switch boxes - systems which can only control a single railway point. Authors formally modelled the system with the RAISE [13] specification language which allowed to develop a formal model incrementally using a refinement process and prove refinement and safety properties with available justification tools. The timing properties of the design were considered in the extended work [22]. Similar ideas for distributed railway interlocking system were also presented in [8,15] where authors used Statecharts and Petri Nets to model and verify decentralised railway interlocking.

At the same time André Platzer introduced an alternative approach to exploring a state-space with model checkers in verifying systems safety. A developed formalism and logic for reasoning about hybrid systems uses a deductive verification and can be implemented in a KeyMaera X verification tool [24,26]. The later work presented a case study where differential dynamic logic was applied for a safety verification of the European Train Control System [27]. Differential Dynamic Logic was also used to model and verify a handover protocol between two trackside train control systems (radio-block centres) by Liu et al. [21]. In a work by Cimatti et al. [11] authors proposed a different logic based on the temporal logic with regular expressions. Their motivation was driven by a need of the automatic verification method for verifying hybrid requirements for hybrid railway system. A more recent work by Iliasov et al. [17] proposed a domain specific language - Unified Train Driving Policy. The formal notation allows to express both static and dynamic properties of railway in readable syntax which can be interpreted by railway engineers without prior knowledge of formal methods. A few recent formal methods projects on cyber-physical systems applied their novel techniques for modelling and verification of hybrid railway systems [16,28,29].

In the previous project on modelling and verification of railway interlocking systems we discussed possible future PhD study directions for addressing the safety of heterogeneous railway networks [32]. The two year project focused on developing an expressive railway oriented simulator which would enable modelling and analysing complex railway including railway systems with mixed signalling. In the future we plan to use the system-level simulator as a specification front-end for our modelling framework discussed in the following paragraph.

This PhD research aims to focus on theories and techniques for formal modelling and verification of classes of distributed hybrid railway systems which are in fact what we define as heterogeneous railway networks. In particular we are interested in developing a railway oriented formal modelling framework which could capture dynamic distributed hybrid systems. A similar work [12,20] has been completed for more general cooperating agent based systems by exploring design patterns or more focused on dynamic distributed hybrid systems in [25]. In our work we would like to continue in this direction but by restricting our methodology to the railway domain. First of all to develop such a formal framework to reason about distributed hybrid railway networks one needs to understand and formally define a general railway design structure. The formal framework should not only capture existing railway operation principles for which a number of domain-specific languages already exists but also allow modelling moving block signalling systems. In the previous paragraphs we also emphasised the necessity to consider a cyber-physical nature of railway for safety reasoning. Therefore an important requirement for the modelling formal framework is to allow capturing continuous evolution of agents and for that we can use existing approaches for instance hybrid automata. The modelling notation should not only have executional semantics which is exactly the simulation of railway operation but it also should offer proof semantics. The work by Damm et al. [12] proposed a generic proof-rules for reducing the complexity of the reasoning about collision avoidance systems. In this PhD research we will attempt to further improve this approach by specifically addressing the railway domain. To enable reasoning about safety of heterogeneous railway signalling we will need to include new safety rules for a system transition reasoning - a similar but more generic to presented in [21]. Lastly in order to ensure that results have potential to be useful in the industrial setting this research will be conducted in a close cooperation with Siemens Rail Automation.

In the following section we present an ongoing work which aims to develop a generic design pattern for distributed railway networks. For that we use the Event-B modelling language as a back-end formal notation which offers a refinement based modelling language. It allows to start with an abstract model for instance the skeleton of a dynamic distributed railway system and then include new details through a number of correctness preserving refinement steps for instance details of a specific signalling system. In this paper we will not discuss hybrid modelling part of the framework but we will base our work on existing methods developed for Event-B [5,7].

3   Distributed Formal Railway Model in Event-B

The Event-B mathematical language used in the system development and analysis is an evolution of the classical B method [1] and Action Systems [6]. Perhaps due to the success of the B method and a good tool support Event-B has also been a popular language choice for modelling railway systems [2,9,19]. The formal specification language offers a fairly high-level mathematical language based on a first-order logic and Zermelo-Fraenkel set theory as well as an economical yet expressive modelling notation. The formalism belongs to a family of state-based modelling languages where a state of a discrete system is simply a collection of variables and constants whereas the transition is a guarded variable transformation.

A cornerstone of the Event-B method is the step-wise development that facilitates a gradual design of a system implementation through a number of correctness preserving refinement steps. The model development starts with a creation of a very abstract specification and the model is completed when all requirements and specifications are covered. The Event-B model is made of two key components - machines and contexts which respectively describe dynamic and static parts of the system. The context contains modeller declared constants and associated axioms which can be made visible in machines. The dynamic part of the model contains variables which are constrained by invariants and initialised by an action. The state variables are then transformed by actions which are part of events and the modeller may use predicate guards to denote when event is triggered (see Fig. 1). Specifying a model is not sufficient one must provide evidence about the correctness of the model as well. The Event-B method is a proof driven specification language where model correctness is demonstrated by generating and discharging proof obligations - theorems in the first-order logic. The model is considered to be correct when all proof obligations are discharged.

The following subsections present an ongoing work on modelling a distributed railway interlocking. In particular we focus on modelling the distributed resource allocation problem where processes can capture and release available resources as it is paramount for a distributed railway interlocking. To develop a protocol for a safe distributed route locking mechanism in further refinements undischarged proof obligations will be used.

```
machine M
    sees Context
    variables v
    invariant I(c, s, v)
    initialisation R(c, s, v')
    events
        E₁ = any vl where g(c, s, vl, v) then S(c, s, vl, v, v') end
        ...
end
```

Fig. 1. Event-B machine structure.

3.1   Abstract Distributed Railway Interlocking Model

First of all we describe the modelling and refinement plan of a distributed railway signalling with main requirements at each step. The initial abstract model specifies the general concept of a distributed resource allocation protocol - processes capturing and releasing available resources. Starting with such a mathematical abstraction allows to simplify the development of a protocol without considering complicated railway requirements at early modelling stages.

Initial model. An abstract model of processes capturing resources.

1. An abstract model context - processes and resources (finite sets).
2. An abstract model contains events for capturing and releasing resources.
3. Processes can only capture not already captured resources.
4. Processes can only release their captured resources.
5. Processes could capture more than a single resource at a time.
6. No two or more processes can have same resources captured.

Refinement 1. Extending the model with events for requesting and granting resources and solving a contention problem.

1. Introducing events for requesting and granting resources.
2. Introducing events for detecting and solving the contention problem.
3. Resources can only be captured if requested and granted by the process.
4. Same resources can be requested by multiple processes at the same time.
5. Resources request from a single process cannot be partially granted.
6. Processes can request any set of resources.
7. Resources can be granted to the process if they have not been requested, granted or captured by other processes or if the conflict has been solved with detect/solve events.

Other Refinements. Introducing graph based resource structures and railway related context (not discussed in this paper).

1. Distributing resources in to separate zones with associated controllers.
2. Introducing a graph based resource structure in to the model.
3. Introducing a railway related context and route locking principles.

Other properties such as a system progress can be addressed by assuming that processes release resources eventually and also by introducing a resource granting queue. In the initial model we only impose a single railway related safety rule which states that collision freedom is ensured if no two or more trains share the same route. This can be simply expressed by the invariant - no two or more processes can have same resources captured.

The modelling was started by creating the abstract context with two carrier sets for processes and resources with two associated axioms stating that these sets are finite. In the dynamic part of the model we defined a global variable mrk (marked) for mapping resources to processes. Furthermore we introduced two events for capturing and releasing resources which are in fact abstract representations of a railway route locking and releasing operations. Both events have similar guards except one can only release resources if they have already been captured.

Event *capture* $\widehat{=}$
> **any**
>> $r,\ p,\ pr$
>
> **where**
>> **grd1** : $r \not\subseteq dom(mrk)$
>> **grd2** : $p \in P$
>> **grd3** : $pr \in r \to \{p\}$
>> **grd4** : $\varnothing \subset pr$
>
> **then**
>> **act1** : $mrk := mrk \cup pr$
>
> **end**

Event *release* $\widehat{=}$
> **any**
>> $r,\ p,\ pr$
>
> **where**
>> **grd1** : $r \subseteq dom(mrk)$
>> **grd2** : $p \in ran(mrk)$
>> **grd3** : $pr \in r \to \{p\}$
>> **grd4** : $\varnothing \subset pr$
>
> **then**
>> **act1** : $mrk := mrk \setminus pr$
>
> **end**

In the next model refinement a logical step then was to introduce two new events for requesting and granting resources and two buffers for storing resourced requests (req) and granted resources (ack). A process can request any subset of resources and grant event then checks whether those resources are not captured or granted for other processes. Because of new events we also needed to update the abstract capture event with stronger guards and additional action to update both buffers.

Event *send_request* $\widehat{=}$
> **any**
>> $r,\ p,\ pr$
>
> **where**
>> **grd1** : $p \in P$
>> **grd2** : $r \subseteq R$
>> **grd3** : $pr \in r \to \{p\}$
>> **grd4** : $\varnothing \subset pr$
>
> **then**
>> **act1** : $req := req \cup pr$
>
> **end**

Event *grant_request* $\widehat{=}$
> **any**
>> p
>
> **where**
>> **grd1** : $p \in ran(req)$
>> **grd2** : $req^{-1}[\{p\}] \cap dom(mrk \rhd \{p\}) = \varnothing$
>> **grd3** : $req^{-1}[\{p\}] \cap dom(req \rhd \{p\}) = \varnothing$
>> **grd4** : $req^{-1}[\{p\}] \cap dom(ack \rhd \{p\}) = \varnothing$
>
> **then**
>> **act1** : $ack := ack \cup (req \rhd \{p\})$
>> **act2** : $req := req \rhd \{p\}$
>
> **end**

The request buffer may contain multiple requests for the same resources from different processes. So the resource grant event will only grant a set of resources to a single process if they have not been requested by other process. In case of multiple requests for the same resources from different processes we needed to introduce another two events for detecting and solving such a situation discussed in the following subsection.

3.2 Contention Problem for Distributed Railway Interlocking

A very common problem in developing distributed systems is the contention problem. In our model the problem can arise when a number of same resources have been requested by different processes. Since we do not allow partial resource allocation because of the safety principle which comes from the railway domain the system deadlocks. To resolve this we simply introduced two new events for detecting and solving this problem. The contention detection event is enabled when there exists a set of processes which all requested common resources and if those resources have not been captured yet. This event action simply copies the set of interested requests to another buffer - cnt (contention).

Event $detect\_contention \;\widehat{=}$
  any
                p
  where
      grd1 : $p = \{x | \exists y \cdot y \neq x \wedge req^{-1}[\{x\}] \cap req^{-1}[\{y\}] \neq \varnothing\}$
      grd2 : $p = \{x | req^{-1}[\{x\}] \cap dom(mrk \rhd \{x\}) = \varnothing\}$
      grd4 : $p \neq \varnothing$
  then
      act1 : $cnt := cnt \cup (req \rhd p)$
  end

After that the following event grant (not shown here) nondeterministically selects a process from that buffer and grants resources for that single process and also removes its requests from the request buffer. The detect/solve process then can be repeated for remaining processes. At this level one does not need to consider which process is given a priority this becomes more important when graph based resource structure is introduced.

4   Conclusions and Future Work

In this paper we presented the main motivation of this PhD research which is the need of new formal methods techniques for modelling distributed dynamic railway networks and reasoning about their safety. The research proposed to develop a new railway oriented modelling framework with proof rules which could capture a cyber-physical nature of the heterogeneous railway networks. Then we presented an ongoing work on modelling a distributed railway signalling system which is necessary in order to explore common distributed railway design patterns and also deduce invariants for heterogeneous railway networks. In the following months we aim to complete this model and focus on hybrid framework part for modelling and reasoning about heterogeneous railway networks.

Acknowledgements. This work is supported by an iCASE studentship (EPSRC and Siemens Rail Automation). We are grateful to our colleagues from Siemens Rail Automation for invaluable feedback. We would also like to thank Guillaume Babin and Yamine Aït-Ameur for useful conversations.

References

1. Abrial, J.-R.: The B-book: Assigning Programs to Meanings. Cambridge University Press, New York (1996)
2. Abrial, J.-R.: Modeling in Event-B: System and Software Engineering. Cambridge University Press, New York (2013)
3. Alur, R.: Formal verification of hybrid systems. In: Proceedings of the Ninth ACM International Conference on Embedded Software, EMSOFT 2011, pp. 273–278. ACM, New York (2011)
4. Alur, R., Courcoubetis, C., Halbwachs, N., Henzinger, T.A., Ho, P.-H., Nicollin, X., Olivero, A., Sifakis, J., Yovine, S.: The algorithmic analysis of hybrid systems. Theor. Comput. Sci. **138**(1), 3–34 (1995)
5. Babin, G., Aït-Ameur, Y., Nakajima, S., Pantel, M.: Refinement and proof based development of systems characterized by continuous functions. In: Li, X., Liu, Z., Yi, W. (eds.) SETTA 2015. LNCS, vol. 9409, pp. 55–70. Springer, Cham (2015). doi:10.1007/978-3-319-25942-0_4
6. Back, R.J.R.: Refinement calculus, part II: parallel and reactive programs. In: Bakker, J.W., Roever, W.-P., Rozenberg, G. (eds.) REX 1989. LNCS, vol. 430, pp. 67–93. Springer, Heidelberg (1990). doi:10.1007/3-540-52559-9_61
7. Banach, R., Butler, M., Qin, S., Verma, N., Zhu, H.: Core hybrid Event-B I: single hybrid event-B machines. Sci. Comput. Program. **105**, 92–123 (2015)
8. Banci, M., Fantechi, A., Gnesi, S.: The role of formal methods in developing a distributed railway interlocking system. In: Proceedings of the 5th Symposium on Formal Methods for Automation and Safety in Railway and Automotive Systems (FORMS/FORMAT 2004), pp. 220–230 (2004)
9. Butler, M.: A system-based approach to the formal development of embedded controllers for a railway. Des. Autom. Embed. Syst. **6**(4), 355–366 (2002)
10. Cimatti, A., Pieraccini, P.L., Sebastiani, R., Traverso, P., Villafiorita, A.: Formal specification and validation of a vital communication protocol. In: Wing, J.M., Woodcock, J., Davies, J. (eds.) FM 1999. LNCS, vol. 1709, pp. 1584–1604. Springer, Heidelberg (1999). doi:10.1007/3-540-48118-4_34
11. Cimatti, A., Roveri, M., Tonetta, S.: Requirements validation for hybrid systems. In: Bouajjani, A., Maler, O. (eds.) CAV 2009. LNCS, vol. 5643, pp. 188–203. Springer, Heidelberg (2009). doi:10.1007/978-3-642-02658-4_17
12. Damm, W., Hungar, H., Olderog, E.R.: Verification of cooperating traffic agents. Int. J. Control **79**(5), 395–421 (2006)
13. George, C., Haxthausen, A.E., Hughes, S., Milne, R., Prehn, S., Pedersen, J.S.: The RAISE Development Method. Prentice Hall International (1995)
14. Haxthausen, A.E., Peleska, J.: Formal development and verification of a distributed railway control system. IEEE Trans. Software Eng. **26**(8), 687–701 (2000)
15. Hei, X., Takahashi, S., Hideo, N.: Toward developing a decentralized railway signalling system using petri nets. In: Proceedings of the IEEE Conference on Robotics, Automation and Mechatronics, pp. 851–855 (2008)
16. Hermanns, H., Jansen, D.N., Usenko, Y.S.: A comparative reliability analysis of ETCS train radio communications. Reports of SFB/TR 14 AVACS 2, SFB/TR 14 AVACS, February 2005. ISSN: 1860-9821. http://www.avacs.org
17. Iliasov, A., Lopatkin, I., Romanovsky, A.: Unified Train Driving Policy, pp. 447–474. Wiley (2014)
18. Kim, K.D., Kumar, P.R.: Cyber-physical systems: a perspective at the centennial. Proc. IEEE **100**(Special Centennial Issue), 1287–1308 (2012)

19. Kiss, T., Jánosi-Rancz, K.T.: Developing railway interlocking systems with session types and Event-B. In: Proceedings of the IEEE 11th International Symposium on Applied Computational Intelligence and Informatics (SACI), pp. 93–98, May 2016
20. Knudsen, J., Ravn, A.P., Skou, A.: Design verification patterns. In: Jones, C.B., Liu, Z., Woodcock, J. (eds.) Formal Methods and Hybrid Real-Time Systems. LNCS, vol. 4700, pp. 399–413. Springer, Heidelberg (2007). doi:10.1007/978-3-540-75221-9_18
21. Liu, Y., Tang, T., Liu, J., Zhao, L., Xu, T.: Formal modeling and verification of RBC handover of ETCS using differential dynamic logic. In: Proceedings of the International Symposium on the Autonomous Decentralized Systems (ISADS), pp. 67–72. IEEE (2011)
22. Madsen, M.S., Bæk, M.M.: Modelling a distributed railway control system. Master's thesis, Technical University of Denmark, DTU, DK-2800 Kgs, Lyngby, Denmark (2005)
23. Morley, M.J.: Safety assurance in interlocking design. PhD thesis (1996)
24. Platzer, A.: Differential dynamic logic for hybrid systems. J. Autom. Reason. **41**(2), 143–189 (2008)
25. Platzer, A.: Quantified differential dynamic logic for distributed hybrid systems. In: Dawar, A., Veith, H. (eds.) CSL 2010. LNCS, vol. 6247, pp. 469–483. Springer, Heidelberg (2010). doi:10.1007/978-3-642-15205-4_36
26. Platzer, A., Quesel, J.-D.: KeYmaera: a hybrid theorem prover for hybrid systems (system description). In: Armando, A., Baumgartner, P., Dowek, G. (eds.) IJCAR 2008. LNCS, vol. 5195, pp. 171–178. Springer, Heidelberg (2008). doi:10.1007/978-3-540-71070-7_15
27. Platzer, A., Quesel, J.-D.: European train control system: a case study in formal verification. In: Breitman, K., Cavalcanti, A. (eds.) ICFEM 2009. LNCS, vol. 5885, pp. 246–265. Springer, Heidelberg (2009). doi:10.1007/978-3-642-10373-5_13
28. ADVANCE project: Final report on application on railway domai, deliverable d1.4 workpackage 1. Technical report, 30 November 2014
29. INTO-CPS project: Case studies 2, deliverable d1.2. Technical report, November 2016
30. Sha, L., Gopalakrishnan, S., Liu, X., Wang, Q.: Cyber-physical systems: a new frontier. In: Proceedings of the IEEE International Conference on Sensor Networks, Ubiquitous, and Trustworthy Computing, SUTC 2008, pp. 1–9, June 2008
31. Silva, B.I., Stursberg, O., Krogh, B.H., Engell, S.: An assessment of the current status of algorithmic approaches to the verification of hybrid systems. In: Proceedings of the 40th IEEE Conference on Decision and Control, vol. 3, pp. 2867–2874. IEEE (2001)
32. Stankaitis, P., Iliasov, A.: Safety verification of heterogeneous railway networks. In: Lecomte, T., Pinger, R., Romanovsky, A. (eds.) RSSRail 2016. LNCS, vol. 9707, pp. 150–159. Springer, Cham (2016). doi:10.1007/978-3-319-33951-1_11

Are Standards an Ambiguity-Free Reference for Product Validation?

Alessio Ferrari, Mario Fusani$^{(\boxtimes)}$, and Stefania Gnesi

ISTI-CNR, Pisa, Italy
{alessio.ferrari,mario.fusani,stefania.gnesi}@isti.cnr.it

Abstract. The increased use of standards as references for safety-critical applications is drawing the attention of researchers on the fact that the responsibility for the safety of standard-compliant systems may depend not only on developers and assessors, but also on the standards themselves. This paper is focused particularly on some quality aspects of standard *clauses*, i.e., the natural language statements that are expressed by the standards, and to which a standard-compliant process or product is required to adhere. Various railway standards are considered, and some linguistic issues, potentially leading to ambiguity of clause interpretation, are discovered with the aid of natural language processing (NLP) tools. Real cases of problems in clause interpretation, taken from industrial experience, are reported, to show the possible impact in products and processes that must be validated against such clauses, and to justify the importance of the analysis.

Keywords: Standard · Clause · Requirement · Ambiguity · Railway · Natural language · NLP · Defect detection · Vagueness · Generality

1 Introduction

Railway systems in Europe shall be developed according to the *process* standards issues by the CENELEC committee[1]. These are a set of norms and methods to be followed when developing a certain safety-critical railway product.

Perhaps it is not explicitly declared in their foreword sections, but railway standards bear a nice deal of responsibility for the characteristics of the *products* that are expected to comply. Indeed, to the vast majority of their users, typical process-related standards are undisputed reference for "the methods which need to be used in order to provide software which meets the demands for safety integrity..." – quoting the introduction of EN50128:2011 [8], the specific CENELEC norm for software development.

Nevertheless, even standards are no immutable reference. To cope with the evolution of technology, they are periodically submitted to a long, regulated revision process. Reasons for change are also recognised by the standardizing organisms as improvement opportunities across successive revisions, regarding

---

[1] European Committee for Electrotechnical Standardization. https://www.cenelec.eu.

© Springer International Publishing AG 2017
A. Fantechi et al. (Eds.): RSSRail 2017, LNCS 10598, pp. 251 264, 2017.
https://doi.org/10.1007/978-3-319-68499-4_17

"the coherency and consistency of the standard, the concept of safety management and the practical usage..." – quoting what would likely be the introduction of a new revision of EN50126 [9]), the specific CENELEC norm for the RAMS Reliability, Availability, Maintainability and Safety process.

Other potential entities exist that could manifest reasons for standards improvement. Such entities are different from the standardizing organizations, such as CENELEC, and from the target users explicitly mentioned in the norms – i.e., Duty Holders and Suppliers. They are governmental organisms and safety/security agencies, who are interested in representing end-users. Furthermore, these entities include research and academic institutions, who are interested in providing standards with sound scientific grounds. These latter made their suggestions public at conferences and in scientific journals [16, 17, 26, 30].

This paper aims to be part of the small but continuing stream of research on the effectiveness of standards, and focuses on a set of quality properties that may affect the ambiguity of the statements declared by the standards, which are generally expressed in natural language (NL) – e.g., English, Italian –, and are named *clauses*[2]. This research theme takes from a more mature work done in the field of requirements engineering (RE), in which natural language processing (NLP) techniques have been developed to detect NL defects in requirements specification documents [15, 24, 32, 34]. Within this context, the purpose of the paper is twofold:

1. To show, with examples, that lack of linguistic qualities in clause-based documents, such as standards, can have an impact on the quality characteristics – e.g., project development time, safety of developed systems, lifecycle costs – of the projects expected to be standard-compliant;
2. To show, using a NLP methodology supported by tools, that some popular standards, adopted in railways applications, are not immune from those defects.

It is not in the paper intents to criticize in any way the analysed standards: they have been the base for safety certification of countless actual well performing products. The work that may result from this investigation is aimed to possibly improve some aspects of current and future standards revisions. Furthermore, there are other kinds of issues about standards that are outside the scope of this work. Reported problems introduced by (non-functional) standard compliance are broad scale, ranging from measurability of prescribed objects [17], to unfocused target determination among process-product-resource [17], to inopportunely mixing levels of abstraction and doping pure requirements with implementation aspects or technicalities at risk of obsolescence [6].

The paper is organised as follows. In Sect. 2, two independent literature streams are discussed. The first one concerns investigations on standards efficacy. The second one concerns methods and tools developed in the RE field for

---

[2] Some authors, e.g., Fenton and Neil [17], refer to these statements as *requirements*. Here, we use the term clause, to distinguish the statements of the standards from those used in requirements specification documents.

discovering linguistic defects in requirements documents. In Sect. 3, the essentials of a quality model for natural language, created in late 1990's with the purpose of analysing the text of system and software requirements, are described as background information.

In Sect. 4 various reasons for justifying linguistic analysis of standards are sketched. In Sect. 5 results from analyses of popular railway standards, performed by a tool in conformity with the model described in Sect. 3, are shown and discussed. In Sect. 6 conclusions are drawn.

2   Related Literature

The works related to the current paper can be broadly partitioned into two research lines. The first one is aimed straight at improving standards, especially safety-related ones, in a variety of aspects. The second one, much more prolific in articles, is concerned with the linguistic aspects that affect the correct interpretation of sentences in general texts and, more specifically, in system and software requirements documents.

2.1   Works on Standards Evaluation

The history of the sporadic but relevant literature of the first line evolved in two steps, widely separated by a couple of decades.

The first step is basically concentrated in the late 1990s, with the works of Norman Fenton and several co-authors [16,17,30] are the ones worth of notice. Especially in [17], in which a systematic standard analysis is presented, the importance of clarity and objectivity in requirements is highlighted, among other aspects. More specifically, Fenton and Neil [17], presents a reference framework for standards' interpretation, and an associated structured approach that guides a reader towards an objective interpretation of the standard clauses, even in presence of vague statements. Furthermore, the authors also suggest an approach to improve the standards, by introducing the notion of *ministandards*, i.e., "coherent subsets of requirements all relating to the same specific process, product, or resource" [17]. While Fenton and Neil focus on improving the structure of the standards, by partitioning them into more manageable subsets, in our work we focus on improving the language of single clauses. In also is worth noticing that Fenton and co-authors also examine how the characteristics of the standards impact in different kind of users, typically, developers and assessors – we will also briefly discuss this aspect in Sect. 4.

The second step did not happen until 2014. On the awareness of the increasing interest in safety-related standards of different domains (such as avionics, automotive, rail, nuclear power plants and others), a workshop was called by Patrick Graydon at the annual European Dependable Computing Conference (EDCC) in Newcastle[3]. A group of experts gathered to examine and discuss the efficacy of

---

[3] Proceedings of Planning the Unplanned Experiment: Assessing the Efficacy of Standards for Safety Critical Software (AESSCS), May 2014.

safety Related standards from different perspectives, also presenting several position papers. The basic outcome was that the situation of the standards was not sensibly improved since Fenton's analysis and suggestions – perhaps disregarded or, likely, unnoticed. The safety-related standards, and the consequent work of compliance implementation and demonstration, are still considered as an "unplanned experiment": there is little evidence about how and why standards *do work*, that is, they are such that safety expectations can be satisfied in products declared standard-compliant. A NASA Memorandum [25] was issued in 2015 by Graydon and Holloway, where the inputs from the workshop are elaborated and a list of research questions, as well as defined investigations and experiments, are proposed. The Memorandum also refers all the position papers.

In 2010, the ongoing research on requirements at our institute produced a work on ambiguity evaluation of the standard clauses [6], which in some way was across the two research lines mentioned in this Section. At the time it was basically an exercise of tool application, since we did not perceive in full what the successive 2014 workshop wanted to examine, and why.

2.2 Works on Requirements Evaluation Using NLP

The second line of research concerns the analysis of linguistic aspects that affect the quality of requirements documents. As mentioned, several works were produced in the requirements engineering (RE) area proposing techniques to address the problem of requirements defects, with a particular focus on linguistic ambiguity. Part of the techniques suggests to use formal, semi-formal languages or constrained NL to prevent or limit ambiguity. Other techniques start from unconstrained NL and generally aims at detecting ambiguity.

In particular, strategies were defined to *prevent* ambiguities by means of formal approaches [1, 27, 29] or constrained natural languages [2, 28]. The works of Kof [27], tools like Circe-Cico [1], LOLITA [29], and NL2ACTL [14], which transform requirements into formal/semi-formal models and languages, have ambiguity prevention among their objectives. Concerning the use of constrained natural languages, the EARS template [28] and the Rupp's template [31] are well known constrained formats for editing requirements. Arora et al. [2] defined an approach to check the conformance of requirements to these templates.

Also in the railway domain, works were performed to translate requirements into formal models, normally by means of manual procedures. Among these works, in Ferrari *et al.* [18], railway requirements for an automatic train protection (ATP) system were manually translated into statecharts models from which safety-critical code was automatically generated. Instead, Ghazel [21] and Cimatti *et al.* [11] formalised a subset of the ERTMS/ETCS standard by means of the NuSMV language. In these latter cases, the goal was formal verification by means of model checking.

Other approaches aim to *detect* ambiguities in requirements. These approaches are mainly *rule-based*, i.e., based on linguistic patterns to be matched within requirements [3]. Most of these works stem from the typically defective terms and constructions classified in the ambiguity handbook of Berry *et al.* [3].

Based on these studies, tools such as QuARS [24], SREE [34] and the tool of Gleich *et al.* [23] were developed. More recently, industrial application of these approaches were studied by Femmer *et al.* [15] and by Rosadini *et al.* [32]. As shown also in these studies, rule-based approaches tend to produce a high number of false positive cases – i.e., linguistic ambiguities that have one single reading in practice. Hence, *statistical* approaches were proposed by Chantree *et al.* [10] and by Yang *et al.* [35] to reduce the number of false positive cases, referred as *innocuous ambiguities*.

Among the works on ambiguity detection, the paper of Rosadini *et al.* [32] is one of the few that focus specifically on railway requirements. In this work, consolidated NLP techniques for ambiguity detection inspired from QuARS [24] were introduced in a railway signalling company to verify a large set of about 1800 requirements, showing that the techniques were mature for industrial adoption.

3 Background: A Quality Model for NL-expressed Requirements

In principle, a Quality Model describes an ideal set of properties a real object must possess to achieve some defined goals related to its use. Such properties, usually called quality characteristics, have themselves some global or individual properties, or meta-properties, such as measurability and others. We do not address here the general problem of Quality Model generation, but just recall the concept of quality of requirements expressions. The relevance of the quality of early work products in systems lifecycle has been pointed out by Gilb [22] and by other authors. What is "just" a quality defect in system/software requirements documents, if not resolved in time, can result in technical problems or in vital system functionality loss during validation or service.

As mentioned in the introduction, the aspect of the intrinsic quality of expressions has been studied by the authors in the case of software requirements, a research that has produced the tool QuARS and a specific Quality Model for NL-expressed requirements [33].

This Quality Model can be better described as a set of negative qualities, or defects, that represent the lack of specific, wanted qualities. Some of these defects, here denoted as sub-characteristics, are listed below. Most of them are grouped by the corresponding wanted property, or capability, here denoted as characteristic. Figure 1 shows the complete set.

– **Vagueness:** the sentence contains items having no uniquely quantifiable meaning.
  • *Vagueness-revealing words*: adequate, bad, clear, close, easy, efficient, far, fast, good, in front, near, recent, significant, slow, strong, suitable, ...
– **Subjectivity:** the sentence expresses personal opinion.
  • *Subjectivity-revealing expressions*: similar, taking-into-account.
– **Optionality:** the sentence contains an optional part (i.e. a part that can be considered or not).

Quality Characteristics and Sub-characteristics		
Lexical		
	Un-ambiguity: the capability of each requirement to have a unique interpretation	
	Vagueness: items having a non-uniquely quantifiable meaning appear in a requirement	
	Subjectivity: personal opinions or feelings are expressed in a requirement	
	Optionality: optional parts (i.e. a parts that may or may not be considered) are contained in a requirement	
	Weakness: weak verbs (e.g. may, might, to manage, to process, ..) are used in a requirement	
Syntactical		
	Implicity: subjects or objects are not expressed by means of their specific name but by pronouns or other indirect references in a requirement	
	Specification Completion: the capability of each requirement to uniquely identify its object or subject	
	Under-specification: Generic terms are used instead of specific ones in a requirement	
	Understandability: the capability of each requirement to be fully understood when used for developing software	
	Multiplicity: more than one main verb or subject occur in a requirement	

Fig. 1. Representation of a NL quality model.

- *Optionality-revealing words*: possibly, eventually, in case, if possible, if appropriate, if needed, ...
- **Under-specification:** the sentence contains terms that are general, and need to be specified in more detail to clarify their meaning in the context of the sentence.
  - *Underspecification-revealing words*: function, document, process, unit, interface, manual.

3.1   QuARS

QuARS (Quality Analyzer for Requirements Specifications) was introduced as an automatic analyzer of NL requirement documents for the automatic detection of potential linguistic defects that can determine ambiguity problems. **QuARS** performs an analysis at sentence level, both syntactical and lexical, whose aim is to find the evidence of indicators of the characteristics and sub-characteristics of the above Quality Model in the sentence. These indicators are either elements (verbs, adjectives) of defined dictionaries for the lexical characteristics, or other elements and constructs for the syntactical characteristics. The dictionaries, whose composition typically depends on the particular knowledge domain the object of the analysis belongs to, can be defined by the user. **QuARS** performs a linguistic analysis of a requirements document in plain text format and points out sentences that are potentially defective according to the expressiveness quality model. The defect identification process is split in two parts: (i) the "lexical analysis" capturing *optionality, subjectivity, vagueness and weakness* defects, by identifying candidate defective words that are identified into a corresponding set of dictionaries; and (ii) the "syntactical analysis" capturing *implicitness, multiplicity and under-specification* defects. In the same way, detected defects may however be *false defects*. This may occur mainly for three reasons: (i) a correct usage of a candidate defective word, (ii) a usage of a candidate defective wording which is not usually considered a defect in the specific system or domain, and (iii) a possible source of ambiguity inserted on purpose to give more freedom to implementors. For this reason, a false positive masking feature is also provided by the tool.

Applying the analysis supported by QuARS to project requirements helps achieving the mentioned qualities: the tool warns about all potential defects it is programmed for, and the human inspector just has to confirm/reject the tool proposal on the basis of semantics insight and experience. This might seem hard-work, but some studies showed a gain in defect detection of 2/3, by a time-saving up to the 80% (that also includes manual resolution of false-positives after automated analysis) with respect to a completely manual process [12, 20]. Also, introducing NLP tools in a working team demands limited resource: as shown in [32], a NLP tool can be proficiently used by practitioners with little training.

4   Motivation for a Linguistic Analysis of Standards

In this Section, some reasons for which the linguistic quality of the standards deserves specific investigation are sketched, which are related to the CELELEC recommendations, and to historical cases that illustrate the impact of NL defects in standards. Furthermore, we also provide some discussion on the differences between product requirements and standard clauses (Sect. 4.1).

CENELEC Recommendations. The organizations that publish standards also issue guidelines on how their products should be written. In the railway domain, the CENELEC Guide 17 [7] is aimed at this purpose. Among other recommendations, it contains a sub-section, named "clear language", that gives some advice about writing text.

We want to be more precise and propose an analysis, described in Sect. 5, which it is more articulated, verifiable and provides a metrics-based approach. We have no notion about any other specific work investigating how and to what extent a standard can enjoy clear language properties.

Impact of Standards Defects. Perhaps the most important motivation regards the impact of a safety-related standard defective in clarity and other linguistic qualities. Determining such an impact is similar to perform a preliminary hazard analysis (PHA) for safety-related systems, a typical *what if* search. Quite a difficult laborious job if performed analytically, it can be done empirically, by looking for real cases in which textual quality issues led to unwanted situations. So far, we do not have but one record of facts related to standards, as most of them regard system/software requirements. On the other hand, the *what if* paradigm warns us that similar cases can happen, so that it is worth it to adopt counter-measures whenever feasible.

These cases are drawn from the experience of the second author in the development of standards, and from his participation in standardisation committees.

- *Case 1*: In baseline 19 (Final Draft) of the functional safety standard ISO 26162, that has been a voluntary reference for years in the automotive domain, the expression [software] "requirements verification" has two distinct meanings in the context of (1) Part 6, clauses 6.4 and Table 9; and (2) Part 8, clause 9. In (1) requirements are considered as a reference against which to verify software modules. In (2) requirements are an object of verification – against other requirements and other non mentioned properties. The impact of this issue could be delay in development of in conformity assessment, or missing requirements analysis. Although baseline 19 was no International Standatd yet, it was pretty popular and adopted by car makers in contracts with suppliers.
- *Case 2:* During development of a brake system for a city train in the US (2000 to 2003), the term "parameter" in a document has had, for several months, different meanings for different roles. For the owners of the software requirements it was intended as a set of configuration data to be externally provided during defined vehicle tests. Instead, some developers interpreted it as a list of arguments for some functions to be compiled. We see in next Sections that this is an occurrence of an *under-specification* defect – also referred as generality in the literature [5] –, where an entity (here, 'parameter') is not sufficiently specified. To a certain extent, these defects can be detected also by automated tools [24]. This problem caused misunderstandings among stakeholders and sensible delay in the project.
- *Case 3*: During a training course (2005) on software inspection processes and techniques for an European automotive supplier of various different car brands, it was decided to use the documentation of some of the current projects as material for exercises. While running a manual checklist on a set of software requirements, a lively discussion on the meaning of a requirement (on the control of the catalytic converter) started between developers and testing engineers. This had an impact on the real project, because the owner of the requirements was out for a mission and could not get involved in any explanatory meeting than many days after.

4.1 Difference Between Product Requirements and Standard Clauses

In order to orient methods and tools towards specific standard analysis, further investigation should be done on the root causes that would make standard clauses different from software/system requirements. Some differences are the following.

- Developers can try to negotiate on requirements with their customers and often collaborate with them to make requirements clearer, but they cannot *correct* possibly defective standards. The meaning of a clause can be determined by comparing it with similar ones, by analysing the context in which it is expressed and by consulting the informative documentation that usually comes with the normative parts. This effort takes time and is often skipped, increasing the risk of non-standard-compliant implementation.

- As already noticed, the audience of a standard is the whole community of developer and of assessors, while product requirements as expressed by a customer are often limited to a single developing environment.
- Standard documents are issued after years of discussions in a community of experts and are often accompanied by books, guides and conferences. Instead, product requirements documents are the result of a more limited group of interested stakeholders, and are sometimes the only source of information about the product, before this is developed and accompanied with manuals.

There are, of course, documents that are standards, i.e., issued by international organisations, and are also product related, instead of process related, as, e.g., the ERTM systems specification that will be used in our analysis presented in Sect. 5. In principle, the differences outlined above make product standards more similar to process standards than to product requirements. However, we will see that differences exist in the language used by the different types of standards, and in the types of defects identified.

5 Analysis

The mere existence of the facts mentioned in Sect. 4, no matter how frequent they are, tells us that some impact of standard textual quality in the behavior of standard-compliant processes and products cannot be denied. In this section, the model used in Sect. 3 is adopted as a reference for an analysis of standards, which showcases how NLP techniques can be useful for standards' improvement. In particular, we show that, even with the help of a moderately simple tools as QuARS, developed years before the current work [24], it is possible to highlight potential linguistic defects in standards. This is not the only outcome. The analysis presented here also shows that the tool reports defects, but also unimportant findings and even expected and wanted properties. This aspect can be better understood if we try to examine the results of analyses made on different standards. Often, such results are more interesting if compared with those obtained from different standards and not as absolute quantities. Furthermore, we know that counts and percentages are affected by false positives – defects identified by the tool, that are not defects in practice –, and a patient work of manual inspection becomes necessary to prune the results lists. However, if we want to check if an indicator of a potential defect is more present in a text than in another one, it may be unnecessary to remove false positives.

Here we examine two different types of railway standards, namely, a process standard, and a product standards. One is the popular CENELEC EN 50128:2011 [8], related to the software life-cycle. The other contains the functional requirements specifications for ERTMS Systems issued by the European Railway Agency (ERA) [13].

QuARS ANALYSIS	EN 50128: 2011 - Clauses			ERA ERTMS		
	sentences	flagged	%	sentences	flagged	%
Lexical						
Optionality	624	4	0,6	645	5	0,8
Subjectivity	624	8	1,3	645	5	0,8
Vagueness	624	141	22,6	645	86	13,3
weakness	624	41	6,6	645	36	5,6
Syntactic						
Implicity	624	54	8,7	645	29	4,5
Multiplicity	624	253	40,5	645	105	16,3
Underspecification	624	115	18,4	645	11	1,7

Fig. 2. An example of comparative metrics.

The results of the tool application are reported in Fig. 2. For each sub-characteristic of the adopted quality model, the number of potentially defective sentences and percentage of such sentences over the total number of sentences are given. We will first discuss some issues associated to the numerical differences that can be observed, and then we will present some relevant cases of potential defects in the considered standards.

Even before doing the job to eliminate false positives, we notice that for the ERTMS clauses, the percentage of potential defects is generally lower than for CENELEC. In particular, if we look at under-specification, the difference becomes evident. We can consider this as no surprise, since the EN50128:2011 is a reference for lifecycle processes. Hence, its content shall be general enough so that several process implementations are able to comply to the same clauses. This is not the case for ERTMS systems, for which we have strict inter-operability requirements – due to the nature of the project – which shall not allow too much freedom of implementation to different suppliers. We argue that, for this reason, ERTMS clauses show a lower degree of under-specification, and the under-specification observed in EN50128:2011 may be, in general, a desirable property.

It is worth reflecting on the different roles that may be played by under-specification cases. The situation presented in Case 2 of Sect. 4, and associated to the under-specified term "parameter", was a project risk, while in EN50128:2001 under-specification may be a desirable property. under-specification in standards can in some cases give an useful indication of possible variability, either in design choice, in implementation choices or configurability, which may be finalised in the products' development. In [25] it was argued that removing linguistic ambiguity from standards could affect the important goal for a standard of not being an obstacle for technical evolution in society. Yet, situations like those mentioned above in Case 2 of Sect. 4 should be avoided. How can an automatic tool distinguish between wanted and unwanted ambiguity is a question on which much investigation must still be carried out [19].

As pointed out, there are findings related to under-specification and other potential defects that can create problems with developers. For reasons of space, only a few from EN50128:2011 are reported here.

Figure 3 shows an item (related to Clause 7.3.4.19 on interfaces description) out of the 115 listed by QuARS for under.specification. In this case, it can be agreed that the term "functions" needs more specification, both in type (programming language functions? functions associated to one or more requirements? safety functions?) and in identification (what functions of a certain type?). The users of the standard may come to a conclusion with a certain degree of confidence, with the aid of the context of the clause and a careful study of the standard itself.

It is worth noticing that, in our analysis, many findings related to under-specification refer to plural nouns. As noted by Berry and Kamsties [4], plurals are ambiguous, and should be avoided. Indeed, "the use of plural to describe a property of elements of a set or of sets makes it difficult to determine whether the property is that of each element or of the whole set" [4].

Other findings, regarding *vagueness*, are reported in Figs. 4 and 5. The finding shown in Fig. 4 (related to Clause 8.4.4.8) can be discarded by manual inspection as a false positive after noticing that there are internal references that can clarify the meaning of the word "general". Sometimes, however, internal references may not be this helpful or can even contribute to generate comprehension problems. In any case, to deal with the false positive problem both analyser's experience and careful readings of the context in which the clause is located are advised. Instead, in Fig. 5 (related to Clause 8.4.8.6) "relevant" is appropriately flagged as a vague word, since no explicit criterion is mentioned to assess whether a certain combination of data and algorithms is relevant or not.

The line number:
⌐ 131. *g) existence of synchronization mechanisms between functions (see e)).*
<u>**contains a unspecified sentence because the term:**</u> function

Fig. 3. QuARS Finding about under-specification.

The line number:
554. a) that the application test specification meets the general requirements for readability and traceability (5.3.2.7 to 5.3.2.10 and 6.5.4.14 to 6.5.4.17) as well as the specific requirements expressed in the sub-clause (8.4.4.6),
is defective because it contains the wording: general

Fig. 4. QuARS finding about vagueness (false positive case).

The line number:
581. 8.4.8.6 care must be taken in the verification process and validation test phase of the generic software in order to assure that all relevant combinations of data and algorithms are considered.
is defective because it contains the wording: relevant

Fig. 5. QuARS finding about vagueness.

> The line number:
> 500. 6.7.4.9 where automatic code generation or similar automatic translation takes place, the suitability of the automatic translator for safety-related software development shall be evaluated at the point in the development lifecycle where development support tools are selected.
> is defective because it contains the wording: similar |

Fig. 6. QuARS finding about subjectivity.

> The line number:
> 392. a) the documentation needed for problem reporting and/or corrective actions, with the aim of giving feedback to the responsible management;
> is defective because it contains the wording: and/or

Fig. 7. QuARS finding about optionality.

In Fig. 6, (related to Clause 6.7.4.9) a finding is shown about *subjectivity*. The interpretation of the term "similar" is, indeed, subjective. One may consider a compiler, or a test-suite generation tool, as similar to an automatic code generator, since they are all automatic translators. However, a doubt remains whether all these different types of tools are subject to the same clause.

In Fig. 7 (related to Clause 7, 6.6.4.1) a finding is shown about *optionality*. In this case, we cannot know if only one or both items, i.e., documentation on "problems" and documentation on "corrective actions", must be provided.

6   Conclusions

The quality of the language used by railway standards has an impact on the processes and products that have to abide to the standards. In this paper, we discuss potential issues that may be raised by vague or ambiguous terminology used in standards, and we showcase how automated tools can be employed to detect these language quality defects. In particular, the experience of one author, involved for many years in standard working groups (ISO/IEC, CENELEC) has joined with that of two authors, who have been active since long in the application of natural language processing (NLP) to technical documents, to produce a simple but significant case study. Clauses of two popular standards in the railway domain have been analysed with a NLP tool. The results of this analysis have been discussed to demonstrate on one side that the risk exists of interpreting standard clauses in an incorrect way, and on another side that the efficacy of different standards can be compared with the aid of the same analysis. Encouraged by some expressions of interest coming from conveners of working groups, we hope that NLP methods and tools will be considered and adopted by the international experts working at the current and future revisions of the standards in the railway domain.

References

1. Ambriola, V., Gervasi, V.: On the systematic analysis of natural language requirements with CIRCE. ASE **13**, 107–167 (2006)
2. Arora, C., Sabetzadeh, M., Briand, L., Zimmer, F.: Automated checking of conformance to requirements templates using natural language processing. TSE **41**(10), 944–968 (2015)
3. Berry, D.M., Kamsties, E., Krieger, M.M.: From contract drafting to software specification: linguistic sources of ambiguity (2003)
4. Berry, D.M., Kamsties, E.: The syntactically dangerous all and plural in specifications. IEEE Softw. **22**(1), 55–57 (2005)
5. Berry, D.M., Kamsties, E.: Ambiguity in requirements specification. In: do Prado Leite, J.C.S., Doorn, J.H. (eds.) Perspectives on Software Requirements. Springer International Series in Engineering and Computer Science, vol. 753, pp. 7–44. Springer, Boston (2004). doi:10.1007/978-1-4615-0465-8_2
6. Biscoglio, I., Coco, A., Fusani, M., Gnesi, S., Trentanni, G.: An approach to ambiguity analysis in safety-related standards. In: International Conference on the Quality of Information and Communications Technology, QUATIC 2010, pp. 461–466 (2010)
7. CENELEC: Guidance for writing standards taking into account micro, small and medium-sized enterprises (SMEs) needs. Guide (2010)
8. CENELEC: Railway applications - communication, signalling and processing systems - software for railway control and protection systems. Standard (2011)
9. CENELEC: prEN 50126-1:2016 (to be published)
10. Chantree, F., De Bashar Nuseibeh, A.N., Roeck, A.W.: Identifying nocuous ambiguities in natural language requirements. In: RE 2006, pp. 56–65 (2006)
11. Cimatti, A., Corvino, R., Lazzaro, A., Narasamdya, I., Rizzo, T., Roveri, M., Sanseviero, A., Tchaltsev, A.: Formal verification and validation of ERTMS industrial railway train spacing system. In: Madhusudan, P., Seshia, S.A. (eds.) CAV 2012. LNCS, vol. 7358, pp. 378–393. Springer, Heidelberg (2012). doi:10.1007/978-3-642-31424-7_29
12. Setamanit, S., Sethanandha, B., Raffo, D., Ferguson, R.: Evaluating the impact of requirements analysis tools using simulation. Softw. Process Improv. Pract. **13**(91), 63–73 (2008)
13. ERA: ERTMS/ETCS - Functional Requirements Specification, Version 5 (2007)
14. Fantechi, A., Gnesi, S., Ristori, G., Carenini, M., Vanocchi, M., Moreschini, P.: Assisting requirement formalization by means of natural language translation. Form. Methods Syst. Des. **4**(3), 243–263 (1994)
15. Femmer, H., Fernández, D.M., Wagner, S., Eder, S.: Rapid quality assurance with requirements smells. JSS **123**, 190–213 (2017)
16. Fenton, N., Page, S.: Towards the evaluation of software engineering standards. In: Proceedings of the Software Engineering Standards Symposium, pp. 100–107. IEEE (1993)
17. Fenton, N.E., Neil, M.: A strategy for improving safety related software engineering standards. IEEE Trans. Software Eng. **24**(11), 1002–1013 (1998)
18. Ferrari, A., Fantechi, A., Magnani, G., Grasso, D., Tempestini, M.: The Metrô Rio case study. Sci. Comput. Program. **78**(7), 828–842 (2013)
19. Ferrari, A., Spoletini, P., Gnesi, S.: Ambiguity cues in requirements elicitation interviews. In: 2016 IEEE 24th International Requirements Engineering Conference (RE), pp. 56–65. IEEE (2016)

20. Ferguson, R., Lami, G.: An empirical study on the impact of automation on the requirements analysis process. J. Comput. Sci. Technol. **22**(3), 338–347 (2007)

21. Ghazel, M.: Formalizing a subset of ERTMS/ETCS specifications for verification purposes. Transp. Res. Part C Emerg. Technol. **42**, 60–75 (2014)

22. Gilb, T., Graham, D., Finzi, S.: Software Inspection. Addison-Wesley Longman Publishing Co., Inc. (1993)

23. Gleich, B., Creighton, O., Kof, L.: Ambiguity detection: towards a tool explaining ambiguity sources. In: Wieringa, R., Persson, A. (eds.) REFSQ 2010. LNCS, vol. 6182, pp. 218–232. Springer, Heidelberg (2010). doi:10.1007/978-3-642-14192-8_20

24. Gnesi, S., Lami, G., Trentanni, G.: An automatic tool for the analysis of natural language requirements. IJCSSE **20**(1), 53–62 (2005)

25. Graydon, P.J., Holloway, C.M.: Planning the unplanned experiment: assessing the efficacy of standards for safety critical software. NASA/TM-2015-218804, September 2015

26. Graydon, P.J., Kelly, T.P.: Using argumentation to evaluate software assurance standards. Inf. Softw. Technol. **55**(9), 1551–1562 (2013)

27. Kof, L.: From requirements documents to system models: a tool for interactive semi-automatic translation. In: RE 2010 (2010)

28. Mavin, A., Wilkinson, P., Harwood, A., Novak, M.: Easy approach to requirements syntax (ears). In: RE 2009, pp. 317–322. IEEE (2009)

29. Mich, L.: NL-OOPS: from natural language to object oriented requirements using the natural language processing system LOLITA. NLE **2**(2), 161–187 (1996)

30. Pfleeger, S.L., Fenton, N., Page, S.: Evaluating software engineering standards. Computer **27**(9), 71–79 (1994)

31. Pohl, K., Rupp, C.: Requirements Engineering Fundamentals. Rocky Nook Inc. (2011)

32. Rosadini, B., Ferrari, A., Gori, G., Fantechi, A., Gnesi, S., Trotta, I., Bacherini, S.: Using NLP to detect requirements defects: an industrial experience in the railway domain. In: Grünbacher, P., Perini, A. (eds.) REFSQ 2017. LNCS, vol. 10153, pp. 344–360. Springer, Cham (2017). doi:10.1007/978-3-319-54045-0_24

33. Trentanni, G., Fabbrini, F., Fusani, M., Gnesi, S., Lami, G.: An automatic tool for the analysis of natural language requirements. Int. J. Comput. Syst. Sci. Eng. **20**(1) (2005). Special Issue on Automated Tools for Requirements Engineering

34. Tjong, S.F., Berry, D.M.: The design of SREE — a prototype potential ambiguity finder for requirements specifications and lessons learned. In: Doerr, J., Opdahl, A.L. (eds.) REFSQ 2013. LNCS, vol. 7830, pp. 80–95. Springer, Heidelberg (2013). doi:10.1007/978-3-642-37422-7_6

35. Yang, H., De Roeck, A.N., Gervasi, V., Willis, A., Nuseibeh, B.: Analysing anaphoric ambiguity in natural language requirements. Requirements Eng. **16**(3), 163–189 (2011)

Author Index